FLORIDA BROKER PRELICENSING:

1ST EDITION

STEPHEN METTLING
RYAN METTLING

PERFORMANCE
PROGRAMS
COMPANY

6810 190th Street East, Bradenton, FL 34211
info@performanceprogramscompany.com
www.performanceprogramscompany.com

ISBN: 978-1965482667

Florida Broker Prelicensing

Table of Contents

Preface

Welcome to Florida Broker Prelicensing, published by Performance Programs Company. This text is the classroom component of Florida's broker prelicensing course, known as FREC Course II, the 72-hour program that a licensed sales associate must complete to qualify for a Florida real estate broker license. The course prepares candidates to pass the state broker licensing examination and to take on the expanded legal, financial, and supervisory responsibilities that a broker's license carries.

About This Course

A Florida broker operates at a higher level of authority and accountability than a sales associate. A broker may own and manage a brokerage, maintain escrow accounts, supervise associates, and conduct real estate transactions independently. With that authority comes a broader body of required knowledge. This course builds on the principles a candidate learned as a sales associate and extends them into the areas a broker must master: the licensing and operational rules that govern a brokerage, the valuation of real property, the law of agency and contracts, real estate finance and closings, taxation, investment analysis, land use regulation, environmental concerns, and property management. Throughout, national real estate principles are paired with the specific Florida statutes and Florida Real Estate Commission (FREC) rules that control practice in this state.

Topics Covered

The eighteen chapters are organized into four parts. The opening chapters address the business of real estate brokerage: becoming a licensed broker, opening a real estate office, owning and supervising a brokerage, managing escrow, and the disciplinary process and Real Estate Recovery Fund. Part II turns to valuing real property, covering the fundamentals of valuation, the sales comparison, cost, and income approaches, the comparative market analysis, and business valuation. Part III examines listing and selling real property, including brokerage relationships and disclosure, real estate contracts, financing, closings, and federal income tax laws. Part IV covers specialty areas: investment real estate, zoning and planning, environmental issues affecting transactions, and property management.

How to Use This Text

Each chapter opens with a Contents list and a set of Learning Objectives, and closes with a Snapshot Review that summarizes the key rules, definitions, and principles in that chapter. These summaries are built for focused review and examination preparation. Each chapter also ends with a quiz, and a full practice examination appears at the back of the book. Reading each chapter carefully, reviewing the Snapshot before attempting the quiz, and returning to the discussion whenever a question proves difficult is one of the most effective ways to prepare for both the course examination and the state licensing examination.

About the Authors

Stephen Mettling has been a real estate educator and custom training program developer specializing in real estate over the past forty years. During that time, he has written or co-developed over 100 books, professional training programs and texts covering all aspects of residential, commercial, and corporate real estate for national trade organizations and real estate companies. Additionally, Steve has directed numerous statewide real estate schools and served as vice president of Dearborn Financial Services where he headed up the country's largest real estate, securities and insurance license training network. He is perhaps best known for co-writing Principles of Real Estate Practice, a national real estate principles textbook used by tens of thousands of students per year.

Ryan Mettling, partner and publisher of Performance Programs, is an accomplished online curriculum designer, author, and course developer. He is responsible for the company's strategic planning, general management, printing and production, e-pub and retail platforms, and multi-channel marketing. Ryan is a co-author of the Real Estate License Exam Prep (RELEP) Series and Real Estate Math Express. Mr. Mettling is a member of the Real Estate Educators Association (REEA), and graduated as a Valedictorian from the University of Central Florida's College of Business Administration.

PART I:

GETTING STARTED IN THE REAL ESTATE BROKERAGE BUSINESS

CHAPTER 1: BECOMING A LICENSED REAL ESTATE BROKER

Contents

- **Florida Licensees Defined**
- **General Licensure Provisions**
- **Essentials of the License Application**
- **Sales Associate License Requirements**
- **Broker License Requirements**
- **Nonresident License Requirements**
- **License Registration**
- **License Renewal**
- **License Statuses**
- **Multiple Licenses and Group Licenses**
- **Services of Real Estate; Activities Authorized**

Learning Objectives

Upon completion of this chapter, you will be able to:

1. Explain broker applicant requirements and situations that may cause an application to be denied
2. Describe nonresident applicant requirements and explain mutual recognition agreements
3. Explain broker education and experience requirements, and identify exceptions to the course requirements
4. Identify the post-licensing and continuing education requirements for brokers
5. Explain active and inactive status, and the renewal requirements for members of the U.S. armed forces and their spouses, and how it is unlawful to perform real estate services with an expired real estate license, and the consequences of renewing a real estate license without first satisfying the continuing education requirement
6. Distinguish between licensure and registration
7. Distinguish between multiple licenses and a group license.
8. Identify the rules regarding change of address, residency, and change of business address
9. Identify real estate services that require a license and exemptions from licensure
10. Distinguish among the broker, broker associate, and sales associate license categories and the activities each is authorized to perform
11. Identify the general licensure provisions and the essential requirements of a complete license application

Florida Licensees Defined

Florida offers real estate licenses in three categories: broker, sales associate, and broker associate. A broker associate and a sales associate may be licensed as an individual or as a professional corporation, limited liability company, or professional limited liability company, if the individual has obtained authorization to do so from the Department of State. A broker associate and sales associate may not be licensed as a general partner, member, manager, officer, or director of a brokerage firm.

Broker

A broker is someone who is licensed to perform real estate services for another person for compensation or the expectation of compensation. Compensation can be monetary or anything else of value.

Real estate services include the sale, exchange, purchase, rental, appraisal, auction, advertising of real property, business enterprises, or business opportunities, or the offer to perform any of these services. Services also include procuring sellers, buyers, lessors, or lessees.

Although a broker may "appraise" property, such appraising does not equate to appraisal services that must be performed by a registered or licensed appraiser.

The broker category of licensure also includes any individual who is a general partner, officer, or director of a partnership or corporation that acts as a broker.

Sales associate

A sales associate is someone who performs the same real estate services as a broker but who works under the direction, control, and management of a specified broker or owner-developer. A sales associate must meet additional licensure requirements to become a broker or broker associate.

Broker associate

A broker associate is someone who has obtained a broker license but performs real estate services as a sales associate under the direction, control, and management of a specified broker.

General Licensure Provisions

General qualifications

To qualify for a real estate license in Florida, an individual must be at least 18 years old; hold a high school diploma or its equivalent; and be honest, truthful, trustworthy, and of good character. He or she must have a good reputation for fair dealing and be competent to handle real estate transactions. Being a U.S. citizen or a Florida resident is not required for licensure, provided the individual meets all other licensure requirements. However, applicants must have a Social Security number. A Social Security number or equivalent is not required for tax purposes, but it is required to ensure that the applicant is not behind on spousal or child support.

Required disclosures

An applicant must disclose any alias or also-known-as (aka) name. The applicant must also disclose whether he or she

- is under investigation for any crime or violation
- has been convicted or entered a plea of nolo contendere, no contest, or guilty for any crime
- has been denied licensure or registration for a regulated profession
- has been disciplined or is pending discipline in any jurisdiction
- has surrendered a license or had a license suspended or revoked

- has been guilty of any conduct that would be grounds for license suspension or revocation. (F.S. 475)

Reasons for licensure denial

An applicant may not qualify for licensure if he or she has been denied a license, had a license revoked or suspended, or has committed offenses that would be grounds for license revocation or suspension. In such cases, when considerable time has passed since the offense or if the applicant has since demonstrated conduct good enough to assure he or she is of no danger to the public, FREC may determine that he or she is then qualified to apply for licensure.

The applicant may also be denied licensure if the applicant acted as a licensee in performing real estate activities or presented himself or herself as a licensee within one year prior to applying for a license.

Applicants may not be denied licensure based on conviction of a crime that occurred five or more years prior to submission of the application unless the crime was related to the practice of real estate or related to the absence of good moral character.

Essentials of the License Application

Application requirements

Application fees. License examination fees and fingerprint processing fees are paid directly to the testing vendor. If, for any reason, the application for licensure is not completely processed, the application fee may be refunded.

Maximum limits are set for each fee based on the estimated funds the Commission needs for operations. In case of an excess in the funds collected, the Department may waive license renewal fees for up to 2 years. If funds run low, the fee amount can be increased, or FREC can charge a one-time fee to each active and inactive licensee to cover the deficit.

Application form. Applicants for a Florida real estate license must submit the designated DBPR application form as provided on the DBPR's website. The application must include the applicant's Social Security number and name as they appear on the applicant's Social Security card.

The applicant must also submit any additional documentation required by the Department, including education, work history, criminal history, disciplinary history, fingerprints, and other relevant information.

Fingerprints. Applicants may use any approved Level 2 FDLE Livescan fingerprinting vendor to submit their fingerprints. When submitting fingerprints, the applicant must also submit the Originating Agency Identification (ORI) number (which can be found on the www.myfloridalicense.com website).

Background check. On receiving the applicant's fingerprints, the Department will forward them to the Florida Department of Law Enforcement and the FBI for use in conducting a criminal history check on the applicant. Both agencies will send their background reports to the DBPR, usually within 3-5 days. To allow adequate processing time, applicants should submit their fingerprints at least 5 days before submitting the license application. The DBPR will use these reports to determine if the applicant is qualified for examination and licensure based on the presence or lack of a criminal history.

Criminal history. If the background report indicates a criminal history, it is best if the applicant has already provided all associated information to the Department along with the application. This is accomplished by answering all application background questions completely and honestly and by including documentation detailing any investigations, convictions, guilty pleas, or nolo contendere pleas, including dates, findings, and penalties.

If the penalties have already been satisfied, the applicant should include documentation proving the satisfaction for each conviction.

Any applicant currently on probation as a result of a conviction should also include an official letter from the probation officer regarding the status of the current probation. The applicant may also want to include at least three character references with the application and other documentation. One reference letter may be from a family member, but all others must be from other people who know the applicant and can attest to his or her character.

Summary of applicants. If an applicant's background check indicates a criminal history, the application is placed on a Summary of Applicants list and submitted to FREC for review in its monthly meeting. During the review, FREC will determine if the applicant is approvable for examination and licensure or if the application requires additional consideration and information.

Additional information on digital fingerprinting and the approved vendors can be found on the DBPR's website at www.myfloridalicense.com . An applicant may order a criminal background report on himself or herself on the Florida Department of Law Enforcement's website at http://www.fdle.state.fl.us.

Application omissions

If an applicant makes an error or omits pertinent information on the application, the licensing Department must notify the applicant within 30 days of receiving the application. The notice should include any additional information needed and a time period for the applicant to make the corrections and submit any additional information. If the Department does not send the notice within 30 days, it may not deny the application for the uncorrected errors and omissions.

Application approval

The Department must approve or deny a license application within 90 days of receiving it. If the Department fails to meet that deadline, the application is considered approved by default. Applicants who are approved by default are to notify the Department in writing of their intent to rely on the default approval. If the Commission denies the application, it must notify the applicant in writing of the denial and the reasons for the denial. The notice must inform the applicant of his or her appeal rights.

Appealing licensure denials. If an application has been denied, the applicant will receive a Notice of Intent to Deny. He or she then has the right to choose to:

- accept the denial and forfeit the opportunity to become licensed
- petition for an informal hearing before FREC to present arguments against the reasons for denial
- petition for a formal hearing before an administrative law judge to review the denial order

An applicant who chooses to request a hearing on the denial must file a petition with the DRE within 21 days of receiving the denial notice.

Application, exam validity period

Initial application. The initial license application remains valid for two years after the date it was received by the DBPR.

Exam eligibility The applicant has two years after completing the pre-license coursework to pass the licensure examination. If the applicant fails to pass the examination within those two years, the completed coursework becomes invalid.

Students with a 4-year degree or higher are exempt from post-licensing requirements for both Sales Associates and brokers. They will immediately start the 14-hour continuing education requirements.

A pre-license student may demonstrate FREC-approved minimal competencies to qualify for licensure, serving as a substitute for completing specific classroom hours.

Education exemptions

Persons seeking licensure who are exempt from the pre-license education requirement include the following.

- An active attorney in good standing with the Florida Bar who is qualified under real estate license law may obtain a real estate sales associate license without completing pre-license education courses. However, attorneys must pass the licensure examination.
- Anyone who has earned a 4-year degree or higher in real estate from a school of higher education may obtain a real estate license without completing pre-license education courses. However, individuals with this degree must pass the licensure examination.
- A nonresident licensed in a state that has a mutual recognition agreement with Florida may obtain a real estate license without completing pre-license education courses. However, these nonresidents must pass a 40-question licensure examination.

Sales Associate License Requirements

General license requirements

To qualify for a Florida sales associate license, the applicant must

- have a Social Security number
- receive approval of the license application
- pay all required fees
- meet all general licensure provisions, including age, education, character, competency, submission of associated background history and fingerprints, as discussed in a previous section.

Pre-license course

Applicants for a sales associate license must complete 63 classroom hours of a FREC-approved pre-license course, referred to as Course I, to be taken at an accredited college, career center, or registered real estate school. The course includes the fundamentals of real estate principles and practices, real estate law and license law, and associated mathematics. The required hours consist of 60 hours of instruction, either in the classroom or through distance learning, and three hours allowed for the end-of-course examination.

State license examination

After completing the pre-license coursework and passing the end-of-course examination, an applicant has 2 years to take and pass the state licensure examination. If the applicant waits longer than 2 years, he or she must retake the pre-license course to be eligible to take the licensure examination.

Applicants must schedule the exam directly with the testing vendor and pay the exam fee at that time. Prior to taking the exam, the applicant must present the pre-license course completion certificate and two forms of identification, one of which is to be government-issued and include a photo.

Failing the examination. If an applicant fails the examination, the testing center will provide a photo-bearing exam report showing the exam score and a breakdown of what they missed. The report will also provide instructions on reviewing what they missed on their examination.

License issuance. The testing center provides a photo-bearing exam report to applicants who pass the exam. The applicant's score will also be provided to the DBPR, which will issue a sales associate license number and provide instructions for printing the license.

The license is issued in an inactive status. To activate the license, the sales associate must establish an association with a broker and then either activate his or her own license by printing the DBPR RE 11 Sales Associate or Broker Sales Associate – Become Active form and having the broker sign it or by having the broker add the sales associate to the broker's online account.

The sales associate must be licensed, associated with a broker or owner/developer, and activated prior to performing any real estate services that require a license.

You can find the RE 11 form online at http://www.myfloridalicense.com/dbpr/re/documents/DBPR_RE_11_Change_of_Status_Associates.pdf.

Broker License Requirements

General license requirements

Just as with a sales associate license, an applicant for a Florida broker license must meet certain general licensure requirements. To qualify for a broker license, the applicant must

- have a Social Security number
- submit and receive approval of the DBPR RE-2 license application
- pay all required fees
- meet all general licensure provisions, including age, education, character, competency, submission of all associated background history and fingerprints, as discussed in a previous section

An applicant who has been licensed as a sales associate in Florida during the preceding 5 years must complete the sales associate post-license education requirements, as discussed in an upcoming section, prior to applying for the broker license. This post-license education requirement does not apply to applicants who hold an out-of-state sales associate license.

Experience requirement

In addition to meeting the general licensure requirements, the applicant must have held an active real estate sales associate license for at least 2 years during the 5 years prior to applying for a broker license. The applicant must also have

- worked under one or more real estate brokers who are licensed in Florida or any other U.S. state, territory, or jurisdiction or in any foreign national jurisdiction. Time under an owner/developer does not count toward the experience requirement.
- performed real estate services as a salaried employee of a governmental agency, or
- been licensed in any other U.S. state, territory, or jurisdiction or in any foreign national jurisdiction

Applicants who gained their required experience outside Florida must submit a current certification of real estate license history from the licensing agency in that jurisdiction. The certificate must be no more than 30 days old and must be attached to the broker license application.

Pre-license course

A licensed sales associate who is applying for a broker license must complete the required pre-license Course II. The course includes 69 classroom hours and 3 hours for the end-of-course examination. The course covers the fundamentals of real estate appraising, investment, financing, and brokerage and management operations.

Just as with the sales associate pre-license coursework, each classroom hour is 50 minutes of live classroom instruction, live streaming, or video conferencing. The course may be taken at an accredited college, technical center, or registered real estate school, or through interactive distance learning. A student who demonstrates hardship may qualify to take the course through correspondence. The student must not miss more than 8 hours of classroom instruction.

The broker end-of-course exam includes 95 multiple-choice questions: 90 are worth 1 point each, and 5 may cover closing statements or escrow accounts and are worth 2 points each. The student must pass the exam with a score of at least 70% to complete the course. Students who fail the exam may retake it once.

State license examination

After successfully completing the broker pre-license coursework and passing the end-of-course exam, the applicant must take and pass the state licensure examination within 2 years of completing the course. If the applicant waits longer than 2 years, he or she must retake the pre-license course to be eligible to take the licensure examination.

The exam for brokers is based on knowledge, understanding, and application of real estate law and real estate principles and practices, and includes appraising, finance, investment, brokerage management, and real estate mathematics. The exam is divided into 45 points based on law, 40 points on principles and practices, and 15 points on real estate mathematics. The student must pass the exam with a score of at least 75%.

The processes for qualifying for, taking, passing, failing, and retaking the exam are the same as for the sales associate state exam. After passing the state exam, the student must print his or her license. Because the license is issued inactive, the individual must submit a completed DBPR RE 13 Broker Transactions form to activate the license before operating as a broker.

An individual who passes the broker's exam but chooses to continue to work under a broker may register as a broker associate and work under an active Florida Broker.

Nonresident License Requirements

Florida resident defined

Florida statutes define a resident as

- a person who has resided in Florida continuously for a period of 4 calendar months or more, within the preceding one year; or

- a person who presently resides in Florida with the intention to reside continuously in Florida for a period of 4 months or more, commencing on the date that the person began the current period of residence in Florida.

Nonresident applications

Non-resident licensees from states other than Florida can expect to complete most if not all of Florida's standard licensing processes unless they are from a state with which Florida has a mutual recognition agreement.

Mutual recognition

Mutual recognition agreements allow Florida to recognize and accept the pre-license education and experience obtained in the other state as a substitute for the requirements in the state where the nonresident is applying for a license.

The nonresident applicant must pass a written examination on general real estate law and codes with emphasis on Chapters 455, 475 and Chapter 61J2. The Laws and Rules examination contains 40 questions and requires the applicant to correctly answer at least 30 of those questions. Only after passing the examination will the applicant be issued a Florida license. The nonresident licensee is then responsible for completing all post-licensure and continuing education required of a Florida licensee.

Florida licensees may seek licensure in any state that has a mutual recognition agreement with Florida, keeping in mind that each state may have different requirements for nonresident licensure. To apply for a nonresident license, the Florida licensee should contact the other state's real estate commission.

Mutual recognition vs. reciprocity. A ***mutual recognition agreement*** is contracted between two states and sets forth that the states will recognize and accept each other's real estate pre-license education requirements.

Reciprocity is an agreement between states to allow licensees of one state to obtain a license in the other state without completing the full licensing requirements of the other state. While each reciprocal state has its own specific requirements, most do not require the nonresident licensee to pass an examination for licensure in the reciprocal state.

Florida currently has mutual recognition agreements with several states, but does not have reciprocity agreements with any.

The Occupational Opportunity Act

Although Florida does not have reciprocity agreements with other states, the Occupational Opportunity Act (FL House Bill 615, as amended in Chapter 2017-135) mandates that Florida provide reciprocal licensure for military members, their spouses, their surviving spouses, and low-income individuals. The Act covers all professions regulated by the DBPR, including real estate. The purpose of the Act is to make it easier for military members and spouses who hold licenses in the same profession in another state to transfer their licenses to Florida.

To qualify under the Act, military members must either be currently on active duty or have been honorably discharged. Surviving spouses qualify if the military member was on active duty at the time of death. Proof of the member's active duty must be submitted at the time of application. Applicants must be licensed in good standing in another state and must submit fingerprints for a background check at the time of application.

The Act waives initial license fees, but the applicant must pay fingerprint fees. The Act also waives requirements for pre-license education and examination, but the licensee must meet all renewal education and fee requirements. Reciprocity is available for up to 2 years after discharge from active duty to those who qualify under the Act.

License Registration

License information

Real estate licenses issued in Florida include the licensee's name and address, type of license, license issue and expiration dates, and the license number. The license number includes a two-letter prefix that indicates the type of license: BK for broker, SL for sales associate, BL for broker associate, BO for branch office, CQ for corporation or limited liability company, or PR for partnership and limited liability partnership.

Change of address. Florida license law requires all licensees to submit their current mailing address to FREC. If a licensee (sales associate, broker associate, or broker) changes a personal mailing address, he or she must notify FREC within 10 days of the change. The licensee is required to make changes in the licensee's online account at DPBR

Broker change of business address. If a broker changes business address, the broker must notify FREC within 10 days of the change. The broker must use the online portal to make such changes and include the names of all sales associates and broker associates who remain in the broker's employ, as well as those who are no longer employed by the broker. The form notifies FREC of the business address change for the remaining associates. The broker and sales associates' licenses cease to be in force until new licenses are issued for the new address.

Permission to perform real estate services. The license serves as prima facie evidence that the individual holds a current, valid license. When the individual or entity has met all current licensing requirements, the state will issue the license that allows the licensee to perform real estate services for compensation. The license must be renewed in a timely fashion to allow for continued performance of real estate activities.

Registration essentials

Every person or entity who is licensed is required to register with FREC, pay a registration fee, and submit all required information: name and address of the licensee, name and business address of the sales associate licensee's employing broker, license status of the sales associate and his or her employing broker, and whether or not the licensee is an officer, director, or partner of a real estate brokerage. Registrations must be renewed when the license is renewed.

Florida sales associates and broker associates are required to register with the employing broker and may register with only one broker at a time.

Partnerships, limited liability partnerships, limited liability companies, and corporations that act as brokers must register. Partnerships must license and register at least one partner as an active broker. Real estate brokerage corporations must license and register their officers and directors. Brokers must also register all branch offices.

If a licensee changes its name or trade name, the license must be reissued in the new name and re-registered. Trade names are to be shown on both the license and the registration.

Licensees and companies are registered when they provide the appropriate completed form to DBPR, giving their name, address, and other information. Persons do not have licensure until they have completed all the education and testing requirements. At that time, they will receive their license.

License Renewal

Post-license requirement

Course completion. All *sales associate* licensees are required to complete a post-licensing course before the first license renewal, even if the license is inactive. The course is 45 classroom hours and includes an end-of-course examination. The course emphasizes the development of skills for licensees to operate effectively and to increase public protection. Any sales associate licensee who applies for broker licensure must have completed all sales associate post-license requirements.

All *broker* licensees are required to complete post-license education, which includes either one 60-hour course or two 30-hour courses, and the related exams. All post-license requirements must be met prior to their first broker license renewal date.

The course is to be taken at an accredited college, technical center, registered real estate school, FREC-approved sponsor, or through a distance learning program. A licensee who is absent from more than 10% of the classroom hours will not be given credit for completing the course. The licensee must pass the end-of-course exam with a score of 75% or higher.

Exam failure. If a licensee fails the course exam, they may retake it. However, the licensee may retake the exam only one time during the year after failing. A licensee who does not pass the exam within that year must then repeat the post-license course. If the licensee does not complete the post-license course and pass the exam prior to the first license renewal date, his or her license will be deemed null and void.

To re-qualify for licensure, the individual must retake the entire pre-license course, pass the end-of-course exam, and pass the state licensure exam again. However, a broker who does not meet the broker post-license requirements may be issued a sales associate license by completing a 14-hour continuing education course within 6 months of the expiration of the broker license.

Exemption. Licensees who hold a four-year degree in real estate from an accredited institute of higher learning are exempt from post-license education requirements.

Hardship cases. FREC may allow a six-month extension past the first license renewal date for a licensee to complete post-license requirements if the licensee cannot meet the education completion deadline due to a personal hardship. FREC administrative code qualifies the following as hardships:

- the long-term illness of the licensee or a close relative or person for whom the licensee has caregiving responsibilities
- the lack of reasonable availability of the required course
- the licensee's economic or technological hardship that substantially interferes with the ability to complete education requirements
- the licensee's economic inability to meet reasonable basic living expenses

To obtain the time extension, the licensee must submit a written request to the Commission explaining the basis for the alleged hardship and submit any documentation the Commission requires as support and/or proof.

Licensees may also claim hardship in completing post-license education through correspondence if they cannot attend the classroom course or do not have access to distance-learning courses.

License renewal procedures

Issue and expiration. Licenses are issued for 2-year periods; at the end of each period, they must be renewed to prevent expiration. All licenses expire on and must be renewed by either March 31 or September 30, depending on the date of issue. Consequently, the initial licensure period will be between 18 and 24 months. To calculate when the initial license expires, add 2 years to the last expiration date, March 31 or September 30, before the issue date.

For example, if John's sales associate license was initially issued on February 28, 2029, a 2-year license period would mean his license would expire at midnight on February 27, 2031. However, since all licenses expire on March 31 or September 30, John's license would expire on September 30, 2030, providing John with 19 months of initial licensure, thereby complying with the 18 to 24-month requirement. Once John renews his license the first time, each license period thereafter will be 24 months (2 years), with his license expiring on September 30 each time.

License renewal. The DBPR sends a license renewal notice to the licensee at least 90 days before the license expiration date. The notice is sent to both active and inactive licensees at the last known address or e-mail address.

The licensee must then submit a completed renewal application, the renewal fee, and proof of completing either the post-license or continuing education courses. The licensee must indicate whether to renew in active or inactive status (discussed in an upcoming section). Once the licensee has met all renewal requirements, the DBPR will issue a renewed license with the appropriate expiration date.

If the licensee does not renew by the expiration date, the license automatically becomes involuntarily inactive and may only be renewed when applicable requirements are met (discussed in an upcoming section). The license is deemed delinquent for the following license period. The licensee is not allowed to practice real estate while on inactive status. If the licensee was on active status at the license expiration date, he or she may renew the license within 24 months by meeting renewal requirements and paying a late fee. If the licensee fails to renew within that time period, the license is rendered void.

Members of the armed forces. Active duty members of the U.S. armed forces who are in good standing with FREC are exempt from license renewal requirements. This exemption is extended to 2 years after the member is discharged from active duty. However, if the member is engaged in real estate for profit in the private sector within Florida while on active duty and for 2 years after discharge from active duty, he or she must meet all renewal requirements but is exempt from paying the renewal fee.

The military member's spouse or the surviving spouse of a member who died while on active duty is also exempt from license renewal requirements if the member's active duty is outside of Florida. The spouse must be in good standing with FREC and not be practicing in the private sector for profit. This exemption is in effect while the member is on active duty and for 6 months after the member's discharge.

Continuing education

Course completion. Florida real estate licenses are issued for 2-year periods and must be renewed every 2 years. During the initial licensing period, licensees must complete post-licensing education based on the type of license held. During that same initial period, licensees are not required to complete continuing education, but they must complete it every 2-year licensing period thereafter.

During each licensing period, active and inactive sales associates and brokers must complete 14 continuing education hours, including at least 3 hours of Core Law education, 3 hours of Business Ethics, and 8 hours of specialty education.

Continuing education courses may be taken in the classroom, through distance learning, or by correspondence (if the licensee qualifies for a hardship). The licensee must attend at least 90% of each classroom hour to receive the notice of completion. The DBPR may deny license renewal for any licensee who fails to complete continuing education requirements. Failure to provide proof of continuing education or providing false proof are grounds for disciplinary action.

Course credits. Because Core Law covers Florida real estate license law, Commission rules, and agency law, and provides an introduction to other state laws, federal laws, and taxes affecting real estate, it is advisable for the licensee to take a 3-hour Core Law course every year to stay up to date on the laws and rules.

Any licensee who takes the course each year will be awarded 3 hours of Core Law education and 3 hours of specialty education. Licensees whose licenses expire after September 30, 2018, are also required to complete a 3-hour Business Ethics course during each license period. Licensees who take the Business Ethics course each year will be awarded 3 hours of Business Ethics education and 3 hours of specialty education. The remaining hours required towards the total 14 hours may be taken in specialty education courses, also known as electives.

Once during each license period, the licensee may be awarded 3 classroom hours for attending an A FREC legal agenda session. To receive credit, the licensee must notify the Division of Real Estate of their intent to attend the session. No credit will be awarded if the licensee attends the session as a party to a disciplinary action.

The courses must be completed by either March 31 or September 30, based on the license expiration date. A 6-month extension past the renewal date may be available if the licensee cannot meet the education completion deadline due to a personal hardship.

Exemption. These continuing education requirements do not apply to attorneys in good standing with the Florida Bar.

Reactivation education

A licensee who has been on involuntary inactive status for 12 to 24 months may complete A FREC-prescribed 28-hour education course towards reactivating the license. The course covers material from the sales associate pre-license course. The course may be taken in the classroom, through distance learning, or by correspondence if the licensee qualifies for a hardship. Completion of the course does not entitle the licensee to reactivate the license until he or she has met all other requirements.

The licensee must also pass the end-of-course exam with a score of 70% or higher. Licensees must attend at least 90% of the instruction hours to be eligible to take the exam. Licensees who fail the exam may retake it once within a year of the failure. If the licensee fails the retake exam, he or she must retake the reactivation course and the end-of-course exam.

Licensees who meet the qualifications of a hardship may request a 6-month extension after license expiration by submitting the hardship basis to FREC.

License Statuses

Active vs. inactive license status

Active status. Sales associate or broker licenses are initially issued on inactive status. Since licensees may practice real estate only if their licenses are active, they must activate their licenses before offering or providing real estate services. Their licenses must also be in active status before the licensee can accept commissions or other fees for real estate services.

A sales associate can activate the license by registering under an employing broker or by having the employing broker activate the license through the broker's online account. Anyone who practices without an active status license is violating licensing law and may be disciplined. At any time after a license is issued, the licensee may place the active license in inactive status. During the license renewal process, the licensee may choose to renew in either active or inactive status. Again, while on inactive status, the licensee may not practice real estate activities.

Voluntary inactive status. There are multiple ways a license may become voluntarily inactive: the licensee does not activate the license when it is initially issued; the licensee chooses to renew an active license on inactive status; or a licensee requests the DBPR place the license on inactive status. Most often, licensees choose voluntary inactive status because they have decided not to practice real estate for a period of time.

When a license is in voluntary inactive status, the licensee may reactivate the license at any time by applying to the DBPR, paying a reactivation fee, and meeting all post-license or continuing education requirements.

Just as with active licenses, voluntarily inactive licenses must be renewed every two years to remain valid. The inactive licensee needs to apply for renewal in inactive status, complete 14 hours of continuing education for each 2-year period the license was inactive, and pay the renewal fee.

Involuntary inactive status. If the licensee does not renew the active or voluntarily inactive license by the expiration date, the license status automatically becomes involuntarily inactive. The license is also deemed delinquent.

The DBPR will send a notice of involuntary inactive status at least 90 days prior to the license expiration date. If a broker's license is suspended or revoked, all sales associates and broker associates registered under that broker will automatically become involuntarily inactive. Their licenses will remain in that status until the broker is reinstated or until they register under a new broker.

If these licensees decide not to practice real estate, they may change their involuntarily inactive status to voluntarily inactive through their online DBPR account.

Once in involuntary inactive status for nonrenewal, the license can be renewed if the licensee applies to the DBPR, pays the renewal fee for each year the license was involuntarily inactive plus any associated late fees, and completes the required continuing education based on the time frame of inactive status.

The licensee can renew as either active or voluntarily inactive, but must do so within 2 years of becoming involuntarily inactive. If the licensee fails to renew during the 2 years, the license automatically expires and becomes null and void.

Null and void license status

A license may become null and void under any of the following conditions.

- The sales associate does not complete post-license education prior to the renewal date for the initial licensure period. To reengage in real estate activities, the individual must requalify for licensure by retaking the prelicensure education and exams and passing the state examination.
- A licensee on involuntary inactive status does not renew the license within 2 years of becoming involuntarily inactive. FREC may reinstate this license if the individual applies to the Commission within 6 months of becoming null and void, shows proof of a physical or financial hardship, completes continuing education, and pays all required fees.
- If the licensee receives the hardship extension, the license will remain null and void until the individual submits a reinstatement application, related fees, and proof of reactivation education completion.
- A license is revoked for disciplinary reasons. Revoked licenses may never be reinstated, and the individual may never reapply for licensure.
- A licensee relinquishes the license unrelated to any disciplinary actions or investigations. The licensee must notify the DBPR of the intent to relinquish the license.

Null and void licenses are those that no longer exist unless they are reactivated under the above allowable conditions.

Reinstatement to active status. The licensee can renew as either active or voluntarily inactive, but must do so within 2 years of becoming involuntarily inactive. If the licensee fails to renew during the 2 years, the license automatically expires and becomes null and void

Reactivation education. A licensee who has been on involuntary inactive status for 12 to 24 months may complete a FREC-prescribed 28-hour education course towards reactivating the license. The course covers material from the sales associate pre-license course. The course may be taken in the classroom, through distance learning, or by correspondence if the licensee qualifies for a hardship. Completion of the course does not entitle the licensee to reactivate the license until he or she has met all other requirements.

The licensee must also pass the end-of-course exam with a score of 70% or higher. Licensees must attend at least 90% of the instruction hours to be eligible to take the exam. Licensees who fail the exam may retake it once within a year of the failure. If the licensee fails the retake exam, he or she must retake the reactivation course and the end-of-course exam.

Licensees who meet the qualifications of a hardship may request a 6-month extension after license expiration by submitting the hardship basis to FREC.

Reporting address changes. A broker must notify the Commission within 10 days of any change to their business address. Until the Commission is notified of the address change, the broker's license ceases to be in force. While the license is in that status, the broker may not engage in real estate activities.

The notice of change of address must include the names of any associates who are no longer employed by the broker. The notice will also serve as a change-of-address notification for associates who are still employed by the broker. These licensees can notify the Commission of the changes on a Commission-provided form or through their online portal.

All licensees must notify the DBPR in writing of their *current residential mailing address and current email address*. They must notify the Department within 10 days of any changes to residential mailing addresses. Failure to do so can result in a disciplinary fine.

Any Florida resident licensee who becomes a nonresident by moving out of the state is required to notify the Commission within 60 days of the change of residency. If the licensee wishes to continue practicing in Florida, he or she must comply with all nonresident requirements. Failure to notify the Commission and comply with the requirements is a violation of license law and can result in disciplinary penalties.

Multiple Licenses and Group Licenses

Multiple licenses. Brokers are required to hold a separate individual license for each entity or business they serve. A broker who serves multiple entities needs multiple licenses. The broker must show that the multiple licenses are necessary to conduct the brokerage business and that the licenses will not be harmful or prejudicial to anyone. Each license must be renewed separately.

The Commission may deny a multiple license for the same reasons it can deny individual licenses. Any discipline against the broker's primary license will apply equally to his or her multiple licenses. Multiple licenses are not transferable to new relationships unless the broker ends all current relationships at the same time and then moves only one license to a new relationship.

Sales associates and broker associates are not eligible for multiple licenses because they may work for only one broker or brokerage at a time.

Group licenses. Property owners/developers are exempt from licensure. Consequently, they employ licensed sales associates or broker associates to sell their properties. Sometimes, an owner/developer owns properties through multiple business entities with different names. When those entities are connected (for example, subsidiaries) and owned or controlled by a single individual or group, any licensee employed by the owner/developer may obtain a group license to sell for all of the entities.

Remember that a sales associate or broker associate may only be employed by one broker or owner/developer at a time. The group license allows the licensee to be employed by one owner/developer while still selling properties for multiple entities, provided all entities are owned or controlled by the employing owner/developer.

Services of Real Estate; Activities Authorized

Real estate services

Florida law does not specifically define "real estate services," but it does infer a definition based on the activities that require a real estate license. Licensees who, "**for another and for compensation**," perform or offer to perform any transactional tasks (negotiating, selling, buying, renting, or leasing **real property**), listing and marketing services, property management services, or business and compensation-related activities. Unlicensed individuals may not hold themselves out to be licensed.

Note that certain transactions are exempt, including performing a transaction on one's own property, performing tasks for employers or government entities, salaried employees who do not receive commissions, and condominium or cooperative apartment employees who rent individual units for terms of a year or less.

Others who are exempt include individuals who sell cemetery lots, rent spaces in mobile home parks, hold an attorney or CPA license (when acting within the scope of their licenses), and those who act as required by the courts through guardianship or power of attorney.

Snapshot Review for Chapter 1

The following review summarizes the key rules and concepts from Chapter 1.

LICENSURE

Florida Licensees, Defined

- Florida license categories: broker, broker associate, sales associate
- broker typically manages brokerage firm and supervises affiliated licensees
- broker associate holds broker's license, works under broker's supervision
- sales associate works under broker's direction and control
- sales associate and broker associates: licensed as individuals, professional corporations, LLCs, or PLLCs
- Florida Department of State authorizes licensure

General Licensure Provisions

- minimum 18 years of age
- high school diploma or equivalent
- good reputation for fair dealing
- competent to handle real estate transactions
- must have Social Security number
- must disclose current criminal or violation investigations, convictions, licensure disciplinary actions
- application denial allowed for licensure disciplinary actions, acting without a license,

Essentials of the License Application

- process includes completed application, fees, fingerprints, background/criminal history check
- additional documentation as required by Department
- Department to notify applicant of omitted information within 30 days of receipt
- Department must approve or deny application within 90 days of receipt; failure to meet deadline results in automatic approval
- applicants may appeal licensure denials
- initial license application valid for 2 years after receipt
- must take licensing exam within 2 years of prelicensing course completion
- exemptions from pre-license education (must pass exam), attorneys, individuals with 4-year real estate degree, nonresidents under mutual recognition

License-specific Requirements

- salesperson: 63 hours pre-license course, pass exam, affiliate with broker
- broker: 2 years active sales associate experience, 72 hours pre-license course, pass exam, post-license course
- non-resident: mutual recognition agreements with 10 other states; qualified applicants complete only a 40-question Florida law exam
- Occupational Opportunity Act: reciprocal licensing permitted, with license fees, education, and exam requirements waived for military members and spouses, military surviving spouses, and low-income individuals

License Registration

- all licensees must register with the state and maintain current contact information
- registration info includes name, address, license type, issue/expiration date, and license number

License Renewal

- sales associates complete 45 hours post-licensed education; brokers, 60 hours
- licenses valid for 2 years, expiring March 31 or September 30
- failure to renew results in licensee becoming involuntarily inactive
- all licensees complete 14 prescribed CE hours every 2 years
- inactive licensees complete 28-hour course and pass exam if inactive for 12-24 months

License Statuses

- active – can perform real estate services
- inactive – cannot perform real estate services
- voluntary inactive – chosen by licensee, requires CE for renewal
- involuntary inactive – failure to renew, requires fees and education to renew
- null and void – post-license education not completed; inactive >2 years; license revoked; license voluntarily relinquished

Multiple and Group Licenses

- multiple – broker only – separate license per entity, justify need, discipline applies to all licenses
- group – for owners/developers with multiple entities; allows one licensee to sell for multiple related entities

Services of Real Estate

- activities requiring licensure: selling, leasing, renting, negotiating transactions, marketing/listing property, property management FOR ANOTHER and FOR COMPENSATION
- some exemptions from licensing, including individuals selling their own property, certain employees, attorneys/CPAs (within scope), court-appointed individuals, and certain rental or cemetery transactions

Chapter 1 Quiz: Becoming a Licensed Real Estate Broker

1.1 Which of the following best describes the three categories of real estate licenses offered in Florida?

a. Broker, Realtor®, and sales associate
b. Broker, sales associate, and broker associate
c. Broker, property manager, and sales associate
d. Broker, owner-developer, and sales associate

1.2 Which individual may perform real estate services independently for compensation?

a. Sales associate
b. Broker associate
c. Broker
d. Unlicensed assistant

1.3 A broker associate differs from a sales associate because a broker associate ______.

a. may work for multiple brokers
b. has obtained a broker's license
c. does not require supervision
d. cannot earn commissions

1.4 Which activity is considered a real estate service under Florida law?

a. Selling one's own personal residence
b. Advertising real property for another for compensation
c. Renting one's own apartment
d. Acting as a salaried government employee

1.5 Which statement about appraisals performed by brokers is TRUE?

a. Brokers may perform licensed appraisal services.
b. Brokers may appraise property only if certified.
c. Broker appraisals do not substitute for licensed appraisal services.
d. Brokers may not estimate property value.

1.6 Which individual is included in the broker category of licensure?

a. Any sales associate with 2 years' experience
b. A general partner of a brokerage partnership
c. An unlicensed office manager
d. A real estate instructor

1.7 Which of the following is NOT a general qualification for licensure in Florida?

a. Be at least 18 years of age
b. Be a Florida resident
c. Have a high school diploma or equivalent
d. Be of good moral character

1.8 Why must an applicant provide a Social Security number when applying for licensure?

a. For income tax reporting
b. To verify employment history
c. To ensure compliance with child or spousal support
d. To establish Florida residency

1.9 Which item must be disclosed on a Florida real estate license application?

a. Political affiliation
b. Prior aliases or "also-known-as" names
c. Credit score
d. Employment references

1.10 An applicant may be denied licensure if he or she ______.

a. has a criminal conviction older than 10 years
b. falsely acted as a licensee within one year prior to applying
c. is a non-resident of Florida
d. failed the exam more than once

1.11 How long does the DBPR have to approve or deny a complete license application?

a. 30 days
b. 60 days
c. 90 days
d. 120 days

1.12 How long is an initial Florida real estate license application valid?

a. One year
b. Eighteen months
c. Two years
d. Four years

1.13 How many classroom hours are required for the sales associate pre-license course?

a. 45 hours
b. 60 hours
c. 63 hours
d. 69 hours

1.14 A sales associate license is initially issued in what status?

a. Active
b. Voluntarily inactive
c. Involuntarily inactive
d. Inactive

1.15 Which requirement must be met before a sales associate may perform real estate services?

a. Pass the post-license course
b. Associate with a broker and activate the license
c. Complete continuing education
d. Hold the license for six months

1.16 To qualify for a Florida broker license, an applicant must have ______.

a. held an inactive sales associate license for 5 years
b. held an active sales associate license for 2 years within the past 5 years
c. completed post-license education after applying
d. worked exclusively under an owner/developer

1.17 Which experience does NOT count toward the broker experience requirement?

a. Time working under a Florida broker
b. Time working under an out-of-state broker
c. Working as a salaried real estate assistant for a government agency
d. Time working under an owner/developer

1.18 How many continuing education hours are required each renewal period after initial licensure and completion of post-licensing coursework?

a. 12 hours
b. 14 hours
c. 21 hours
d. 28 hours

1.19 Which license status allows a licensee to legally practice real estate?

a. Voluntarily inactive
b. Involuntarily inactive
c. Active
d. Null and void

1.20 Which statement about multiple licenses is TRUE?

a. Sales associates may hold multiple licenses.
b. Broker associates may work for more than one broker.
c. Brokers must renew each multiple license separately.
d. Multiple licenses are freely transferable.

1.21 A broker who holds an active license in a state that has a mutual recognition agreement with Florida wants to become licensed in Florida. Mutual recognition allows the broker to ______.

a. obtain a Florida license without completing Florida's pre-license education requirement
b. practice in Florida using only his or her out-of-state license
c. skip both the education and the examination requirements entirely
d. obtain a Florida license only after establishing Florida residency

1.22 Which statement best describes reciprocity?

a. It requires every applicant to complete Florida's full pre-license course.
b. It applies only to applicants who are Florida residents.
c. It is an agreement allowing licensees of one state to obtain a license in another state without completing the full licensing process.
d. It permits unlicensed persons to perform real estate services temporarily.

1.23 A developer owns several separate corporations, each holding property for sale, and wants one sales associate to represent all of them. Which type of license permits this arrangement?

a. A multiple license
b. A group license
c. A broker associate license
d. A temporary license

1.24 Before the first renewal of a sales associate license, the licensee must ______.

a. complete 14 hours of continuing education
b. accumulate two years of active experience
c. pass a second state examination
d. complete a 45-hour post-license course

1.25 Florida real estate licenses are issued for two-year periods and expire on ______.

a. March 31 or September 30
b. January 1 or July 1
c. the anniversary of the licensee's date of birth
d. December 31 only

1.26 A real estate license becomes null and void when ______.

a. the licensee changes his or her mailing address
b. the licensee chooses voluntary inactive status
c. a licensee on involuntary inactive status fails to renew within two years
d. the licensee completes post-license education late but within the renewal period

1.27 A sales associate moves to a new home. Within how many days must he or she notify FREC of the new mailing address?

a. 5 days
b. 10 days
c. 30 days
d. 60 days

1.28 Which individual is exempt from the requirement to hold a Florida real estate license?

a. A person who, for a fee, negotiates the sale of another owner's property
b. A person who advertises another's property for compensation
c. A person who leases property owned by others for a commission
d. An owner who sells his or her own real property

1.29 A sales associate does not renew her license by its expiration date. Immediately after the expiration date, her license status becomes ______.

a. involuntarily inactive
b. voluntarily inactive
c. null and void
d. revoked

1.30 A licensee has been on involuntary inactive status for 18 months and wants to return to active status. To reactivate, he or she must complete ______.

a. only the 14-hour continuing education course
b. a new 63-hour pre-license course
c. a FREC-prescribed 28-hour education course and pass the end-of-course exam
d. two years of additional experience

CHAPTER 2:
OPENING A REAL ESTATE OFFICE

Contents

Learning Objectives

Upon completion of this chapter, you will be able to:

1. Describe the characteristics of the various business structures that may be registered as brokerage entities; the characteristics of officers, directors, and partners of real estate brokerage corporations and partnerships; and the statutes/rules pertaining to operating under a broker's own name
2. Identify the rules regarding vacancy of office and appointing a temporary broker
3. Recognize the various business forms that may not register as real estate brokerage entities
4. Identify the requirements associated with registering a trade name with DBPR, requirements of the Fictitious Name Act, and exemptions from filing under the Fictitious Name Act.
5. Identify the rules and requirements regarding real estate brokerage offices, branch offices, and temporary shelters
6. Identify the rules and requirements related to entrance signs
7. Identify the accessibility requirements outlined in the Americans with Disabilities Act pertaining to public accommodations and commercial facilities and the Florida Americans with Disabilities Accessibility Implementation Act
8. Explain the statutes and rules pertaining to classified advertising, self-promotion, team advertising, internet sites, unauthorized use of association names, licensees selling property by owner, and rental lists
9. Explain the Fair Housing Act and protected classes as it applies to advertising, exemptions for housing for older persons, and the display of the equal housing opportunity poster
10. Explain the provisions of the Telephone Consumer Protection Act, Federal Communications Commission's (FCC) do-not-call rules, and describe the applicable exemptions under Florida's Telephone Solicitation Law, and explain the provisions of the CAN-SPAM Act

Business Structures That May Be Registered as Brokerages

Sole proprietorships

A business or brokerage owned by a single individual is called a sole proprietorship. A licensed broker may form a sole proprietorship by filing with the Florida Department of State (FDOS) and registering with the DBPR. The sole broker is responsible for all business and employee activities

General partnership

Two or more individuals may form a general partnership and share in the partnership's business activities, finances, and profits. The partnership must be registered with the DBPR. At least one partner must be a licensed broker, and all partners who deal with the public to perform real estate services must hold valid broker licenses. Every active broker partner is responsible for ensuring that each partner who must be registered and licensed is registered and licensed.

If the only licensed broker dies or withdraws from the partnership, another licensed broker must be appointed within 14 days, or the partnership's registration will be canceled, and all licenses within the partnership will be placed on involuntary inactive status. New brokerage business may not be performed during those 14 days until the new licensed broker is appointed. FREC must be notified immediately of the death or removal of the licensed broker, and of the steps taken to fill the vacancy.

Limited partnership

Limited partnerships are created by filing with the FDOS and must be registered with the DBPR. They must include at least one general partner, with all general partners required to register with the DBPR. At least one general partner must be a licensed broker. All general partners who deal with the public to perform real estate services must also be licensed brokers. The limited partnership must also include at least one limited partner who must invest cash or property, but not services. Limited partners are not liable for the partnership's debts unless their names are part of the partnership's name or they participate in managing the business.

Limited liability partnership

(LLP) An LLP is a business entity that requires a written partnership agreement between the partners. Unlike limited partnerships, all partners in an LLP can participate in managing the business with no one partner having explicit control. New partners can be added and existing partners removed in accordance with the provisions of the partnership agreement. Liability is split among the partners in that each partner is liable for his or her own acts and those of the partner's employees, and no partner is responsible for the errors or acts of another partner. The partners are not liable for debts incurred by another partner.

The LLP is a pass-through entity wherein the partners receive untaxed profits and then pay their own income taxes. As with other entities, an LLP must be registered with the FDOS.

Sales associates and broker associates are prohibited from being officers, members, managers, or directors in a real estate brokerage corporation or a general partner in a brokerage limited or general partnership.

Broker associates or sales associates are licensed as individuals, but can be licensed as a professional corporation, limited liability company, or professional limited liability company if the licensee submits authorization from the Department of State to FREC.

The new broker's name must be registered with the Florida Department of State (FDOS) for the business. Because this process takes time, FREC now allows a temporary broker to be named and registered with DBPR within 14 days. This temporary broker may remain in place for 60 days. Within that timeframe, a new broker must be registered with the FDOS and DBPR.

Corporation

For-profit corporation. A corporation is created by one or more individuals who file articles of incorporation with the FDOS and who are the corporation's owners and stockholders. Corporations may be domestic or foreign. Domestic corporations are incorporated in Florida and conduct business within

Florida. Foreign corporations, on the other hand, are incorporated outside of Florida but conduct business within Florida. The corporation is managed by a board of directors elected by the owners/stockholders.

To become a real estate brokerage, the corporation must register with the DBPR as a brokerage entity by submitting a brokerage corporation application. The corporation must have at least one officer or director who is licensed as an active broker. The corporation may have licensed, unlicensed, and inactive brokers serve as officers or directors, but all who provide real estate services to the public must be licensed active brokers. The corporation must also register all unlicensed officers and directors for identification purposes. The brokerage corporation application includes a section for this purpose.

If the brokerage does not have at least one registered, licensed active broker, the corporation's registration will be automatically canceled until the license and registration are deemed in force.

Sales associates and broker associates may not be officers or directors within a corporation, but they may be shareholders.

Not-for-profit corporation. Florida not-for-profit corporations are created by filing a Florida Not-for-Profit Corporations application. The specific purpose of the corporation must be included, as well as whether or not the corporation will be seeking 501(c)(3) federal tax-exempt status. The corporation is required to file an annual report to maintain its active status. Failure to file the report will result in the corporation's administrative dissolution.

The corporation may have one or more classes of members or no members at all, but it must have at least three directors. Unlike for-profit corporations, these corporations are prohibited from paying dividends or any part of their income or profit to the corporation's members, directors, or officers.

Limited liability company(LLC)

LLCs are separate and distinct legal entities wherein the owners are not personally liable for the entity's debts and liabilities. It allows owners to separate their business dealings from their personal affairs. Like other business entities, an LLC must be filed with the FDOS.

An LLC can be taxed as a regular corporation or as a pass-through entity, such as a sole proprietorship or a partnership. With the pass-through, the owners pay taxes only once on the profits, whereas a regular corporation's income is taxed twice – once on its net income and then again on the profit distribution to stockholders.

LLCs can be converted to corporations if the owners so choose.

Business Structures That May Not Register

Corporation sole

A corporation sole is made up of one individual occupying one incorporated office and may consist of only one member at a time. This one member is typically a bishop or other church official. While the corporation sole is typically a church organization, it can also be a political organization.

The purpose of the entity is to ensure the continuity of ownership of property that has been dedicated to the benefit of a particular religious organization. The one member holds title to the property but does not personally own the property. If one member dies or is removed, the property title passes to a successor, not to the previous member's heirs.

Not all states recognize the corporation sole status, and although the Supreme Court of Florida recognizes it, a corporation sole cannot be registered as a real estate broker.

Joint venture

This business arrangement is formed when two or more individuals or entities join together to carry out a single business activity or a designated number of activities. The arrangement is not permanent and requires the participating individuals to have joint control and to share in the profits and losses. Under Florida law, each partner owes the duties of care and loyalty to the venture and the other partners.

In a real estate joint venture, each individual must be an active licensed broker. Consequently, the venture is not registered as an entity with the FDOS because there is no written arrangement, and the licensed brokers are already registered.

Business trust

A business trust is typically set up when the assets and property of a business corporation are entrusted to an appointed trustee. The trustee then manages the business's operations and assets for the benefit and profit of the beneficiaries.

A real estate business trust is used for transactions involving the trust's own property. Each individual invests in the entity so the trust can buy, develop, and/or sell property. The title to any property purchased is filed in the trustee's name, but the property does not belong to the trustee. All property and assets belong to the trust itself.

While every participant in the trust who performs real estate services must be licensed and registered, the trust itself does not register with the DBPR as a real estate broker.

Cooperative association

A cooperative association is a business organization that is formed, owned, and operated by its members for their mutual benefit. The association may buy or sell its own property, but it is not registered as a real estate broker. Each member is a shareholder with equal ownership and control of the association, and each shareholder has one vote. Profits earned by the association are distributed to shareholders.

Unincorporated association

An unincorporated association is a group of people who form the association for a common non-business purpose and to create a legally binding relationship among themselves. The associations are easy to form and extremely flexible. They can, for example, be a small neighborhood group or a national organization.

Because they are unincorporated, they are not permitted to own property in their own name or to enter into contracts. Consequently, they may not be registered as real estate brokers.

Ostensible Partnerships

The State of Florida prohibits ostensible partnerships because they are not actually partnerships. Instead, they occur when two or more people deceive others by acting as though a business partnership exists. For example, if two unassociated brokers work in the same office but do not have separate signs, they are giving the appearance of a business partnership when one does not exist.

Trade Names

Brokers register their brokerages under the broker's legal name or the business's legal name. They may also register under a trade name, a fictitious name other than their own name that the broker would like to use for the brokerage, as long as they comply with Florida's Fictitious Name Act. The trade name must appear on the broker's license application and license or registration, and must be unique from any other business or trade name.

Note that there are exemptions to fictitious name registration, but they do not apply to the real estate industry.

The broker may register under only one trade name and must obtain a new license if he or she changes it. The registered trade name must appear on all brokerage signage and advertising.

LLC registration and trade name usage. DBPR allows sales associates and broker associates to register as limited liability companies (LLCs) or professional associations (PAs) with the FDOS. It does not permit them to use a trade name or fictitious name. They must register with their real names and have only their real names show on the license. For example, John Kennedy may form an LLC and be licensed as John Kennedy, LLC. This is the name he must operate under, and that must appear on all official documents. All money must be deposited into an account under this name.

It is recommended that sales associates and broker associates consult with a certified public accountant (CPA) or a lawyer to ensure they understand all the consequences and requirements of this form of registration.

Display of names. FREC administrative rules prohibit licensees from using or displaying any name, insignia, or designation of a real estate association or organization unless they are authorized to do so.

Office Requirements

Officing requirements

Florida statute mandates that each active broker maintain an office located in a building of "stationary construction." The law further mandates that only brokers can own and maintain an office. Sales associates and broker associates may not have their own offices.

Brokers' offices must be registered with the Department of Business and Professional Regulation (DBPR). The office must include at least one enclosed room and have space to conduct private transactions. Additionally, the broker is required to keep any real estate files and records (physical or electronic) in the office so they are immediately available for inspection by FREC or other governing authority.

A broker may have an office that is located outside the state of Florida if the broker agrees in writing to cooperate with any investigation conducted in accordance with Florida statutes and rules. The broker must also register the out-of-state office with the DBPR.

If local zoning allows, the broker may set up the office in a residential location, such as the broker's home, as long as all office requirements are met, including display of the broker's sign.

Under the law, a brokerage office is considered both a public accommodation and a commercial facility. Consequently, the office must comply with federal and state laws regarding accessibility for people with physical or mental disabilities. The office will need clearly marked handicapped parking spaces and wheelchair accessible ramps and doorways. These requirements also apply to residential offices.

Branch offices

If a broker conducts business at a location other than the main office, the broker may be required to register the additional office as a branch office and pay the required registration fee for each such office. All branch offices must be registered.

Additionally, if the broker or brokerage's name or advertising is displayed on an office other than the main office in such a way as to lead the public to believe the office is owned or operated by that same broker, then that office must be registered as a branch office.

If a broker decides to close a branch office and open a new one at a different location, the broker must register the new office and pay the registration fee for it. The registration for the closed branch office may not be transferred to the new branch office. If the broker decides to re-open the closed branch office within that office's license period, no additional fee will be required.

Entrance sign requirements

Every main and branch office must display a sign at the entrance that is easily visible and legible to anyone entering the office. The sign can be on the exterior or interior entrance of the office. Florida law requires the sign to contain the broker's name and any trade name. If the brokerage is a partnership or corporation, the sign must contain the partnership or corporation's name or trade name, as well as at least one of the brokers. The words "Licensed Real Estate Broker" or "Lic. Real Estate Broker" must be included on the entrance sign of any real estate brokerage or business entity.

Sunshine State Realty, LLC
John Kennedy
Licensed Real Estate Broker

The law does not require that sales or broker associates' names be included on entrance signs. If the broker chooses to include them, the names must be below the broker's name, with a space between the broker's name and the associates' names. The associates' names must also include "Sales Associate" or "Broker Associate," as appropriate.

Sunshine State Realty, LLC
John Kennedy
Lic. Real Estate Broker

Sally Kenney, Broker's Associate

Temporary shelters

Brokers sometimes set up temporary shelters in subdivisions they are selling to protect associates and customers. If the shelter is to be deemed temporary, associates may not be permanently assigned there, and the location may not be used for closings. In that case, the shelter need not be registered as a branch office. However, the permanence, use, and type of activities conducted at the shelter determine whether or not it must be registered. If, for example, transactions are closed within the shelter, it must be treated as a branch office and registered as such.

Sales associate officing

At initial licensure, a sales associate must be registered with an employing broker. The sales associate must work under the direction, control, and management of the specified broker or an owner-developer. The associate must work out of an office maintained by that same broker. The sales associate may be registered under only one broker at a time and may not operate as a broker or operate for any other broker who is not the associate's registered employing broker.

Americans with Disability Act

Purpose. The Americans with Disabilities Act (ADA), enacted in 1990, is a civil rights law that prohibits discrimination against individuals with disabilities in all areas of public life, including employment, education, transportation, and facilities open to the general public. The purpose of the law is to make sure that people with disabilities have the same rights and opportunities as everyone else.

Coverage. The Americans with Disabilities Act Amendments Act (ADAAA) became effective on January 1, 2009. Among other things, the ADAAA clarified that a disability is "a physical or mental impairment that substantially limits one or more major life activities." This definition applies to all titles of the ADA and covers private employers with 15 or more employees, state and local governments, employment agencies, labor unions, agents of the employer, joint management-labor committees, and private entities that are places of public accommodation. Examples of the latter include hotels, restaurants, retail stores, doctors' offices, golf courses, private schools, day care centers, health clubs, sports stadiums, and movie theaters.

Requirements. Key requirements of the ADA include establishing and maintaining accessible entrances and routes, including ramps, door width, maneuvering clearance, and accessible parking spaces.

Restrooms must have grab bars, a wheelchair-accessible turning radius, and accessible sinks and fixtures.

Lowered transaction counters for accessibility in service areas are required.

Existing buildings must remove architectural barriers when it is "readily achievable. New construction and alterations must fully comply with ADA standards, renovations must make altered areas accessible, and an accessible path of travel must be provided to altered areas (to the extent required).

Reasonable modifications must be made to policies when necessary. This is particularly important for property managers, who must reasonably modify parking policies and permit service animals.

Industry impact. In the real estate industry, the ADA impacts primarily brokerage firms, not individual licensees (because firms have a physical presence that may be required to comply with ADA regulations). Licensees who perform commercial property management functions will also be impacted.

Florida ADA Implementation Act. To ensure compliance with ADA requirements, Florida implemented the Florida Americans with Disabilities Accessibility Implementation Act. This act explicitly incorporates ADA requirements and guidelines into Florida law, particularly as they apply to building and construction accessibility.

This means that architectural accessibility requirements must meet standards that align with, or be more stringent than, federal ADA rules. The act also establishes and maintains the Florida Accessibility Code for Building Construction, which sets the technical accessibility rules for design, construction, and alteration of buildings and facilities in Florida. These requirements apply during new construction, renovations, and additions.

Fair housing

Federal and state governments have enacted laws prohibiting discrimination in the national housing market. The aim of these fair housing laws, or equal opportunity housing laws, is to give all people in the country an equal opportunity to live wherever they wish, provided they can afford to do so, without impediments of discrimination in the purchase, sale, rental, or financing of property.

State Fair Housing Laws. While states have enacted fair housing laws that generally reflect the provisions of national law, each state may have slight modifications. For that reason, it is incumbent upon Florida real estate students to learn the Florida laws and, in particular, note where these laws differ from national fair housing laws.

Fair Housing and Local Zoning. The Fair Housing Act prohibits a broad range of practices that discriminate against individuals on the basis of race, color, religion, sex, national origin, familial status, and disability. The Act does not pre-empt local zoning laws. However, the Act applies to municipalities and other local government entities and prohibits them from making zoning or land-use decisions or implementing land-use policies that exclude or otherwise discriminate against protected persons, including individuals with disabilities.

Advertising Guidelines

Prohibitions

False or misleading advertising. Florida law prohibits licensees from placing or causing to be placed any advertisement for property or services that is fraudulent, false, deceptive, misleading, or exaggerated. This includes written, television, and radio ads that are used to induce the sale, purchase, or rental of real property.

Penalties. False, deceptive, fraudulent, or misleading advertising can result in administrative fines and license suspension.

Blind advertising. Florida law requires that all advertisements include the brokerage's licensed name so any reasonable person would know the ad is from a real estate licensee. The broker's nickname may be included in the advertising as long as his or her legally registered name is also included. The broker's personal name may also be included in the ad, as long as the broker's last name, as it appears on the DBPR records, is included. Ads that do not include the brokerage's name are considered blind advertising and are prohibited.

Sales associates advertising or conducting business in own name. Brokerage services include advertising. Consequently, anyone placing advertisements must be a broker. Sales associates may create or place advertisements only under the supervision and in the name of their employing broker. Sales associates may not advertise in their own names. Any form of advertising created by a sales associate must include the brokerage's licensed name.

Sales associates and brokers' associates may sell their own property under their own name with their broker's permission. If selling under their own name and phone number, they do not need to display the brokerage name in the advertisement. However, the associates must disclose to anyone they plan to show the property to that they are licensed real estate agents.

Team advertising

Teams within a brokerage firm may advertise only under the supervision of the broker and in the name of the brokerage firm. To prevent confusion among the public, certain words, such as "brokerage," "realty," and the like, are not allowed in team names. The team's name must be in a font no larger than that used for the registered broker's name or logo. The team name must also be adjacent to the brokerage's name. For example, the team name cannot be at the top of the page and the brokerage name at the bottom. They must both appear either at the top or the bottom of the page.

Wording of advertisements

In addition to including the brokerage's name, real estate advertisements must be worded so that any reasonable person knows that the advertiser is a real estate licensee. They may not be worded in a way that makes the public believe the ad is from someone other than a real estate licensee.

Advertisements must be worded so that responding buyers or renters know who they are calling when they answer the ad. Consider the following sets of ad copy:

> "Three-bedroom, 2-bath ranch-style home in a good neighborhood. $350,000. Contact John Kennedy, Sunshine State Realty (816) 259-7802."

Here, it is unclear who the buyer should contact, John Kennedy or Sunshine State Realty. Consider a clearer version:

> "Three-bedroom, 2-bath ranch-style home in good neighborhood. $350,000. Sunshine State Realty. Contact John Kennedy, cell (816) 259-7802."

In this ad, it is clear that John Kennedy is associated with the Sunshine State real estate company, and phone calls will go to John Kennedy.

Internet advertising

Just as with any other form of advertising, the brokerage's name must appear within all internet advertisements. Florida administrative rule requires the name to be placed adjacent to, immediately above, or immediately below the point of contact information. Again, this prevents blind advertising and any related penalties.

Point of contact information. Information on how to contact the brokerage firm or the individual licensee is referred to as "point of contact information." Such contact information includes mailing address, physical street address, e-mail address, telephone number, and facsimile (fax) telephone number.

Telephone solicitation laws

Telephone Consumer Protection Act. The TCPA (Telephone Consumer Protection Act) regulates unsolicited telemarketing phone calls. Rules include the following:

- Telephone solicitors are banned from using an artificial or a pre-recorded voice to a residential line without prior express consent.
- Robocalls (prerecorded calls) from telemarketers or debt collectors without prior express consumer consent are banned.
- Solicitors are banned from using a fax or computer to fax unsolicited advertisements.
- Solicitors are banned from using an auto dialer to send text messages to cell phones without prior express consumer consent.
- Calls after 9 p.m. and before 8 a.m. in the consumer's time zone are banned.
- telephone solicitors must identify themselves, on whose behalf they are calling, and how they can be contacted
- telemarketers must comply with any do-not-call request made during the solicitation call
- consumers can place their home and wireless phone numbers on a national Do-Not-Call list, which is maintained by the Federal Trade Commission and which prohibits future solicitations from telemarketers.

- Information on the national registry can be found online at https://www.consumer.ftc.gov/articles/0108-national-do-not-call-registry or https://www.donotcall.gov/ .
- Robocalls must provide an automated opt-out function during the call.
- Consumers may sue companies that violate the law on a per-call basis.

Exemptions from the Act.

- Debt collection calls with express consent (not written) and without any advertisements.
- Calls from nonprofit organizations, political organizations, and healthcare organizations.
- Certain exigent circumstances calls, such as fraud or cyber breach warnings.
- Federal debt collectors up to three times per month.
- A real estate licensee who has an actual buyer for an advertised "for sale by owner" property, only to negotiate a sale or to arrange a showing for a current customer.
- A real estate licensee with an established business relationship with a customer, even if the customer's number is on the national do-not-call list. Here, one may call for up to 18 months after the relationship began.
- A real estate licensee who has accepted a business inquiry or application from a customer within the last 3 months.

Florida Telephone Solicitation Act. In addition to the federal rules above, Florida imposes its own, often stricter, limits through the Florida Telephone Solicitation Act (Section 501.059, F.S.). The Act requires a telephone solicitor to obtain the called party's prior express written consent before making a sales call that uses an automated system to dial numbers or to play a recorded message, and it applies to text messages as well as voice calls. It limits sales calls to the hours between 8 a.m. and 8 p.m. in the called party's time zone, restricts how many times a solicitor may call the same person about the same subject within a 24-hour period, and prohibits disguising the origin of a call through caller-ID spoofing. Florida also maintains a no-sales-solicitation-calls list, administered by the Department of Agriculture and Consumer Services, and a person who receives calls in violation of the Act may sue for statutory damages. A licensee who prospects using autodialing or mass-texting tools should confirm the practice complies with both the federal TCPA and the Florida Act.

CAN-SPAM Act. The CAN-SPAM Act (Controlling the Assault of Non-Solicited Pornography and Marketing Act of 2003) supplements the Telephone Consumer Protection Act (TCPA) by covering solicitations through email. It

- bans sending unwanted email 'commercial messages' to wireless devices
- requires express prior authorization
- requires giving an 'opt out' choice to terminate the sender's messages

Junk Fax Prevention Act. Both the Junk Fax Prevention Act and the Federal Communications Commission (FCC) address the use of faxing for solicitations. Faxing unsolicited advertisements to residential or business fax machines is prohibited unless the consumer has given prior express consent. Both solicited and unsolicited faxes must include the following:

- the date and time the fax was sent
- the sending company's registered name
- the sending company's telephone number or the sending fax machine's telephone number
- an opt-out option on unsolicited faxes

Florida telemarketing laws

Florida state telemarketing laws apply to businesses located in Florida and to businesses outside the state that call Florida residents. The laws include the Florida Telemarketing Act and the Florida Telephonic Sales law. They are administered by the Florida Department of Agriculture and Consumer Affairs (FDACS) and the Attorney General, who investigate violations and assess penalties. Penalties for violations are assessed on a per-call basis. The maximum fine is $10,000 per call. The laws include the following:

- Telephone solicitors must obtain a license from the Florida Division of Consumer Services before operating in Florida.
- Solicitors must restrict their calls to 8 a.m. to 9 p.m.
- Solicitors may not block caller ID.
- Solicitors may not accept only credit card payments.
- The solicitor has 30 seconds to state his or her true name, the name of the company the telemarketer represents, and the goods or services being sold.
- Solicitors must tell consumers about their right to cancel any agreement to purchase the goods or services being offered.

Florida has its own do-not-call list that prohibits telemarketers from calling residential phones, cell phones, or paging devices. The FDACS is required to merge all Florida listings within the national do-not-call list with the Florida do-not-call list. Additional information and the registry can be found online at https://www.fdacs.gov/Consumer-Resources/Florida-Do-Not-Call .

Exemptions from the Florida laws. The following are exempted from Florida's telemarketing laws in some cases:

- licensed insurance professionals
- nonprofit and religious organizations
- political organizations
- certain newspapers
- certain banks

Real estate licensees are also exempt when they are calling a property seller in response to a yard sign or other advertisement placed by the seller. However, a licensee is not exempt if the seller is a "for sale by owner" advertiser who has placed his or her telephone number on the national do-not-call list.

Brokers are required to develop written procedures for solicitation calling policies. They must obtain do-not-call lists and train their employees and independent contractors (ICs) on how to use and maintain the lists. The lists should be reviewed periodically for new additions so licensees can remove them from their own solicitation call lists. Reviewing the national list is critical since federal law does not exempt real estate licensees. If a number is on the national list, whether or not it is on the state list, real estate licensees must not call that number.

Snapshot Review for Chapter 2

The following review summarizes the key rules and concepts from Chapter 2.

Brokerage Business Structures

- sole proprietorships – file with FDOS and register with DBPR
- general partnership – register with DBPR, one partner must be licensed broker
- limited partnership – create through FDOS, register with DBPR, at least one general partner must be licensed broker, limited partners invest capital only
- limited liability partnership – register with FDOS, requires written partnership agreement, all partners may manage business
- corporation (for profit or not-for-profit) – created via articles of incorporation with FDOS, register with DBPR, at least one officer/director must be active licensed broker, owned by stockholders, managed by board of directors
- limited liability company – register with FDOS, separate and distinct legal entity

Prohibited Brokerage Business Structures

- corporation sole – typically used for church organization
- joint venture – impermanent arrangement, not registered with FDOS because no written arrangement exists
- business trust – all participants in trust must be licensed and registered; trust itself is not register
- cooperative association – formed, owned, and operated by members; may buy and sell own property; not registered as a broker
- unincorporated association – may not own property or enter into contracts; not registered as broker

Trade Names

- brokers may register under legal name, business name, trade name
- must comply with Fictitious Name Act
- must be unique and appear on license and advertising
- only one trade name allowed
- LLC and Associates must use legal name only

Office Requirements

- stationary structured registered with DBPR
- enclosed room with private transaction space
- maintain appropriate records
- branch office required if business conducted at additional location; registered with Department
- entrance signs must be visible and legible, include broker name, trade name (if applicable), and "Licensed Real Estate Broker"
- temporary shelters may be used in subdivisions; not considered branch office if temporary and no closing are conducted there
- sales associates work under one broker and operate from broker's office; cannot have independent office or work for multiple brokers

Americans with Disabilities Act (ADA)

- prevents discrimination against individuals with disabilities
- applies to employers with 15+ employees; governs public accommodations, including brokerage offices
- requires accessibility, removal of barriers when feasible, reasonable policy modifications
- Florida ADA Implementation Act aligns Florida law with federal ADA

Fair Housing

- protects individuals against discrimination based on race, color, sex, national origin, familial status, disability
- applies to sales, rentals, financing
- does not override zoning laws, does prohibit discriminatory zoning decisions

Advertising Guidelines

- no false, misleading, deceptive, or exaggerated advertising
- penalties include fines and license suspension
- blind ads must include brokerage name
- sales associate marketing must be under broker supervision, include brokerage name
- team advertising must include brokerage name, avoid terms indicating team is a brokerage, cannot dominate brokerage name
- all ads must include broker name and contact info
- internet ads must include brokerage name near contact information
- telephone solicitation laws prohibit robocalls without consent, calls outside 8 a.m. – 9 p.m.; requires do-not-call compliance
- CAN-SPAM Act applies to all email marketing; requires consent and opt-out option
- Junk fax prevention act requires consent for fax ads, identification info, opt-out option
- Florida telemarketing laws enforced by FDACS and Attorney General; marketers must be licensed, identify themselves within 30 seconds, respect do-not-call laws

Chapter 2 Quiz: Opening a Real Estate Office

2.1 Which business structure is owned by a single individual who is fully responsible for all business activities and employees?

a. Limited liability partnership
b. Corporation
c. Sole proprietorship
d. General partnership

2.2 Which requirement must be met for a general partnership to be registered as a real estate brokerage in Florida?

a. All partners must be sales associates
b. At least one partner must be a licensed broker
c. The partnership must file articles of incorporation
d. Limited partners must invest capital

2.3 If the only licensed broker in a general partnership withdraws, what happens if no replacement is appointed within 14 days?

a. The partnership converts to an LLP.
b. Business may continue under supervision.
c. All licenses remain active for 60 days.
d. The partnership registration is canceled.

2.4 Which statement BEST describes the liability of limited partners in a limited partnership?

a. They are liable for all partnership debts.
b. They have no liability under any circumstances.
c. They are liable only if they manage the business or are named.
d. They are liable for acts of the general partner.

2.5 Which characteristic distinguishes a limited liability partnership (LLP) from a limited partnership?

a. Only one partner may manage the business
b. All partners may participate in management
c. Profits are taxed twice
d. Limited partners may not exist

2.6 In an LLP, a partner is liable for which of the following?

a. All debts of the partnership
b. Acts of all other partners
c. Only the broker's actions
d. Their own acts and their employees' acts

2.7 Which individuals are prohibited from serving as officers or directors of a brokerage corporation?

a. Inactive brokers
b. Sales associates and broker associates
c. Licensed active brokers
d. Shareholders

2.8 How long may a temporary broker remain in place while a permanent broker is being registered with FDOS and DBPR?

a. 14 days
b. 30 days
c. 60 days
d. 90 days

2.9 Which requirement applies to a for-profit corporate brokerage?

a. All directors must be licensed brokers.
b. At least one officer or director must be an active broker.
c. Sales associates may act as directors.
d. Only domestic corporations may register.

2.10 Which statement is TRUE for not-for-profit corporations in Florida?

a. They may distribute profits to members
b. They require only one director
c. They must file annual reports
d. They are exempt from dissolution

2.11 Which business structure CANNOT be registered as a real estate brokerage in Florida?

a. Limited liability company
b. Corporation sole
c. General partnership
d. Limited partnership

2.12 A joint venture in real estate is NOT registered with FDOS because ______.

a. It lacks partners.
b. It is permanent.
c. The brokers are already licensed.
d. It cannot earn profits.

2.13 Why are ostensible partnerships prohibited in Florida?

a. They lack tax identification numbers.
b. They are unprofitable
c. They involve unlicensed activity.
d. They mislead the public.

2.14 A broker who changes a registered trade name must do which of the following?

a. Notify FREC within 10 days
b. Obtain a new license
c. File a partnership agreement
d. Register a second trade name

2.15 How must a sales associate registered as an LLC appear on the license and all official documents?

a. Using a fictitious name
b. Using the brokerage's trade name
c. Using the associate's real name only
d. Using a team name

2.16 Which statement regarding broker office requirements is CORRECT?

a. Sales associates may maintain independent offices.
b. Offices may be mobile if records are electronic.
c. Office must be in stationary construction.
d. Records may be kept off-site without notice.

2.17 When must a temporary shelter be registered as a branch office?

a. When it has a visible sign
b. When associates are present
c. When closings are conducted there
d. When it is located in a subdivision

2.18 Which of the following is true regarding the 14-day period after the only licensed broker in a partnership dies or withdraws?

a. New brokerage business may continue
b. The partnership automatically dissolves
c. New brokerage business may not be performed
d. Sales associates may operate independently

2.19 A broker may register under how many trade names?

a. None
b. One
c. Two
d. Unlimited

2.20 A brokerage corporation must have at least one officer or director who is ______.

a. a limited partner
b. a sales associate
c. an active licensed broker
d. a CPA

2.21 Which agency enforces Florida telemarketing laws?

a. FREC only
b. DBPR only
c. The Department of State
d. FDACS and the Attorney General

2.22 Real estate brokerage offices must contain which of the following?

a. No private space
b. At least one enclosed room
c. Outdoor seating
d. Shared cubicles only

2.23 A sales associate may do which of the following?

a. Work under multiple brokers
b. Operate independently
c. Work under one employing broker
d. Maintain own office

2.24 Blind advertising occurs when ______.

a. the price is omitted
b. the brokerage name is omitted
c. team names are listed
d. a logo is used

2.25 CAN-SPAM requires ______.

a. no opt-out options
b. opt-out options
c. phone consent
d. broker approval

CHAPTER 3: OWNING, MANAGING AND SUPERVISING A REAL ESTATE OFFICE

Contents

- **Start-up Finances**
- **The Business Plan**
- **Brokerage Affiliation: Franchise or Independent**
- **Recordkeeping and Tax Considerations**
- **Personnel Management**

Learning Objectives

Upon completion of this chapter, you will be able to:

1. Describe what considerations are involved in developing a business plan and what types of initial start-up costs are involved in opening a real estate business
2. Describe factors to consider when projecting income and expenses of a real estate business, and list typical fixed and variable expenses incurred by a real estate business
3. Compare the advantages of purchasing a franchise versus remaining an independent broker
4. Distinguish between cash basis accounting and accrual basis accounting
5. Identify I.R.S. treatment concerning employees versus independent contractors
6. Describe considerations when hiring sales managers and personal assistants, and recruiting sales associates
7. Identify the equal employment opportunity laws and ADA requirements regarding hiring personnel
8. Describe the considerations regarding the development of employment agreements, including the various commission structure plans and what fees and payments are typically deducted from the associate's commission
9. Identify important topics to include in a training program for sales associates and what should be included in a policy and procedures manual
10. Describe the start-up finances of a new brokerage, including the capital and operating funds needed to cover expenses during the initial period

Start-up Finances

DBPR regulation

Unlike some industries, the real estate industry in Florida is not subject to a minimum capital requirement for new brokerages. Owners and managers should carefully consider the costs of starting and operating the firm until it becomes profitable.

The DBPR does consider financial responsibility related to broker licensure. Broker license applicants often must demonstrate financial responsibility and stability.

Capital cost coverage

Most experts recommend that new business owners have sufficient capital to cover initial start-up costs as well as a minimum of six months of operating expenses. Depending on the business structure, this capital may consist of funds from the individual broker/owner, investors, or partners. Firms that depend on investors or partners for funding or management should engage an attorney to ensure all parties are protected.

Initial start-up costs

Individuals should consider the following start-up costs:

Licensing, registration, and legal fees. New brokerage firms will face costs for the firm's initial licensing with the DBPR, broker license activation, business entity formation (including filing with the Florida Division of Corporations, if necessary), and legal and accounting setup (including operating agreements, compliance advice, software purchases, membership fees in appropriate multiple listing services, legal library purchases, and draft independent contractor and other agreements.

Office Space and Facilities. The DBPR requires that brokerage firms have a permanent location. New firms will either lease or purchase office space and equip that space. If renting, a security deposit and the first month's rent are typically required, and deposits for utilities and technology services, such as internet and telephones, will likely be required.

Insurance and risk management. The brokerage firm and all affiliated licensees, including the broker, must obtain errors and omissions insurance. In addition, the firm should carry general liability insurance and, if hiring staff, workers' compensation insurance.

Technology and communication. If the firm will house licensees or unlicensed staff, owners will incur costs for computers, printers, scanners, and other technology-based equipment, as well as for providers and software. Most firms have some form of brokerage management software and a records management system.

Marketing and branding. As you are aware, new firms must register the brokerage firm's name. In addition, most independent firms will need logo design and tagline/slogan development. Firms may wish to develop a website and register a domain name to protect the firm's identity.

Introducing the firm to the community is a necessity, and can be accomplished through initial advertising and promotion. Though this can be costly, it is imperative to the firm's initial success. Some firms provide yard signs, business cards, stationery, and other branding materials to affiliated licensees, while other firms require licensees to absorb those costs individually.

MLS start-up fees and association dues are also a critical cost consideration.

Staffing and compensation. Most firms rely on independent contractor licensees, thereby avoiding any costs typically required to engage employees. However, the firm may choose to hire salaried licensees or unlicensed assistants to support the firm. This staffing engenders recruiting expenses. Additional costs will be incurred to develop training materials, policy manuals, and onboarding processes.

Escrow and accounting setup. The brokerage firm will establish necessary escrow/trust and operating accounts. Banks may require an initial minimum deposit for these accounts, and costs for checks and deposit slips must be considered. Many firms will implement computerized accounting and bookkeeping systems to simplify recordkeeping and ensure compliance with trust accounting requirements.

Operating capital. As noted above, start-up firms should ensure they have adequate capital to cover expenses for at least 6 months, allowing time for commissions to stabilize. This capital requirement should address continuing marketing, rent, insurance, and payroll costs.

The Business Plan

Purpose and content

A business plan is a written roadmap that explains what a business is, how it will operate, and how it will succeed financially. Not only is this document important for planning purposes, but it is also a critical component of any financing application.

In general, a business plan defines goals and direction; guides decision-making and daily operations; demonstrates feasibility and profitability to lenders, investors, or partners; identifies risks and risk-management strategies; and provides a benchmark for measuring performance and growth.

Executive summary. The business plan usually follows a somewhat standardized format, beginning with an executive summary that provides a brief overview of the business, key objectives, and a mission statement. Most topics addressed in the executive summary will be expanded on in later sections of the business plan.

The mission statement summarizes the firm's purpose and what it hopes to achieve. For example, "Our mission is to deliver ethical, professional real estate services that protect the public and help clients achieve their real estate goals with integrity and transparency."

Business description. The executive summary also describes the business type, ownership structure, and services offered.

Market analysis. To succeed, a business must identify its target market, competitors, and market demand. Armed with this information, the firm can develop appropriate marketing strategies, define how it will outperform the competition, and address how the firm fits into the overall market/area.

Organization and management. Who owns the firm? What is the management structure? What are key personnel roles? Answers to these questions define how the firm will operate.

Services provided. Brokerage firms have multiple options regarding the services they will provide. While most will represent both buyers and sellers, some firms focus on one or the other. Firms must determine which agency relationships they will offer and whether they will provide any third-party services (such as an in-house closing operation or title services). The market analysis and other planning steps help the firm define how its services will meet the needs of its proposed target market.

Marketing and sales strategy. The section of the executive summary briefly describes how the firm will price its services (commission or flat fee), the types of advertising it will implement, and how it will acquire clients, especially in the start-up phase.

Operations plan. A summary of the firm's day-to-day operations, policies, procedures, and compliance systems appears in this section of the executive summary.

Financial plan. A brief summary of the firm's financial plan here (including startup costs, operating expenses, revenue projections, and cash flow) will be addressed more fully in subsequent sections of the business plan.

Risk analysis and contingency plans. It is critical for firms to identify areas of risk and the strategies they will implement to address them.

Income projections

Brokers must consider multiple factors when developing income projections for the firm. Naturally, the firm's size and geographic area (scope of operations) will dictate income to a great degree. Both revenue and revenue timing (cash flow) projections are critical.

Projections should take into account start-up phase considerations, legal and regulatory compliance costs, commissions and commission splits, and anticipated salaries.

A market analysis should provide information on local real estate activity, particularly in the firm's proposed target market, including average sales price, average days on market, sales volume, list-to-sale price ratios, interest rates, overall economic conditions, and seasonal trends (especially in coastal communities). It is important to note that the factors involved in income projections are fluid. Market conditions can change rapidly, and the firm must be Knowledgeable and flexible enough to adapt to those changes.

It is better to undervalue income projections and overvalue expenses to some extent to ensure a more realistic financial picture.

Income sources

Most brokerage firms rely solely on commissions earned from representing buyers and sellers. Some firms expand into property management services, which can provide an additional revenue stream. Referral fees, consulting and advisory fees, desk and other fees paid by affiliated agents, and broker price opinions are alternative revenue sources. All revenue is strictly regulated by the DBPR.

Operating expense projections

A significant gauge of a new business's potential success is how accurately it projects expenses. Fortunately, the types of expenses firms encounter are relatively standard. The challenge lies in identifying exactly how that aligns with the firm's other projections and goals.

Firms must identify both fixed and variable expenses.

Fixed expenses

Fixed expenses remain relatively constant over time, regardless of the level of business activity. Thus, rent or mortgage payments, insurance premiums, licensing fees, equipment rentals, association fees, any local or state business taxes, technology subscriptions, and administrative salaries fall into this category. Expenses in this category are reasonably simple to identify for projection purposes.

Variable expenses

Variable expenses fluctuate based on transaction volume or business activity. These expenses include marketing and advertising, commission splits, transaction fees, office supplies, MLS listing fees, utilities, and printing.

Sample business plan

Sample Business Plan
ABC Realty Group, LLC
Florida Real Estate Brokerage

---

1. Executive Summary

ABC Realty Group, LLC is a Florida real estate brokerage registered with the **Florida Department of Business and Professional Regulation (DBPR)** and regulated by the **Florida Real Estate Commission (FREC)**. The brokerage will operate under the direction of an **actively licensed Florida broker** and will provide residential real estate services in compliance with **Chapter 475, Florida Statutes**, and **FREC administrative rules**. The firm's objective is to establish lawful operations, protect the public interest, and achieve profitability through ethical brokerage practices.

---

2. Business Description

ABC Realty Group, LLC is organized as a **limited liability company** registered with the **Florida Department of State** and licensed as a real estate brokerage by the DBPR. The brokerage will maintain a **registered office location** and conduct real estate brokerage activities, including listing, selling, and negotiating real property transactions. All brokerage activities will be conducted under the supervision of the broker of record.

---

3. Mission Statement

Our mission is to provide ethical and professional real estate brokerage services in compliance with Florida law while protecting the public and serving customers and clients with honesty, integrity, and transparency.

---

4. Market Analysis

The brokerage will serve a defined Florida residential market area with consistent demand for brokerage services. Target customers and clients include homebuyers, sellers, and small investors. The brokerage will compete with **franchise and independent brokerages** by emphasizing local market knowledge, broker supervision, and compliance-focused service.

---

5. Organization and Management

The brokerage will be operated by a **licensed Florida real estate broker** acting as the **broker of record**, who is responsible for:

- Supervision of all licensed sales associates and broker associates
- Compliance with FREC rules and Chapter 475, Florida Statutes
- Maintenance of transaction records and escrow accounts
- Training and oversight of licensees

Initially, the brokerage will register and employ **licensed sales associates** who will perform brokerage services under the broker's direction and control.

---

6. Brokerage Services

ABC Realty Group, LLC will provide the following brokerage services as defined under Florida law:

- Listing real property for sale or lease
- Representing buyers and sellers as customers or clients
- Preparing comparative market analyses (CMAs)
- Negotiating contracts and assisting with transaction coordination

The brokerage will comply with all **agency disclosure requirements**, including the use of **Florida-approved disclosure forms**.

---

7. Marketing and Advertising

All advertising will comply with **FREC advertising rules**, including the requirement that the **brokerage name** be clearly identified. Marketing methods will include online advertising, MLS participation, social media, signage, and networking. Sales associates' advertising will be reviewed and approved by the broker of record.

---

8. Operations, Escrow, and Record-Keeping

The brokerage will:

- Maintain **escrow (trust) accounts** in a Florida financial institution, as required
- Keep **transaction records, escrow records, and brokerage documents** for the required retention periods
- Use secure electronic record-keeping systems permitted by FREC
- Conduct periodic internal reviews to ensure compliance

All escrow handling and record-keeping will comply with FREC rules and DBPR requirements.

---

9. Financial Plan

Startup costs will include DBPR licensing fees, Department of State filing fees, office expenses, insurance, technology systems, and marketing. Ongoing expenses will include operating costs and compliance-related expenses. Brokerage income will be generated through **commission-based compensation** earned on real estate transactions.

---

10. Risk Management and Compliance

The brokerage will manage risk by:

- Maintaining required **errors and omissions insurance**
- Conducting ongoing licensee education and supervision
- Monitoring changes to Florida real estate laws and FREC rules
- Implementing written office policies and procedures

The broker of record will ensure the brokerage operates in a manner that **protects the public interest**, as required by FREC.

Brokerage Affiliation: Franchise or Independent

Franchise fee programs

A critical decision that new firms must make very early in the planning process is whether to act as a franchised or independent firm. Several regional and national franchised firms exist, and many brokers choose to affiliate with a franchise. Many others choose to operate independently. Each option has advantages and disadvantages.

Franchise advantages

Brand recognition is one of the primary advantages of affiliating a new firm with a franchise operation. Access to franchise-wide training and support programs is a second advantage. In addition, many large franchises have developed standardized processes, transaction management systems, and compliance tools that meet regulatory requirements. Franchises typically offer national or regional advertising campaigns and promotional materials, and affiliation provides access to a large network of other agents and offices, which can increase referrals and collaboration.

Franchise disadvantages

The primary disadvantage of affiliating with a franchise is the cost. Brokerage firms must pay franchise fees to affiliate with a franchised company, which can significantly increase expenses. In addition, firms or individual licensees may have to pay royalty fees, marketing fees for franchise-supplied marketing and advertising campaigns, and technology or desk fees for various systems, including lead generation tools.

Additionally, some brokers prefer the flexibility and autonomy of operating an independent firm.

Recordkeeping and Tax Considerations

Recordkeeping

Brokerage firms face the challenge of maintaining multiple types of records.

Transaction records. The DBPR mandates how long licensees must retain transaction records. These records include contracts, listings, purchase agreements, and closing documents. Such records must be retained, either electronically or in hard copy, for at least 5 years after the transaction date. Licensees should also document all communications, disclosures, and agency relationships and retain these documents with the standard transaction files.

Advertising and marketing records. Licensees must retain copies of all advertisements (print, digital, and social media) for at least five years. Typically, retaining these records serves as a defense if the firm is accused of discrimination or of violating any other advertising rules.

Employee and associate records. Firms must retain commission agreements, employment or independent contractor agreements, training and supervision records, payroll records, and licensing status for all sales and broker associates. Again, the retention length is at least five years.

Internal policies and procedures. Additional recordkeeping requirements apply to office policies for supervision, compliance, and risk management. Firms must document compliance with FREC rules, especially regarding agency disclosure and escrow handling.

Escrow accounts

The DBPR invokes strict compliance rules regarding the use of and accounting for escrow/trust accounts. Brokerage firms that hold client funds or accept lease/rental security deposits must open and maintain appropriate escrow accounts. You will learn more about the specific requirements in a subsequent chapter. For now, keep in mind that detailed ledger records of deposits, withdrawals, and disbursements are required.

Accounting records

Another critical decision a brokerage firm must make before operations begin is the type of accounting system to implement. Brokers should always consult an accountant familiar with the real estate field to discuss options.

Two main options are whether to use a **cash or accrual-based system**. Note that this refers to how revenue is reported, not the form of payment received. Many small businesses elect the cash system because it is much simpler and less time-consuming than accrual-based accounting.

Under the **cash system**, expenses are recorded when paid, and revenue when received.

Under the **accrual system**, expenses are recorded when they become due, and revenue is recorded when it becomes due. The benefit of this type of system is that it allows businesses to match revenue received during a specific period with the expenses required to generate it. However, this system requires considerably more time and effort than the cash system.

Tax considerations

Brokerage firms face multiple tax considerations.

Business taxes. Brokerage entities must file state and federal income tax returns, in addition to those filed by individuals. The entity type impacts how income is taxed. Again, this is an important conversation to have with an accountant during the planning stages of the new firm.

Employment taxes. If the firm has employees, brokers must withhold and remit federal and state payroll taxes, including income and workers' compensation taxes. Sales and broker associates are usually independent contractors, but firms and individual licensees must ensure compliance with all IRS guidelines regarding independent contractor status.

Deductible expenses. Operating expenses are typically deductible for income tax purposes, so appropriate accounting procedures are critical to ensure the firm can utilize every possible deduction and support all deductions in the event of an audit.

Escrow and trust funds. Funds held in escrow are not income, and therefore are not taxable to the broker unless they include commission funds. In that situation, the funds become taxable when received (cash accounting) or earned (accrual accounting).

Personnel Management

Support staff

Small, independent firms may have little to no support staff. As the firm grows and adds sales staff (or is larger to begin with), it may become necessary to hire administrative assistants, unlicensed/personal assistants, transaction coordinators, and accounting or recordkeeping staff. In addition, though less common, some firms engage licensees as employees rather than independent contractors.

Sales manager. Brokers should monitor the firm's growth and activity and consider hiring a sales manager when it becomes difficult for them to manage staffing and supervision on their own. These managers may be compensated through salary, salary plus commission (if the manager is to remain active in representing clients), or commission only.

Compliance. Brokerage firms must comply with all federal, state, and local employment laws. They are responsible for withholding appropriate accounting, tax withholding, and supervision. The firm's broker is ultimately responsible for these tasks, though they may be delegated to others within the firm.

Sales associates

Unless a firm is operated solely by a broker acting as the lone sales associate, it must engage the services of sales associates to meet the production goals stated in the business plan. Just as hiring the "right" employees is critical to a firm's success, engaging the "right" independent contractor sales associates is critical to a firm's success.

Attributes that signal success. Each associate who affiliates with a firm should, of course, be able to sell themselves, the firm, and listings. They should be coachable, excited about learning, and willing to accept personal accountability. They should demonstrate professional communication skills, including prompt responses to emails, phone calls, and texts. They should be able to explain concepts simply. They must demonstrate a respect for rules and procedures and possess a clean or explainable license history. An entrepreneurial mindset is important, as is the willingness and ability to work well with others.

Key challenges. Hiring sales associates in Florida presents challenges, both those common to hiring in any geographic area and those specific to Florida. Real estate in general has a notoriously high churn rate. Many new licensees fail to recognize and plan for the difficulty of finding and closing early deals, building a client base, and the resulting financial instability during the early years.

Florida's real estate market is among several known for being highly competitive (due to a large supply of licensees relative to available listings). This oversaturation leads many agents to leave the industry early due to income volatility. Brokers may choose to focus on engaging licensees with proven production or strong potential.

Miscellaneous contract services

Larger firms may choose to engage other contract providers, such as janitorial services, sign delivery and construction services, and technology services. They may engage trainers for specific topics. Note that these contractors will be managed somewhat differently than licensee contractors for the reasons noted previously.

Recruitment and selection

Brokers face various challenges when recruiting sales associates who will align with the firm's goals and strategies. Many brokers partner with local real estate schools to recruit new licensees. Firms that gravitate toward more experienced licensees may use local job boards, networking events, and associations to generate recruits. Encouraging staff to refer skilled friends and family members and urging affiliated licensees to recruit other high-caliber colleagues is another potential resource.

Wherever the brokerage identifies potential candidates, it should clearly communicate the affiliation process and provide support and guidance to promising candidates as they navigate the Florida licensing process.

Recruitment tools. Traditional recruitment perks are unlikely to attract high-quality licensees. In fact, many "traditional" perks (such as insurance, paid time off, and sick pay) are not available to independent contractors. Brokers are challenged to develop a compensation plan that attracts quality licensees while balancing firm profitability. Some tools firms use to attract licensees include tiered commission splits, lead or marketing support, reduced desk fees, performance incentives, and access to technology and CRM tools.

Career nights. A career night is a recruiting event a brokerage hosts to attract prospective associates. The firm invites people who are considering, or are new to, a real estate career to an informational session describing the profession, the firm's training and support, and its commission structure and culture, with the goal of recruiting promising candidates.

Brand and value differentiation. Many brokerages appear similar to potential recruits, making it difficult to stand out. Brokers must articulate and market a unique value proposition that resonates with both top producers and newcomers.

As previously noted, brokers must align production goals with the number of licensees needed. While not an exact science, identifying the estimated dollar value of commissions earned by a licensee in general and mathematically comparing that to the firm's revenue goals is a start.

Brokerage firms may offer desk space to licensees, and the number of available work areas also dictates the number of licensees that can join the firm. However, many licensees elect to work remotely but must ensure the brokerage firm serves as the office of record.

Brokers should carefully evaluate the effectiveness of hiring part-time licensees. While many licensees work part-time in real estate until they begin to generate a decent level of income, they may have difficulty attending meetings or training unless their "other" job is flexible. Some clients may have concerns about working with part-time licensees.

Strong onboarding and ongoing skill development are crucial to new licensees' success. Consider pairing new hires with seasoned mentors. Frequent workshops on market trends, technology tools, and effective sales practices help all affiliated licensees become more productive.

Application Process

Brokers must never lose sight of regulations governing the application and hiring process. For example, firms must comply with equal employment opportunity and ADA regulations. All procedures must be the same for each candidate. For example, if one applicant is required to submit an application, all applicants should be required to do the same. Employment law is complex; brokers should seek expert help to avoid legal complications.

Equal employment laws and the ADA. Federal equal employment laws focus primarily on preventing discrimination in hiring. Firms should establish and adhere to hiring practices that treat all applicants equally. Applicants should be evaluated based on their skills, experience, and ability to perform the required tasks. ADA regulations require that firms provide reasonable accommodations for qualified applicants with disabilities when required.

Hiring criteria. Brokerage firms must establish clear hiring and evaluation criteria and ensure they comply with all regulations. Firms should use standardized application forms for all applicants, which become part of the individual's permanent record.

Job descriptions. A job description is a written statement of the duties, responsibilities, and performance expectations of a particular position. Clear job descriptions help the broker recruit and hire suitable people, set expectations, supervise consistently, and evaluate performance fairly.

Organizational chart. An organizational chart is a diagram of the office's structure. It shows the positions in the firm, broker, sales managers, associates, and administrative staff, and the reporting relationships among them, so that everyone understands the lines of authority and accountability.

References. Another standard procedure is to check references. Experienced licensees should be able to produce references directly related to their work in the industry. New licensees may rely on references who can attest to the characteristics required of a successful licensee.

License status. Brokers must verify a licensee's license status, including any disciplinary actions, keeping in mind that new licensees may have an inactive license if they have not yet affiliated with a broker.

Interviews. Many interview methods exist, and each broker should implement a system that is most likely to identify candidates who are a good fit for the firm. Once again, consistency is important. The same interview process and questions should be used in each interview.

Employment arrangements

Brokers must be thoroughly familiar with the differences between hiring/managing staff and engaging independent contractors. In the real estate industry, managing independent contractors is different from managing contractors in other industries, too, because brokers are more responsible for the actions of their affiliated licensees than managers in other types of firms are for contractors they hire.

Employee relationships. Employee relationships are characterized by the amount and type of control the employer maintains over the employee. The hiring party controls how, when, and where work is performed. The employee is paid a salary or an hourly wage.

Independent contractor relationships. Strict IRS regulations govern who can and cannot be classified as an independent contractor. In general, employers cannot control how, when, or where independent contractors work. Contractors pay their own expenses and taxes, own their own tools and equipment, have the opportunity for profit or loss, and are not reimbursed for routine expenses. In the real estate industry, brokers do have the right to ensure that independent contractors are properly trained and supervised. They must verify licensure and ensure the licensee maintains an active license.

Independent contractor agreement. While Florida law does not require brokers to use an independent contractor agreement with sales associates, they are strongly encouraged to do so. This agreement not only outlines the broker's expectations of the licensee, but it also serves as evidence that the licensee is indeed a contractor, not an employee. Brokers may be able to obtain a sample agreement from their REALTORS® Association.

This agreement should state that the individual is an independent contractor and thus responsible for all related taxes. It should spell out commission splits, fees, advertising rules, association membership rules, use of brokerage systems and branding, and termination procedures.

Without this agreement and proper treatment, both the broker and the licensee risk misclassification claims, which can be financially devastating for both parties.

Compensation

Brokers with unlicensed staff will have to navigate two compensation methods.

Unlicensed staff. Non-commission employees submit a W-4 to the employer. This form identifies how much the broker should withhold for state and federal income taxes. Brokers pay unlicensed staff wages (hourly or salary) and deduct, submit, and report state and federal taxes from employee compensation. They may offer benefits such as health insurance, paid time off, and retirement accounts. Employees receive a W-2 at the end of the year to use for filing income tax returns.

Licensed independent contractors. Most licensees work on a commission basis, earning revenue only when the firm earns a commission from representing a client. Contractors earn a percentage of the commission the brokerage negotiated with the client in the agency agreement. The licensee's commission earned is based on the compensation plan outlined in the independent contractor agreement.

Traditional commission split. One common commission structure is a straight commission split percentage, such as 70/30. The first number in the split is the amount the licensee receives.

For example, Abrams Realty earned a 2.5% commission by representing a buyer in a transaction that closed at $250,000. Thus, the total commission earned was $6,250. The broker's agreement with the licensee provides for a 70/30 split, meaning the licensee receives 70% of the earned commission, or $ 4,375 in this case. The firm retains the remaining $1,875.

One disadvantage of this compensation method is that high producers may not feel adequately rewarded for their productivity.

Graduated or tiered split. This method is similar to the traditional split, but the split paid to the licensee increases based on graduated productivity levels.

For example, the firm may offer a 60/40 split for sales up to $50,000; a 70/30 split for sales between $50,000 and $100,000; and an 80/20 split for sales over $100,000.

This method incentivizes productivity but requires more complex accounting.

Commission cap. With this model, the agent keeps all commissions after the broker reaches a pre-determined cap.

Under this structure, the broker and contractor could agree that, after the broker has earned $25,000 in commissions under a traditional split, the licensee keeps 100% of the brokerage-earned commissions.

Flat fee/100% commission. Under this model, agents keep all or nearly all of the commissions earned on each transaction, but will likely pay a desk fee, a transaction fee, and a technology or compliance fee.

As an example, a licensee under this method earns $74,500 by closing 10 transactions. The licensee keeps the commissions but pays a $475 fee for each transaction. Some brokers charge for both sides of the transaction, i.e., if the licensee represents both the buyer and the seller, the transaction fee would be $950.

Other commission structures exist, but these are the most common.

Contractors provide the broker with a W-9 form, which includes the contractor's legal name, address, and Social Security or Employer ID number. Brokers provide the IRS and the independent contractor with a 1099 at the end of the year that details the commission amount the licensee received.

Training and supervision

Similar to all states, Florida strictly regulates broker supervision of affiliated licensees. Brokers are required to provide "adequate" supervision of licensees. The concept of adequate supervision in Florida is grounded in the broker's duty to direct, control, and manage the licensed activities of the people they sponsor.

Activities required of brokers include the following:

- monitor sales activities (review listings, contracts, and transaction progress)
- ensure office policy compliance
- provide training and support
- be available to licensees at reasonable times
- supervise advertising
- review transaction files for accuracy and compliance

Florida treats supervision as a broker obligation. Brokers can be disciplined for failing to provide adequate supervision under the concept of vicarious liability. For example, if a licensee is disciplined for failing to properly disclose an agency relationship, the broker may also be disciplined.

Brokers can protect themselves against some issues by documenting policies and procedures, providing training, and offering mentoring. Requiring licensee signatures on policy and procedure manuals can demonstrate that the licensee received, read, and understood them.

Policy and procedures manual

Florida statute does not require a policy and procedures manual, but brokers are encouraged to develop and maintain one. A Florida real estate brokerage policy and procedures manual should address two primary issues: 1) legal compliance with FREC/DBPR rules and 2) clear, practical guidance for brokers and sales associates.

While each firm should determine the exact content of its manual, common topics include the following:

- brokerage structure and authority
- licensure and affiliation policies
- broker supervision and office management
- independent contractor and employment policies
- trust account and escrow procedures
- transaction management processes
- advertising and marketing compliance
- ethics, fair housing, and professional conduct
- recordkeeping and document retention
- risk management and legal compliance
- education and training requirements
- technology and data security
- termination, transfers, and dispute resolution

Broker/sales manager Responsibilities

The firm's broker is ultimately responsible for all brokerage-related activities, including tasks delegated to others. You may recall a previous mention of vicarious liability. Florida places direct responsibility on the broker for escrow handling, local, state, and federal regulatory compliance, and general supervision.

Brokers must actively oversee day-to-day licensee activities, including reviewing contracts, listing agreements, and other transaction documents; ensuring proper disclosures are made; supervising escrow and trust account processes; and ensuring all sales staff are properly licensed.

In short, the broker is the point of accountability for all brokerage operations.

Snapshot Review for Chapter 3

The following review summarizes the key rules and concepts from Chapter 3.

CAPITAL REGULATION BY DBPR

Start-up Finances

- Florida does not require minimum capital for brokerages; brokers must demonstrate financial responsibility, per DBPR
- initial start-up costs: DBPR licensing and registration fees, legal/accounting setup and escrow/trust account setup, MLS memberships, office rent, utilities, internet, and phones, computers, software, and recordkeeping systems; recruiting/training costs, marketing, branding, signs, website, and advertising, insurance: errors and omissions, liability, workers' compensation.

Business Plan

- business plan = roadmap for business operations and profitability, helps obtain financing and attract investors, defines goals, risks, and growth strategies
- key business plan components: executive summary and mission statement, business description and ownership structure, market analysis and target market, management structure and staffing, services offered, marketing and sales strategy, operations and compliance systems, financial plan and risk management
- income projections based on market activity, sales volume, pricing, and expenses, should account for cash flow timing, and better to underestimate income and overestimate expenses
- income sources: commissions, property management fees, referral fees, consulting services, desk and transaction fees
- operating expenses: fixed expenses: rent, insurance, salaries, licensing fees, subscriptions; variable expenses: marketing, commission splits, MLS fees, office supplies, utilities

Franchise vs. Independent

Brokerage

- franchise advantages: brand recognition, training and support systems, standardized compliance tools, referral networks and advertising support
- franchise disadvantages: franchise, royalty, and marketing fees, less flexibility and autonomy
- independent brokerage advantages: greater control and independence, avoids franchise-related costs

Recordkeeping and Tax Considerations

- transaction, advertising, and employment records retained at least 5 years, paper/electronic records allowed; firms must document disclosures and agency relationships
- DBPR/FREC rules govern escrow handling; detailed records of deposits and disbursements required
- accounting systems: cash basis = income/expenses recorded when received or paid; accrual basis = income/ recorded when earned or due
- tax considerations: brokerages file state/federal tax returns, employees require payroll tax withholding, most sales associates treated as independent contractors, operating expenses generally tax deductible

Personnel Management

- hiring and recruiting through schools, networking, referrals, and job boards; firms must follow equal employment and ADA laws; applicants evaluated consistently using standard procedures
- independent contractors vs. employees: employees receive wages and benefits, independent contractors control their own work and taxes, brokers should use written independent contractor agreements

- commission structures: traditional split, graduated/tiered split, flat-fee, or 100% commission plans, commission cap
- brokers responsible for adequate supervision, providing ongoing training and policy guidance, supervision of advertising, contracts, disclosures, and escrow
- policy and procedures manual addresses supervision, escrow handling, advertising compliance, ethics and fair housing, recordkeeping, training and dispute resolution
- recruiting tools include career nights to attract prospective associates
- organizational chart shows positions and reporting relationships
- written job descriptions set duties and performance expectations

Chapter 3 Quiz: Owning, Managing, and Supervising a Real Estate Office

3.1 What amount does Florida require new real estate brokerages to maintain as a minimum capital amount?

a. $10,000
b. $50,000
c. An amount set by FREC
d. No specific minimum capital requirement

3.2 Broker applicants must demonstrate which of the following?

a. Franchise affiliation
b. Financial responsibility and stability
c. A minimum MLS balance
d. Six months of commission history

3.3 Most experts recommend new brokerages maintain enough capital to cover start-up costs plus at least ______.

a. 30 days of expenses
b. 3 months of expenses
c. 6 months of expenses
d. 12 months of payroll

3.4 Filing a new brokerage entity with the Florida Division of Corporations is part of what costs?

a. Marketing
b. Licensing and registration
c. Variable expenses
d. Commission splits

3.5 Which of the following will a brokerage that leases office space typically pay?

a. Royalty fees only
b. A security deposit and first month's rent
c. Commission advances
d. Transaction bonuses

3.6 A brokerage is typically required to carry what type of insurance?

a. Errors and omissions
b. Health insurance for contractors
c. Automobile liability for agents' personal vehicles
d. Franchise bonding insurance

3.7 MLS start-up fees and association dues are classified as which of the following?

a. Optional luxury expenses
b. Capital investments
c. Critical start-up cost consideration
d. Personal expenses of licensees only

3.8 What is the primary purpose of a business plan?

a. Satisfy FREC recordkeeping rules
b. Provide a roadmap for operations and financial success
c. Replace escrow procedures
d. Establish commission splits

3.9 Which of the following does the executive summary of a business plan typically include?

a. Detailed trust account ledgers
b. Mission statement and key objectives
c. All commission agreements
d. MLS statistics

3.10 What should a mission statement primarily describe?

a. Commission percentages
b. Office lease terms
c. The firm's purpose and goals
d. Payroll structure

3.11 Which of these factors should a market analysis examine?

a. Only franchise competitors
b. Average sales price and days on market
c. Internal staffing only
d. Advertising copy formats

3.12 Income projections should consider revenue timing because it affects ______.

a. advertising design
b. cash flow
c. office décor
d. commission caps

3.13 It is generally safer to do which of the following when preparing projections?

a. Overestimate income
b. Underestimate expenses
c. Overestimate expenses and undervalue income
d. Ignore seasonal trends

3.14 Which of the following is a common additional income source for brokerages?

a. Property management fees
b. Escrow deposits
c. Security deposits
d. Licensing penalties

3.15 Which of the following best describes fixed expenses?

a. They increase with transaction volume.
b. They remain relatively constant regardless of activity.
c. They occur only during closings.
d. They are optional.

3.16 Commission splits paid to sales associates are generally categorized as which of these?
a. Fixed expenses
b. Capital investments
c. Variable expenses
d. Trust liabilities

3.17 What is a major advantage of a franchise affiliation?
a. Elimination of all fees
b. Guaranteed profit
c. Brand recognition and standardized systems
d. Exemption from FREC and DBPR regulation

3.18 Which of these is a primary disadvantage of franchise affiliation?
a. Lack of supervision
b. Royalty and franchise fees
c. Limited access to referrals
d. No market support

3.19 For what minimum length of time should brokerages retain transaction records?
a. 3 years
b. 4 years
c. 5 years
d. 7 years

3.20 Copies of all advertisements must be retained for what length of time?
a. 1 year
b. 2 years
c. 3 years
d. 5 years

3.21 Which of the following is true regarding funds held in escrow?
a. They are immediately classified as taxable income.
b. They are considered broker profit.
c. They are not considered income unless they include commission funds.
d. They are subject to payroll tax.

3.22 Under the cash accounting system, when is revenue recorded?
a. When it is earned
b. When it is due
c. When it is received
d. When it is negotiated

3.23 In Florida, which one of these is brokers required to provide?
a. Minimal supervision of affiliated licensees
b. Adequate supervision of affiliated licensees
c. No oversight of independent contractors
d. Supervision only for new agents

3.24 One sign of a potentially successful sales associate is ______.

a. Resistance to coaching
b. Poor communication habits
c. Respect for rules and procedures
d. Frequent license violations

3.25 Under a 70/30 commission split, the 70% represents the portion paid to which of these parties?

a. Licensee
b. Broker
c. Franchise
d. MLS

3.26 A brokerage engages its sales associates as independent contractors. Even so, Florida requires the broker to ______.

a. ensure the associates are properly trained and supervised
b. withhold income taxes from the associates' commissions
c. pay the associates an hourly wage
d. control the daily hours and location of the associates' work

3.27 Under a commission-cap arrangement, once the broker has collected a predetermined amount from an associate's production during the year, the associate ______.

a. must renegotiate the listing agreement
b. reverts to a 50/50 split
c. loses eligibility for further commissions
d. keeps 100% of subsequent commissions

3.28 A broker may be disciplined for a sales associate's violation when the broker failed to provide adequate supervision. This principle is known as ______.

a. respondeat inferior
b. vicarious liability
c. constructive notice
d. procuring cause

CHAPTER 4: ESCROW MANAGEMENT

Contents

- **Handling Escrow Deposits**
- **Escrow Disputes and Settlement**
- **Commingling and Conversion**
- **Title Company and Attorney Escrow Accounts**
- **Broker's Recordkeeping**

Learning Objectives

Upon completion of this chapter, you will be able to:

1. Describe the purpose of escrow accounts, the types of monies that must be held in escrow, and authorized depositories for establishing escrow accounts
2. Distinguish between commingling of funds and conversion
3. Describe the requirements for timely deposit of escrow funds and interest-bearing escrow accounts
4. Describe the requirements for placing escrow deposits with title companies and attorneys
5. Calculate the broker's trust liability, reconciled bank balance, and prepare a monthly reconciliation statement
6. Explain what a broker must do when a good-faith doubt or conflicting demands arise over an escrow deposit, including the notice given to FREC and the applicable timeframes
7. Describe the settlement procedures for resolving an escrow dispute: mediation, arbitration, litigation, and an escrow disbursement order

Handling Escrow Deposits

Deposit requirements compliance

Definition of escrow account. An escrow account, also known as a trust account, is an account established at a qualified depository institution in Florida, such as a bank, credit union, or savings and loan association. These accounts are established to hold funds belonging to others until they are disbursed for a specific purpose. The account is held by a third party to a transaction and holds money, such as earnest money from a property buyer, until property ownership is transferred at closing. Brokers do NOT have to open and maintain a trust account if they do not intend to hold funds for others. For sales transactions, brokers may rely on a title company or attorney to hold funds in escrow.

Escrow accounts may be used to hold rental property deposits and rent payments; however, while not required, brokers should maintain sales funds and rental funds in separate escrow accounts. The funds deposited into the escrow account most commonly include cash, checks, money orders, and drafts.

Florida law mandates that a trust account hold only third-party funds. **No licensee's personal funds should be commingled with trust funds.** However, the law permits brokers to deposit up to $1,000 in a sales escrow account or $5,000 in a property management escrow account to cover transaction fees.

Escrow funds must be held in the escrow account until the transaction closes or one of the proper settlement procedures is completed. (See following Settlement procedures section)

One of the duties owed to any client or customer is to account for all funds. Acceptable trust fund management requires that the client or customer be kept informed of the funds' location at all times.

Sales associate funds delivery requirements. If a property buyer gives earnest money or any other deposit to a sales associate in relation to a real estate transaction, the sales associate is required to turn the money over to his or her employing broker no later than the end of the next business day, not counting Saturdays, Sundays, or legal holidays. The same timing applies to rental deposits.

For example, Buyer Susan gives Sales Associate John an earnest money check on Monday morning. John must turn the check over to Broker Justin by the end of the day on Tuesday. Let's say that Tuesday is a legal holiday. That means John needs to turn the check over to Justin by the end of the day on Wednesday.

Definition of "immediately" for a broker. Florida administrative rules state that brokers who receive any form of funds from their sales associates related to a real estate transaction must immediately deposit them into an escrow account. The rule defines "immediately" as no later than the end of the third business day following receipt of the item to be deposited, with Saturdays, Sundays, and legal holidays not considered business days. The three business days begin when the sales associate receives the funds, not when the broker receives them from the sales associate.

Here's how this works: If the funds are received on Monday, Tuesday is the first business day "following receipt of the item to be deposited." Wednesday is the second business day after receipt of the deposit, and Thursday is the third business day, on which the funds must be deposited into the escrow account.

So, given the previous example, if associate John receives an earnest money check on Monday and turns it over to broker Justin on Tuesday, Justin must deposit it into his escrow account by the end of the day on Thursday. If Tuesday is a holiday and John turns the check over to Justin on Wednesday, Justin deposit the funds by the end of the day on Friday.

Requirements if deposited with a title company or attorney. Funds related to a real estate transaction may be deposited or placed in escrow with a title company or an attorney. When this happens, the company's or attorney's name, address, and telephone number must be noted on the sales contract by the licensee who prepared it. All deposit requirements for the broker's escrow account also apply to deposits made with a title company or attorney.

When funds are due for deposit, the licensee's broker has 10 business days to request in writing that the title company or attorney provide written verification that the funds were received and deposited. Then, within 10 business days of that request, the broker must provide the seller's broker either a copy of the written verification that the funds were received and deposited or a written notice that the broker did not receive verification of the funds and deposit. This verification is not necessary if the title company or attorney was nominated in writing by the seller or the seller's agent. If the seller is not represented by a broker, the buyer's broker is to notify the seller directly.

If the funds have been placed in escrow with a title company or an attorney, there is no Florida statute that regulates those accounts. Consequently, FREC will not step in to resolve any conflict over the disbursement of the funds if the transaction does not close. To settle the dispute, the parties will need to rely on the appropriate court and bear the expense of doing so.

Managing escrow accounts

Escrow account signatory. Florida administrative rules require the broker to be the signatory on all escrow accounts. If there is more than one broker licensee within the brokerage, then any one of those licensees may be the designated signatory.

Escrow account maintenance. The broker is responsible for reconciling the accounts each month and ensuring they comply with Florida law. The broker must also provide a monthly written statement comparing the broker's total liability with the bank balances of all escrow accounts.

The statement needs to include the date the account reconciliation was completed, the date used to reconcile the balances, the name of the bank and the account, the account number, account balance and date, any deposits in transit, outstanding checks, and an itemized list of the broker's trust liability.

The broker must keep records of all deposits, the source of funds, and each account, and provide those records and transaction-related agreements to the DBPR when requested. The records must be kept for at least 5 years.

Requirements for interest distribution. The broker may hold escrow funds in an insured, interest-bearing account at a banking facility located in Florida. All parties associated with the particular transaction must agree in writing to use an interest-bearing account. They must also agree regarding to whom and when the interest will be disbursed.

Requirements for conflicting demands for escrow funds. When a real estate transaction does not close, the earnest money and any other related funds must be disbursed to the appropriate party. If the parties to the transaction dispute who should receive the funds and both parties make demands for the funds, the broker must notify FREC of the conflict within 15 business days of the last demand. The broker should use the Notice of Escrow Dispute/Good Faith Doubt form available on the DBPR website.

The broker must also proceed with a settlement procedure (see below) within 30 business days after the last demand and notify FREC of the procedure being used to resolve the conflict. The notification timing requirements for both the conflict and settlement procedures begin on the same day.

For example, if the broker received the last demand for escrow funds on June 1, the 15-business-day period for notifying FREC of the conflict begins on June 1. The 30-business-day period for notifying FREC of the settlement procedure starts on July 1.

Good-faith doubt procedure and situations. The term "good faith" refers to a sincere, honest motive, free of malice or intent to defraud. People enter into contracts, such as real estate sales contracts, with a presumption of good faith that the parties will be honest and fair and not negatively impact the other party's right to benefit from the contract. When one party appears not to be behaving in good faith, the behavior creates doubt in that party's good faith. If that doubt is sincere and honest, it is referred to as good-faith doubt.

If a broker has a good-faith doubt as to who is entitled to the funds held in the broker's escrow account, he or she should first look to the sales contract for the escrow instructions. If the contract does not resolve the doubt, the broker must notify FREC within 15 business days of the doubt, using the Notice of Escrow Dispute/Good Faith Doubt form. The broker may have a good-faith doubt based on any of many situations.

For example, one party indicates he does not plan to comply with the closing schedule and terms but does not provide the broker with instructions for disbursing the trust funds, or provides instructions that do not match those in the sales contract.

Another example is that the transaction closes, and the parties provide different instructions for disbursing the funds.

Yet another situation leading to good-faith doubt for the broker would be if the transaction fails to close and one party does not respond to the broker's request for disbursement instructions, thus requiring the broker to send notice to that party that the funds will be released to the other party if he or she does not respond by a given date.

Once the broker develops good-faith doubt, he or she must begin the settlement procedure (see below) within 30 business days of developing such doubt. The determination of good faith doubt is based upon the facts of each case brought before FREC.

Escrow Disputes and Settlement

Mediation

Mediation defined. Mediation is an informal conflict resolution process conducted by a qualified third party.

The purpose of mediation is to bring the parties together and, with the mediator's guidance, reach a mutually agreeable resolution. Mediation may be used to resolve the conflict if all parties give written consent. Once an agreement is reached, it is documented in writing and signed by both parties, becoming a binding contract.

If the parties do not all consent to mediation or if the conflict is not resolved in mediation within 90 days of the last demand, the broker must employ one of the other settlement procedures. All statements made during mediation are confidential and may not be used in any other proceeding.

Arbitration

Arbitration defined. Arbitration is a dispute settlement procedure conducted by one or more (usually three) third-party arbitrators acting as judges.

Typically, each side chooses one arbitrator, and the two then select a third. The arbitrators hear evidence, make decisions, and give written opinions. The arbitrators' decisions are binding. The parties must agree in writing to submit the matter to arbitration and to comply with the arbitrators' final decision.

Litigation

Litigation is a legal procedure either party may use if parties do not agree to mediation or arbitration

In this case, one party would file a lawsuit to have the dispute heard in court and resolved. However, because mediation is so successful and cost-effective, Florida courts require most lawsuits to be mediated before a court will hear the case. Litigation can involve either of the following procedures:

- ***interpleader action*** – an interpleader action is a means for the broker holding the escrow funds to be removed from the dispute over the disbursement of the funds

The funds are placed in the court depository, and it is up to the court to determine who will receive them. This also removes the broker from any potential liability arising from the final disbursement. Contracts often include provisions for the interpleader action costs to be paid with the escrow funds or for the loser of the case to pay the other party's attorney fees.

- ***declaratory judgment*** – a declaratory judgment is requested when the broker claims part of the escrow funds

The broker would file for a declaratory relief or judgment to have the appropriate trial court decide each party's rights to the escrow funds.

Escrow disbursement order (EDO)

An Escrow Disbursement Order (EDO) is a determination made by FREC as to who is entitled to the escrow funds.

If the funds are held by the broker, he or she can request that FREC issue an EDO. If the EDO is denied, the broker must use another settlement procedure and notify FREC of the procedure to be used. If the funds are held by an attorney or title company, FREC will not issue an EDO.

Even if the broker is using one of the settlement procedures, either party may still choose to file a civil lawsuit to resolve the matter. If the broker has requested an EDO but the parties settle the matter by another means before the EDO is issued, the broker must notify FREC of the settlement within 10 business days.

If the broker follows the notice and settlement procedures under the required timeframes and follows the resulting order or judgment, no administrative complaint may be filed against the broker for failure to account for, deliver, or maintain the escrowed property.

Notice and settlement procedures exceptions

Not all situations regarding the disbursement of escrow funds require the broker to give notice or employ any of the settlement procedures. Florida statute and administrative rule allow three specific exceptions:

- If the buyer of a residential condominium gives the broker a written sales contract cancellation notice in accordance with Florida Condominium law, the broker may release the escrowed funds to the buyer without notifying FREC or employing any of the settlement procedures.
- If a real property good-faith buyer fails to meet the financing provisions within the sales contract, the broker may release the escrowed funds to the buyer without notifying FREC or employing any of the settlement procedures.
- If a broker receives an earnest money deposit as a result of a Department of Housing and Urban Development (HUD) residential sales contract for the sale of a HUD-owned property, the broker is not required to follow the notice or settlement procedures. Rather, the broker must follow HUD's Agreement to Abide, Broker Participation Requirements, and the HUD Act of 1968 (24 C.F.R. s. 291.135) as they pertain to the proper disbursement of earnest money deposits.

Commingling and Conversion

Commingling

Commingling involves mixing funds that belong to one party with the funds of another party; i.e., depositing a licensee's personal or business funds into the same escrow account that holds clients' funds.

You previously learned that Florida regulations permit brokers to deposit a limited amount of funds in a trust account for maintenance purposes. Any amount in excess of the permitted limit, or any other mixing of operating or personal funds with trust funds, is strictly prohibited, regardless of which account is used for the commingled funds (operating, personal, or trust).

Conversion

Conversion refers to one party's use, alteration, or destruction of another party's property or funds for the first party's own purposes; i.e., a licensee's personal use of a client or customer's funds.

For example, a licensee cannot use trust funds to pay expenses, even if the intent is to "repay" the funds. Additionally, a broker may not retain a buyer's earnest money deposit without legal entitlement or following escrow dispute procedures.

Note that while commingling and conversion are both illegal, the DBPR may treat conversion more harshly because it involves actual misuse of trust funds.

Title Company and Attorney Escrow Accounts

Deposit procedures; deadlines

Brokers who rely on a title company or attorney to hold earnest money funds must transmit or deliver any funds received within the same timeframe as if they were depositing them to an escrow account. The purchase contract must clearly state this and include the third party's name, address, and phone number.

Either the buyer or the buyer's brokerage may deliver earnest money funds to the named third party. The title company or attorney must provide a receipt.

When a deposit will be held by a title company or an attorney, the licensee who prepares or presents the sales contract must list the name, address, and phone number of that title company or attorney in the contract.

Within 10 business days after the deposit is due, the licensee's broker must ask the title company or attorney in writing to confirm that the deposit was received, unless the title company or attorney was chosen in writing by the seller or the seller's agent.

Within 10 business days after making that request, the licensee's broker must give the seller's broker either:

- a copy of the written confirmation showing the deposit was received, or
- written notice stating that no confirmation was received.

If the seller does not have a broker, the licensee's broker must send this notice directly to the seller.

If more than one earnest money deposit is required by contract, each deposit must comply with these deposit regulations. Note that FREC does not have jurisdiction over title companies or attorneys used as escrow agents.

Broker's Recordkeeping

Recordkeeping requirements

Recordkeeping and accounting for escrow/trust accounts are strictly regulated by FREC and the DBPR. Brokers must maintain complete, detailed records of all escrow transactions. Accounting records must include a journal for each escrow/trust account, showing all receipts and disbursements in chronological order. Records must also include individual ledgers for each client or transaction that reflect the funds held. The total amount of funds in the ledgers must always reflect the actual escrow account balance.

All journal and ledger entries should include the date and amount of each deposit and disbursement, the source of funds, and the purpose of the transaction. Each ledger account should include a running balance.

All accounting records should be maintained in a way that supports a clear audit trail and enables verification of trust funds at any time.

Retention. Brokers must retain escrow records for at least 5 years. This includes all supporting documentation such as bank statements, reconciliations, receipts, correspondence, and settlement records, as well as the journal and ledgers.

If any funds are related to an ongoing dispute or audit, records should remain available until the matter is resolved.

Storage and format. The required records may be kept on paper or in electronic form, provided they remain legible, complete, and readily available for inspection by FREC or the DBPR. Whatever the format, the records for each deposit must be sufficient to trace the funds, showing the date received, the party who provided them, the property or transaction involved, the amount, the depository holding the funds, and the date and details of any disbursement.

Recording timelines. Journal and ledger entries must be recorded promptly, usually by the end of the next business day after receiving or disbursing funds.

Broker's trust liability

Under Florida statutes and FREC rules, a broker's trust liability refers to the broker's accounting liability for escrow funds. In practice, any broker who maintains a sales trust account has trust liability equal to the sum of all escrow funds owed to others, as demonstrated by the individual trust ledgers and the escrow journal. The broker's liability must be fully supported by the escrow account balance, accurately documented in the broker's records, and verifiable through monthly reconciliation.

For brokers who hold property management funds, the trust liability is equal to the total of security deposits collected and not yet returned, undisbursed rental payments, and owner reserves.

Reconciliation

Brokers must perform a monthly reconciliation of their escrow accounts to ensure that bank statements match the brokerage firm's records and that the sum of all individual ledgers matches total escrow account liabilities.

To reconcile a sales trust account, the broker identifies the bank balance as of a specific date (usually the date of the bank statement). This balance, minus any operating funds in the account, equals net escrow funds.

Net escrow funds must equal the escrow journal balance AND the total of all individual escrow liabilities.

Operating funds limitations

As previously noted, Florida law permits brokers to deposit and maintain up to $1,000 in a sales escrow account or $5,000 in a property management escrow account to cover transaction fees. Deposits to, or operating funds in, a trust account in excess of these amounts may be considered commingling.

Snapshot Review for Chapter 4

The following review summarizes the key rules and concepts from Chapter 4.

Handling Escrow Deposits

- escrow/trust accounts hold funds belonging to others: earnest money, rent, security deposits, etc.
- account must be maintained at qualified Florida depositories; brokers not required to have escrow account if they never hold funds
- account rules: only third-party funds may be held in escrow; brokers may keep up to $1,000 in sales escrow account, up to $5,000 in property management escrow account; solely for account maintenance expenses; sales and rental escrow funds should be separated
- sales associate must deliver escrow funds to broker by end of next business day; broker must deposit funds by end of third business day after receipt by associate
- title company/attorney escrow: contracts must include escrow holder's name, address, phone number; broker must request written verification of deposit within 10 business days; FREC has no jurisdiction over attorney/title company escrow disputes

Managing Escrow Accounts

- broker must be escrow account signatory and maintain journals, ledgers, bank records, and transaction documents, conduct monthly reconciliation, and retain records for at least 5 years
- interest-bearing trust accounts only allowed with written consent of all parties who must agree in writing on interest distribution
- conflicting demands: broker must notify FREC within 15 business days, settlement procedure must begin within 30 business days, and broker uses Notice of Escrow Dispute/Good Faith Doubt form
- good faith doubt exists when broker sincerely doubts entitlement to escrow funds; broker must follow settlement procedures if contract does not resolve issue

Escrow Disputes and Settlement

- mediation is an informal negotiation process with neutral third party and requires written consent of all parties; settlement agreement becomes binding contract
- arbitration is a dispute resolved by arbitrators acting as judges, in which parties agree in writing to accept decision; decision is binding
- litigation is a dispute resolved in court; may involve interpleader action or declaratory judgment
- escrow disbursement order (EDO): FREC determines who receives escrow funds; available only when broker holds escrow funds
- exceptions to notice/settlement procedures: condominium rescission rights, financing contingency failures, HUD-owned property transactions

Commingling and Conversion

- commingling: mixing personal/business funds with escrow funds, illegal except permitted maintenance amounts
- conversion: unauthorized use of another party's escrow funds, considered more serious than commingling

Title Company and Escrow Accounts

- deposit procedures: sales contract must identify the title company/attorney holding escrow, including name, address, and phone number; earnest money may be delivered by buyer or broker directly to escrow holder; receipt should be obtained; funds must be delivered within same timeframe as broker-held escrow
- deadlines: broker must request written confirmation of deposit within 10 business days; broker must notify seller's broker within 10 business days whether confirmation was received
- FREC has no jurisdiction over title company/attorney escrow accounts

Broker Recordkeeping

- recordkeeping requirements: all escrow accounts require journals and ledgers, records must create clear audit trail, and entries should include dates, amounts, source of funds, and the purpose of transaction
- broker trust liability: total escrow funds owed to others must equal escrow account balances and ledger totals
- monthly reconciliation: escrow account balance must match the escrow journal and total individual ledgers, performed monthly to ensure compliance
- operating funds exceeding permitted amounts may constitute commingling
- records kept on paper or electronically, legible and available for inspection; each deposit traces date, payer, property, amount, depository, and disbursement

Chapter 4 Quiz: Escrow Management

4.1 Which of the following best describes a Florida escrow account?

a. An account used for broker operating expenses, including payroll
b. An account held by a third party to hold funds belonging to others
c. A brokerage savings account used primarily for commission payments
d. A personal account used to temporarily deposit funds

4.2 A broker who does not intend to hold funds for others ______.

a. must maintain a trust account
b. must maintain two trust accounts
c. is not required to open a trust account
d. must maintain a rental escrow account only

4.3 Florida law permits a broker to keep how much personal money in a sales escrow account for maintenance?

a. $5,000
b. $2,500
c. $1,000
d. No personal funds are permitted

4.4 If a sales associate receives an earnest money deposit on Friday (not a holiday), it must be delivered to the broker by ______.

a. end of day Monday
b. end of day Saturday
c. end of day Tuesday
d. within 3 business days

4.5 Under Florida rules, a broker must deposit escrow funds "immediately." What does this mean?

a. Within 24 hours
b. By the end of the third business day following receipt
c. Within 7 calendar days
d. Before closing

4.6 When does the three-business-day period for broker escrow deposits begin?

a. When the broker receives funds from the sales associate
b. When the buyer signs the contract
c. When the sales associate receives the funds
d. When the check clears the bank

4.7 Which of the following must be included in the sales contract when escrow funds are to be held by a title company or attorney?

a. The broker's commission agreement
b. The escrow amount only
c. The third party's name, address, and phone number
d. A copy of the title insurance policy

4.8 Within how many days after a deposit is due must the broker request written verification from a title company or attorney (if required)?

a. 5 business days
b. 15 business days
c. 30 business days
d. 10 business days

4.9 FREC will NOT issue an Escrow Disbursement Order (EDO) when ______.

a. the broker holds the funds
b. the parties agree in writing
c. the funds are held by a title company or attorney
d. the broker requests one

4.10 Within what time period must a broker notify FREC of an earnest money dispute?

a. 10 business days of the first demand
b. 15 business days of the last demand
c. 30 calendar days
d. 3 business days

4.11 After the last demand in an escrow dispute, the broker must begin a settlement procedure within ______.

a. 60 days
b. 90 days
c. 30 business days
d. 15 calendar days

4.12 When does mediation become binding?

a. The mediator announces a decision.
b. FREC approves it.
c. The parties reach a written agreement signed by both.
d. 90 days have passed.

4.13 Which of the following is true regarding arbitration decisions?

a. They are binding if agreed to in writing.
b. They are advisory only.
c. They are confidential but nonbinding.
d. They are subject to broker approval.

4.14 What does an interpleader action do?

a. It allows the broker to retain part of the disputed escrow funds.
b. It permits the broker to transfer the funds to FREC until the courts determine who is entitled to the funds.
c. It allows the broker to personally mediate the dispute.
d. It requires the broker to deposit funds with the court, removing the broker from the dispute.

4.15 When is a declaratory judgment typically used?

a. The buyer cancels under condominium law
b. The broker claims part of the escrow funds
c. Both parties consent to mediation
d. The title company holds the funds

4.16 A broker may release escrow funds without notice to FREC if which of the following occurs?

a. The buyer and seller argue
b. The transaction fails to close
c. A condominium buyer timely cancels under Florida Condominium law
d. The broker suspects bad faith

4.17 Which of the following best exemplifies commingling?

a. A broker mixes personal or business funds with trust funds beyond permitted limits.
b. A broker uses escrow funds for personal purposes, intending to pay them back.
c. A broker fails to reconcile escrow accounts monthly.
d. A broker holds rental and sales funds in the same account.

4.18 Conversion is ______.

a. Depositing too much maintenance money into an account
b. Using another party's escrow funds for personal purposes
c. Failing to document a ledger entry in the escrow accounts
d. Failing to notify FREC of a mediation action

4.19 During monthly reconciliation of a sales trust account, net escrow funds must equal which of the following?

a. The broker's operating account balance
b. Escrow journal balance and the total of all individual escrow liabilities
c. Only the bank statement balance
d. The broker's commission total

4.20 Broker's trust liability in a sales escrow account equals ______.

a. the broker's commission due
b. the bank statement balance
c. the sum of all escrow funds owed to others as shown in ledgers and the journal
d. the amount of operating and personal funds held by the broker/brokerage firm

4.21 A broker holds an earnest money deposit and sincerely doubts which party is entitled to it. This good-faith doubt requires the broker to ______.

a. release the funds to the buyer
b. notify FREC and follow one of the settlement procedures
c. keep the funds indefinitely
d. deposit the funds into the operating account

4.22 A broker may place escrow funds in an interest-bearing account only when ______.

a. the broker keeps the interest as a service fee
b. FREC issues written approval
c. the amount exceeds a set threshold
d. all parties consent in writing and agree on who receives the interest

4.23 A broker who manages rental properties may keep how much of his or her own money in the property management escrow account to cover bank charges?

a. no personal funds at all
b. up to $1,000
c. up to $5,000
d. up to $10,000

CHAPTER 5:
OFFICE INSPECTIONS, DISCIPLINARY PROCESS AND THE REAL ESTATE RECOVERY FUND

Contents

Learning Objectives

Upon completion of this chapter, you will be able to:

1. Describe the investigation process and what information and records must be made available to the inspector during a routine office inspection and escrow account audit
2. Describe the steps involved in the complaint process
3. Explain the grounds for denial of an application and the result of a revocation without prejudice
4. Explain the various types of administrative penalties, the use and purpose of a notice of noncompliance, and describe the grounds and penalties for suspension and revocation of a real estate license
5. Describe the purpose and requirements associated with the Real Estate Recovery Fund, including payment limits for claims, assessment of fees, and persons not qualified to make a claim
6. Explain the requirements for self-reporting a criminal conviction
7. Define the key terms of license law enforcement and identify the regulatory roles of the DBPR, the Division of Real Estate, and FREC
8. Explain how probable cause is established and distinguish between formal and informal hearings in a disciplinary proceeding
9. Distinguish among the major categories of license law violations, including culpable negligence, concealment, breach of trust, and fraud
10. Explain the process for appealing a Commission final order, including judicial review by the District Court of Appeal

Definitions

Administrative complaint – an initial written summary of allegations of license law violation(s) filed against a licensee

Breach of trust – failure to carry out promises or obligations owed to another person, whether intentional or negligent

Commingling – mixing funds that belong to one party with the funds of another party; depositing a licensee's personal or business funds into the same escrow account that holds clients' funds

Concealment – the failure to disclose material facts or information as required by law; an act that prevents or hinders the discovery of facts that could potentially affect the decision to move forward with a contract

Conversion – one party's use, alteration, or destruction of another party's property or funds for the first party's own purposes; a licensee's personal use of a client or customer's funds

Culpable negligence – actions or lack of actions that negatively or harmfully affect others; failure to consider the potential results of one's actions

Formal complaint – an administrative complaint that lists all of the charges against a licensee and which is filed when the Probable Cause Panel determines that probable cause exists for prosecution by the DBPR

Formal hearing – a hearing chosen by an offender when there are disputed facts after probable cause has been determined to exist; held before an administrative law judge, and allows the offender to present his or her side of the case

Fraud – the deliberate deception for the purpose of unfair or unlawful personal gain; use of a dishonest action to deprive another person of his or her money, property, or legal right

Good faith – a sincere belief, motive, or intention to deal honestly with others without malice or unfair advantage

Informal hearing – a hearing chosen by an offender when there are no disputed facts after probable cause has been determined to exist; held during a regular meeting of FREC

Material fact – significant or essential information that may affect a property's value and/or a person's willingness to enter into a contract or transaction

Misrepresentation – one party providing a false or misleading statement that can affect another party's decision to enter into a contract or transaction

Moral turpitude – a type of act or behavior that is considered vile or depraved and goes against accepted moral standards and/or insults general morality; for example, murder, robbery, counterfeiting, and arson

Nolo contendere or no contest – a plea made by a defendant in a criminal case that accepts conviction without admitting guilt

Probable cause – a reasonable basis or concrete evidence to indicate that a crime may have been committed

Summary suspension – an emergency suspension order issued when the public is in immediate danger from the actions of a licensee

Disciplinary Process

Office inspections

The DBPR is authorized to conduct office inspections as a regulatory compliance check of a brokerage firm's operations. Such inspections are initiated as periodic checks, audits (primarily related to escrow issues), or in response to a complaint.

Inspections may be announced or unannounced. If a complaint has been filed, the broker is often notified using an inspection notice or an investigative letter.

On-site inspection. During an on-site investigation, an investigator visits the brokerage to evaluate multiple compliance issues, including the following:

- presence of a physical, stationary office with at least one enclosed room for recordkeeping and conducting business negotiations
- appropriate signage

- licenses
- proper disclosure processes

Escrow audit. The escrow audit is a critical component of most office inspections. Inspectors will review accounting documentation, lease agreements, and trust account activity. The purpose of this inspection is to identify any commingling or conversion activities and to ensure proper reconciliation processes.

Records review. Inspectors will also review the firm's transaction records, including transaction files and contracts, to ensure that all required transaction records are present and accurate.

Findings and reports. After the inspection, the broker receives a copy of the inspection report outlining any compliance issues and the related corrective actions. Depending on the severity of issues identified, the brokerage may receive a corrective request, a follow-up inspection, a formal investigation, or an administrative complaint, with any necessary probable cause review and/or administrative hearing. Penalties may include fines, license suspensions, and license revocations.

The complaint

Any person who believes a licensee, applicant, or unlicensed person has violated Florida real estate licensing laws may file a complaint with the Department of Business and Professional Regulation (DBPR). The complaint must be in writing, signed by the complainant, and legally sufficient. That is, the complaint must include ultimate facts that show a violation of Florida statutes and/or FREC administrative rules. The DBPR may require supporting documentation to determine legal sufficiency.

An administrative complaint alleging a violation by a broker, broker associate, or sales associate must be filed within 5 years of the violation, or within 5 years of when the violation was discovered or should have been discovered. If the complaint is filed with the DBPR or FREC against a sales associate, the associate's employing broker will be notified of the complaint in writing. However, the notice will not be sent until 10 days after the Probable Cause Panel finds probable cause, or until the licensee waives his or her confidentiality privilege, whichever occurs first.

Investigate if warranted. If the DBPR determines the allegations constitute a violation, the Department will initiate an investigation and send a copy of the complaint to the violating licensee or the licensee's attorney. The DBPR will also notify the complainant of whether probable cause was found and the status of the investigation and administrative proceedings. If the complaint results from a criminal act by the offender, the Department is not required to notify anyone about the investigation. Further, if those conducting the investigation agree in writing that notifications would adversely affect the investigation, notifications may be withheld.

If the complaint concerns a first-time minor violation, the DBPR may simply issue a notice of noncompliance to the offender. However, if the DBPR believes the public is in immediate danger from the offender's actions, the Department's secretary may issue a summary suspension.

DBPR investigation

The Department of Business and Professional Regulation (DBPR) may investigate the following:

- an anonymous complaint, as long as the complaint is in writing and legally sufficient, and if the alleged violation is substantial and the department believes the allegations are true
- a complaint from a confidential informant, as long as the complaint is in writing and legally sufficient, and if the alleged violation is substantial and the department believes the allegations are true
- a complaint that the original complainant withdraws or tries to dissuade the DBPR from investigating or prosecuting

- the DBPR or FREC's own reasonable belief that a licensee or group of licensees has violated a Florida statute or rule

After the Department has initiated an investigation and notified the violating licensee or the licensee's attorney, the licensee has 20 days to submit a written response. The response is forwarded to the Probable Cause Panel for consideration.

When the Department completes the investigation, it will submit an investigative report to the Panel, including the investigative findings and recommendations regarding probable cause. However, if the Department determines that there is insufficient evidence to support the allegations, it may submit a report to the Panel, dismiss the case, and notify the subject of the complaint.

Probable-cause panel

Based on the volume of cases to be handled, FREC may provide multiple probable cause panels. Each panel will consist of at least two members who meet the following requirements:

- one or more may be former Commission members
- one must be a current Commission member
- one must be a former or current consumer Commission member
- one must be a former or current professional Commission member who holds an active, valid real estate license

Members of the panel serve varying terms or may repeat service, as determined by FREC.

The sole purpose of the Panel is to determine whether probable cause exists for any complaint investigated by the DBPR. The determination is made by a majority vote of Panel members. To make an informed determination, the Panel may request additional investigative information from the DBPR within 15 days of receiving a case's investigative report. The Panel must then make its determination of probable cause within 30 days of receiving a final investigative report. The Department's secretary may grant extensions to the 15- and 30-day timelines.

If the Panel finds there is no probable cause, it may dismiss the case with or without a Letter of Guidance suggesting what action the subject of the complaint should take. If the Panel does not determine probable cause or issue a letter of guidance within the 30 days, the DBPR will make a determination one way or the other within the next 10 days. If either the Panel or the DBPR finds probable cause, a formal complaint will be filed against the offender and his or her employing broker, and the complainant will be notified.

Probable cause proceedings are confidential and therefore are not open to the public or to FREC members who are not on the Panel, because those members must remain objective if they are to participate in an informal hearing on the matter.

Formal/administrative complaint

The filing of a formal complaint will result in the DBPR prosecuting it. However, if the Department believes the Panel was faulty or careless in finding probable cause, the Department may decide not to prosecute.

The formal complaint will be sent to the offender either by regular mail, certified mail, or email. It is the responsibility of the licensee to ensure that the Department has a record of the licensee's current mailing address, email address, and place of practice. The formal complaint lists the charges and includes an Election of Rights, which provides options for how the offender may respond. The offender may choose

- not to dispute the allegations of fact and to request an informal hearing
- to dispute the allegations of fact and to request a formal hearing, or
- not to dispute the allegations of fact and to waive the right to be heard

The offending licensee must submit his or her Election of Rights choice within 21 days from the date it was received and be given at least a 14-day notice of a hearing date. Failing to respond within the required timeframe results in the licensee waiving the right to choose. Consequently, the case will be heard informally before FREC.

Stipulation

Rather than attend a hearing when the licensee does not dispute the facts, he or she may agree to meet with the Division of Real Estate to discuss an agreement that will end the case. The agreement, called a stipulation, will take into account the facts of the case and any penalties both parties agree to. The stipulation must be approved by FREC before it becomes effective. If FREC denies the terms of the stipulation, it can recommend changes to the penalties that it considers more appropriate.

Voluntary relinquishment

Another decision the offending licensee may make to avoid a complaint hearing is voluntary relinquishment, which results in permanent revocation of his or her license. Doing so will permanently revoke the license and prohibit the licensee from ever practicing real estate in Florida again. The relinquishment will replace any penalties that may have been deemed appropriate as a result of a hearing. The relinquishment must be approved by FREC, which will notify the offender of its approval through a final order.

Complaint Deliberation

If neither a stipulation agreement nor a voluntary relinquishment for permanent revocation is agreeable to the offending licensee, then the complaint case must be heard in an informal or formal hearing.

Informal hearing

If the licensee chooses not to dispute the allegations presented in a formal complaint, he or she may request an informal hearing before FREC. The meeting is held during a FREC meeting. The licensee may present his or her side of the case and have an attorney and/or witnesses attend on his or her behalf. Only those FREC members who did not serve on the Probable Cause Panel may attend the hearing.

After hearing the case, the Commission will determine the licensee's guilt or innocence and, if appropriate, impose a penalty. The Commission will send a formal notice to the licensee in the form of a final order. If any dispute arises during the informal hearing, the hearing will be terminated, and the case will be moved to a formal hearing.

Formal hearing

A formal hearing may be held in either of two situations: the offending licensee 1) disputes the allegations and requests a formal hearing, or 2) disputes that arise during an informal hearing result in the case being heard in a formal hearing. The hearing is similar to how a case is tried in a civil or criminal court, with each party presenting facts and witnesses.

As in an informal hearing, the licensee may have an attorney and/or witnesses on his or her behalf. If necessary, the judge may subpoena witnesses.

After the case is heard, the judge will issue a recommended order to FREC and provide a copy to the licensee. The order will include the judge's findings, conclusions, and any recommended penalties. Parties of record in the case may submit written exceptions to the judge's recommended order that clearly identify the legal basis for the exception.

FREC-issued final order

After receiving the recommended order from the formal hearing judge, the Commission will review all information from the informal and formal hearings as well as any stipulations, voluntary relinquishments, and exceptions to determine if guilt has been established and if discipline is warranted. The Commission may reject, modify, or accept the recommended order as the final order.

If penalties are deemed warranted, the Commission can impose fines, suspend or revoke licenses, or permanently bar the offender from practicing real estate in Florida. At any point in the complaint process where the offender's actions are considered dangerous to the public, the DBPR Secretary may issue a summary suspension of the offender's license.

After the Commission has reviewed the case and ruled on guilt or innocence and discipline, it will issue a final order within 90 days of receiving the recommended order. The final order will include a ruling on each previously submitted exception.

The Commission will then send a copy of the final order to all parties to the case and inform them of the process to appeal the ruling. A copy of the final order must also be sent to the DRE within 15 days after the order is filed with the clerk. The final order can be used as prima facie evidence in any resulting civil case arising from the complaint and the final ruling.

Judicial review

A licensee who disagrees with the final order may file an appeal with the DBPR and the District Court of Appeals within 30 days of receiving the order. The licensee may also file a stay of enforcement to stop the enforcement of the final order until the appeal is completed. When the stay request is filed, the court issues a writ of supersedeas, which overrides the Commission's final order and allows the licensee to continue practicing real estate until the appeal is completed.

During the appeal, if the court finds that the Commission committed a material error, it will require the Commission to take corrective action. However, with no finding of error by FREC and no other legitimate grounds for modifying or dismissing the final order, the court must find in support of FREC's final order. If the court finds in favor of the licensee, the licensee's rights must be restored. The court may award the licensee attorney's fees and court costs.

Violations and Penalties

FREC authority for punitive actions

The Commission has the authority to set guidelines for penalties to be imposed on a licensee who violates Florida's real estate laws, specifically Chapter 455 and Chapter 475, as well as FREC Administrative Code. Because the Commission's jurisdiction is limited to the practice of real estate in Florida, it may only impose administrative penalties related to that practice. Criminal and civil penalties must be imposed by the courts. Restitution to an injured party is a civil matter and, therefore, cannot be granted by FREC.

FREC is authorized to carry out the following actions (administrative penalties):

- **deny a license application**

  Grounds for application or licensure denial include errors on the application, failure to meet application or licensure qualifications, failure to pay applicable fees, lack of required character, acts that would warrant suspension or revocation of a license, or being caught cheating on the licensure examination.

- **refuse to renew a license**

  Grounds for refusing to renew an existing license are much the same as those for denying the license application

- **reprimand**

  Similar to a notice of noncompliance, a letter of reprimand may be issued to a licensee who has violated real estate law or code.

- **issue notice of noncompliance**

  As established by the Commission, violations of certain statutes and rules are considered minor violations

  These laws do not cause economic or physical harm, do not negatively affect the public's health, safety, or welfare, or create a threat of harm.

  First-time violators of these laws can receive a notice of noncompliance that identifies the law violated and contains instructions on how and by when to correct the violation. The law gives these violators 14 days to correct the violation. Failure to correct the violation may result in a citation or further disciplinary action.

  The list of statutes and rules can be found by searching for Florida's Administrative Code 61J2-24.003.

- **impose an administrative fine**

  Fines range from $100 to $5,000 per violation for certain violations.

- **impose probation**

  In addition to other disciplinary penalties, the Commission may place a licensee on probation. The Commission will designate the time period and conditions it deems appropriate.

  Standard probationary conditions may include requiring the licensee to complete a pre- or post-licensing course, to successfully complete the state-administered examination, and/or be periodically interviewed by a DBPR investigator.

  Brokers on probation may have their licenses placed on a broker associate status or be required to file escrow account status reports with the Commission or with a DBPR investigator at prescribed intervals.

- **issue citations**

  Citations are issued for specific violations that do not pose a substantial threat to the public health, safety, and welfare. DBPR investigators and FREC may issue a maximum citation of $500. Citations must be paid or disputed within 30 days. If disputed, the matter will be forwarded for a formal hearing before an administrative law judge.

- **suspend a license**

  Based on disciplinary guidelines and associated penalties, a license may be suspended for law and code violations for up to 10 years.

- **revoke a license**

  Based on disciplinary guidelines and associated penalties, this penalty is intended to permanently remove the violator from the practice of real estate; however, further language in the law states that FREC may approve an application from a previously revoked licensee if "because of lapse of time and subsequent good conduct and reputation, or other reason deemed sufficient, it appears to the commission that the interest of the public and investors will not likely be endangered."

Regardless of this language in the law, FREC maintains its policy not to license previously revoked licensees.

- **revoke without prejudice**

  If the license was issued in error or through the Commission's inadvertence, it can be revoked or canceled without prejudicing a later application by the same individual.

- **mediation**

  Violations that are economic in nature and involve disputes are subject to referral to mediation for resolution.

  Such violations include: a broker's failure to maintain an office or entrance sign, failure to register a branch office, and failure to pay a licensee the amount of commission designated in a civil judgment.

Violations and penalties

Florida Administrative Code contains an exhaustive list of actions that constitute real estate law violations and the penalties for first and subsequent violations. The list may be found online at

https://www2.myfloridalicense.com/servop/testing/documents/FREC_printable_LawBook.pdf

The following are examples of violations and associated penalties from that list.

Violation	First Violation	Subsequent Violations
Fraud, misrepresentation, and dishonest dealing	administrative fine and 30-day suspension to revocation	administrative fine and 6-month suspension to revocation
False, deceptive, or misleading advertising	administrative fine and 30- to 90-day suspension	administrative fine and 90-day suspension to revocation
Culpable negligence or breach of trust	administrative fine and 30-day suspension to revocation	administrative fine and 6-month suspension to revocation
Failure, as a broker, to deposit any money in an escrow account immediately upon receipt until disbursement is properly authorized;. as a sales associate, to place any money to be escrowed with his registered employer	administrative fine and 30-day suspension to revocation	administrative fine and suspension to revocation
Failure to report in writing to the Commission within 30 days after the licensee is convicted or found guilty of, or entered a plea of nolo contendere or guilty to, regardless of adjudication, a crime in any jurisdiction.	administrative fine and suspension to revocation	administrative fine and suspension to revocation
Collection, by a sales associate, of any money in connection with any real estate brokerage transaction except in the name of the employer	administrative fine and suspension to revocation	administrative fine and suspension to revocation
Rendering an opinion that the title to property sold is good or merchantable when not based on the opinion of a licensed attorney	administrative fine and 30-day suspension to revocation	administrative fine and suspension to revocation

These penalties are typically imposed during an informal or formal hearing. The order of penalties for violations, ranging from lowest to highest, is reprimand, fine, probation, suspension, and revocation or denial. Any of these penalties may be combined.

The penalties are as listed unless aggravating or mitigating circumstances are demonstrated during a hearing, in which case the Commission may deviate from the penalty guidelines in the Administrative Code.

Additional violations and grounds for discipline are contained in Chapter 455.227.

The following are examples of violations that may result in a citation. The entire list is found in 61J2-24.002 F.A.C.

Section 475.25(1)(q), F.S.	failed to give the appropriate disclosure or notice at the appropriate time under the provisions of Section 475.2755 or 475.278, F.S. (A citation may only be given for a first-time violation.)
Section 475.25(1)(r), F.S.	failed to include the required information in a listing agreement; failed to give a copy to a principal within 24 hours; contains a self-renewal clause
Section 475.4511(2), F.S.	advertised false, inaccurate, misleading, or exaggerated information
Rule 61J2-10.025, F.A.C.	advertised in a manner in which a reasonable person would not know one is dealing with a real estate licensee or brokerage; failed to include the registered name of the brokerage firm in the advertisement; failed to use the licensee's last name as registered with the Commission in an advertisement
Rule 61J2-10.038, F.A.C	failed to timely notify the DBPR of the current mailing address or any change in the current mailing address
Subsection 61J2-14.012(2), F.A.C.	failed to properly reconcile an escrow account when the account balances

Penalties issued by court of law

Civil penalties. Civil penalties are monetary punishments for violating a statute or administrative code and are imposed as restitution for wrongdoing. The penalty can be a fine, surcharge, or compensation imposed to enforce regulations and/or recover funds owed. Civil penalties are not the result of a private suit between two private parties. Those suits result in civil damages, not penalties. Civil penalties are imposed by the courts for such violations as writing bad checks, practicing real estate without a license, filing a false complaint against a licensee, failure to pay an imposed fine, etc.

Criminal penalties. Criminal penalties are a result of violations of local, state, or federal laws that prohibit certain conduct. The penalty may be a fine, an arrest, or jail/prison time. These penalties are imposed by criminal courts. Neither FREC nor the DBPR has the authority to impose criminal penalties. However, the DBPR is required to refer criminal matters to the Florida Attorney General's office. Criminal offenses fall into separate classes:

- **misdemeanor of the first degree** results in a penalty of a fine up to $1,000 and/or up to 1 year in jail; offenses such as failing to provide accurate and current rental information for a fee are misdemeanors of the first degree
- **misdemeanor of the second degree** results in a penalty of a fine up to $500 and/or up to 60 days in jail; offenses such as false advertising, filing false statements to FREC, or other violations of Chapter 475 F.S. are misdemeanors of the second degree

- **felony of the third degree** results in a penalty of a fine up to $5,000 and/or 5 years in jail; offenses such as stealing or copying the state licensure examination, making misleading statements on a licensure application, and practicing real estate without a valid license are felonies of the third degree

Any licensee who pleads guilty or **nolo contendere** or is found guilty of a misdemeanor or felony must notify the Commission within 30 days of the plea or conviction. Failure to report the plea or conviction may result in disciplinary action against the licensee.

Reporting licensees should use Florida's Criminal Self-Reporting Document, which can be found online at

https://www2.myfloridalicense.com/criminal-self-reporting/

Real Estate Recovery Fund

Brokerage transactions

The purpose of the Florida Real Estate Recovery Fund is to reimburse individuals or business entities for monetary damages caused by the actions of a real estate licensee in relation to a real estate transaction. Payments from the Fund will be approved by FREC if

- the licensee held a current, valid, active real estate license at the time the act was committed
- the licensee was neither the seller, buyer, landlord, or tenant nor an officer, director, partner, nor member of a business entity that was the seller, buyer, landlord, or tenant in the transaction
- the licensee was acting solely as a real estate licensee in the transaction; and
- the act was a violation of Chapter 475 F.S

Furthermore, the damaged claimant will be eligible for monetary reimbursement from the Fund if

- the claimant has filed suit in a civil court and obtained a final judgment against the licensee for his or her actions during the course of a real estate transaction
- the claimant has notified FREC of the licensee's actions
- the claim for recovery is made within 2 years of the date of the action or the date the action was discovered
- the claim for recovery is not made more than 4 years after the date of the alleged action was committed
- the claimant obtains a writ of execution on the judgment and executes an affidavit showing the claimant has made a concerted effort to find sufficient personal or real property belonging to the licensee that could be used to satisfy the judgment; and
- the claimant executes an affidavit showing the final judgment is not on appeal, or an appeal has concluded

Additionally, a real estate licensee is eligible for monetary reimbursement from the Fund if the licensee:

- was the buyer, seller, landlord, or tenant in the transaction as a consumer and not as a licensee handling the transaction; and
- suffers monetary damages as a result of acts committed by the licensee/agent handling the transaction

Persons unqualified to make claim

An individual or business entity is not eligible to make a claim for payment from the Fund if

- the claimant is the spouse of the offending licensee or a personal representative of the spouse
- the claimant is a licensed broker or sales associate who performed as a single agent or transaction broker in the subject transaction
- the claim is based on a transaction in which the offending licensee owned or controlled the property in the subject transaction or in which the licensee was not acting as a broker or sales associate
- the claim is based on a transaction in which the offending broker or sales associate did not hold a current, valid license; and/or
- the judgment is against a real estate brokerage corporation, partnership, LLC, or LLP

Additionally, those seeking punitive damages in lieu of compensatory damages are not eligible for payment from the Fund.

Payment for claims

An injured party who meets all of the eligibility requirements may apply to FREC for a reimbursement payment from the Fund. Florida statutes limit each payment to the lesser of the amount of the unsatisfied judgment or $50,000. Multiple claims for payments based on the same transaction are limited to a total of $50,000, regardless of the number of claims, claimants, or land parcels involved. Multiple claims against any one licensee are limited to a total of $150,000.

The license of a licensee whose actions have resulted in a reimbursement to a claimant is suspended from the date of the payment until the licensee has repaid with interest the total amount paid by the Fund.

Statutes limit the payments to compensatory or actual damages and do not pay treble damages, court costs, attorney fees, or interest unless the claimant is a licensee who is ordered by the court to pay monetary damages as a result of an escrow disbursement order (EDO) issued by FREC. In that case, treble damages, court costs, attorney fees, and interest may be paid to the licensee. Again, the payment is limited to the amount of the judgment against the licensee or $50,000, whichever is less.

Fund limit and fees

The Florida Real Estate Recovery Fund is funded by fees charged to licensees. A $3.50 annual fee is charged for new and renewal broker licenses. A $1.50 annual fee applies to new and renewal sales associate licenses. All moneys collected from disciplinary fines are also deposited into the fund.

If the fund's balance reaches $1 million, the special fee for new and renewal licenses is temporarily discontinued. Once the balance reaches $500,000 due to payments, the fees will resume.

Self-reporting of Criminal Violations

Self-reporting criminal violations

Florida law requires all professional licensees to self-report certain criminal events to the DBPR within 30 days after any of the following occurs in any jurisdiction (including out-of-state violations).

A licensee must report any criminal offense that results in:

- a guilty plea
- a no contents (nolo contendre) plea

- a conviction, regardless of adjudication

This applies to felonies, misdemeanors, and Florida or out-of-state federal offenses. Licensees must report within 30 days of the plea or conviction. Failing to report or missing the deadline is itself a separate disciplinary violation.

A copy of the reporting form, available from the DBPR website, appears below.

CRIMINAL SELF-REPORTING DOCUMENT
Department of Business and Professional Regulation (DBPR)

Note: Effective October 1, 2009, Section 455.227(1)(t), Florida Statutes, requires that a licensee must report to the board or, if there is no board, to the department within 30 days after a licensee is convicted or found guilty of, or entered a plea of nolo contendere (no contest) or guilty to, regardless of adjudication, a crime in any jurisdiction. *If you previously reported a criminal conviction or plea to DBPR, you do not need to report it again.*

1. Last Name (Surname), First Name, Middle Name	2. Date of Birth

3. Address	4. City	5. State	6. Zip

7. Telephone (Home)	8. Telephone (Cell)	9. E-mail

10. Profession(s) – list all DBPR licenses:	11. Professional license number(s) – list all DBPR license numbers:
a.	a.
b.	b.
c.	c.

12. Have you pled guilty or nolo contendere (no contest) to any crime in any jurisdiction? Please check one: ☐Yes ☐ No	13. Have you been convicted or found guilty in any jurisdiction, regardless of adjudication, of any crime in any jurisdiction? Please check one: ☐Yes ☐ No

14. For each crime to which you pled guilty or nolo contendere (no contest), or for which you were convicted or found guilty in any jurisdiction, regardless of adjudication, please state the following:

a. Name of court:
b. Address of court:
c. Case number:
d. Date of plea or conviction:
e. Name of crime:

a. Name of court:
b. Address of court:
c. Case number:
d. Date of plea or conviction:
e. Name of crime:

Note: If you have more than two convictions to report, please attach an additional sheet including the above information.

Date:	Signature of Licensee:

Please submit this form to the appropriate mailing address.

Mailing Address: **Architecture & Interior Design** Manausa, Shaw & Minacci, P.A. 140-D West First Street St. George Island, FL 32328	Mailing Address: **CPA** Division of Certified Public Accounting 240 NW 76th Drive, Suite A Gainesville, FL 32607
Mailing Address: **Real Estate** Division of Real Estate 400 West Robinson Street, N801 Orlando, FL 32801	Mailing Address: **All Others** Division of Regulation 2601 Blair Stone Road Tallahassee, FL 32399-0782

DBPR Form No. TBD | Page 1 of 1 | Criminal Self Reporting Document

Snapshot Review for Chapter 5

The following review summarizes the key rules and concepts from Chapter 5.

DISCIPLINARY PROCEDURE

Office Inspections

- announced or unannounced DBPR inspections
- review of licenses, signage, disclosures, contracts, transaction files, escrow accounts, and reconciliations
- escrow audits focus on commingling, conversion, and improper accounting practices
- possible outcomes: corrective action request, investigation, administrative complaint, fines, suspension, revocation

Complaint Process

- complaints must be written, signed, legally sufficient
- DBPR may investigate anonymous complaints, confidential informants, withdrawn complaints
- licensee response required within 20 days
- minor first offense: notice of noncompliance
- emergency situations: summary suspension by DBPR Secretary
- Probable Cause Panel: determines existence of probable cause; proceedings confidential
- hearings: informal, no disputed facts; formal, disputed facts before administrative law judge; after formal hearing, judge issues recommended order to FREC
- FREC final orders: dismissal, reprimand, fine, probation, suspension, revocation
- appeals filed within 30 days

Violations and Penalties

- common violations: fraud, misrepresentation, breach of trust; false advertising; escrow violations; failure to report convictions
- FREC authority (only administrative penalties): deny applications, refuse renewals, issue notice of noncompliance/citations/reprimands, fines of $100–$5,000, probation, suspension up to 10 years, revocation, mediation
- FREC cannot impose civil or criminal penalties; those must be imposed by the courts
- civil penalties: court-imposed monetary punishments imposed for law/rule violation as restitution for wrongdoing
- criminal penalties imposed by courts: 1st-degree misdemeanor, up to $1,000 and/or 1 year jail; 2nd-degree misdemeanor, up to $500 and/or 60 days jail; 3rd-degree felony, up to $5,000 and/or 5 years prison
- self-reporting required within 30 days: guilty plea, nolo contendere plea, conviction

Real Estate Recovery Fund

- reimburses monetary losses caused by licensee misconduct related to a real estate transaction
- requirements:
- active license at time of violation
- licensee acting as agent, not principal, in transaction
- civil judgment obtained
- writ of execution attempted
- FREC has been notified of licensee's actions
- claim for recovery is made within 2 years of the action or date it was discovered, and not made more than 4 years after the date of the action occurred

- payment limits: $50,000 per transaction; $150,000 per licensee
- compensatory damages only
- ineligible claimants: spouses of offending licensees, brokerage entities, claims involving inactive/unlicensed individuals
- funded by license fees and disciplinary fines
- licensee whose actions led to a fund payout has their license suspended until they repay the fund with interest

Chapter 5 Quiz: Office Inspections, Disciplinary Process, and the Real Estate Recovery Fund

5.1 Which of these is the best description of an administrative complaint?

a. A civil lawsuit filed by an injured party against an active licensee
b. An emergency order issued by FREC
c. An initial written summary of alleged license law violation
d. A final disciplinary order

5.2 Which of these actions could result in a charge of commingling?

a. Failing to reconcile an escrow account with the bank statement
b. Depositing excess personal or business funds in an escrow account
c. Using escrow funds for personal expenses with the intent to repay it
d. Failing to report a criminal conviction

5.3 What does conversion involve?

a. Mixing operating funds with escrow funds
b. Failing to disclose a material defect
c. Negligently advertising property
d. A licensee's personal use of a client's escrow funds

5.4 A material fact is information that ______.

a. must be disclosed only if requested
b. is trivial and unlikely to affect value
c. may affect a party's decision to enter a transaction
d. d.relates only to zoning

5.5 What does a plea of nolo contendre mean for the defendant?

a. It is a written admission of guilt.
b. The defendant refuses to appear in court.
c. The defendant accepts a conviction without admitting guilt.
d. The defendant denies all allegations.

5.6 What is a summary suspension?

a. A fine imposed after a hearing
b. An emergency suspension to prevent public danger
c. A voluntary relinquishment of a license
d. A penalty imposed by a civil court

5.7 A complaint filed with the DBPR must be ______.

a. Oral and confidential
b. Filed within 1 year of the alleged action
c. In writing, signed, and legally sufficient
d. Submitted by another licensee in the same firm

5.8 After receiving a notice of an investigation, a licensee has how many days to submit a written response?

a. 10 days
b. 30 days
c. 21 days
d. 20 days

5.9 What is the purpose of a Probable Cause Panel?

a. Decide whether probable cause exists
b. Determine guilt and impose penalties
c. Negotiate stipulations
d. Conduct formal hearings

5.10 Which of the following may result if a Probable Cause Panel finds no probable cause?

a. Automatic license suspension
b. Dismissal of the case
c. Referral to criminal court
d. Issuance of a final order

5.11 Which of the following does a formal complaint include?

a. A subpoena for witnesses
b. An Election of Rights form
c. A civil judgment
d. A Writ of supersedeas

5.12 If a licensee disputes material facts in a formal complaint, the case proceeds to which venue?

a. Mediation
b. Informal hearing
c. Formal hearing
d. Immediate revocation

5.13 A stipulation in a disciplinary case becomes effective when which event occurs?

a. The licensee signs it
b. FREC approves it
c. It is filed with the court
d. It is recommended by the DBPR investigator

5.14 Voluntary relinquishment of a license during an investigative process results in which outcome?

a. Temporary license suspension
b. Permanent license revocation
c. A reduced fine
d. Probation

5.15 An informal hearing occurs under which circumstance?

a. When facts are disputed before a judge
b. When only attorneys may speak; no witness statements are taken
c. When the Probable Cause Panel presides over the hearing
d. When the case is heard before FREC, and material facts are not disputed

5.16 After a formal hearing, the administrative law judge issues which document?

a. A summary suspension
b. A recommended order
c. A final court judgment
d. A citation

5.17 A licensee may appeal a final order within how many days?

a. 15 days
b. 30 days
c. 60 days
d. 90 days

5.18 Which of the following penalties may FREC impose??

a. A jail sentence
b. Criminal restitution
c. Revocation of license
d. Prison probation

5.19 A first-time minor violation that causes no harm may result in which disciplinary action?

a. Notice of noncompliance with 14 days to correct
b. Automatic license revocation
c. Criminal prosecution
d. Immediate license suspension

5.20 A third-degree felony in Florida may result in which penalty?

a. Up to $500 fine and/or 60 days in jail
b. Up to $1,000 fine and/or 1 year in jail
c. Up to $5,000 fine and/or 5 years in prison
d. Administrative fine only

5.21 The Florida Real Estate Recovery Fund will reimburse a claimant only if which condition is met?

a. The licensee was acting as a principal in the transaction.
b. The claimant obtained a final civil judgment and met statutory requirements.
c. The claim is for punitive damages
d. The transaction involved an unlicensed person

5.22 Payment from the Recovery Fund for a single transaction is limited to what amount?

a. $150,000 per claimant
b. The full amount of the judgment
c. $500,000 per licensee
d. $50,000 total per transaction

5.23 If the Recovery Fund pays a claim due to a licensee's misconduct, what happens to the licensee?

a. The license is suspended until repayment with interest
b. The license is automatically renewed
c. The broker is fined $500
d. The claimant must repay the fund

5.24 A person is not eligible to claim from the Recovery Fund if which condition exists?

a. The licensee held an active license
b. The claimant is the spouse of the offending licensee
c. The claimant obtained a writ of execution
d. The claimant filed within 2 years of the offense

5.25 Florida licensees must self-report to the DBPR within 30 days after which event?

a. Being investigated for any civil or criminal offense
b. The filing of any civil lawsuit
c. A guilty plea, nolo contendre plea, or conviction in any jurisdiction
d. Receiving and failing to pay a traffic ticket

5.26 Which statement about DBPR office inspections is TRUE?

a. They may be either announced or unannounced.
b. They may be conducted only after a complaint is filed.
c. They require at least 30 days' advance written notice.
d. They may be performed only by FREC members.

5.27 Total payments from the Real Estate Recovery Fund against a single licensee are limited to ______.

a. $25,000
b. $50,000
c. $150,000
d. no maximum

5.28 The Real Estate Recovery Fund is funded primarily by ______.

a. fees charged to licensees
b. state general tax revenue
c. fees paid by consumers filing claims
d. proceeds from the sale of seized property

5.29 A licensee who disagrees with a FREC final order may seek judicial review by appealing to ______.

a. the DBPR secretary
b. the District Court of Appeal
c. the Florida Supreme Court directly
d. the local small claims court

5.30 For a claim to be paid from the Recovery Fund, the offending licensee must have ______.

a. been convicted of a felony
b. voluntarily surrendered the license
c. carried errors-and-omissions insurance
d. held a current, valid, active real estate license when the act was committed

5.31 Each probable cause panel established by FREC must consist of at least ______.

a. one member
b. two members
c. five members
d. seven members

5.32 Probable cause is best defined as ______.

a. proof beyond a reasonable doubt
b. an admission of guilt
c. a reasonable basis or concrete evidence that a violation may have been committed
d. any complaint filed with the DBPR

5.33 A licensee who fails to act with reasonable care, without considering potential harm to others, may be charged with ______.

a. culpable negligence
b. concealment
c. false advertising
d. conversion

5.34 A licensee's failure to carry out promises or obligations owed to another person, intentional or negligent, is ______.

a. misrepresentation
b. commingling
c. fraud
d. breach of trust

5.35 A licensee deliberately deceives a buyer to gain an unlawful advantage. This is best described as ______.

a. simple negligence
b. concealment
c. fraud
d. a stipulation

PART II: VALUING REAL PROPERTY

CHAPTER 6: OVERVIEW OF REAL ESTATE VALUATION

Contents

- **Physical Characteristics of Real Estate**
- **Economic Characteristics of Real Estate**
- **Regulation of Appraisal**
- **Concepts of Value**
- **Types of Appraisal Reports**

Learning Objectives

Upon completion of this chapter, you will be able to:

1. Differentiate between land and real estate
2. Identify examples of natural attachments and improvements
3. List the three physical characteristics of land
4. Define immobility, indestructibility, heterogeneity, and "highest and best use"
5. State the four economic characteristics of real estate markets
6. Describe the basic relationships between supply, demand, and price
7. List key factors that influence housing supply and demand
8. Identify whether a market is a buyer's or seller's market based on simple indicators like price and supply levels
9. Describe the purpose of an appraisal
10. Describe the appraisal certification and licensure classifications
11. Recognize which appraisal assignments must be performed by state-certified or state-licensed appraisers and that real estate licensees must comply with the USPAP when conducting appraisals, but not CMAs or BPOs
12. Distinguish among value, price, cost, and various types of value
13. Define various market value definitions
14. Distinguish among the various principles of value and understand how each influences value
15. Define highest and best use
16. Describe the two different types of appraisal reports and describe different reporting methods

Physical Characteristics of Real Estate

To fully understand real estate valuation, you must first understand a number of underlying real estate concepts and definitions.

Legal concepts of land and real estate

Land. As discussed in an earlier section, the legal concept of land encompasses

- the surface area of the earth

- everything beneath the surface of the earth extending downward to its center
- all *natural* things permanently attached to the earth
- the air above the surface of the earth extending outward to infinity.

Land, therefore, includes minerals beneath the earth's surface, water on or below the earth's surface, and the air above the surface. In addition, land includes all plants attached to or growing in the ground, such as trees and grass.

Real estate. The concept of real estate, in addition to land, encompasses man-made structures, known as improvements, that are "permanently" attached to the land. "Permanently attached," as mentioned earlier, is a question of intention; if a person constructs a house with the intention of creating a permanent dwelling, the house is considered real estate. If a camper affixes a tent to the land with the intention of moving it to another camp in a week, the tent is not considered real estate.

Unique physical features of land

The unique physical characteristics of land, also mentioned earlier, are: *immobility, indestructibility, and heterogeneity.*

Immobility and location. Land is immobile, since a parcel of land cannot be moved from one site to another. In other words, the geographical location of a tract of land is fixed and cannot be changed. One can transport portions of the land, such as mined coal, dirt, or cut plants. However, once such elements are detached from the land, they are no longer considered land.

As the upcoming appraisal section will demonstrate, the economics of land reflect the effects of immobility and location in the following ways:

- valuation of land and real estate is heavily influenced by conditions and changes in the surrounding area
- highest and best use, a valuation concept, is fundamentally determined by the locational and environmental value of a site to different potential users intending different uses

The use and user that yield the greatest value for the site constitute the highest and best use. A decline in this value relative to other uses often leads to a change in the site's highest and best use and in its actual land use.

Indestructibility. Land is indestructible in the sense that one would have to remove a segment of the planet all the way to the core in order to destroy it. Even then, the portion extending upward to infinity would remain. For the same reason, land is considered to be permanent.

The indestructibility of land is reflected in real estate investment, tax accounting, and insurance, in that

- real estate investors tend to regard real estate as a long-term investment, meaning they hold onto their investments for a long time
- land does not depreciate (while improvements do)
- improvements, but not land, are covered by property insurance

Heterogeneity. Land is non-homogeneous because no two parcels are identical. Admittedly, two adjacent parcels may be very similar and have the same economic value. However, they are inherently different because each parcel has a unique location.

Economic Characteristics of Real Estate

Real estate as an economic product

As an economic commodity, real estate is bought, sold, traded, and leased as a product within a real estate market. Like other products and services, real estate is:

- subject to the laws of supply and demand
- governed in the market by the price mechanism
- influenced by the producer's costs to bring the product to market
- influenced by the determinants of value: utility, scarcity, desire, and purchasing power

Distinguishing features. Compared with other economic products and services, real estate has unique characteristics. These include:

- **inherent product value**
  Land is a scarce resource as well as a required factor of production. Like gold and silver, it has both inherent and utility value.
- **unique appeal of product**
  Since no two parcels of real estate can be alike (each has a different location), every parcel of real property has its own appeal. Likewise, no two parcels of real estate can have exactly the same value, except by coincidence.
- **demand must come to the supply**
  Since real property cannot be moved, real property investors and users must come to the supply. This creates risk because if demand drops, the supply cannot be transported to a higher-demand market.
- **illiquid**
  Real estate is a relatively illiquid economic product, meaning it cannot always be readily sold for cash. Since it is a large, long-term investment that has no exact duplicate, buyers must go through a complex process to evaluate and purchase the right parcel of real estate.
- **slow to respond to changes**
  Real estate is relatively slow to respond to market imbalances. Because new construction is a large-scale, time-consuming process, the market is slow to respond to increases in demand. The market is similarly slow to respond to sharp declines in demand, since the product cannot be moved and sold elsewhere. Instead, owners must wait out slow periods and simply hope for the best.
- **decentralized, local market**
  A real property cannot be shipped to a large, central real estate marketplace. Real estate markets are thus local in nature and highly susceptible to swings in the local economy.

Relationship between supply, demand, and price

In a market economy, the primary interactions between supply, demand, and price are:

- if supply increases relative to demand, price decreases
- if supply decreases relative to demand, price increases
- if demand increases relative to supply, price increases
- if demand decreases relative to supply, price decreases

These relationships reflect simple common sense: if a valued product becomes increasingly scarce, its value and price go up as consumers compete for the limited supply. If there is an overabundance of a product, the price falls, as demand is largely met. On the other side, if demand for a product or service increases in relation to supply, prices will go up as consumers compete for the popular item. If demand diminishes, the price drops with it.

The inverse of these principles also applies. By tracking a price trend, one can draw conclusions about supply and demand trends:

- if price decreases, demand declines in relation to supply
- if price increases, demand increases in relation to supply

To assess price movements, the supply and demand of a product or service must always be considered together. It is always possible for demand and supply to rise and fall together at the same rate, with no detectable change in price.

For example, if demand for bicycles jumps by a million units and manufacturers can easily increase production to meet the new demand, there may be no price increase. The price may even go down as manufacturers obtain better prices on the larger quantities of raw materials they now use.

Supply factors

Supply. In real estate, supply is the inventory of properties that sellers or landlords are willing and able to offer for sale or rent at any given time. The units used to quantify the amount of property available differ across property categories. These supply units, by property type, are:

- residential: dwelling units
- commercial and industrial: square feet
- agricultural: acreage

Factors influencing supply. In addition to the influences of demand and the underlying determinants of value, real estate supply responds to

- development costs, particularly labor
- availability of financing
- investment returns
- a community's master plan
- government police powers and regulation

Demand factors

Demand. Real estate demand is the amount of property buyers and tenants wish to acquire by purchase, lease, or trade at any given time. Units of demand by property classification are:

- residential: households
- commercial and industrial: square feet
- agricultural: acreage

The unit of residential demand is the household, which is an individual or family that would occupy a dwelling unit. Residential demand can be further broken down into demand to lease versus buy, and demand for single-family homes versus apartments.

Residential demand can be very difficult to quantify. One measure is the number of buyers employing agents to locate property. Another measure is the net population change in an area, plus the number of families that attempted to move in but could not.

The unit of commercial (retail and office) and industrial real estate demand is the square foot, further broken down into demand for leased space versus purchased space. In most instances, the area demanded refers to the improved area rather than the total lot area.

Demand for office and industrial real estate is calculated by identifying employment growth or shrinkage in a market, then multiplying the employment change by the average floor area per employee. For example, consider an office property market where employment in the community increases by 500 employees. If each employee uses an average of 120 square feet, the increased demand for space is 60,000 square feet.

Factors affecting demand. The demand for particular types of real estate reflects users' specific concerns. These concerns revolve around the components of value: desire, utility, scarcity, and purchasing power.

Residential users are concerned with:

- employment
- quality of life
- neighborhood quality
- convenience and access to services and other facilities
- dwelling amenities in relation to household size, lifestyle, and costs

Retail users are concerned with:

- sufficient trade area population and income
- the level of trade area competition
- sales volume per square foot of rented area
- consumer spending patterns
- growth patterns in the trade area

Office users are concerned with:

- costs of occupancy to the business
- efficiency of the building and the suite in accommodating the business's functions
- accessibility by employees and suppliers
- matching building quality to the image and function of the business

Industrial users are concerned with:

- functionality
- the availability and proximity of the labor pool
- compliance with environmental regulations
- permissible zoning
- health and safety of the workers
- access to suppliers and distribution channels

Base employment and total employment. The engine that drives demand for real estate of all types in a market is employment, base employment and total employment.

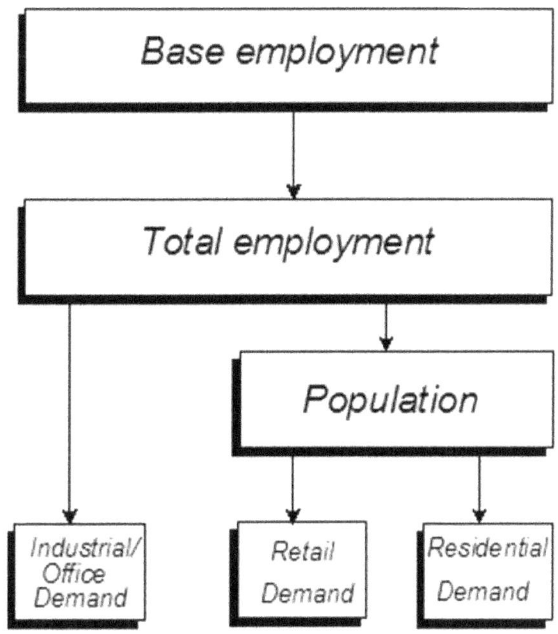

Basis of Real Estate Demand

Base employment is the number of people employed in businesses that form the area's economic foundation. For example, the auto industry has traditionally been the primary employer base in the Detroit metropolitan area.

Base industries lead to the rise of supporting and secondary industries in the market. If the auto industry is the base, auto parts manufacturers and assembly industries will develop to support the auto manufacturing plants. In addition, service businesses emerge to support the many needs of the local population engaged in primary and secondary employment.

Thus, base employment feeds total employment. Total employment in a market includes base, secondary, and support industries. Total employment creates a demand for a labor force. From total employment, demand for industrial and office space arises; as employment grows, so does the population, leading to demand for housing and retail support. In addition to creating demand for real estate, employment provides the purchasing power households need to acquire dwellings and retail products.

Without employment, the real estate market evaporates, as there is no demand for commercial or industrial facilities, retail services, or housing. The best example of this phenomenon is a gold rush boom town: Once the gold runs out, there is no more mining. Without mining employment, everyone moves away, and the town becomes a ghost town.

Market influences on supply and demand

Numerous factors in a market influence the real estate cycle to speed up or slow down. These influences can be local or national, and can come from the public or private sectors.

Local market influences. Since the real estate market is local by definition, local factors heavily influence its conditions. Among these are:

- cost of financing
- availability of developable land
- construction costs
- capacity of the municipality's infrastructure to handle growth
- governmental regulation and police powers
- changes in the economic base

- in- and out-migrations of major employers

National trends. Regional and national economic forces influence the local real estate market in the form of:

- changes in money supply
- inflation
- national economic cycles

In recent years, international economic trends have increasingly influenced local real estate markets, particularly in border states, large metropolitan areas, and markets with an economic base tied to foreign trade. In these instances, currency fluctuations significantly affect the local economy.

Governmental influences. Governments at every level exert significant influence over local real estate markets. The primary forms of government influence are:

- local zoning power
- local control and permitting of new development
- local taxing power
- federal influence on interest rates
- environmental legislation and regulations

A good example of government influence over the local real estate market is a city government's power to declare a moratorium on new construction, regardless of demand. Such officially declared stoppages may occur due to water or power shortages, insufficient thoroughfares, or incompatibility with the master plan.

Interpreting market indicators

Real estate supply and demand, like supply and demand for other economic products, interact in the marketplace to produce *price movements*.

Real Estate Supply-Demand Cycle

As the exhibit illustrates, prices, construction, and vacancy fluctuate over the cycle. Construction represents the addition of a new supply. **Vacancy** is the amount of total real estate inventory of a certain type that is unoccupied at a given time. **Absorption** is the amount of available property that becomes occupied over a period of time.

Starting the cycle with undersupply or high demand, vacancy is low, and prices are high. This situation stimulates suppliers to construct additional housing or commercial space. New construction increases supply, causing vacancies to rise and prices to fall until the supply-and-demand equilibrium is reached. As more new space is added, supply begins to outstrip demand, vacancy continues to rise, and prices continue to fall. At the bottom of the cycle, prices and vacancy are at unacceptable levels, and construction ceases. The market "dies" until excess supply can be absorbed. The absorption process continues through the equilibrium point until price and vacancy conditions are sufficiently attractive to encourage renewed construction. Then the cycle repeats.

Thus, by considering indicators such as vacancy rates, construction numbers, building permits, supply and demand factors, sales volume, and price levels over time, one can identify where a market is in the supply-demand cycle and gain some insight into what is coming next, whether prices will rise or fall, tending to favor buyers (buyers' market) or sellers (sellers' market); and by comparing submarkets within a market, one can identify trends in area preferences: which local areas are now or soon likely will be most sought out, which ones are falling into disfavor, and so on.

Regulation of Appraisal

FIRREA

In 1989, Congress passed the Financial Institutions Reform, Recovery, and Enforcement Act (FIRREA) in response to the savings and loan crisis. This act included provisions to regulate appraisal.

Title XI of FIRREA requires that competent individuals whose professional conduct is properly supervised perform all appraisals used in federally related transactions. Such federally-related appraisals must be performed only by state-certified appraisers. A state-certified appraiser has passed the examinations and met the competency standards established by the state in which licensure is sought. State standards are created in accordance with the federal standards set forth in FIRREA and USPAP (Uniform Standards of Professional Appraisal Practice). The minimum certification criteria must follow those established by the Appraiser Qualifications Board of the Appraisal Foundation.

The Appraisal Foundation

The Appraisal Foundation and USPAP. In the 1980s, a team of professional appraisal organizations agreed on a set of appraisal standards, known as the Uniform Standards of Professional Appraisal Practice (USPAP), and in 1987 established The Appraisal Foundation (TAF) as a not-for-profit organization to administer those standards and generally advance the profession of appraisal.

TAF provides consulting, citation development, standards of practice procedures, implementation guidelines, and other appraisal-related services. To support its mission, TAF established the

- Appraiser Qualifications Board (AQB)
- Appraisal Standards Board (ASB)
- Appraisal Practices Board (APB) (as of July 1, 2010)
- Board of Trustees (BOT)

- Appraisal Subcommittee

Appraisal Qualifications Board. The Appraiser Qualifications Board (AQB) is the education and licensing arm of USPAP. This board creates and maintains the National Appraisal Examination, administers the National USPAP courses, and certifies national USPAP instructors.

Appraisal Standards Board. The Appraisal Standards Board (ASB) is the primary source for the content and substance of USPAP standards. It establishes the standards, issues advisory opinions, and works with the AQB to develop courses and certify instructors.

Appraisal Subcommittee. The ASC oversees TAF and state licensing agencies. It also maintains a registry of all state-certified and licensed appraisers qualified to appraise properties subject to federally related transactions.

USPAP

USPAP standards. The Uniform Standards of Professional Appraisal Practice (USPAP) is a set of standards, guidelines, and provisions for the appraisal industry. It resulted from the cooperation of nine national appraisal organizations in 1985.

The "competence" provision requires appraisers to assess whether they have the necessary knowledge and competence to perform a specific assignment. If they do not, they must disclose this fact.

The "departure" provision permits appraisers to perform an appraisal that does not meet all the USPAP guidelines, provided they have informed the client of the limitations of the incomplete appraisal and ensured that the partial appraisal will not be misleading.

The "standards" concern:

- recognized appraisal methods
- definition of due diligence
- how appraisal results are reported
- disclosures and assumptions
- appraisal review
- real estate analysis
- mass appraisals
- personal property appraisals
- business appraisals
- compliance with USPAP
- compliance with the Code of Professional Ethics and Standards of Professional Practice

Florida appraiser licensing and certification requires at least 15 hours of prelicensure education on USPAP and additional post-licensure coursework on USPAP.

State-licensed and certified appraisers

Florida statute mandates that a person may not use the titles "certified real estate appraiser," " licensed real estate appraiser," or "registered trainee real estate appraiser," or any words or titles similar to these, nor may a person issue an appraisal report unless the person is certified, licensed, or registered under the requirements of F.S. 475.612. However, someone who is not certified, licensed, or registered may perform the work necessary to complete an appraisal report if that person is supervised, the work is approved, and the report is signed by a certified or licensed appraiser. Only the certified or licensed appraiser may receive direct compensation for providing valuation services for the report.

Certified appraisers include ***certified residential appraisers,*** who issue appraisal reports for residential properties consisting of one to four units, and ***certified general appraisers,*** who issue appraisal reports for any type of property.

However, Florida-licensed real estate brokers, sales associates, and broker associates may provide valuation services for compensation, provided they do not represent themselves as certified or licensed appraisers or registered appraiser trainees. Real estate licensees may also prepare comparative market analyses, price opinions, and opinions of real estate value, provided they do not represent any of these as an appraisal.

Requirements for federally-related transactions. Federal banking law defines a federally-related transaction as "any real estate-related financial transaction that a federal financial institution's regulatory agency or the Resolution Trust Corporation engages in, contracts for, or regulates, and which requires the services of a state-licensed or state-certified appraiser." The financial transaction must require the services of a certified appraiser to be considered a federally related transaction. This definition is reiterated in Florida statute.

Federal banking law expands the definition to include a real-estate-related financial transaction as "Any transaction involving:

> (A) the sale, lease, purchase, investment in, or exchange of real property, including interests in property, or the financing thereof;
>
> (B) the refinancing of real property or interests in real property; and
>
> (C) the use of real property or interests in property as security for a loan or investment, including mortgage-backed securities."

To be determined a federally-related transaction, the transaction must satisfy the following requirements:

- meet the definition of a real estate-related financial transaction
- be engaged in, contracted for, or regulated by any of the five federal financial institutions regulatory agencies: the Board of Governors of the Federal Reserve System, the Federal Deposit Insurance Corporation, the Office of the Comptroller of the Currency, the Office of Thrift Supervision, or the National Credit Union Administration
- require the services of an appraiser

Under FIRREA, all financial transactions involving Freddie Mac, Fannie Mae, FHA, and VA require certified appraisals.

Out-of-state appraiser licenses and certifications are recognized in Florida on a temporary basis if the nonresident appraiser is appraising property for a federally related transaction.

Certified appraisal reports. A certified appraisal involves recording, photographing, measuring, checking, and verifying information for accuracy. This information is to be included in a certified appraisal report as a legal document that will hold up in court.

Florida statute defines an appraisal report as "any communication, written or oral, of an appraisal, appraisal review, appraisal consulting service, analysis, opinion, or conclusion relating to the nature, quality, value, or utility of a specified interest in, or aspect of, identified real property, and includes any report communicating an appraisal analysis, opinion, or conclusion of value, regardless of title." The report is certified when it is signed by the authorized appraiser who, by signing the report, is attesting that its facts and procedures are true and correct.

To be recognized in a federally related transaction, an appraisal report must be in writing and conform to USPAP.

The appraisal defined. Florida law (Section 475.611, F.S.) defines an appraisal as the act or process of developing an opinion of value of real property. An appraisal is a supportable, defensible, and impartial opinion of value, not a guarantee, developed as of a specific date for a specific purpose. The purpose of an appraisal is the value question the appraiser is engaged to answer, that is, what type of value, such as market value or investment value, is to be estimated and for what problem.

Client, intended use, and intended user. The client is the party who engages the appraiser for a specific assignment, by employment or contract. The intended use is the way the appraiser's reported opinions and conclusions will be used, as identified at the time of the assignment, for example mortgage-loan underwriting, a buying or selling decision, estate-tax valuation, or portfolio analysis. The intended users are the client and any other parties the appraiser identifies, by name or type, as users of the report. Because both the scope of work and the form of the report depend on these identifications, the appraiser settles them with the client before beginning.

Appraisal service of real estate

Florida real estate brokers, broker associates, and sales associates are licensed and regulated by F.S. Chapter 475, Part I. In this chapter, brokers and sales associates are defined as individuals who perform services for others in exchange for compensation, with the understanding that sales associates must work under a broker. The services listed in the definition are many, but include selling, buying, renting, exchanging, and appraising.

As licensed real estate professionals, brokers and sales associates are not required to be licensed or certified appraisers to perform appraisals. However, they may not appraise federally-related transactions or represent themselves as certified or licensed appraisers. They also may not perform appraisals, which require a state-licensed or certified appraiser, or appraisals that may be performed by a registered trainee appraiser. When performing an appraisal, real estate licensees should obtain a written statement from the client that no federally-related transaction is involved and that a certified appraiser is not required for the appraisal.

Appraisal reports must conform to USPAP. To perform appraisals and prepare appraisal reports, real estate licensees must be familiar with and comply with USPAP standards.

Individuals who apply for registration or certification as appraisers must sign a pledge to comply with USPAP. In complying with the standards of practice, appraisers must set aside their personal interests and exercise impartiality, objectivity, and independence in performing appraisals. Ethical standards prohibit appraisers from accepting or charging compensation based on the property's value. Failure to comply with USPAP may result in disciplinary action against the appraiser or real estate licensee.

Comparative Market Analysis (CMA). Real estate licensees routinely prepare comparative market analyses in the course of their business practice. Although licensees are required to comply with USPAP when preparing appraisals, they are exempt from the standards when performing comparative market analyses, provided these services are not referred to as appraisals.

Broker Price Opinion (BPO). Real estate licensees also routinely prepare broker price opinions. Again, while they are required to comply with USPAP for appraisal services, they are exempt from the standards when performing broker price opinions or opinions of real estate value, provided these services are not referred to as appraisals.

Concepts of Value

Market cost, price, and value

What is a market? A market is a place where supply and demand meet: Suppliers sell or trade their goods and services to demanders, who are consumers and buyers. It is a transaction arena where the price mechanism continually defines and quantifies the value produced by the relative forces of supply and demand.

Supply and demand. The goal of an economic system is to produce and distribute a supply of goods and services to satisfy the demand of its constituents. Economic activity, therefore, centers on the production, distribution, and sale of goods and services to meet consumer demand. Consumers demand goods and services; suppliers and sellers produce and distribute them for a negotiated price.

Cost, price, and value. To produce a good or service, a supplier incurs costs, which are the expenses necessary to generate and deliver the item to the market. Essential production costs include capital, materials and supplies, labor, management, and overhead.

Costs play an important role in the dynamics of supply, demand, and value. Since producers have limited resources, it is imperative to maximize production efficiency and minimize costs. Moreover, because consumers will pay the lowest possible price for comparable goods and services, producers must be price-competitive to stay in business. A competitor who can produce an item of similar quality at a lower price will eventually drive higher-priced items out of the market. At that point, the elements of value, desire, utility, scarcity, and purchasing power, do not matter: if the consumer wants the item at all, he or she must cover the producer's costs and profit.

In addition to supply and demand, the other critical component of an economic system is the price mechanism, or simply, price. A price is the amount of money or other asset that a buyer has agreed to pay and a seller has agreed to accept to complete the exchange of a good or service. It is a quantification of the value of an item traded.

Price in this context means the final trading price; it is not the seller's preliminary asking price nor the purchaser's initial bidding price. Asking and bidding prices are pricing positions in a negotiation between the parties prior to the exchange. The true price of an item or service is the final number the parties agree to.

Real estate value types

The purpose of an appraisal influences an estimate of the value of a parcel of real estate. This is because different types of value relate to different appraisal purposes. Some of the possibilities are listed below.

- market
- reproduction
- replacement
- going concern
- salvage
- plottage
- assessed
- condemned
- depreciated
- appraised
- rental

- leasehold
- insured
- book
- mortgage

Market value. Market value is an estimate of the price at which a property will sell at a particular time. This type of value is generally sought in appraisals and used by brokers in their estimates of value. It is an opinion of the price that a willing seller and a willing buyer would probably agree on for a property at a given time if:

- the transaction is a cash transaction
- the property is exposed on the open market for a reasonable period
- buyer and seller have full information about market conditions and about potential uses
- there is no abnormal pressure on either party to complete the transaction
- buyer and seller are not related (it is an "arm's length" transaction)
- title is marketable and conveyable by the seller
- the price is a "normal consideration," that is, it does not include hidden influences such as special financing deals, concessions, terms, services, fees, credits, costs, or other types of consideration

Reproduction value. Reproduction value is the cost to construct a precise duplicate of the subject property's improvements, assuming current construction costs.

Replacement value. Replacement value is the cost to construct a functional equivalent of the subject property's improvements, based on current construction costs.

Going concern value. The total worth of a business that is expected to continue operating profitably, including both tangible and intangible assets.

Salvage value. Salvage value refers to the nominal value of a property that has reached the end of its economic life. Salvage value is also an estimate of the price at which a structure will sell if it is dismantled and moved.

Plottage value. Plottage value is an estimate of the value that the process of assemblage adds to the combined values of the assembled properties.

Assessed value. Assessed value is the value of a property as estimated by a taxing authority as the basis for ad valorem taxation.

Condemned value. Condemned value is the value set by a county or municipal authority for a property that may be taken by eminent domain.

Depreciated value. Depreciated value is the amount remaining after subtracting accumulated depreciation from the property's purchase price.

Appraised value. Appraised value is an appraiser's opinion of a property's value.

Rental value. Rental value is an estimate of the rental rate a property can command for a specific period.

Leasehold value. Leasehold value is an estimate of the market value of a lessee's interest in a property.

Insured value. Insured value is the face amount a casualty or hazard insurance policy will pay in case a property is rendered unusable.

Book value. Book value is the value of the property as carried on the accounts of the owner. The value is generally equal to the acquisition price plus capital improvements minus accumulated depreciation.

Liquidated value. The value of the property when converted to cash.

Investment value. Investment value is the value of a property to a particular investor, based on that investor's individual requirements, financing, tax position, and return expectations. Because it reflects one investor's circumstances rather than the typical buyer's, investment value may be higher or lower than market value.

Value in use. Value in use is the value of a property for a specific use, often its current use to its present owner, rather than for its highest and best use. A specialized facility, such as a manufacturing plant built around one company's process, may have a high value in use to that owner but a much lower market value to a typical buyer.

Fundamental value characteristics

Value characteristics. Price is not something of value in itself. It is only a number that quantifies value. The economic issue underlying the interplay of supply and demand is how trading parties determine the value of a good or service, as reflected in its price.

Consider consumer demand for air conditioners. Why do air conditioners have value? How do they command the price they do?

The value of something is based on the answers to four questions:

- How much do I desire it?
- How useful is it?
- How scarce is it?
- Am I able to pay for it?

Demand/desire. One determinant of value is how dear the item is to the purchaser. Returning to the air conditioner example, the question becomes "how much do I desire to be cool, dry, and comfortable?" To a person who lives in the tropics, it is safe to say that air conditioning is more valuable than a heating system. It is also safe to say the opposite is true for residents of northern Alaska.

Utility. The second determinant of value is the product's ability to do the job. Can the air conditioner satisfy my need to stay cool? How cool does it make my house? Does it even work properly? Of course, I won't pay as much if it is old or ineffectual.

Scarcity. The third critical element of value is a product's availability in relation to demand. The air conditioner is quite valuable if there are only five units in the entire city and everyone is hot. On the other hand, the value of an air conditioner declines when there are 10,000 units for sale in a 500-person market.

Purchasing power. A fourth component of value is the consumer's ability to pay for the item. If one cannot afford to buy the air conditioner, the value of the air

conditioner is diminished, since it is financially out of reach. If all air conditioners are too expensive, consumers are forced to consider alternatives such as ceiling fans.

In the marketplace, the relative presence or absence of the four elements of value is constantly changing due to innumerable factors. Since price reflects the total value of all underlying factors at any given time, changes in those factors drive changes in price.

Valuation principles

A number of economic forces interact in the marketplace to contribute to real estate value. Appraisers must consider these forces when estimating a property's value. Among the most recognized of these principles are those listed below.

Substitution. According to the principle of substitution, a buyer will pay no more for a property than the buyer would have to pay for an equally desirable and available substitute property. For example, if three houses for sale are essentially similar in size, quality, and location, a potential buyer is unlikely to choose the one that is priced significantly higher than the other two

Highest and best use. This principle holds that, in theory, there is a single use of a property that yields the highest income and return. A property achieves its maximum value when it is put to this use. If the actual use is not the highest and best use, the value of the property is correspondingly less than optimal. Technically, highest and best use must be legally permissible, physically possible, financially feasible, and maximally productive.

For example, a property with an old house on it may not be in its highest and best use if it is surrounded by retail properties. If zoning permits the property to be converted to a retail use, its highest and best use may well be retail rather than residential.

The appraiser actually analyzes highest and best use in two ways. Highest and best use *as though vacant* asks what use would be most profitable if the site were bare; this determines the land's value and whether any existing improvement should be removed. Highest and best use *as improved* asks whether the existing building should be kept as is, renovated, or demolished, given what the site could otherwise support. When the value of the property as improved is less than the value of the site as though vacant (minus the cost to demolish), the improvement has reached the end of its economic contribution.

Conformity. This principle holds that a property's maximum value is achieved when its form and use are in harmony with surrounding properties and uses. For example, a two-bedroom, one-bathroom house surrounded by four-bedroom, three-bathroom homes may derive maximal value from a room addition.

Supply and demand. The availability of certain properties interacts with the strength of the demand for those properties to establish prices. When demand for properties exceeds supply, scarcity exists, and real estate values rise. When supply exceeds demand, a surplus exists, and real estate values decline. When supply and demand are generally in balance, the market is considered to be in equilibrium, and real estate values stabilize.

Utility. The fact that a property has a use in a particular marketplace increases its demand. Use is not the same as function. For instance, a swampy area may have an ecological function as a wetland, but it may have no economic utility if it cannot be put to some use that people in the marketplace are willing to pay for.

Anticipation. The benefits a buyer *expects to derive from a property over a holding period* influence what the buyer is willing to pay for it. For example, if an investor anticipates an annual rental income from a leased property to be one million dollars, this expected sum has a direct bearing on what the investor will pay for the property.

Contribution. The principle of contribution focuses on the degree to which a particular improvement affects the market value of the overall property. In essence, the contribution of the improvement equals the change in market value it *causes*. For example, adding a bathroom to a house may add $15,000 to the appraised value. Thus, the contribution of the bathroom is $15,000. Note that an improvement's contribution to value has little to do with the improvement's cost. The foregoing bathroom may have cost $5,000 or $20,000. *Contribution is what the market recognizes as the change in value, not what an item cost.* If continuous improvements are made to a property, it is possible that, at some point, the cost of adding improvements to a property no longer contributes a corresponding increase in the value of the property. When this occurs, the property suffers from *diminishing marginal return,* where the costs to improve exceed the contribution.

It is also important to understand that not all "improvements" to a property increase its value. For example, replacing a sewer line may be necessary and costly, but because it is part of the infrastructure expected to be in working order, it does not necessarily add value.

Progression and regression. The value of a property influences, and is influenced by, the values of neighboring properties. If a property is surrounded by properties with higher values, its value tends to rise (progression); if it is surrounded by properties with lower values, its value tends to fall (regression).

Assemblage and plottage. Assemblage, or the conjoining of adjacent properties, sometimes creates a combined value that is greater than the values of the unassembled properties. The excess value created by assemblage is called **plottage value**.

Subdivision. Dividing a single property into smaller properties can also result in a higher total value. For instance, a one-acre suburban site appraised at $50,000 may be subdivided into four quarter-acre lots, each worth $30,000. This principle contributes significantly to the financial feasibility of subdivision development.

Increasing and decreasing returns. As successive increments of investment are added to a property, value rises at first (increasing returns), but beyond a certain point each added increment returns less than it costs (decreasing returns). An improvement that costs more than it adds to value is an over-improvement.

External economies and diseconomies. Influences outside a property's own boundaries also affect its value. Favorable surroundings, such as nearby parks, good schools, and strong employment, are external economies that support value; unfavorable surroundings, such as an adjacent landfill, heavy through-traffic, or a declining neighborhood, are external diseconomies that depress it.

The Appraisal Process

An appraisal is not a single calculation but an orderly process that USPAP requires the appraiser to follow so that the value opinion is credible and well supported. The process moves through the following steps.

Identify the problem. The appraiser first determines exactly what is to be valued and why. This includes identifying the client and intended users, the intended use of the appraisal, the type and definition of value sought, the effective date of the opinion, and the subject property and its relevant characteristics, including the real property interest to be valued and any easements, leases, or other items affecting it. The appraiser also notes any extraordinary assumptions or hypothetical conditions the assignment requires.

Determine the scope of work. The scope of work is the type and extent of the research and analysis the appraiser performs to produce credible results. It covers how thoroughly the property is identified and inspected, the type and extent of data gathered, and the depth of analysis applied. The work must be enough to meet the expectations of parties who regularly use appraisals for similar assignments and to match what an appraiser's peers would do in the same situation; the scope may be more or less extensive from one assignment to another, but it must be sufficient for a credible result.

Collect and analyze the data. The appraiser gathers general data about the region, community, and neighborhood that affect value, and specific data about the subject and comparable properties. From this analysis the appraiser forms an opinion of the property's highest and best use, which guides the rest of the valuation.

Apply the approaches to value. The appraiser develops the applicable approaches, the sales comparison approach, the cost approach, and the income approach, each of which yields a separate indication of value. Not every approach fits every property, and the appraiser explains the exclusion of any approach not used.

Reconcile and report. Finally, the appraiser reconciles the separate value indications, weighing the quality and quantity of the data behind each, into a single final opinion of value. The appraiser does not simply average the indications but judges which are most reliable for the assignment. The conclusion is then communicated in an appraisal report, the formats of which are described in the next section.

Types of Appraisal Reports

Oral appraisals

While it is most common for appraisers to present written reports, under USPAP, an appraisal can be oral or written. An appraiser may communicate value conclusions orally, but must maintain a workfile that supports those conclusions.

Purpose and uses. Oral reports are rare and are usually used only for preliminary opinions of value, consultations, and situations in which a written report follows the verbal communication.

Note that the moment a value conclusion is communicated, even verbally, it is considered an appraisal.

Written appraisals

USPAP recognizes two types of written appraisal reports: an appraisal report and a restricted appraisal report.

Appraisal report. The appraisal report is the default, standard written report. It contains sufficient information to enable the intended user to understand the appraisal and the reasoning behind the value conclusion.

A standard appraisal report includes the following:

- summaries of the analyses performed
- summaries of the appraisal methods and techniques used
- summaries of the information analyzed
- explanations of reasoning that support the value conclusion
- discussion of assumptions and limited conditions in context
- explanation of how the approaches to value were applied and reconciled

This standard appraisal report is most commonly used for lending, litigation, and general valuation purposes.

Restricted appraisal report. This type of report provides less detail. It is intended only for a client, with no other intended users. The report must still be credible and prepared using appropriate, recognized methods by a qualified appraiser. It must be supported by the workfile.

A restricted appraisal report does NOT include the summaries or explanations included in the standard report. It may state only the results, relying entirely on the workfile to contain all supporting details.

The restricted appraisal report is typically used when the client does not need full reporting detail. For example, a seller may wish to appraise a property before setting a listing price. The appraisal cannot be used for financing purposes, so a restricted appraisal report would be sufficient.

Appraisal report formats

USPAP does not require a particular format for written appraisal reports, so appraisers may use a narrative format, a form such as the URAR, checklists, or any combination of these.

In practice, most appraisers use the URAR to standardize presentations. Many lenders require the use of the URAR, which streamlines the process by providing checkboxes and specific fields for various content, as illustrated on the following page.

UNIFORM RESIDENTIAL APPRAISAL REPORT File No.

Property Description

SUBJECT

Property Address | City | State | Zip Code
Legal Description | County
Assessor's Parcel No. | Tax Year | R.E. Taxes $ | Special Assessments $
Borrower | Current Owner | Occupant: Owner / Tenant / Vacant
Property rights appraised: Fee Simple / Leasehold | Project Type: PUD / Condominium (HUD/VA only) | HOA $ /Mo.
Neighborhood or Project Name | Map Reference | Census Tract
Sale Price $ | Date of Sale | Description and $ amount of loan charges/concessions to be paid by seller
Lender/Client | Address
Appraiser | Address

NEIGHBORHOOD

Location	Urban	Suburban	Rural	**Predominant occupancy**	**Single family housing** PRICE $(000)	AGE (yrs)	**Present land use %**	**Land use change**
Built up	Over 75%	25-75%	Under 25%				One family	Not likely / Likely
Growth rate	Rapid	Stable	Slow	Owner	Low		2-4 family	In process
Property values	Increasing	Stable	Declining	Tenant	High		Multi-family	To:
Demand/supply	Shortage	In balance	Over supply	Vacant (0-5%)	Predominant		Commercial	
Marketing time	Under 3 mos.	3-6 mos.	Over 6 mos.	Vac. (over 5%)				

Note: Race and the racial composition of the neighborhood are not appraisal factors.

Neighborhood boundaries and characteristics:

Factors that affect the marketability of the properties in the neighborhood (proximity to employment and amenities, employment stability, appeal to market, etc.):

Market conditions in the subject neighborhood (including support for the above conclusions related to the trend of property values, demand/supply, and marketing time -- such as data on competitive properties for sale in the neighborhood, description of the prevalence of sales and financing concessions, etc.):

PUD

Project Information for PUDs (If applicable) - - Is the developer/builder in control of the Home Owners' Association (HOA)? Yes No
Approximate total number of units in the subject project | Approximate total number of units for sale in the subject project
Describe common elements and recreational facilities:

SITE

Dimensions | Topography
Site area | Corner Lot: Yes No | Size
Specific zoning classification and description | Shape
Zoning compliance: Legal / Legal nonconforming (Grandfathered use) / Illegal / No zoning | Drainage
Highest & best use as improved: Present use / Other use (explain) | View

Utilities	Public	Other	**Off-site Improvements**	Type	Public	Private	
Electricity			Street				Landscaping
Gas			Curb/gutter				Driveway Surface
Water			Sidewalk				Apparent easements
Sanitary sewer			Street lights				FEMA Special Flood Hazard Area: Yes No
Storm sewer			Alley				FEMA Zone / Map Date
							FEMA Map No.

Comments (apparent adverse easements, encroachments, special assessments, slide areas, illegal or legal nonconforming zoning use, etc.):

DESCRIPTION OF IMPROVEMENTS

GENERAL DESCRIPTION	EXTERIOR DESCRIPTION	FOUNDATION	BASEMENT	INSULATION
No. of Units	Foundation	Slab	Area Sq. Ft.	Roof
No. of Stories	Exterior Walls	Crawl Space	% Finished	Ceiling
Type (Det./Att.)	Roof Surface	Basement	Ceiling	Walls
Design (Style)	Gutters & Dwnspts.	Sump Pump	Walls	Floor
Existing/Proposed	Window Type	Dampness	Floor	None
Age (Yrs.)	Storm/Screens	Settlement	Outside Entry	Unknown
Effective Age (Yrs.)	Manufactured House	Infestation		

ROOMS	Foyer	Living	Dining	Kitchen	Den	Family Rm.	Rec. Rm.	Bedrooms	# Baths	Laundry	Other	Area Sq. Ft.
Basement												
Level 1												
Level 2												

Finished area **above** grade contains: Rooms; Bedroom(s); Bath(s); Square Feet of Gross Living Area

INTERIOR	Materials/Condition	HEATING	KITCHEN EQUIP.	ATTIC	AMENITIES	CAR STORAGE
Floors		Type	Refrigerator	None	Fireplace(s) #	None
Walls		Fuel	Range/Oven	Stairs	Patio	Garage # of cars
Trim/Finish		Condition	Disposal	Drop Stair	Deck	Attached
Bath Floor		COOLING	Dishwasher	Scuttle	Porch	Detached
Bath Wainscot		Central	Fan/Hood	Floor	Fence	Built-In
Doors		Other	Microwave	Heated	Pool	Carport
		Condition	Washer/Dryer	Finished		Driveway

COMMENTS

Additional features (special energy efficient items, etc.):

Condition of the improvements, depreciation (physical, functional, and external), repairs needed, quality of construction, remodeling/additions, etc.:

Adverse environmental conditions (such as, but not limited to, hazardous wastes, toxic substances, etc.) present in the improvements, on the site, or in the immediate vicinity of the subject property:

Freddie Mac Form 70 6/93 | PAGE 1 OF 2 | Fannie Mae Form 1004 6/93

Form UA2 — "TOTAL for Windows" appraisal software by a la mode, inc. — 1-800-ALAMODE

Appraisers may elect to use a different format for purposes such as estate planning, litigation, divorce, or consulting. Specialty properties that don't align with the URAR fields may require a different format, and restricted appraisal reports do not follow the URAR format.

Snapshot Review for Chapter 6

The following review summarizes the key rules and concepts from Chapter 6.

VALUATION

Physical Characteristics

Of Real Estate

- land = surface + subsurface + airspace + natural attachments
- real estate = land + permanent improvements
- land characteristics: immobility (cannot be moved), indestructibility (cannot be destroyed), heterogeneity (no two parcels are identical)
- highest and best use: principle holds that there's a single use of a property that yields the highest income and return; strongly influenced by location and demand
- natural attachments: trees, water, minerals
- improvements = manmade additions to land

Economic Characteristics of Real Estate

- market forces: real estate affected by supply, demand, and price; local, illiquid market that responds slowly to change; rising demand or limited supply leads to higher prices; excess supply or weak demand leads to lower prices
- supply and demand factors: supply affected by construction costs, financing, zoning, regulation; demand driven by employment, population, purchasing power, amenities; vacancy, absorption, and construction trends indicate market conditions

Regulation of Appraisal

- FIRREA regulates federally related appraisals
- USPAP establishes appraisal ethics and standards
- federally related transactions require certified appraisers
- The Appraisal Foundation's AQB, ASB, and ASC oversee licensing and standards

Florida Appraisal Rules

- certified residential appraisers: 1–4 residential units
- certified general appraisers: all property types
- licensees may prepare CMAs and BPOs, but these are not appraisals
- appraisal reports must comply with USPAP
- appraisal (s. 475.611): an opinion of value developed for a stated purpose and effective date
- client engages the appraiser; intended use and intended users are identified before work begins

CONCEPTS OF VALUE

Value Basics

- cost = expense to produce; price = amount paid; value = market worth
- market value = probable selling price under normal conditions
- value is based on desire, utility, scarcity, and purchasing power
- types of value: market, assessed, insured, rental, replacement, reproduction, leasehold, salvage, etc.
- investment value: worth to a specific investor based on individual requirements
- value in use: worth for a specific use, which may differ from market value

Principles of Value

- substitution: a buyer will pay no more for a property than the buyer would have to pay for an equally desirable and available substitute property
- conformity: property's maximum value is achieved when its form and use are in harmony with surrounding area
- anticipation: the benefits a buyer expects to derive from a property over a holding period influence what the buyer is willing to pay
- contribution: the degree to which a particular improvement affects the market value of the overall property
- if a property is surrounded by properties with higher values, its value tends to rise (progression); if it is surrounded by properties with lower values, its value tends to fall (regression)
- assemblage: the conjoining of adjacent properties, sometimes creates a combined value that is greater than the values of the unassembled properties; plottage: excess value created by assemblage
- highest and best use maximizes property value
- highest and best use is analyzed both as though vacant and as improved
- increasing and decreasing returns: added investment eventually returns less than its cost (over-improvement)
- external economies and diseconomies: off-site influences that raise or lower value

The Appraisal Process

- identify the problem; determine the scope of work; collect and analyze data
- form an opinion of highest and best use; apply the three approaches to value
- reconcile the indications into one final value opinion, then report it
- scope of work: the extent of identification, inspection, data, and analysis needed for credible results

Types of Appraisal Reports

- oral (verbal) appraisals require supporting workfile
- appraisal report = detailed written report
- restricted appraisal report = limited-use report for client only
- URAR commonly used for residential lending reports

Chapter 6 Quiz: Overview of Real Estate Valuation

6.1 The legal concept of land includes which of the following components?

a. Only the surface of the earth and man-made improvements
b. The surface of the earth, everything beneath it to the center, natural attachments, and the air above extending outward
c. Only minerals and water below the surface
d. The surface area and any temporary structures attached to it

6.2 A house built with the intention of serving as a permanent dwelling is classified as real estate because it is considered which of the following?

a. A fixture that is permanently attached to the land
b. Personal property until it is sold
c. A temporary structure subject to relocation
d. A trade fixture owned by the builder

6.3 The physical characteristic of land that refers to the fact that no two parcels are identical is known as which of the following?

a. Indestructibility
b. Progression
c. Heterogeneity
d. Substitution

6.4 When supply increases relative to demand in a real estate market, what typically happens to prices?

a. Prices increase due to competition among buyers
b. Prices remain stable regardless of supply
c. Prices decrease as the market becomes saturated
d. Prices fluctuate randomly without pattern

6.5 In real estate markets, the unit commonly used to measure residential supply is which of the following?

a. Acreage
b. Square footage
c. Households
d. Dwelling units

6.6 The principle that a buyer will pay no more for a property than the cost of an equally desirable substitute property is known as which valuation principle?

a. Contribution
b. Conformity
c. Substitution
d. Anticipation

6.7 Under the Financial Institutions Reform, Recovery and Enforcement Act, appraisals performed for federally related transactions must be completed by which of the following individuals?

a. Any licensed real estate broker
b. A state-certified appraiser
c. A registered trainee appraiser working independently
d. Any person supervised by a lender

6.8 The Uniform Standards of Professional Appraisal Practice are administered by which organization?

a. The Federal Deposit Insurance Corporation
b. The National Credit Union Administration
c. The Resolution Trust Corporation
d. The Appraisal Foundation

6.9 A restricted appraisal report differs from a standard appraisal report because it does which of the following?

a. Provides detailed explanations of appraisal methods and reasoning
b. Eliminates the need for a supporting workfile
c. Contains only the results and is intended solely for the client
d. Is required for all federally related transactions

6.10 Market value is best defined as which of the following?

a. The assessed value determined for property tax purposes
b. The price agreed upon under normal conditions in an arm's length transaction
c. The cost to reproduce a property exactly as it currently exists, with no substitutions
d. The insured value listed in a casualty insurance policy

6.11 The physical characteristic of land meaning that a parcel cannot be moved from one site to another is ______.

a. immobility
b. scarcity
c. heterogeneity
d. indestructibility

6.12 The four determinants that give real estate value are utility, scarcity, desire, and ______.

a. transferability
b. mobility
c. durability
d. purchasing power

6.13 Highest and best use is best described as the use that ______.

a. the current owner personally prefers
b. requires the least investment
c. yields the greatest value for the site
d. matches the property's original zoning

6.14 A large, custom four-bedroom home is built in a neighborhood of modest two-bedroom houses, and it does not return its full cost. This is explained by the principle of ______.

a. anticipation
b. contribution
c. substitution
d. conformity

6.15 An investor pays a premium for a property because she expects a new highway interchange to raise its value. Her willingness to pay reflects the principle of ______.

a. anticipation
b. regression
c. plottage
d. substitution

6.16 A homeowner adds a swimming pool costing $60,000, but it raises the home's market value by only $25,000. This illustrates the principle of ______.

a. progression
b. contribution
c. conformity
d. anticipation

6.17 A modest home located among larger, more expensive homes tends to be worth more than it would be elsewhere. This effect is called ______.

a. regression
b. plottage
c. progression
d. assemblage

6.18 The increase in value that can result from combining two or more adjacent parcels under one owner is called ______.

a. progression
b. assessed value
c. salvage value
d. plottage value

6.19 The total expenses a builder incurs to construct improvements are referred to as ______.

a. price
b. cost
c. market value
d. investment value

6.20 The cost to construct an exact duplicate of a building, using the same materials and design, is its ______.

a. replacement value
b. assessed value
c. reproduction value
d. going-concern value

6.21 A particular investor values a property higher than the typical buyer would because of her favorable tax position and financing. The value to that specific investor is called ______.

a. market value
b. assessed value
c. salvage value
d. investment value

6.22 The value a county property appraiser places on real estate as the basis for ad valorem taxes is its ______.

a. market value
b. assessed value
c. insurable value
d. going-concern value

6.23 A specialized manufacturing plant designed around one company's process is worth far more to that owner than to a typical buyer. The value to the current owner for its specific use is called ______.

a. value in use
b. market value
c. plottage value
d. reproduction value

6.24 The first step in the appraisal process is to ______.

a. reconcile the value indications
b. identify the problem to be solved
c. apply the three approaches to value
d. report the final opinion of value

6.25 In an appraisal assignment, the party who engages the appraiser by employment or contract is the ______.

a. intended user
b. borrower
c. client
d. mortgagee

CHAPTER 7:
SALES COMPARISON, COST-DEPRECIATION AND INCOME APPROACHES

Contents

Learning Objectives

Upon completion of this chapter, you will be able to:

1. Describe the assumptions underlying the sales comparison approach
2. Construct a sales comparison adjustment grid using the proper sequence of adjustments
3. Distinguish among normal sale price, market conditions-adjusted normal sale price, and final adjusted sale price
4. Describe considerations regarding the applicability of the cost approach
5. Identify the steps in the cost approach
6. Distinguish between reproduction cost and replacement cost and describe the methods for estimating costs
7. Distinguish among the three types of accrued depreciation and describe the methods of estimating accrued depreciation
8. Describe the process for a GIM analysis
9. Reconcile the various approaches to value into a final value estimate
10. Explain the income capitalization approach and estimate value using net operating income and a capitalization rate

Sales Comparison Approach

The sales comparison approach, also known as the market data approach, is used for almost all properties. It also serves as the basis for a broker's opinion of value. It is based on multiple assumptions. The principle of substitution, that a buyer will pay no more for the subject property than would be sufficient to purchase a comparable property, is the foundation of the entire approach. Contribution means that specific characteristics add value to a property.

Other underlying assumptions in this approach are that an active and competitive market exists, buyers and sellers act rationally (they are informed and acting in their own best interests), and the transaction is arms-length.

The sales comparison approach is widely used because it considers the subject property's specific amenities relative to competing properties. In addition, because of the currency of its data, the approach incorporates present market realities.

The sales comparison approach is limited in that every property is unique. As a result, it is difficult to find good comparables, especially for special-purpose properties. In addition, the market must be active; otherwise, sale prices lack currency and reliability.

Steps in the approach

The sales comparison approach involves comparing the sale prices of recently sold properties comparable to the subject and making dollar adjustments to each comparable's price to account for competitive differences between the comparable and the subject. After identifying the adjusted value for each comparable, the appraiser weights the reliability of each comparable and the factors underlying the adjustments. The weighting yields a final value range based on the most reliable factors in the analysis.

Steps in the Sales Comparison Approach

1. Identify comparable sales.
2. Compare comparables to the subject and make adjustments to comparables.
3. Weight values indicated by adjusted comparables for the final value estimate of the subject.

Identifying comparables

To qualify as a comparable, a property must:

- resemble the subject in size, shape, design, utility, and location
- have sold recently, generally within six months of the appraisal
- have sold in an arm's-length transaction

An appraiser considers three to six comparables, and usually includes at least three in the appraisal report.

Appraisers have specific guidelines within the foregoing criteria for selecting comparables, many of which are set by secondary market organizations such as FNMA. For example, to qualify as a comparable for a mortgage appraisal, a property might have to be located within 1 mile of the subject property. Or perhaps the comparable's size must be within a certain percentage of the improved area relative to the subject.

The time-of-sale criterion is important because transactions that occurred too far in the past will not reflect appreciation or recent changes in market conditions.

An arm's-length sale involves objective, disinterested parties who are presumed to have negotiated a market price for the property. If a house were sold between a father and a daughter, for example, one might assume the transaction did not reflect market value.

Principal sources of data for generating the sales comparison are tax records, title records, and the local multiple listing service.

Adjusting comparables

The appraiser adjusts the sale prices of comparables to account for competitive differences relative to the subject property. Note that the sale prices of the comparables are known, while the value and price of the subject are not. Therefore, adjustments can be made only to the comparables' prices, not to the subject's. Adjustments to the comparables are made through value deductions or additions.

Adding or deducting value. If the comparable is better than the subject in a particular characteristic, an amount is deducted from the comparable's sale price. This neutralizes the comparable's competitive advantage in an adjustment category.

For example, a comparable has a swimming pool, and the subject does not. To equalize the difference, the appraiser deducts an amount, say $26,000, from the comparable's sale price. Note that the adjustment reflects the swimming pool's contribution to market value. The adjustment amount is not the pool's cost or its depreciated value.

If the comparable is inferior to the subject in some characteristic, an amount is added to the price of the comparable. This adjustment equalizes the subject's competitive advantage in this area.

Adjustment criteria. The principal factors for comparison and adjustment are *time of sale, location, physical characteristics, and transaction characteristics.*

- **time of sale**

  An adjustment may be made if market conditions, market prices, or financing availability have changed significantly since the comparable's sale date. Most often, this adjustment is to account for appreciation.

- **location**

  An adjustment may be made if there are differences between the comparable's location and the subject's, including neighborhood desirability and appearance, zoning restrictions, and general price levels.

- **physical characteristics**

  Adjustments may be made for marketable differences between the comparable's and subject's lot size, square feet of livable area (or other appropriate measure for the property type), number of rooms, layout, age, condition, construction type and quality, landscaping, and special amenities.

- **transaction characteristics**

  An adjustment may be made for such differences as mortgage loan terms, mortgage assumability, and owner financing.

Transactional elements of comparison

Beyond the broad categories above, an appraiser examines several transactional elements that can cause a comparable's sale price to differ from what the property would bring in a normal market sale. Each is adjusted before the price is used as evidence of the subject's value.

Conditions of sale. This element accounts for the motivations of the buyer and seller. A normal, arm's-length sale assumes a willing buyer and a willing seller, each acting knowledgeably and without undue pressure. When a sale is not arm's-length, for example a sale between family members, a sale to settle an estate, or a forced or distressed sale, the price may be above or below market, and an adjustment is required, or the comparable is rejected.

Financing terms and cash equivalency. A sale financed on unusually favorable terms, such as a below-market interest rate bought down by the seller or an assumable low-rate mortgage, often sells for more than it would on market terms. To remove this distortion, the appraiser makes a *cash-equivalency* adjustment, restating the comparable's price as if the buyer had paid cash or obtained market-rate financing. The amount is usually estimated by market abstraction, comparing otherwise similar sales made with and without the special financing.

Sales concessions. Sometimes a seller gives the buyer something of value outside normal terms, such as paying the buyer's closing costs, providing a decorating allowance, or including personal property. Like favorable financing, concessions tend to inflate the recorded sale price, so the appraiser deducts the value of the concession, leaving the price of the real property alone.

Personal property. Only the real property is valued in the appraisal, so the appraiser removes the value of any personal property included in a comparable sale. This requires distinguishing a fixture from a trade fixture. A *fixture* is an item of personal property that has been so attached to the real estate that it is considered part of it and conveys with the property, such as a built-in dishwasher. A *trade fixture* is an article attached to leased premises by a tenant for use in a business; it remains the tenant's personal property and does not convey with the real estate. Fixtures are part of the realty being appraised; trade fixtures and other personal property are not.

Paired-sales analysis

Whenever possible, an appraiser derives the dollar amount of an adjustment from the market itself rather than from judgment alone, using *paired-sales analysis* (also called matched-pairs analysis). The appraiser locates two comparable sales that are alike in every significant respect except for the single feature being measured; the difference in their sale prices is taken as the market's measure of that feature's contribution to value. For example, if two nearly identical homes sell for $400,000 and $415,000 and the only meaningful difference is that the higher-priced home has a swimming pool, paired-sales analysis indicates a pool adjustment of about $15,000. Because perfectly matched pairs are rare, the appraiser usually analyzes several pairs and reconciles the results.

Note the following terminology:

- normal sale price – the actual price the comparable property sold for under typical, arms-length conditions
- market conditions/adjusted normal sale price – the comparable's sales price adjusted only for changes in market conditions over time
- final adjusted sales price – the comparable's price after all adjustments have been applied

Weighting comparables

Adding and subtracting the appropriate adjustments to the sale price of each comparable results in an adjusted price for the comparables that indicates the value of the subject. The last step in the approach is to perform a weighted analysis of the indicated values of each comparable. The appraiser, in other words, must identify which comparable values are more indicative of the subject and which are less indicative.

An appraiser primarily relies on experience and judgment to weight comparables. There is no formula for selecting a value from the range of all analyzed comparables. However, there are three quantitative guidelines: the total number of adjustments, the amount of each adjustment, and the net change in value from all adjustments.

As a rule, *the fewer the total number of adjustments, the smaller the adjustment amounts, and the less the total adjustment amount, the more reliable the comparable.*

Number of adjustments. In terms of total adjustments, the comparable with the fewest adjustments tends to be the most similar to the subject, making it the best indicator of value. If a comparable requires excessive adjustments, it is increasingly less reliable as an indicator of value. The underlying rationale is that any adjustment involves a margin of error. Whenever multiple adjustments are required, the margin of error increases. By the time six or seven adjustments are made, the margin becomes significant, and the reliability of the final value estimate is greatly reduced.

Single adjustment amounts. The dollar amount of an adjustment represents the variance between the subject and the comparable for a given item. If a large adjustment is called for, the comparable becomes a less reliable indicator of value. The smaller the adjustment, the better the comparable is as an indicator of value. If an appraisal is performed for mortgage qualification, the appraiser may be restricted from making adjustments in excess of a certain amount, for example, anything in excess of 10-15% of the sale price of the comparable. If such an adjustment were necessary, the property would no longer be considered comparable.

Total net adjustment amount. The third reliability factor in the weighting of comparables is the total net value change across all adjustments. If a comparable's total adjustments alter the indicated value only slightly, the comparable is a good indicator of value. If total adjustments result in a large dollar difference between the sale price and the adjusted value, the comparable is a poorer indicator of value. Fannie Mae, for instance, will not accept a comparable where total net adjustments exceed 15% of the sale price.

For example, an appraiser is considering a property that sold for $1,000,000 as a comparable. After all adjustments are made, the comparable's indicated value is $1,210,000, a 21% difference from its sale price. This property, if allowed at all, would be a weak indicator of value.

Cost Approach

The cost approach is most often used for recently built properties where the actual costs of development and construction are known. It is also used for special-purpose buildings that cannot be valued using other methods due to a lack of comparable sales or income data.

The strengths of the cost approach are that it:

- provides an upper limit for the subject's value based on the undepreciated cost of reproducing the improvements
- is very accurate for a property with new improvements, which are the highest and best use of the property.

The limitations of the cost approach are that:

- the cost to create improvements is not necessarily the same as market value
- depreciation is difficult to measure, especially for older buildings

Types of cost appraisal

The cost approach generally aims to estimate either the reproduction cost or the *replacement cost* of the subject property.

Reproduction cost is the cost, at current prices, of constructing a precise duplicate of the subject improvements. **Replacement cost** is the cost of constructing, at current prices and using current materials and methods, a functional equivalent of the subject improvements.

Replacement cost is primarily used to appraise older structures, since it is impractical to consider reproducing outmoded features and materials. However, reproduction cost is preferable whenever possible because it facilitates calculating depreciation on a structure.

Depreciation

A cornerstone of the cost approach is the concept of depreciation. Depreciation is the *loss of value in an improvement over time*. Since land is assumed to retain its value indefinitely, depreciation only applies to the improved portion of real property. The loss of an improvement's value can come from any cause, such as deterioration, obsolescence, or changes in the neighborhood. The sum of depreciation from all causes is accrued depreciation.

An appraiser considers depreciation as having three causes: physical deterioration, functional obsolescence, and economic obsolescence.

Physical deterioration. Physical deterioration is wear and tear from use, decay, and structural deterioration. Such deterioration may be either curable or incurable.

Curable deterioration occurs when the costs of repair of the item are less than or equal to the resulting increase in the property's value. For example, if a paint job costs $6,000, and the resulting value increase is $8,000, the deterioration is considered curable. Incurable deterioration is the opposite: the repair will cost more than can be recovered from its contribution to the building's value. For example, if the foregoing paint job cost $10,000, the deterioration would be considered incurable.

Functional obsolescence. Functional obsolescence occurs when a property has outmoded physical or design features that are no longer desirable to current users. If the obsolescence is curable, the cost of replacing or redesigning the outmoded feature would be offset by the contribution to overall value, for example, a lack of central air conditioning. If the functional obsolescence is incurable, the cost of the cure would exceed its contribution to overall value; for example, a floor layout with a poor traffic pattern would cost three times as much to repair as the cure would add to overall value.

Economic obsolescence. Economic (or **external**) obsolescence is the loss of value due to adverse changes in the surroundings of the subject property that make the subject less desirable. Since such changes are usually beyond the property owner's control, economic obsolescence is considered an incurable loss of value. Examples of economic obsolescence include a deteriorating neighborhood, a rezoning of adjacent properties, or the bankruptcy of a large employer.

Steps in the approach

The cost approach consists of estimating the value of the land "as if vacant," estimating the cost of improvements, estimating and deducting accrued depreciation, and adding the estimated land value to the estimated depreciated cost of the improvements.

Steps in the Cost Approach

1. Estimate land value.
2. Estimate reproduction or replacement cost of improvements.
3. Estimate accrued depreciation.
4. Subtract accrued depreciation from reproduction or replacement cost.
5. Add land value to depreciated reproduction or replacement cost.

Estimate land value. To estimate land value, the appraiser uses the sales comparison method: find comparable properties to the subject property in terms of land and adjust the sale prices of the comparables to account for competitive differences with the subject property. Common adjustments concern location, physical characteristics, and time of sale. The indicated values of the comparable properties are used to estimate the land value of the subject. The implicit assumption is that the subject land is vacant (unimproved) and available for the highest and best use.

Estimate reproduction or replacement cost of improvements. There are several methods for estimating the reproduction or replacement cost of improvements. These are as follows.

- **Unit comparison method (square-foot method)**

  The appraiser examines one or more new structures that are similar to the subject's improvements, determines a cost per unit for the benchmark structures, and multiplies that cost per unit by the number of units in the subject. The unit of measurement is most commonly denominated in square feet.

- **Unit-in-place method**

  The appraiser uses materials cost manuals and estimates of labor costs, overhead, and builder's profit to estimate the cost of constructing separate components of the subject. The overall cost estimate is the sum of the estimated costs of individual components.

- **Quantity survey method**

  The appraiser considers in detail all materials, labor, supplies, overhead, and profit to arrive at an accurate estimate of the cost to build the improvement. More thorough than the unit-in-place method, this method is used less often by appraisers than by engineers and architects.

- **Cost indexing method**

  The original cost of constructing the improvement is updated by applying a percentage increase factor to account for increases in nominal costs over time.

Estimate accrued depreciation. Accrued depreciation is often estimated by the **straight-line** method, also called the **economic age-life method**. This method assumes depreciation occurs at a steady rate over the structure's economic life. Therefore, a property suffers the same incremental loss of value each year.

The **economic life** is the period during which the structure is expected to remain useful in its original use. The cost of the structure is divided by the number of years of economic life to determine the annual depreciation amount. The straight-line method is primarily relevant to depreciation from physical deterioration.

In applying the age-life method, the appraiser uses the structure's *effective age* rather than its actual, or chronological, age. Effective age is the age the structure appears to be, given its condition and modernization. A well-maintained building may have an effective age lower than its actual age, while a neglected one may have an effective age higher than its actual age. The ratio of effective age to total economic life, applied to the reproduction or replacement cost, estimates accrued depreciation.

The age-life method is not the only way to estimate depreciation. Two other methods are common:

Market-extraction method. The appraiser derives depreciation directly from comparable sales. By subtracting land value and the depreciated improvement value implied by a comparable's sale price from the cost of the improvements when new, the appraiser extracts the total accrued depreciation the market has recognized and expresses it as an annual rate. Like paired-sales analysis, this method grounds the estimate in market evidence.

Breakdown method. The appraiser estimates each type of depreciation separately, physical deterioration (curable and incurable), functional obsolescence (curable and incurable), and external obsolescence, then adds them together. Although the most detailed and time-consuming method, it is the most precise for older or complex properties, where a single age-life rate would be unreliable.

Subtract accrued depreciation from reproduction or replacement cost. The sum of accrued depreciation from all sources is subtracted from the estimated cost of reproducing or replacing the structure. This produces an estimate of the current value of the improvements.

Add land value to depreciated reproduction or replacement cost. To complete the cost approach, the estimated value of the land "as if vacant" is added to the estimated value of the depreciated reproduction or replacement cost of the improvements. This yields the final estimate of the property's value using the cost approach.

Cost Approach Illustration

I. LAND VALUE	
Land value, by direct sales comparison	80,000
II. IMPROVEMENTS COST	
Main building (by one or more of the four methods)	260,000
Plus: other structures	16,000
Total cost new	276,000
III. ACCRUED DEPRECIATION	
Physical depreciation	
Curable	10,000
Incurable	14,000
Functional obsolescence	6,000
External obsolescence	
Total depreciation	30,000
IV. IMPROVEMENTS COST MINUS DEPRECIATION	
Total cost new	276,000
Less: total depreciation	30,000
Depreciated value of improvements	246,000
V. OVERALL ESTIMATED VALUE	
Total land value	80,000
Depreciated value of improvements	246,000
Indicated value by cost approach	326,000

Income Approach

The income capitalization approach, or income approach, is used for income properties and sometimes for other properties in a rental market where the appraiser can find rental data. The approach is based on the principle of anticipation: the expected future income stream of a property determines what an investor will pay for it. It is also based on the principle of substitution: that an investor will pay no more for a subject property with a given income stream than for another property with a similar income stream.

The strength of the income approach is that it helps investors determine how much to pay for a property. Thus, in the right circumstances, it provides a good basis for estimating market value.

The income capitalization approach is limited in two ways. First, it is difficult to determine an appropriate capitalization rate. This is often a matter of judgment and experience on the part of the appraiser. Secondly, the income approach relies on market data on income and expenses, which can be difficult to obtain.

Steps in the approach

The income capitalization method involves estimating the subject property's annual net operating income and applying a capitalization rate to it. This produces a principal amount that the investor would pay for the property.

Steps in the Income Capitalization Approach

1. Estimate potential gross income.
2. Estimate effective gross income.
3. Estimate net operating income.
4. Select a capitalization rate.
5. Apply the capitalization rate.

Estimate potential gross income. Potential gross income is the scheduled rent of the subject plus income from miscellaneous sources such as vending machines and telephones. Scheduled rent is the total rent a property will produce if fully leased at the established rental rates.

Scheduled rent

+ Other income

Potential gross income

An appraiser may estimate potential gross rental income using current market rental rates (market rent), the rent specified by leases in effect on the property (contract rent), or a combination of both. Market rent is determined through market studies, a process similar to the sales comparison method. Contract rent is used primarily when existing leases are not due to expire in the short term and the tenants are unlikely to default or leave the lease.

Estimate effective gross income. Effective gross income is potential gross income minus an allowance for vacancy and credit losses.

Potential gross income

- Vacancy & credit losses

Effective Gross Income

Vacancy loss is the amount of potential income lost due to unrented space. Credit loss is the amount lost due to tenants' failure to pay rent for any reason. Both are estimated based on the subject property's history, comparable properties in the market, and typical management quality. The allowance for vacancy and credit loss is usually estimated as a percentage of potential gross income.

Estimate net operating income. Net operating income is effective gross income minus total operating expenses.

Effective gross income

- Total operating expenses

Net operating income

Operating expenses include both fixed and variable costs. Fixed expenses are those incurred whether the property is occupied or vacant, such as real estate taxes and hazard insurance. Variable expenses are those related to the building's actual operation, such as utilities, janitorial services, management, and repairs.

Operating expenses typically include an annual reserve fund for replacing equipment and other items that wear out, such as carpets and heating systems. Operating expenses do not include debt service, capital improvement expenditures, or expenses unrelated to the operation of the property.

Reconstructed operating statement

Before applying a capitalization rate, the appraiser prepares a *reconstructed operating statement*, a restatement of the property's income and expenses adjusted to reflect typical, stabilized operation rather than the current owner's actual figures. Income is stated at market levels, vacancy and collection loss is deducted to reach effective gross income, and only the expenses necessary to operate the property are included. The reconstructed statement uses three categories of operating expense:

- *fixed expenses*, such as real estate taxes and hazard insurance, which continue whether or not the property is occupied
- *variable expenses*, such as utilities, management, maintenance, and trash removal, which change with occupancy and use
- a *reserve for replacements*, an annual allowance for items that wear out periodically, such as roofs, carpeting, appliances, and heating and cooling systems

Certain items are deliberately *excluded* because they do not reflect the property's operating performance: debt service (mortgage principal and interest), income taxes, book depreciation, capital improvements, and the owner's personal expenses. Deducting the included operating expenses from effective gross income yields net operating income, the figure to which the capitalization rate is applied.

Select a capitalization rate. The capitalization rate is an estimate of the rate of return an investor will demand on the investment of capital in a property such as the subject. The appraiser's judgment and market knowledge play an essential role in selecting an appropriate rate for the subject property. In most cases, the appraiser will research capitalization rates used on similar properties in the market.

Apply the capitalization rate. An appraiser now obtains an indication of value from the income capitalization method by dividing the estimated net operating income for the subject by the selected capitalization rate

$$\frac{NOI}{capitalization\ rate} = value$$

Using traditional symbols for income (I), rate (R), and value (V), the formula for value is

$$\frac{I}{R} = V$$

Income approach – case illustration

Case Illustration: Income Capitalization

I. ESTIMATE POTENTIAL GROSS INCOME

Potential gross rental income	192,000
Plus: other income	2,000
Potential gross income	194,000

II. ESTIMATE EFFECTIVE GROSS INCOME

Less: vacancy and collection losses	9,600
Effective gross income	184,400

III. ESTIMATE NET OPERATING INCOME

Operating expenses	
Real estate taxes	32,000
Insurance	4,400
Utilities	12,000
Repairs	4,000
Maintenance	16,000
Management	12,000
Reserves	1,600
Legal and accounting	2,000
Total expenses	84,000
Effective gross income	184,400
Less: total expenses	84,000
Net operating income	100,400

IV. SELECT CAPITALIZATION RATE

Capitalization rate: 7%

V. APPLY CAPITALIZATION RATE

$$\frac{I}{R} = V = \frac{100{,}400}{.07} = 1{,}434{,}300 \text{ (rounded)}$$

Indicated value by income approach: 1,434,300

Reconciliation and Final Estimate

Evaluation of value indications

When reconciling an appraisal, the appraiser evaluates the value indications (estimates) from each applicable approach (sales comparison, cost, and income) to determine which is most reliable for the specific property and assignment. This process involves analyzing the quality and quantity of data, the relevance of each approach to the property type and market conditions, the consistency of adjustments, and the strength of underlying assumptions.

Weighting of Value indications

In an appraisal, the weighting of value indicators refers to the importance the appraiser assigns to each valuation approach when forming a final opinion of value.

After developing the sales comparison, cost, and/or income approaches (as applicable), the appraiser evaluates the strengths and weaknesses of each. Appraisers assign more weight to the approach that is 1) most relevant to the property type, 2) supported by the most reliable and complete data, 3) most consistent with current market behavior, and 4) based on the fewest and most reasonable assumptions.

The appraiser does not simply average the values; instead, each indication is weighted based on its credibility and applicability. The final opinion of value reflects the appraiser's reasoned judgment about which approach (or combination of approaches) provides the most accurate and supportable estimate of market value.

Gross rent approach and gross income multiplier approach

The gross rent multiplier (GRM) and gross income multiplier (GIM) approaches are simplified income-based methods used primarily for properties that produce or might produce income but are not primarily income properties. Examples are single-family homes and duplexes.

The methods involve applying a multiplier to the subject's estimated gross income or gross rent. The multiplier is derived from market data on sale prices and gross income or gross rent.

The advantage of the income multiplier is that it provides a relatively quick indication of value through an informal method. However, the approach excludes many variables, such as vacancies, credit losses, and operating expenses. In addition, the appraiser must have market rental data to establish multipliers.

Gross rent multiplier approach

Steps in the gross rent multiplier approach. There are two steps in the gross rent multiplier approach.

First, select a gross rent multiplier by examining the sale prices and monthly rents of comparable properties that have sold recently. The appraiser's judgment and market knowledge are critical in determining an appropriate gross rent multiplier for the subject. The gross rent multiplier for a property is:

$$\frac{Price}{Monthly\ rent} = GRM$$

Second, estimate the value of the subject by multiplying the selected GRM by the subject's monthly income.

GRM x Subject monthly rent = estimated value

Gross Rent Multiplier Illustration

Property	Sale price	Monthly rent	GRM
Comparable A	500,000	1,660	151
Comparable B	248,000	1,500	165
Comparable C	324,000	2,200	147
Comparable D	304,000	1,800	169
Subject	320,000	2,000	160

In the illustration, the indicated GRM for the subject is 160, based on the appraiser's research and judgment. Applying the GRM to a rental rate of $2,000 yields an indicated value of $320,000 for the subject.

Gross income multiplier approach

Steps in the gross income multiplier approach. The GIM approach is identical to the GRM approach, except that a different denominator is used in the formula. Step one is to select a gross income multiplier by examining the sale prices and gross annual incomes of comparable properties that have sold recently. The gross income multiplier for a property is:

$$\frac{Price}{Gross\ annual\ income} = GIM$$

Step two is to estimate the value of the subject by multiplying the selected GIM by the subject's gross annual income:

GIM x Subject gross annual income = estimated value

Gross Income Multiplier Illustration

Property	Sale price	Gross income	GIM
Comparable A	250,000	19,920	12.55
Comparable B	248,000	18,000	13.78
Comparable C	324,000	26,400	12.27
Comparable D	304,000	21,600	14.07
Subject	324,000	24,000	13.50

In the illustration, the indicated GIM for the subject is 13.5, based on the appraiser's research and judgment. Applying the GIM to the property's gross annual income yields an indicated value of $324,000 for the subject.

Snapshot Review for Chapter 7

The following review summarizes the key rules and concepts from Chapter 7.

Sales Comparison/market

Data Approach

- based on the substitution principle
- compares subject property to recently sold comparables
- assumes active market and arm's-length transactions
- commonly used for residential property valuation and CMAs

Comparable Adjustments

- adjustments made only to comparables, not to subject property
- if a superior comparable, then subtract value
- if an inferior comparable, then add value
- adjustment factors: time, location, physical features, financing terms
- conditions of sale, financing/cash equivalency, and sales concessions adjusted before use
- personal property removed; a fixture conveys with the realty, a trade fixture is the tenant's
- paired-sales (matched-pairs) analysis derives adjustment amounts from the market
- weighting comparables: fewer adjustments = more reliable comparable; small adjustment amounts preferred; large net adjustments reduce reliability

Cost Approach

- most useful for new or special-purpose properties
- estimates value by land value + depreciated improvement cost
- based on reproduction or replacement cost
- depreciation types: physical deterioration – wear and tear; functional obsolescence – outdated features/design; economic obsolescence – outside negative influences
- cost approach steps:
- estimate land value
- estimate replacement/reproduction cost
- estimate accrued depreciation
- subtract depreciation from improvement cost
- add land value to depreciated improvement value
- effective age (apparent age from condition), not actual age, drives the age-life method
- depreciation-estimating methods: age-life, market-extraction, and breakdown

Income Capitalization Approach

- used primarily for income-producing properties
- based on anticipation principle
- value determined by expected future income
- income calculations:

Income Calculations

- PGI (potential gross income) = scheduled rent + other income
- EGI (effective gross income) = PGI – vacancy/credit losses
- NOI (net operating income) = EGI – operating expenses
- value = NOI ÷ capitalization rate

- operating expenses: taxes, insurance, utilities, repairs, management, reserves; excludes debt service and capital improvements
- reconstructed operating statement restates income and expenses at stabilized market levels
- includes fixed, variable, and reserve for replacements; excludes debt service, income taxes, depreciation, capital improvements

Reconciliation of Value

- appraiser compares all applicable approaches
- greatest weight given to most reliable and relevant method
- appraiser does not simply average values
- final estimate based on judgment and market support

Gross Rent/income Multipliers

- simplified income valuation methods
- commonly used for small residential income properties
- GRM (gross rent multiplier) uses monthly rent
- GIM (gross income multiplier) uses annual gross income
- estimated value = multiplier × income

Reconciliation and Final Value Estimate

- appraiser reviews value estimates from applicable approaches: sales comparison, cost, and income
- strongest weight goes to the approach most relevant to the property type and best supported by reliable data
- appraiser considers market behavior, adjustment consistency, and strength of assumptions
- final value is not an average; it is the appraiser's reasoned judgment of the most supportable market value

Chapter 7 Quiz: Sales Comparison, Cost-Depreciation, and Income Approaches

7.1 The sales comparison approach is also commonly known as which of the following?

a. The income approach
b. The capitalization approach
c. The market data approach
d. The quantity survey approach

7.2 The sales comparison approach is based on the principle that a buyer will pay no more for a property than the cost of a comparable alternative, which is known as what principle?

a. Conformity
b. Anticipation
c. Progression
d. Substitution

7.3 One of the required steps in the sales comparison approach is which of the following?

a. Estimating potential gross income
b. Identifying comparable sales
c. Calculating accrued depreciation
d. Selecting a capitalization rate

7.4 To qualify as a comparable, a property generally must have sold within what typical time frame of the appraisal date?

a. Within 2 years
b. Within one year
c. Within six months
d. Within 30 days

7.5 Which of these is an example of an arm's length transaction?

a. A seller lists a home on the open market and sells it to an unrelated buyer.
b. A homeowner sells her property to her brother at a discounted price.
c. A bank transfers a foreclosed property to its subsidiary corporation.
d. A parent deeds a property to a child as a gift.

7.6 The three primary quantitative guidelines used in weighting comparables include the number of adjustments, the amount of each adjustment, and which of the following?

a. Market absorption rate
b. Total net value of all adjustments
c. Gross living area
d. Capitalization rate

7.7 The cost approach is most often used for which type of property?

a. Vacant agricultural land
b. Recently constructed properties
c. Properties with long-term leases
d. Distressed foreclosure properties

7.8 Depreciation in the cost approach applies only to which component of real property?

a. The land
b. The neighborhood
c. The zoning classification
d. The improvements

7.9 The straight-line method of estimating depreciation assumes which of the following?

a. Depreciation accelerates over time.
b. Depreciation occurs only in early years.
c. Depreciation occurs at a constant rate over the economic life.
d. Depreciation is unrelated to economic life.

7.10 Net operating income is determined by subtracting which of the following from effective gross income?

a. Mortgage payments
b. Capital improvements
c. Depreciation expense
d. Total operating expenses

7.11 If a comparable is inferior to the subject in some feature, the appraiser ______.

a. adds an amount to the comparable's price
b. subtracts from the comparable's price
c. adds to the subject's price
d. makes no adjustment

7.12 If a comparable is superior to the subject, the appraiser ______.

a. adds to the comparable's price
b. raises the subject's value
c. subtracts from the comparable's price
d. makes no adjustment

7.13 Adjustments are made to the comparables rather than the subject because ______.

a. the comparables are always worth more
b. the subject cannot legally be adjusted
c. buyers prefer comparables
d. the sale prices of the comparables are known while the subject's value is not

7.14 An appraiser compares two nearly identical sales differing only by a swimming pool to isolate the pool's value. This is ______.

a. paired-sales analysis
b. the cost approach
c. gross rent multiplier analysis
d. reconciliation

7.15 Which is a transactional element of comparison?

a. lot size
b. number of bedrooms
c. construction quality
d. financing terms

7.16 Reproduction cost is the cost to construct ______.

a. a functional equivalent using modern materials
b. an exact duplicate of the improvements
c. the land as if vacant
d. only the curable items

7.17 Replacement cost is primarily used to appraise ______.

a. brand-new construction
b. vacant land
c. older structures with outmoded features
d. income property only

7.18 The most detailed and comprehensive cost-estimating method is ______.

a. the square-foot (unit comparison) method
b. the unit-in-place method
c. the index method
d. the quantity survey method

7.19 The three causes of depreciation are physical deterioration, functional obsolescence, and ______.

a. economic obsolescence
b. accrued appreciation
c. capitalization
d. market conditions

7.20 A house with a poor floor plan and outdated design features buyers no longer want suffers from ______.

a. physical deterioration
b. functional obsolescence
c. economic obsolescence
d. curable appreciation

7.21 A home loses value because a noisy industrial plant is built nearby. This is ______.

a. physical deterioration
b. functional obsolescence
c. economic (external) obsolescence
d. curable deterioration

7.22 In the cost approach, the appraiser estimates land value as if vacant, then adds ______.

a. the original purchase price
b. the depreciated cost of the improvements
c. the gross rent multiplier
d. the capitalization rate

7.23 In direct capitalization, value equals ______.

a. net operating income multiplied by the cap rate
b. net operating income divided by the cap rate
c. gross income divided by the sale price
d. potential gross income minus expenses

7.24 A property produces net operating income of $60,000 and the market cap rate is 8%. Its indicated value is ______.

a. $480,000
b. $600,000
c. $750,000
d. $4,800,000

7.25 Effective gross income equals potential gross income minus ______.

a. debt service
b. vacancy and collection losses
c. depreciation
d. the capitalization rate

7.26 A reconstructed operating statement excludes ______.

a. property taxes
b. insurance
c. management fees
d. debt service (mortgage payments)

7.27 The gross rent multiplier (GRM) for residential income property is based on ______.

a. monthly rent
b. annual net income
c. the cap rate
d. the sale price of land

7.28 The gross income multiplier (GIM) differs from the GRM in that it uses ______.

a. monthly rent
b. net operating income
c. annual gross income
d. depreciated cost

7.29 In the reconciliation step, the appraiser ______.

a. averages the three value indications
b. selects the highest indication
c. discards the sales comparison approach
d. weighs the indications according to their reliability

7.30 For a typical single-family residence, which approach is generally given the most weight?

a. the sales comparison approach
b. the cost approach
c. the income capitalization approach
d. the gross income multiplier approach

CHAPTER 8: COMPARATIVE MARKET ANALYSIS

Contents

Learning Objectives

Upon completion of this chapter, you will be able to:

1. Distinguish between a formal appraisal and a comparative market analysis (CMA) and broker price opinion (BPO)
2. Explain the three major sections of a typical CMA report form
3. Identify what information is necessary to prepare a CMA or BPO
4. Identify the best sources to find the information necessary to prepare a CMA or BPO
5. Explain the major elements of comparison between the comparable property and the subject property
6. Calculate the square footage of a building
7. Prepare a CMA that would allow a seller or buyer to understand values in the
8. neighborhood
9. Prepare a BPO that would allow a lender or asset manager to understand the subject
10. property and market area

Defining Market Value

A CMA estimates the price at which a property is likely to sell in the current market. That probable selling price is grounded in the concept of market value, the price a willing, informed buyer and seller would agree on with no undue pressure, which is defined in full in Chapter 6. A CMA, however, is not a formal appraisal and does not produce a USPAP opinion of market value; it produces a broker's opinion of a competitive listing or offering price.

It helps to distinguish market value from market price. Market price is what a property actually sells for. In theory, market price equals market value when all the conditions of a market-value sale are present, but in practice market price may not reflect the analysis of comparables that underlies an estimate of value.

Broker's opinion of value. A broker's opinion of value may resemble an appraisal, but it differs in that it is not necessarily performed by a disinterested third party or a licensed appraiser, it generally uses only a limited form of one of the three approaches to value, and it is not subject to USPAP or other professional appraisal standards.

Comparative Market Analysis Essentials

CMAs versus appraisals

After gathering the appropriate information about the property, the licensee will want to identify and select comparable properties for comparison.

Current property listings are a good source of information on the pricing of similar properties. Comparing common elements across similar properties and their listing prices provides a basis for setting a competitive listing price for the subject property. MLS listings are a good source for detailed information.

Recently sold properties and those with pending contracts indicate market values for similar properties, what buyers are willing to pay, and how long the properties were listed before selling.

Properties whose listings have expired without a sale provide valuable information about appropriate pricing. Listings often expire without selling because the price is too high. A number of recently expired listings is a good indicator that the market trend is changing, and market values are decreasing.

Generating the CMA

Snapshot of the CMA

Underlying the CMA is the sales comparison approach to value in full operation. This approach, which also serves as the basis for a broker's opinion of value, (BPO) is based on the principle of substitution-- that a buyer will pay no more for the subject property than would be sufficient to purchase a comparable property, The value principle of contribution is also involved., to wit that specific characteristics of a property feature add or detract value to the property.

The sales comparison approach is widely used because it considers the subject property's specific amenities relative to competing properties. In addition, because its data are current, the CMA incorporates current market realities.

The CMA value comparison is necessarily limited in that every property is unique. As a result, finding good comparables can be challenging, especially for special-purpose properties. Optimally, the market should be active; otherwise, comparable sale prices lack currency and reliability.

Comparison. The sales comparison approach used to generate CMAs involves comparing the sale prices of recently sold properties comparable to the subject and making dollar adjustments to each comparable's price to account for competitive differences with the subject.

Weighting. After identifying the adjusted value for each comparable, the appraiser assesses the reliability of each comparable and the factors underlying the adjustments. The weighting yields a final value range based on the most reliable factors in the analysis.

Steps in Developing the CMA

Steps in Developing the CMA

1. Identify and select comparable sales.
2. Compare comparables to the subject and make adjustments to comparables.
3. Weight values indicated by adjusted comparables for the final value estimate of the subject.

Identifying comparables

In selecting comparables, the licensee uses the information gathered on the subject at the start of the CMA (location, size, number of rooms, age, and special features) and looks for recently traded properties whose attributes are as similar as possible to the subject's. The mechanics of selecting and adjusting comparables follow the sales comparison approach presented in Chapter 7. What distinguishes a CMA is the broker's purpose and sources: a CMA estimates a competitive listing or selling price for the current market, and it is not a formal appraisal.

For that reason, a licensee preparing a CMA draws on a broader range of listings than an appraiser, who relies almost entirely on closed sales. The three categories of CMA comparables are:

- properties currently on the market, which represent the subject's direct competition
- recently sold properties, which show what buyers have actually paid
- recently expired or withdrawn listings, which often signal prices the market rejected

Pending sales are also useful, since they indicate where the market is heading before the sale closes. To serve as a useful comparable, a property should resemble the subject in size, shape, design, utility, and location; sit in the same market area, ideally the same neighborhood or subdivision; and reflect current conditions, generally having sold or been listed within the past six months. Because the time of sale strongly affects price, comparables that closed too far in the past may not reflect recent appreciation or changes in market conditions. The principal sources of CMA data are the local multiple listing service, tax records, and title records.

Adjusting comparables

The licensee adjusts the prices of the comparables to account for competitive differences with the subject. Because the sale or list prices of the comparables are known while the subject's value is not, adjustments are always made to the comparables, never to the subject. If a comparable is superior to the subject in some feature, an amount is deducted from the comparable's price; if it is inferior, an amount is added.

For example, a comparable has a swimming pool and the subject does not. To equalize the difference, the licensee deducts an amount, say $26,000, from the comparable's price. Note that the adjustment reflects the pool's contribution to market value, not the cost of the pool or its depreciated value.

A CMA weighs the same elements of comparison an appraiser uses in the sales comparison approach (Chapter 7), but the broker applies them practically, focusing on the features buyers in the area actually pay for. Common elements of comparison include:

- location and lot size, shape, and landscaping
- construction quality, style, design, and age
- square feet of gross living area; number of rooms, bedrooms, and bathrooms
- condition of the interior and exterior, garage, and other improvements
- financing or transaction terms, such as seller concessions or favorable assumable financing

Weighting comparables; reconciliation

After adjusting each comparable, the licensee weighs the results to arrive at a competitive price range for the subject rather than a single value opinion. There is no formula for this; it relies on judgment about which comparables are most like the subject. As a rule, the fewer and smaller the adjustments a comparable requires, the more reliable it is as an indicator of price, because every adjustment carries a margin of error that compounds as adjustments accumulate. A comparable needing many or large adjustments is, by the same logic, a weaker indicator and may not truly be comparable at all. (Chapter 7 covers the formal reconciliation of value indications and the adjustment limits an appraiser observes in a mortgage appraisal.)

CASE ILLUSTRATION OF A CMA

The following exhibit illustrates the development of a typical CMA. A licensee is estimating market value for a subject property. Four comparables are selected and adjusted to find an indicated value for the subject. The grid following the property data shows the adjustments for differences between the four comparables and the subject.

The CMA Illustrated

Comparables Data

Subject property:	8 rooms-- 3 bedrooms, two baths, kitchen, living room, family room; 2,000 square feet of gross living area; 2-car attached garage; landscaping is good. Construction is frame with aluminum siding.
Comparable A:	Sold for 1,000,000 within previous month; conventional financing at current rates; located in subject's neighborhood with similar locational advantages; house approximately same age as subject; lot size smaller than subject; view similar to subject; design less appealing than subject's; construction similar to subject; condition similar to subject; 7 rooms-- two bedrooms, one bath; 1,900 square feet of gross living area; 2-car attached garage; landscaping similar to subject.
Comparable B:	Sold for 1,200,000 within previous month; conventional financing at current rates; located in subject's neighborhood with similar locational advantages; house six years newer than subject; lot size smaller than subject; view is better than the subject’s; design is more appealing than subject's; construction (brick and frame) better than subject's; better condition than subject; 10 rooms-four bedrooms, three baths; 2,300 square feet of gross living area; 2-car attached garage; landscaping similar to subject.
Comparable C:	Sold for 1,150,000 within previous month; conventional financing at current rates; located in subject's neighborhood with similar locational advantages; house five years older than subject; lot size larger than subject; view similar to subject; design and appeal similar to subject's; construction similar to subject; condition

similar to subject; 8 rooms-- three bedrooms, two baths; 2,000 square feet of gross living area; 2-car attached garage; landscaping similar to subject.

Comparable D: Sold for 1,090,000 within previous month; conventional financing at current rates; located in a neighborhood close to subject's, but more desirable than subject's; house approximately same age as subject; lot size same as subject; view similar to subject; design less appealing than subject's; construction (frame) poorer than subject's; poorer condition than subject; 7 rooms-- two bedrooms, one and one half baths; 1,900 square feet of gross living area; 2-car attached garage; landscaping similar to subject.

CMA Illustration: tabulated comparables data

Adjustments

	Subject	A	B	C	D
Sale price		1,000,000	1,200,000	1,150,000	1,090,000
Financing terms		standard	standard	standard	standard
Sale date	NOW	equal	equal	equal	equal
Location		equal	equal	equal	-20,000
Age		equal	-12,000	+10,000	equal
Lot size		+10,000	+10,000	-10,000	equal
Site/view		equal	-10,000	equal	equal
Design/appeal		+10,000	-12,000	equal	+5,000
Construction quality	good	equal	-30,000	equal	+10,000
Condition	good	equal	-50,000	equal	+20,000
No. of rooms	8				
No. of bedrooms	3	+5,000	-5,000	equal	+5,000
No. of baths	2	+10,000	-15,000	equal	+5,000
Gross living area	2,000	+10,000	-20,000	equal	+10,000
Other space					
Garage	2 car/attd.	equal	equal	equal	equal
Other improvements					
Landscaping	good	equal	equal	equal	equal
Net adjustments		+45,000	-144,000	0	+35,000
Indicated value	1,120,000	1,045,000	1,056,000	1,150,000	1,125,000

Reconciliation

For comparable A, the evaluator has made additions to the lot value, design, number of bedrooms and baths, and gross living area. This accounts for the comparable' s *deficiencies* in these areas relative to the subject. A total of five adjustments amount to $45,000, or 4.5% of the purchase price.

For comparable B, the appraiser has deducted values for age, site, design, construction quality, condition, number of bedrooms, number of baths, and living area. This accounts for the comparable's superior qualities relative to the subject. The only addition is the lot size, since the subject's is larger. A total of nine adjustments amount to $144,000, or 12% of the sale price.

For comparable C, the appraiser has added value for the age and deducted value for the lot size. The two adjustments offset each other, resulting in a net adjustment of zero.

For comparable D, one deduction has been made for the comparable's superior location. This is offset by six additions reflecting the various areas where the comparable is inferior to the subject. A total of seven adjustments amount to $35,000, or 3.2% of the sale price.

In view of all adjusted comparables, the appraiser developed a final indication of value of $1,120,000 for the subject. Underlying this conclusion is the fact that Comparable C, with only two minor adjustments that offset each other, is by far the best indicator of value. Comparable D might be the second-best indicator, since the net adjustments are very close to the sale price. Comparable A might be the third-best indicator, since it has the second-fewest number of total adjustments. Comparable B is the least reliable indicator because there are numerous adjustments, three of which are significant. In addition, Comparable B is questionable as a comparable altogether, since total adjustments increase the sale price by 12%.

The Broker Price Opinion (BPO)

BPOs defined

A broker price opinion (BPO) is an estimate of the probable selling price prepared by a real estate licensee instead of an appraiser.

Florida BPO regulations. Florida statutes permit licensees to prepare BPOs for compensation. Sales associates may prepare BPOs only under their broker's direct supervision. However, licensees must take care not to represent the BPO as an appraisal.

Acceptable BPO formats. The format of a BPO varies depending on the preparer and the client's needs. These reports may be prepared as a standardized lender form, a narrative report, a letter, or an exterior (drive-by) or interior inspection report.

BPOs vs. appraisals. A BPO is not an appraisal and is not prepared by a state-certified or licensed appraiser. BPOs may be prepared by real estate licensees, but their scope and use are more limited than those of appraisals. Appraisals must comply with USPAP standards, while BPOs are not regulated. Formal appraisals are most commonly used in mortgage lending, though they may also assist in estate settlement and probate, divorce proceedings, tax assessment appeals, eminent domain cases, and investment analysis.

Disclaimers. Every BPO should clearly state that it is NOT an appraisal, it was NOT prepared by a state-certified or licensed appraiser, and it may NOT be used for federally related transactions or loan origination purposes.

Purpose of the BPO

The primary use of a BPO is to help determine an estimated market price for a property in situations that do not require a formal appraisal. While lenders cannot use a BPO for loan origination, they can use one to evaluate properties in short sales, foreclosures, or REO (real estate owned) inventory. Asset managers may use a BPO to set a listing price for distressed properties, and relocation companies may use one to estimate the likely selling price.

Note that a comparative market analysis (CMA) differs from a BPO in that the CMA is used primarily to help sellers determine a listing price or buyers to determine if a listing price is reasonable. The CMA is also provided free of charge by the representing real estate licensee and will likely be less formal or structured than a BPO.

Computer-generated CMAs and Automated Valuation Models (AVMs)

Computer- generated CMAs

Commonly available CMA software allows licensees to create CMAs and listing presentations quickly and easily. Although a few online programs allow homeowners to fill out a form to gather data on their home, they may not be as accurate as the more robust programs available to licensees through REALTOR® associations. These programs still require the licensee's knowledge to thoroughly gather the appropriate data, enter it into the program, and let the program organize it into the CMA presentation.

Automated valuation models (AVM)

An automated valuation model (AVM) is a service that combines mathematical modeling with databases of existing properties and transactions to calculate property values. Most AVMs compare values of similar properties at the same point in time and perform best in areas where homes are similar rather than in areas where they are more customized and dissimilar. The service is available to real estate licensees, mortgage lenders, and major financial institutions.

Lenders and licensees can quickly obtain AVM reports to generate a price estimate, which typically includes the tax assessor's value, the property's sales history, and the comparables' sales history. They are quicker than appraisals, cost less, and remove subjectivity from the valuation process. What they do not include is the property's condition when determining its value, nor do they include measurements, photographs, and other information included in an appraisal. Consequently, they do not qualify as appraisals and do not comply with USPAP standards. AVM services are available online.

Snapshot Review for Chapter 8

The following review summarizes the key rules and concepts from Chapter 8.

COMPARATIVE MARKET ANALYSIS

Market Value Concepts

- market value = probable price agreed upon by willing buyer and seller
- assumes arm's-length transaction and reasonable market exposure
- market price = actual sale price
- broker's opinion of value differs from formal appraisal

Comparative Market Analysis (CMA)

- CMAs are based on sales comparison approach to value
- uses substitution and contribution principles
- compares subject property to similar recent sales
- incorporates current market conditions and trends

CMAs vs. Appraisals

- CMAs prepared by licensees, not appraisers
- appraisals follow USPAP standards
- expired listings may indicate overpricing or declining market
- MLS, tax, and title records are key data sources

Steps to Develop a CMA

- identify and select comparable properties:
- similar size, design, utility, and location
- recent arm's-length sales preferred, generally within six months
- typically 3–6 comparables used
- properties should reflect current market conditions
- compare and adjust comparables
- make adjustments only to comparables
- if a superior comparable, deduct value
- if an inferior comparable, add value
- adjustment based on time, location, condition, amenities, financing terms
- weight comparables and reconcile final value estimate
- fewer adjustments = stronger comparable
- smaller adjustment amounts increase reliability
- excessive net adjustments reduce credibility
- final value based on judgment and overall market support

Broker Price Opinion (BPO)

- BPO = estimated selling price prepared by licensee
- not an appraisal and not USPAP regulated
- sales associates require broker supervision
- cannot be used for federally related loan transactions

- BPO uses: short sales, foreclosures, REO, and distressed properties; relocation and asset management purposes
- BPO formats: may be interior, exterior, narrative, or standardized report format; typically more formal and detailed than a CMA

Computer-generated CMAs

- CMA software organizes comparable and market data into presentations
- still requires licensee judgment and accurate data input

Automated Valuation Models (AVMs)

- computer-generated value estimates using databases and algorithms
- commonly used by lenders and financial institutions
- faster and less expensive than appraisals
- best for areas with similar properties and consistent market data
- do not evaluate property condition or comply with USPAP standards

Chapter 8 Quiz: Comparative Market Analysis

8.1 Which statement best defines market value in real estate?

a. The amount a seller originally paid for the property
b. The highest price a buyer would pay and the lowest price a seller would accept under normal conditions
c. The value determined only by tax assessments from the taxing authority responsible for the property
d. The exact amount a property sells for in every transaction

8.2 Which condition is necessary for a transaction to reflect market value?

a. The buyer and seller are family members.
b. The transaction includes hidden financing concessions.
c. The property is exposed on the open market for a reasonable time.
d. The seller is under pressure to sell quickly.

8.3 What is the primary difference between market price and market value?

a. Market price is always higher than market value.
b. Market value is based on replacement cost only.
c. Market price is the sales price, while market value is an estimate of probable value.
d. Market value can only be determined by taxing authorities .

8.4 Which source of information is MOST useful for determining what buyers are currently willing to pay for similar properties?

a. Expired listings
b. Recently sold properties
c. Building permits
d. Tax assessor estimates

8.5 Why are expired listings helpful when preparing a CMA?

a. They always reflect increasing market values.
b. They prove that all listed properties eventually sell.
c. They eliminate the need for comparable sales.
d. They may indicate that properties were overpriced for the market.

8.6 Which valuation principle is the basis for the sales comparison approach in a CMA?

a. Assemblage
b. Substitution
c. Balance
d. Conformity

8.7 Which property would BEST qualify as a comparable for a CMA?

a. A recently sold property with similar size, design, and location
b. A property sold five years ago in another city
c. A commercial building in a different market area
d. A property transferred between family members

8.8 If a comparable property is superior to the subject property, how should the appraiser adjust the comparable sales price?

a. Ignore the difference
b. Add value to the subject property
c. Add value to the comparable's sale price
d. Deduct value from the comparable's sale price

8.9 Which adjustment category includes differences in lot size, square footage, and construction quality?

a. Financing characteristics
b. Transaction characteristics
c. Physical characteristics
d. Time-of-sale characteristics

8.10 Which statement correctly describes an automated valuation model (AVM)?

a. An AVM includes a complete interior property inspection.
b. An AVM is considered a formal appraisal under USPAP.
c. An AVM may only be used by government agencies or lending organizations.
d. An AVM uses mathematical modeling and property databases to estimate value.

8.11 A comparative market analysis (CMA) is ______.

a. an estimate of value that is not a formal appraisal
b. prepared only by certified appraisers
c. required to follow USPAP
d. legally binding on the seller

8.12 A broker price opinion (BPO) ______.

a. must be prepared by a state-certified appraiser
b. is the same as a formal appraisal
c. is not an appraisal and may be prepared by a real estate licensee
d. may not be used by lenders

8.13 Lenders most commonly order a BPO to ______.

a. set property tax assessments
b. replace a survey
c. determine zoning
d. help decide on short sales or foreclosures

8.14 When gathering comparables for a CMA, a licensee reviews properties that are currently listed, recently sold, pending, and ______.

a. tax-exempt
b. expired
c. commercial only
d. owner-occupied only

8.15 Currently listed properties are useful in a CMA mainly because they show ______.

a. the exact market value
b. the assessed value
c. the competition the subject will face
d. the replacement cost

8.16 Which comparables best indicate what buyers will actually pay?

a. expired listings
b. currently active listings
c. withdrawn listings
d. recently sold and pending properties

8.17 In a CMA, price adjustments are applied to ______.

a. the subject property
b. the comparable properties
c. the listing commission
d. the tax assessment

8.18 The primary purpose of a CMA is to ______.

a. help a seller establish a realistic listing price
b. guarantee a sale price
c. satisfy federal appraisal requirements
d. determine property taxes

8.19 When reconciling adjusted comparable values in a CMA, the licensee ______.

a. always averages the values
b. selects the highest value
c. weighs the values based on how comparable each property is
d. uses only one comparable

8.20 A limitation of an automated valuation model (AVM) is that it ______.

a. cannot access public records
b. requires a certified appraiser
c. is prohibited in Florida
d. cannot physically inspect the property's condition

CHAPTER 9:
BUSINESS VALUATION

Contents

Learning Objectives

Upon completion of this chapter, you will be able to:

1. Distinguish between real property valuation and business valuation
2. Describe the characteristics of the various business entities
3. Explain the business appraisal process
4. Describe the steps in the analysis of financial statements
5. Describe the elements of a balance sheet and an income statement
6. Describe and calculate current ratio, quick ratio, inventory turnover ratio, debt-to-worth ratio, and net-profit-to-owner capital ratio
7. Describe the various approaches to business valuation
8. Distinguish among the different types of intangible assets and the techniques used to value intangible assets
9. Describe the nature of business brokerage and identify the components that make up the value of a business, including tangible assets, inventory, and goodwill

Overview of Business Brokerage

Business brokerage is *the effecting of a sale or exchange of an existing business*. In most cases, the sale of a business entails the simultaneous transfer of an estate in land, whether a leasehold or a fee. Thus, to sell businesses, a broker must generally hold a real estate license.

Business brokerage may be classified as opportunity brokerage or enterprise brokerage based on the size of the business being sold, although Florida does not make this distinction. **Opportunity brokerage** concerns a small business, usually a proprietorship or partnership, in which the transaction consists of the sale of assets and the assignment of a lease. **Enterprise brokerage** concerns a larger company, usually a corporation, where the transaction involves the sale of stock and multiple real estate parcels leased or owned by the seller.

The process of business brokerage is similar to real estate brokerage: a broker secures a listing, procures a purchaser, and facilitates the closing. Once a ready, willing, and able buyer is found, the broker earns a commission.

Business brokerage vs real property brokerage

The critical difference between selling a business and selling real estate is that selling a business involves the transfer of *business income, personal property, goodwill, and possibly liabilities, in addition to real property.*

Goodwill is an intangible asset tied to a business's reputation and adds value to the business opportunity. Goodwill is discussed further below. Franchises, copyrights, and patents are examples of other intangible assets that add value.

Another non-real-estate value transferred with a business is going-concern value, the monetary value expected from ongoing operations and profits, as opposed to the value of the physical assets alone.

Among the similarities of selling a business and selling real estate are the facts that both usually involve real property or a long-term lease and both require the broker to be licensed in accordance with Florida Statute Chapter 475, Part I., wherein the definition of a broker and the licensure requirements of a broker include "...the sale, exchange, purchase, or rental of business enterprises or business opportunities or any real property ..."

To be competent in this brokerage specialty, a business broker must have specialized skills concerning transactions, accounting, and pricing. A business broker must also rely on a professional team to complete the transaction. Members of this team would include the client's legal counsel, accountant, and, preferably, a professional appraiser.

Transaction knowledge

Types of sale. There are generally two types of business sale transactions for a business broker to be aware of: **asset sales** and stock sales. In an asset sale, the purchaser takes possession of some or all of the business's assets, as well as the real estate, in exchange for the sale price. The purchase usually does not include acquiring the existing business entity or its liabilities. An asset sale is preferred by buyers who want to purchase only portions of a business or who want to avoid the liabilities inherent in a stock purchase.

In a **stock sale**, a purchaser acquires complete ownership of a business, including the legal corporate entity, all assets, all financial liabilities, and any current or future legal liabilities arising from incidents that have occurred prior to the sale. A purchaser may prefer a stock sale to avoid creating a new business entity or to take advantage of a potential tax advantage. In addition, a stock sale preserves a business's identity, which can be very valuable.

Transaction documents. The most common transaction documents in business brokerage are a sale contract, an assignment or real estate sale contract, a no-compete agreement, and a consulting agreement.

A **sale contract** sets forth all terms and conditions of the agreement, including exactly what is being sold. An **assignment** or **real estate sale agreement** is an agreement to transfer all real property involved in the transaction. A **no-compete agreement** is a seller's covenant, for compensation, not to compete with the buyer under prescribed conditions and time periods. A **consulting agreement** is an employment agreement under which the seller is hired to assist the buyer in taking over business operations.

For the most part, transaction documents in business brokerage are not fully standardized. For that reason, a business broker must exercise caution in dealing with document language so as to avoid the unauthorized practice of law.

Accounting

A broker or agent who wants to undertake business brokerage needs basic proficiency in accounting. In particular, one must know how to read and interpret:

- income, expenses, and profit on an income statement
- assets, liabilities, and net worth on a balance sheet

Income, expenses, and profit. A business's profit is the revenue remaining after all expenses are paid. A business broker must evaluate an owner's income and expenses to determine the business's value to a buyer. This often involves interpreting which income and expense items will change after the business is sold.

For example, a seller owns a grocery store and uses family members to perform clerical work without pay. If a buyer is a bachelor without children, much of the clerical work will have to be hired out. The additional payroll significantly changes the store's profitability. Neglecting to consider how income and expenses might change is likely to lead to serious problems in working with buyers.

Business assets. The assets of a business include **tangible** assets and **intangible** assets. Tangible assets include:

- cash and marketable securities
- inventory
- trade fixtures and equipment
- real property
- accounts receivable

Intangible assets include:

- the company name
- trademarks
- copyrights
- patents
- licenses
- contracts for future sales of goods or services
- goodwill
- going concern

When valuing a business, both tangible and intangible assets must be considered, even though intangibles can be difficult to appraise.

Business liabilities. Business liabilities acquired in a corporate stock sale include short-term debt, such as accounts payable, and long-term liabilities, such as mortgages and leases.

Goodwill. Goodwill, mentioned earlier, is a business brokerage term with two meanings. In one sense, goodwill is an intangible asset consisting of factors an owner values in a business, apart from specific assets. For example, goodwill might include reputation, a long history of success in a market, name recognition, a dominant market share, and an excellent business location.

In the second sense, which is more familiar to accountants, goodwill is the difference in value between an owner's price and the value of all other business assets. For example, if an owner wants $400,000 for a business and the total of tangible and intangible assets is valued at $320,000, the goodwill is $80,000.

Determining a price

The most difficult task for a business broker is often finding the right price range for a business. An owner of a small business has probably built it from scratch and tends to overvalue it. Moreover, such an owner may have been less thorough in maintaining business and accounting records, making asset valuation quite difficult. Finally, a business's true income may differ for one owner than for another because of variations in management style and ability.

In any case, the value of the business is a function of the following:

- past, present, and future net profits, and the capitalized value of these
- amount of risk and certainty associated with realizing future profits
- value of all assets as reflected in the books of account
- impact of goodwill on the value of the business
- prices paid for similar businesses
- all other risks associated with the business

Business brokerage regulation

Licensing. A business broker generally must have an active real estate license. In addition, the broker may need to have a valid securities license since a transaction may entail the sale of securities.

Florida licensing of business brokerage. In Florida, brokering the sale of a business is a licensed real estate activity. Chapter 475, Florida Statutes, defines the practice of real estate broadly enough to include business enterprises and business opportunities, so a person who, for compensation, sells or offers to sell a business, or the goodwill and assets that compose it, generally must hold an active Florida real estate license. Such a transaction falls under FREC's jurisdiction, and the licensee owes the same duties and disclosures required in any other brokerage transaction.

Uniform Commercial Code (UCC). The Uniform Commercial Code regulates the sale of personal property on a state-by-state basis and forms the basis for standardized sale documents. Standard documents include promissory notes, security agreements, and bills of sale.

Bulk Sales Act. The Bulk Sales Act protects creditors against loss of collateral in an indebted business through the undisclosed sale of the business's inventory. If a business sells over half of its inventory to a buyer, the sale is deemed a bulk sale and may be an asset sale. Since a creditor could lose security in such a sale, the seller must disclose the names of creditors to the buyer in a Bulk Sales Affidavit. The buyer must notify the creditors of the sale, who may then take appropriate action to secure their loans.

Fundamentals of Business Appraisal

Reasons for a business appraisal

Business appraisal purpose. A business appraisal (business valuation) is conducted to determine the economic value of a business or ownership interest. Common reasons include:

- establish a fair market price for sale or purchase

- support negotiations in mergers or acquisitions
- divide marital assets in a divorce proceeding
- determine estate tax value for estate planning or probate
- set or trigger a contractual price for a purchase agreement
- litigate shareholder disputes or damages claims
- support tax reporting for gifting or IRS compliance
- support loan or equity requests for financing or investors

Business appraisal process

Business appraisal steps. Preparing a business appraisal commonly involves the following steps:

- **definition of the assignment**

  The appraiser clarifies the purpose of the valuation, the standard of value (e.g., fair market value, investment value), and the ownership interest being valued (controlling vs. minority interest).
- **establish the date of the appraisal**

  Because the value of a business can change (sometimes rapidly, sometimes over a longer period), it is important to define the date on which the appraisal is performed.
- **data collection**

  The appraiser collects financial statements (usually 3 – 5 years), tax returns, organizational documents, industry data, and information about operations, management, and market position.
- **analysis of the collected data**

  Financial statements are reviewed and often "normalized" to adjust for unusual, non-recurring, or discretionary expenses.
- **selection and reconciliation of the approaches for the value estimate**

  The appraiser identifies one or more approaches to value (income, market, or asset), performs the necessary calculations, and then reconciles those results to arrive at a final opinion of value.
- **finalization of the appraisal report**

  The appraiser issues a formal report that explains the methodology, assumptions, data sources, and the final value conclusion.

Understanding and Using Financial Statements

Overview of financial statements

Balance Sheet. This statement identifies a firm's financial condition at a specific point in time. It shows a company's assets, liabilities, and equity. It is often called a "snapshot" of the firm's financial position.

Income Statement (Profit and Loss Statement). This statement reports revenues, expenses, and net income over a specific time period, showing the firm's profit or loss.

Cash Flow Statement. This statement tracks the flow of cash into and out of the business. Cash flow is generated through operating processes, investing, and financing activities. This statement highlights the firm's liquidity (the quality of being readily convertible into cash).

Statement of Shareholders' Equity. This statement, prepared only for companies and private businesses with equity investors, identifies changes in ownership interests, including retained earnings and stock transactions.

These statements provide the foundation for business valuation, lending decisions, and operating analysis.

Pitfalls in analyzing financial statements

Financial statement analysis requires the analyst to be aware of several items:

- non-recurring items: one-time revenue, expense, gains, or losses that distort normal profitability
- owner's discretionary expenses: personal or non-essential expenses run through the business
- aggressive accounting practices: overstating revenue, deferring expenses, or improper asset valuation
- incomplete or inaccurate records: missing invoices, unrecorded liabilities, or poor bookkeeping
- timing differences: seasonal fluctuations or mismatched revenue and expense recognition

Failing to adjust for these variables can lead to misleading conclusions about a firm's financial position.

Financial statement analysis and purification

Financial statement analysis. Professional analysis of a firm's financial statements is a method for evaluating a company's financial health, using techniques such as horizontal, vertical, ratio, and trend analyses based on data from multiple periods.

Horizontal analysis refers to comparing financial data across multiple periods to identify trends.

Vertical analysis involves expressing each line item as a percentage of a base figure (typically revenue) to assess structure.

Ratio analysis involves calculating metrics such as liquidity, profitability, debt, and efficiency ratios to assess performance and risk.

Trend analysis involves examining patterns over time to forecast for future performance.

Book value. Book value is the value of an asset, or of the whole business, as carried on the accounting records: original cost less accumulated depreciation. The book value of the business, its net worth or equity, is total assets minus total liabilities as shown on the balance sheet. Book value rarely equals market value, because assets are recorded at historical cost and internally built intangibles such as goodwill usually do not appear at all. It is a starting point for valuation, not the answer.

Key financial ratios. Analysts calculate several ratios over multiple years to gauge a firm's health:

- **Current ratio** = current assets divided by current liabilities; a liquidity measure of the firm's ability to pay short-term debts. A ratio above 1.0 means current assets cover current liabilities.
- **Quick ratio (acid test)** = current assets minus inventory, divided by current liabilities; a stricter liquidity test that excludes inventory, which can be slow to convert to cash.
- **Inventory turnover ratio** = cost of goods sold divided by average inventory; how many times inventory is sold and replaced in a period. Low turnover can signal overstocking or obsolescence.
- **Debt-to-worth ratio** = total liabilities divided by net worth; a leverage measure. The higher the ratio, the more the business is financed by debt rather than owner equity.

- **Net-profit-to-owner-capital ratio** = net profit divided by owner's equity; the return the business earns on the owner's invested capital, comparable to return on equity.

Financial statement purification. Purification is the process of adjusting financial statements to reflect the true economic position of a firm. Common adjustments include the following:

- removing non-recurring or extraordinary items
- adding back the owner's discretionary expenses
- correcting errors or accounting irregularities
- normalizing depreciation, amortization, and rent to market levels

The goal of the purification process is to produce a "normalized" set of financials that accurately reflects the firm's ongoing earning capacity, which is critical for a credible valuation.

Statements prepared for valuation. After purifying the raw statements, the appraiser recasts them into the specific forms a valuation requires:

- **Adjusted balance sheet** restates the book balance sheet to correct errors and reclassify items, while still based on cost.
- **Market (market-value) balance sheet** restates each asset and liability at its current market value rather than book value, producing the adjusted net asset value used in the asset approach.
- **Adjusted income statement** restates historical earnings by removing non-recurring items and normalizing owner's compensation and discretionary expenses to market levels, revealing the business's true ongoing earning power.
- **Pro forma income statement** projects future revenue, expenses, and earnings under stated assumptions, supporting the income approach and any forecast of return.

Approaches to Business Value

A business appraiser develops value through one or more recognized approaches and then reconciles the results, much as a real estate appraiser does.

Asset (cost) approach. This approach values the business as the sum of its assets less its liabilities. The appraiser begins with book value, then restates the assets and liabilities to market value to reach the adjusted net asset value. The asset approach works best for asset-heavy or marginally profitable businesses and generally sets a floor for a profitable going concern, because it captures the tangible assets but not the earning power represented by goodwill.

Market (sales comparison) approach. This approach derives value from the prices at which comparable businesses have sold, expressed as a multiple, for example a multiple of revenue, of earnings, or of seller's discretionary earnings (SDE). The appraiser selects multiples from comparable transactions and applies them to the subject's figures. Its reliability depends on the availability of truly comparable sales.

Income (capitalization) approach. This approach converts the business's expected earnings into value. In direct capitalization, the appraiser divides one year of normalized earnings by a capitalization rate that reflects the risk of the business; a discounted-cash-flow method instead projects several years of cash flow and discounts them to present value. The income approach is usually the most persuasive for a profitable, ongoing business.

Liquidation value approach. This approach estimates the net amount the assets would bring if sold off and the business closed, rather than continued. Orderly liquidation assumes a reasonable selling period; forced liquidation assumes a quick sale at lower prices. Liquidation value is the relevant standard when a business is failing or worth more closed than open.

Valuing intangible assets and goodwill. Much of a successful business's value lies in intangibles, chiefly goodwill, the value above the worth of the identifiable assets. Two methods are common:

- **Excess-profits method** determines a fair return on the adjusted net tangible assets, subtracts that return from the business's normalized earnings, and capitalizes the remainder, the excess earnings, at a higher (riskier) rate; the resulting goodwill is added to the net tangible asset value.
- **Market-residual method** subtracts the value of a comparable business's identifiable tangible and intangible assets from its total sale price; the residual is the market's measure of goodwill, which can then be related to the subject business.

Financial Analysis Conclusions and Valuation Finalization

Analysis conclusions

Develop a defensible forecast, net income, and ROI. The financial analysis conclusions summarize what the company's financial statements reveal about its performance, health, and trends. These conclusions are based on an examination of historical and current data, ratios, and purified statements.

The conclusion integrates information from financial analysis, market conditions, industry data, and valuation approaches. Using that data, the parties can draw conclusions about a number of factors:

- profitability – assessing whether the business generates sustainable earnings
- liquidity and solvency – determining the company's ability to meet short- and long-term obligations
- operational efficiency – evaluating how effectively assets and resources are used
- financial trends – identifying patterns in revenue growth, expense control, and cash flow
- risk assessment – highlighting potential financial or operational weaknesses

A thorough evaluation of these factors allows conclusions to be drawn and a sound forecast of net income and return on investment to be developed, guiding investors, buyers, and even sellers in making decisions.

Business appraisal conclusions

Finalize return ratios (payback, C on C, 3-year forecast). The business appraisal conclusion is the appraiser's opinion of the economic value of the business or an ownership interest in a particular business as of a specific date. This conclusion integrates information from the financial analysis, market conditions, industry data, and valuation approaches. This conclusion incorporates a number of key points:

- value determination – The appraiser reconciles values from different approaches to form a final opinion.
- purpose-specific – The appraisal conclusion depends on the intended use, such as a sale, merger, estate planning, or buy-sell agreement.
- supported by rationale – The final value is accompanied by a detailed explanation of any assumptions made, the methods used, and the adjustments applied.

A thorough analysis of these factors enables relevant parties to finalize and apply key return ratios.

A Sample Business Valuation: PPC Institute of Real Estate

To pull the chapter together, consider the valuation of PPC Institute of Real Estate, a single-owner company that offers prelicensing and exam-prep courses and publishes its own textbooks. An appraiser has been engaged to estimate the fair market value of the business as a going concern as of December 31. The owner reports the following results for the most recent year.

Reported income statement (most recent year)

Revenue	$1,200,000
Cost of sales (printing, instructor fees)	(500,000)
Gross profit	**700,000**
Owner's salary	(200,000)
Rent	(84,000)
Marketing	(90,000)
Administrative and other	(150,000)
One-time litigation expense	(30,000)
Owner's personal vehicle and travel	(16,000)
Reported pretax net income	**130,000**

Step 1 - Adjust (normalize) the income statement. The appraiser removes items that will not carry forward to a buyer and normalizes the owner's pay to a market manager's salary of $100,000.

Reported pretax net income	$130,000
Add back owner's excess compensation ($200,000 - $100,000)	100,000
Add back one-time litigation expense	30,000
Add back owner's discretionary expenses	16,000
Adjusted (normalized) pretax earnings	**276,000**

Adding the market salary back to normalized earnings gives seller's discretionary earnings (SDE) of $376,000 ($276,000 + $100,000).

Step 2 - Build the market-value balance sheet (asset approach). The book balance sheet is restated to current market values.

	Book	**Market**
Cash	$80,000	$80,000
Accounts receivable	100,000	100,000
Inventory (textbooks)	90,000	70,000
Equipment and fixtures	60,000	45,000
Total assets	**330,000**	**295,000**
Less total liabilities	(130,000)	(130,000)
Net worth / net asset value	**200,000**	**165,000**

Book value of equity is $200,000; the adjusted net tangible asset value is $165,000, the asset-approach indication and a floor for a profitable business.

Step 3 - Income (capitalization) approach. Capitalizing the normalized earnings at a 30 percent rate (reflecting the risk of a small, owner-dependent business): $276,000 divided by 0.30 = $920,000.

Step 4 - Market approach. Comparable small education businesses sell at about 2.5 times SDE: $376,000 x 2.5 = $940,000. A revenue check, roughly 0.78 x $1,200,000 = $936,000, agrees.

Step 5 - Excess-profits method (goodwill).

Normalized earnings	$276,000
Less fair return on net tangible assets (12% x $165,000)	(19,800)
Excess earnings (attributable to goodwill)	256,200
Goodwill = excess earnings divided by 0.33	776,000
Total value = $165,000 net assets + $776,000 goodwill	**941,000**

Step 6 - Reconcile. The asset approach ($165,000) only sets a floor, because it ignores the earning power of an established, profitable school. The three earnings-based indications cluster closely:

Approach	**Indicated value**
Asset (net tangible)	$165,000 (floor)
Income (capitalization)	920,000
Market (SDE multiple)	940,000
Excess-profits (assets + goodwill)	941,000

Weighting the income, market, and excess-profits results most heavily, the appraiser concludes a fair market value of approximately $930,000, of which roughly $765,000 is goodwill above the adjusted net tangible assets.

Apply what you learned. Test your understanding against the PPC example.

- What is PPC's book value of equity, and why does it differ from the adjusted net asset value? *Book equity is $200,000; the adjusted figure of $165,000 restates inventory and equipment down to market value.*
- Why is the asset-approach value so much lower than the income and market indications? *The asset approach omits goodwill, the earning power and reputation of a profitable going concern.*
- Compute PPC's current ratio and quick ratio if current assets are $270,000, inventory is $90,000, and current liabilities are $90,000. *Current ratio 3.0; quick ratio 2.0.*
- Why does the appraiser normalize the owner's salary and remove the litigation expense before valuing the business? *To reveal the ongoing earning power a buyer would actually acquire, not one owner's discretionary or one-time figures.*

Snapshot Review for Chapter 9

The following review summarizes the key rules and concepts from Chapter 9.

OVERVIEW OF BUSINESS BROKERAGE

Business Brokerage Basics

- business brokerage = sale or exchange of an existing business
- often includes transfer of real estate or leasehold interest
- brokers generally must hold active real estate license
- opportunity brokerage = smaller businesses; enterprise brokerage = larger companies

Business vs. Real Property Brokerage

- business sales may include goodwill, inventory, equipment, contracts, liabilities
- goodwill = intangible value from reputation, location, market presence
- going-concern value = value of ongoing operations and profits
- business brokers require knowledge of transactions, accounting, and pricing

Types of Business Sales

- asset sale = transfer of selected assets, usually excludes liabilities
- stock sale = transfer of ownership entity, assets, and liabilities
- stock sales preserve business identity and operations

Business Brokerage Regulation

- may require securities license in some transactions
- UCC governs personal property transfer documents
- Bulk Sales Act protects creditors in inventory sales
- brokers must avoid unauthorized practice of law

Fundamentals of Business Appraisal

- reasons for business valuation: establish sale or purchase price; mergers, acquisitions, and financing; divorce, estate planning, probate, tax reporting; shareholder disputes and contractual agreements

Business Appraisal Process

- define assignment and ownership interest
- establish valuation date
- collect financial and operational data
- analyze and normalize financial statements
- apply valuation approaches and reconcile conclusions
- finalize formal appraisal report

Understanding Financial Statements

- balance sheet = assets, liabilities, owner equity at a point in time
- income statement = revenues, expenses, net income over time
- cash flow statement = movement of cash in and out of business
- shareholders' equity statement = ownership and retained earnings changes

Financial Analysis Concerns

- non-recurring items may distort profitability
- discretionary owner expenses affect true income
- inaccurate records and aggressive accounting reduce reliability
- seasonal timing differences may impact analysis

Financial Statement Analysis

- horizontal analysis = compare periods over time
- vertical analysis = compare items as percentages
- ratio analysis = liquidity, debt, profitability, efficiency
- trend analysis = identify long-term performance patterns
- book value = assets minus liabilities at cost; usually below market value
- liquidity: current ratio = current assets / current liabilities; quick ratio excludes inventory
- inventory turnover = COGS / inventory; debt-to-worth = liabilities / net worth; net-profit-to-owner = profit / equity

Financial Statement Purification

- remove extraordinary or non-recurring items
- normalize rent, depreciation, and expenses
- adjust owner discretionary expenses
- create accurate "normalized" earning picture
- adjusted and market-value balance sheets restate assets to market for the asset approach
- adjusted income statement normalizes earnings; pro forma projects future results

Approaches to Business Value

- asset approach: adjusted assets minus liabilities; a floor for a going concern
- market approach: a multiple of revenue, earnings, or SDE from comparable sales
- income approach: capitalize normalized earnings at a risk-based rate, or use DCF
- liquidation approach: net proceeds if the assets are sold and the business closed
- goodwill valued by the excess-profits or market-residual method

Financial Conclusions

- evaluate profitability, liquidity, solvency, and efficiency
- identify revenue, expense, and cash flow trends
- assess operational and financial risk
- develop forecasts for net income and ROI

Business Appraisal Conclusions

- reconcile value indications into final opinion of value
- conclusions depend on intended use of appraisal
- supported by assumptions, methods, and adjustments
- final analysis helps determine investment and pricing decisions

Sample Valuation: PPC Institute

- normalize earnings by adding back excess owner pay, non-recurring, and discretionary items
- reconcile asset, income, market, and excess-profits indications into a final value
- goodwill is the value concluded above the adjusted net tangible assets

Chapter 9 Quiz: Business Valuation

9.1 What is the primary activity involved in business brokerage?

a. Managing rental properties for absent owners
b. Effecting the sale or exchange of an existing business
c. Developing new commercial subdivisions
d. Leasing only real property interests

9.2 Which statement best describes opportunity brokerage?

a. The sale of a large corporation involving multiple parcels of real estate
b. The transfer of stock ownership in a publicly traded company
c. The sale of a small business that usually involves assets and lease assignment
d. The management of distressed commercial assets

9.3 What is a major difference between selling a business and selling real estate?

a. Business sales do not involve real property.
b. Real estate sales require no written agreements.
c. Business brokerage involves transferring goodwill and income.
d. Real estate transactions always involve securities licenses.

9.4 Which item is considered an intangible asset that may add value to a business?

a. Inventory
b. Trade fixtures
c. Accounts receivable
d. Goodwill

9.5 What is meant by "going-concern value" in business brokerage?

a. The liquidation value of physical assets only
b. The value expected from ongoing operations and profits
c. The assessed tax value for a business property
d. The cost to replace all business equipment

9.6 In an asset sale, what does the buyer typically avoid acquiring?

a. Tangible assets
b. Inventory and equipment
c. Existing liabilities
d. Leasehold interests

9.7 In a stock sale, what does the purchaser acquire?

a. Only select business assets
b. The business entity plus liabilities
c. Only the business's real estate holdings
d. A lease assignment without corporate ownership

9.8 Which agreement is designed to prevent a seller from competing against the buyer after the transaction closes?

a. Consulting agreement
b. Listing agreement
c. Assignment agreement
d. Non-compete agreement

9.9 Which financial statement shows a company's assets, liabilities, and equity at a specific point in time?

a. Cash flow statement
b. Income statement
c. Balance sheet
d. Statement of retained earnings

9.10 Which of the following is considered a tangible business asset?

a. Trademark
b. Patent
c. Goodwill
d. Inventory

9.11 Which factor is commonly used in determining the value of a business?

a. The owner's emotional attachment to the business
b. Prices paid for similar businesses
c. The original cost of all equipment
d. The number of years the owner worked there

9.12 Why might a business broker need a securities license in addition to a real estate license?

a. Business transactions may involve the sale of securities such as stocks
b. Real estate licenses are invalid for commercial transactions
c. All leases are considered securities
d. Florida prohibits brokers from selling businesses without a securities license

9.13 What is the purpose of the Bulk Sales Act?

a. To establish appraisal standards for businesses
b. To regulate franchise agreements
c. To protect creditors when a business sells its inventory
d. To require lenders to approve all business sales

9.14 Which step in the business appraisal process involves adjusting financial statements for unusual or discretionary expenses?

a. Establishing the appraisal date
b. Analysis of the collected data
c. Finalization of the appraisal report
d. Definition of the assignment

9.15 Which type of financial analysis compares financial data across multiple periods to identify patterns and changes?

a. Vertical analysis
b. Ratio analysis
c. Trend analysis
d. Horizontal analysis

9.16 The three recognized approaches to valuing a business are the income approach, the market approach, and the ______.

a. gross rent approach
b. replacement approach
c. asset approach
d. straight-line approach

9.17 Which financial statement reports a company's revenues and expenses over a period of time?

a. the balance sheet
b. the income statement
c. the escrow ledger
d. the closing statement

9.18 Before valuing a business, an appraiser often "normalizes" the financial statements to ______.

a. inflate the reported profits
b. remove all tax obligations
c. adjust for unusual, non-recurring, or discretionary expenses
d. convert them to a cash basis only

9.19 The excess-profits method is primarily used to estimate the value of a business's ______.

a. goodwill
b. real property
c. inventory
d. accounts payable

9.20 A business appraisal may be needed for all of the following reasons EXCEPT ______.

a. a proposed sale of the business
b. financing or a loan application
c. litigation or a partnership dispute
d. routine daily bookkeeping

PART III:
LISTING AND SELLING REAL PROPERTY

CHAPTER 10: BROKERAGE RELATIONSHIPS AND DISCLOSURE REQUIREMENTS

Contents

Learning Objectives

Upon completion of this chapter, you will be able to:

1. Describe which provisions of the Brokerage Relationship Disclosure Act apply only to residential real estate sales and list types of real estate activities that are exempt from the disclosure requirements
2. Describe the required content and format of the various disclosure forms
3. Describe the procedure for giving No Broker Relationship Notice
4. Distinguish among the three forms of authorized brokerage relationships
5. List and describe the duties owed in the various authorized relationships
6. Describe the disclosure procedures for the various authorized relationships
7. Identify the procedure for transition from a single agent to a transaction broker
8. Describe the disclosure requirements for non-residential transactions where the buyer and seller have assets of $1 million or more
9. Describe the events that will cause a brokerage relationship to be terminated
10. Explain the essentials of real estate agency, including the roles of principal and agent and the distinctions among universal, general, and special agency
11. Describe the property condition disclosure obligations of sellers and licensees, including the duty to disclose known material defects

Essentials of Real Estate Agency

Historical perspective

The most fundamental relationship in real estate brokerage is that between broker and client, the relationship known in law as the **agency relationship**. The laws controlling agency grow out of two types of law: common law and statutory law. Common law is based on customary usage and the court decrees and judgments. Statutory law is the law written by legislatures. A body of law, generally known as the law of agency, defines and regulates the legal roles in this relationship. The parties to the relationship are the **principal** (a client), the **agent** (a broker), and the **customer** (a third party).

The laws of agency are distinct from contract law, though the two interact. For example, the listing agreement, a contract, establishes an agency relationship. Thus, the relationship is subject to contract law.

However, agency law dictates how the relationship will achieve its purposes, regardless of what the listing contract states.

The essence of the agency relationship is *trust, confidence, and mutual good faith*. The principal trusts the agent to exercise the utmost skill and care in fulfilling the authorized activity and to promote the principal's best interests. The agent undertakes to strive in good faith to achieve the desired objective and to fulfill the fiduciary duties.

It is important to understand that the agency relationship does not require compensation or any form of consideration. Nor does compensation define an agency relationship: a party other than the principal may compensate the agent.

How Florida modifies common-law agency. The agency principles in this section come from the common law and describe the traditional relationship between a principal and an agent. Florida, however, does not leave real estate brokerage to the common law alone. Chapter 475, Part III, Florida Statutes, largely replaces common-law agency with a set of statutory brokerage relationships: the transaction broker, which is the default relationship in Florida; the single agent; and no brokerage relationship. These statutory relationships, and the notices that accompany them, are covered later in this chapter and control how a Florida licensee actually works with buyers and sellers. Read the common-law material that follows as the background from which the Florida statutory model departs.

Basic roles

In an agency relationship, a principal hires an agent as a fiduciary to perform a desired service on the principal's behalf. As a fiduciary, the agent has a legal obligation to fulfill specific fiduciary duties throughout the term of the relationship.

The **principal**, or **client**, is the party who hires the agent. The agent works for the client. The principal may be a seller, a buyer, a landlord, or a tenant.

The **agent** is the principal's fiduciary, hired to perform authorized work and bound to fulfill fiduciary duties. In real estate brokerage, the agent must be a licensed broker.

The **customer** or **prospect** is a third party in the transaction whom the agent does not represent. The agent works with a customer in fulfilling the client's objectives. A seller, buyer, landlord, or tenant may be a customer. A third party who is a potential customer is a **prospect.** Another example of a non-representative relationship is working with a For Sale By Owner (FSBO) prospect.

Types of agency

According to the level of authority delegated to the agent, there are three types of agency: *universal, general, and special*.

Universal agency. In a universal agency relationship, the principal empowers the agent to perform any and all actions that may be legally delegated to an agency representative. The instrument of authorization is the power of attorney.

General agency. In a general agency, the principal delegates ongoing tasks and duties to the agent within a particular business or enterprise. Such delegation may include the authority to enter into contracts.

Special , or limited, agency. Under a special agency agreement, the principal delegates authority to conduct a specific activity, after which the agency relationship terminates. In most cases, the special agent may not bind the principal to a contract. An example of a special agency is the relationship between the sales associate and the buyer or seller the associate represents.

In most instances, real estate brokerage is based on a special agency. The principal hires a licensed broker to procure a ready, willing, and able buyer or seller. When the objective is achieved, the relationship terminates, although certain fiduciary duties survive termination of the relationship.

Creating an agency relationship

An agency relationship may arise from an express oral or written agreement between the principal and the agent, or from the actions of the parties by implication.

Written or oral listing agreement. The most common way to create an agency relationship is through a listing agreement, which may be oral or written. The agreement sets forth the various authorizations and duties, as well as requirements for compensation. A listing agreement establishes an agency for a specified transaction and has a stated expiration.

Implied agency. An agency relationship can arise by implication, by intention (intentionally), or by accident (unintentionally). *Implication* means that the parties act as if there were an agreement. For example, if an agent promises to do everything possible to find a property for a buyer at the lowest possible price and the buyer accepts the offer, there may be an implied agency relationship even without a specific agreement. Even if the agent does not wish to establish an agency relationship, the agent's actions may be construed as implying one.

Whether intended or accidental, the creation of implied agency obligates the agent to fiduciary duties and professional standards of care. If these are not fulfilled, the agent may be held liable

Terminating an agency relationship

Full performance of all obligations by the parties terminates an agency relationship. In addition, the parties may terminate the relationship at any time by *mutual agreement*. Thirdly, the agency relationship automatically terminates on the expiration date, regardless of whether the obligations were performed.

Involuntary termination. An agency relationship may terminate contrary to the wishes of the parties by reason of:

- death or incapacity of either party
- abandonment by the agent
- condemnation or destruction of the property
- renunciation
- breach
- bankruptcy
- revocation of the agent's license

Involuntary termination of the relationship may create legal and financial liability for a party who defaults or cancels. For example, a client may renounce an agreement but then be held liable for the agent's expenses or commission.

Duties Owed the Principals

The agency relationship imposes fiduciary duties on the client and agent, but particularly on the agent. An agent must also observe certain standards of conduct in dealing with customers and other outside parties.

Fiduciary duties to the client

Skill, care, and diligence. The agent is hired to do a job and is therefore expected to do it diligently and with reasonable competence. Competence is generally defined as a level of real estate marketing skills and knowledge comparable to those of other practitioners in the area.

The notion of care extends to observing the limited scope of authority granted to the agent. A conventional listing agreement does not authorize an agent to obligate the client to enter into contracts, nor does it allow the agent to conceal offers to buy, sell, or lease from a customer or another agent. Furthermore, because a client relies on a broker's representations, a broker must exercise care not to offer advice outside his or her field of expertise. Violations of this standard may expose the agent to liability for the unlicensed practice of a profession such as law, engineering, or accounting.

Fiduciary Duties

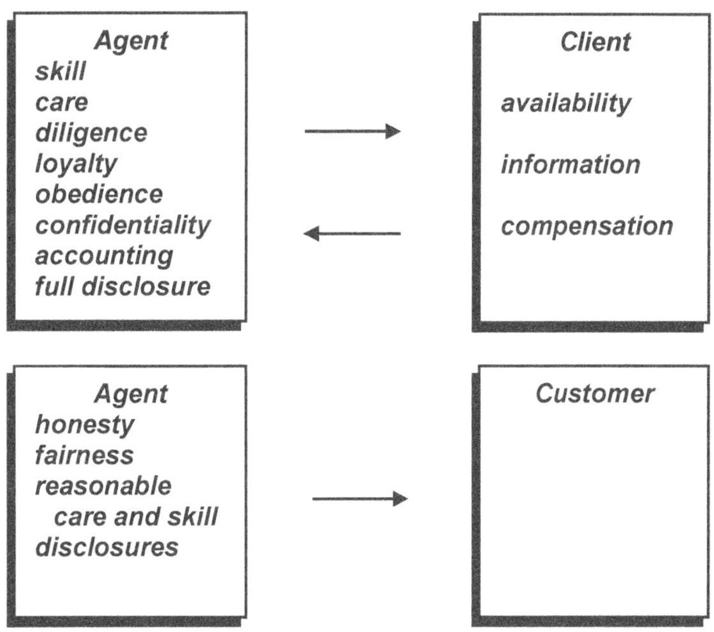

Loyalty. The duty of loyalty requires the agent to place the interests of the client above those of all others, particularly the agent's own. This standard is particularly relevant whenever an agent discusses transaction terms with a prospect.

Obedience. An agent must comply with the client's directions and instructions, *provided they are legal.* An agent who cannot obey a legal directive, for whatever reason, must withdraw from the relationship. If the directive is illegal, the agent must also immediately withdraw.

Confidentiality. An agent must hold in confidence any personal or business information received from the client during the term of employment. An agent may not disclose any information that would harm the client's interests or bargaining position, or anything else the client wishes to keep secret.

The confidentiality standard is one of the duties that extends *beyond the termination of the listing*: at no time in the future may the agent disclose confidential information.

An agent must exercise care in fulfilling this duty: if confidentiality conflicts with the agent's legal requirements to disclose material facts, the agent must inform the client of this obligation and make the required disclosures. If such a conflict cannot be resolved, the agent must withdraw from the relationship.

Accounting. An agent must safeguard and account for all monies, documents, and other property received from a client or customer. Florida licensing law regulates brokers' accounting obligations and escrow practices.

Full disclosure. An agent has the duty to inform the client of all material facts, reports, and rumors that might affect the client's interests in the property transaction.

In recent years, Florida's disclosure standard has been raised to require an agent to disclose items that a practicing agent should know, whether or not the agent actually had that knowledge, and regardless of whether the disclosure furthers or impedes the progress of the transaction.

Examples of a "should have known" disclosure is a property defect, such as a major structural, mechanical, or health-related defect, that should be recognized by a typical agent in the market.

There is no obligation to obtain or disclose information related to a customer's race, creed, color, religion, sex, or national origin: anti-discrimination laws hold such information to be immaterial to the transaction.

Florida law requires a seller to make a written disclosure about a property's condition to a prospective buyer.

Critical material facts for disclosure include:

- the agent's opinion of the property's condition
- information about the buyer's motivations and financial qualifications
- discussions between agent and buyer regarding the possibility of the agent's representing the buyer in another transaction.
- adverse material facts, including property condition, title defects, environmental hazards, and property defects

Agent's duties to the customer

The traditional notion of caveat emptor, let the buyer beware, no longer applies unequivocally to real estate transactions. Agents do have certain obligations to customers, even though they do not represent them. In general, they owe a third party:

- honesty and fair dealing
- reasonable care and skill
- proper disclosure

An agent has a duty to deal fairly and honestly with a customer. Thus, an agent may not deceive, defraud, or otherwise take advantage of a customer.

"Reasonable care and skill" means that an agent will be held to the standards of knowledge, expertise, and ethics commonly maintained by other agents in the area.

Proper disclosure primarily concerns disclosure of agency, property condition, and environmental hazards.

An agent who fails to meet prevailing standards may be held liable for negligence, fraud, or violations of state real estate licensing laws and regulations. Agents should be particularly careful not to misrepresent or offer inappropriate expert advice when working with customers.

Intentional misrepresentation. An agent may defraud a buyer, whether intentionally or unintentionally, by misrepresenting or concealing facts. While it is acceptable to promote a property's features to a buyer or a buyer's virtues to a seller, there is a fine line between promotion and misrepresentation. Silent misrepresentation, which is intentionally failing to reveal a material fact, is just as fraudulent as a false statement.

Negligent misrepresentation. An agent can be held liable for failure to disclose facts the agent was not aware of if it can be demonstrated that the agent should have known such facts. For example, if it is a common practice for agents to inspect property, an agent can be held liable for failing to disclose a leaky roof that was not inspected.

Misrepresentation of expertise. An agent should not act or speak outside the agent's area of expertise. A customer may rely on anything an agent says, and the agent will be held accountable. For example, an agent represents that a property will appreciate. The buyer interprets this as expert investment advice and buys the property. If the property does not appreciate, the buyer may hold the agent liable.

Principal's general duties

The obligations of a principal in an agency relationship concern the following:

Availability. In a special agency, the agent's power and decision-making authority are limited. Therefore, the principal must be available for consultation, direction, and decision-making. Otherwise, the agent cannot complete the job.

Information. The principal must provide the agent with sufficient information to complete the desired activity. This may include property and financial data, as well as the client's timing requirements.

Compensation. If an agreement includes a provision for compensating the agent and the agent performs in accordance with the agreement, the client is obligated to compensate the agent. As indicated earlier, however, the agency relationship does not necessarily include compensation.

The Brokerage Relationships Disclosure Act

Residential transactions applicability

Under the Brokerage Relationship Disclosure Act, all real estate transactions impose certain duties and obligations on licensees. Written disclosures, however, are required only when a brokerage is acting as a single agent or in a no-brokerage relationship in a residential sale transaction.

Residential sale transactions are those involving

- improved residential properties with four or fewer dwelling units
- unimproved residential properties zoned for four or fewer residential units

- agricultural properties of ten acres or less

The requirement for agency disclosures to be written thus excludes

- non-residential transactions
- rental or leasing transactions and sales of business opportunities unless they include an option to purchase a property with four or fewer residential units
- auctions
- appraisals

No written disclosure is required when the brokerage acts as a transaction broker, as this relationship is presumed under Florida law.

Disclosure notices

The mandated disclosures do not include language about whom the agent represents or about the choices of representation the clients or customers have; they simply disclose the duties. However, there are separate disclosures for each relationship that do include the type of representation.

Other disclosure notices include "No Brokerage Relationship Notice" and "Consent to Transition to Transaction Broker." This second disclosure includes the duties owed by the transaction broker to the customer.

The authorized relationships, duties, and disclosure notices are described below.

Under Florida's Brokerage Relationship Disclosure Act, licensees may establish a relationship with a buyer or seller as either a transaction broker or as a single agent. The licensee may also assist a buyer or seller with no brokerage relationship, known as nonrepresentation. The licensee may not establish a dual agency relationship with both a buyer and a seller in the same transaction. The relationship established must be disclosed in writing to the involved party(ies). The licensee may transition from one type of relationship to another with the consent of the buyer and/or seller and the disclosure of the duties owed to the client or customer under the new relationship.

The customer is not required to enter into any brokerage relationship with a licensee.

Nonrepresentation relationships

A licensee may enter into a listing agreement with a seller and be paid a commission or other compensation, even if there is no brokerage relationship with the buyer or seller. In this situation, the licensee owes no loyalty or other fiduciary duties to either party but still owes certain duties to the party or parties as customers. Those duties must be disclosed in writing before the licensee shows a property. F.S. Chapter 475.278(4)(c) mandates the following form and language for the disclosure:

NO BROKERAGE RELATIONSHIP NOTICE

FLORIDA LAW REQUIRES THAT REAL ESTATE LICENSEES WHO HAVE NO BROKERAGE RELATIONSHIP WITH A POTENTIAL SELLER OR BUYER DISCLOSE THEIR DUTIES TO SELLERS AND BUYERS.

As a real estate licensee who has no brokerage relationship with you, (insert name of Real Estate Entity and its Associates) owe to you the following duties:

1. *Dealing honestly and fairly.*
2. *Disclosing all known facts that materially affect the value of the residential property that are not readily observable to the buyer.*
3. *Accounting for all funds entrusted to the licensee.*

A buyer or seller seeking additional duties and a different level of assistance must enter into an agency relationship with the broker.

Single agency relationships

The agent represents one party in a transaction. The client may be either the seller or the buyer.

Seller agency. In the traditional situation, a seller or landlord is the agent's client. A buyer or tenant is the customer.

Buyer agency. Recently, it has become common for an agent to represent a buyer or tenant. In this relationship, the property buyer or tenant is the client and the property owner is the customer.

Dual agency. An agency relationship is established with a brokerage firm and not with any one agent within the firm. Therefore, a dual agency would exist if one agent within the firm represented the seller while another agent in the same firm represented the buyer. ***Dual agency as a form of representation is prohibited in Florida whether it is disclosed or nondisclosed.***

Subagency. In a subagency, a broker associate or sales associate works as the agent of a broker who is the agent of a buyer or seller. In effect, the associate, as agent of the broker, is the subagent of the client. The subagent owes the same duties to the broker's client as the broker does.

The disclosure required for single agency is as follows. The disclosure must be made at the time of entering into a listing agreement or an agreement for representation or before showing the property, whichever occurs first.

SINGLE AGENT NOTICE

FLORIDA LAW REQUIRES THAT REAL ESTATE LICENSEES OPERATING AS SINGLE AGENTS DISCLOSE TO BUYERS AND SELLERS THEIR DUTIES.

- As a single agent, (insert name of Real Estate Entity and its Associates) owe to you the following duties:
- Dealing honestly and fairly;
- Loyalty;
- Confidentiality;
- Obedience;
- Full disclosure;
- Accounting for all funds;
- Skill, care, and diligence in the transaction;
- Presenting all offers and counteroffers in a timely manner, unless a party has previously directed the licensee otherwise in writing; and
- Disclosing all known facts that materially affect the value of residential real property and are not readily observable.

Transaction broker relationships

Florida prohibits both parties to a transaction from being represented by the same licensee or brokerage in a dual-agency relationship. Instead, the transaction broker relationship was created to allow a single brokerage to provide limited representation and duties to both the seller and the buyer in the same transaction. Limited representation means neither party is responsible for the licensee's actions.

In a transaction broker relationship, the broker does not represent either party in a fiduciary capacity or as a single agent. Neither party has the right to the licensee's undivided loyalty. Furthermore, because the broker is not representing either party as a client, all parties to the transaction are considered customers.

The transaction broker relationship is between the brokerage and the client. Consequently, one licensee in the brokerage may represent both the seller and the buyer, or one licensee may represent the seller while another represents the buyer. All licensees in the firm are providing the same limited representation to both parties. Neither the seller nor the buyer may be represented to the detriment of the other party.

Florida law presumes that all licensees operate as transaction brokers unless the broker and the customer have entered into a written single-agent or nonrepresentation agreement. Consequently, transaction brokers are not required to provide customers with a notice or disclosure regarding a transaction broker relationship.

Duties of a transaction broker. As with any Florida agency relationship, the broker must disclose the duties owed to both parties.

- dealing honestly and fairly
- accounting for all funds
- using skill, care, and diligence in the transaction
- disclosing all known material facts that are not readily observable and that affect the property's value
- presenting all offers and counteroffers in a timely manner unless directed otherwise
- providing limited confidentiality unless either party waives in writing

- performing any additional duties agreed upon by both parties

The duty of limited confidentiality prevents the broker or licensee from disclosing any of the following information:

- the seller will accept a price less than the asking or listed price
- the buyer will pay a price greater than the price submitted in a written offer
- the motivation of any party for selling or buying property
- a seller or buyer will agree to financing terms other than those offered
- any other information requested by a party to remain confidential

Duties not imposed on the transaction broker. Since there are no fiduciary duties binding the transaction broker, the broker is held to standards for dealing with customers rather than clients. These include honesty, fair dealing, and reasonable care. The transaction broker is under no obligation to inspect the property for the benefit of a party or verify the accuracy of statements made by a party.

Transitioning to transaction broker

Timing. A single-agency relationship may transition to a transaction broker relationship at any time the agent and principal wish to do so. With the transition, the licensee will provide limited representation and can assist both the buyer and the seller, but will not have dedicated loyalty. The licensee must not represent one party to the detriment of the other party.

Procedure. The licensee must obtain the principal's written consent to the single agency before or at the time of entering into a listing agreement, entering into an agreement for representation, or showing a property, whichever occurs first. Consent **to change the relationship from single agent to transaction representation must be obtained before the change occurs.**

Format. When a relationship change is disclosed in other documents, it must be the same type size or larger and placed conspicuously, with the first sentence in uppercase and bold. It must include its own initials or signature line directly under the disclosure language. The disclosure must also include the duties the licensee owes to the principal. The consent-to-transition form below is also available in F.S. Chapter 475.278.

CONSENT TO TRANSITION TO TRANSACTION BROKER

FLORIDA LAW ALLOWS REAL ESTATE LICENSEES WHO REPRESENT A BUYER OR SELLER AS A SINGLE AGENT TO CHANGE FROM A SINGLE AGENT RELATIONSHIP TO A TRANSACTION BROKERAGE RELATIONSHIP IN ORDER FOR THE LICENSEE TO ASSIST BOTH PARTIES IN A REAL ESTATE TRANSACTION BY PROVIDING A LIMITED FORM OF REPRESENTATION TO BOTH THE BUYER AND THE SELLER. THIS CHANGE IN RELATIONSHIP CANNOT OCCUR WITHOUT YOUR PRIOR WRITTEN CONSENT.

As a transaction broker, (insert name of Real Estate Firm and its Associates), provides to you a limited form of representation that includes the following duties:

- Dealing honestly and fairly;
- Accounting for all funds;
- Using skill, care, and diligence in the transaction;

- Disclosing all known facts that materially affect the value of residential real property and are not readily observable to the buyer;
- Presenting all offers and counteroffers in a timely manner, unless a party has previously directed the licensee otherwise in writing;
- Limited confidentiality, unless waived in writing by a party. This limited confidentiality will prevent disclosure that the seller will accept a price less than the asking or listed price, that the buyer will pay a price greater than the price submitted in a written offer, of the motivation of any party for selling or buying property, that a seller or buyer will agree to financing terms other than those offered, or of any other information requested by a party to remain confidential; and
- Any additional duties that are entered into by this or by separate written agreement.

Limited representation means that a buyer or seller is not responsible for the acts of the licensee. Additionally, the parties are giving up their rights to the licensee's undivided loyalty. This aspect of limited representation allows a licensee to facilitate a real estate transaction by assisting both the buyer and the seller, but a licensee will not act to represent one party to the detriment of the other when acting as a transaction broker for both parties.

I agree that my agent may assume the role and duties of a transaction broker. [must be initialed or signed]

Designated sales associate

Non-residential transaction limitations. When a broker is handling a non-residential transaction in which the buyer and seller have assets of $1 million or more, the customers may request that the broker designate sales associates to act as single agents for each customer in the same transaction. In other words, the broker may designate one sales associate to the buyer and another sales associate to the seller. Each of these sales associates has the same duties to the customer as a single agent does, including disclosures.

Disclosure requirements. While brokers who handle residential sale transactions must comply with mandated disclosure requirements, those who handle non-residential transactions do not face the same requirements. The broker does not have to disclose duties to the customers, but the designated sales associates must disclose their single-agent duties.

Additionally, the buyer and the seller must each sign disclosures stating that their assets meet the $1 million requirement and that they are requesting designated sales associates. The disclosure must include the following language:

FLORIDA LAW PROHIBITS A DESIGNATED SALES ASSOCIATE FROM DISCLOSING, EXCEPT TO THE BROKER OR PERSONS SPECIFIED BY THE BROKER, INFORMATION MADE CONFIDENTIAL BY REQUEST OR AT THE INSTRUCTION OF THE CUSTOMER THE DESIGNATED SALES ASSOCIATE IS REPRESENTING. HOWEVER, FLORIDA LAW ALLOWS A DESIGNATED SALES ASSOCIATE TO DISCLOSE INFORMATION ALLOWED TO BE DISCLOSED OR REQUIRED TO BE DISCLOSED BY LAW AND ALSO ALLOWS A DESIGNATED SALES ASSOCIATE TO DISCLOSE TO HIS OR HER BROKER, OR PERSONS SPECIFIED BY THE BROKER, CONFIDENTIAL INFORMATION OF A CUSTOMER FOR THE PURPOSE OF SEEKING ADVICE OR ASSISTANCE FOR THE BENEFIT OF THE CUSTOMER IN REGARD TO A TRANSACTION. FLORIDA LAW REQUIRES THAT THE BROKER MUST HOLD THIS INFORMATION CONFIDENTIAL AND MAY NOT USE SUCH INFORMATION TO THE DETRIMENT OF THE OTHER PARTY.

Single agent duties. As a designated single agent, the sales associate has the following duties to buyers and sellers:

- dealing honestly and fairly
- loyalty
- confidentiality
- obedience
- full disclosure
- accounting for all funds
- skill, care, and diligence in the transaction
- presenting all offers and counteroffers in a timely manner, unless a party has previously directed the licensee otherwise in writing
- disclosing all known facts that materially affect the value of residential real property and are not readily observable

Documentation Brokers are required to retain their business records for at least 5 years from the date of agreement execution. Disclosure documents related to transactions that resulted in a written contract to sell or purchase must be retained for 5 years.

Any document that has been the subject of or served as evidence in any civil action or appellate proceeding must be retained for at least 2 years after the conclusion of the action or proceeding, but no less than the required 5 years.

Even records related to transactions that did not close should be retained for 5 years.

Property Condition Disclosure

Roles and forms

Seller's disclosure form. Many states require sellers to make a written disclosure about property condition to a prospective buyer. This seller disclosure may or may not relieve the agent of certain disclosure liabilities. The residential property condition disclosure is the seller's written summary of the property's condition at the time of contracting for sale. The disclosure is entered on state-approved forms.

Owner's role. State legislation requires owners of previously occupied single-family homes and buildings containing 1-4 dwelling units to provide prospective buyers with a disclosure if they are selling, exchanging, or optioning their property. Some exceptions and exemptions apply. When required, the disclosure must be transmitted to the prospective buyer no later than when the buyer makes an offer.

A typical form requires the seller to affirm whether or not problems exist in any of the listed features and systems of the property. In denying that a problem exists, the seller claims to have no knowledge of a defect. If a defect does in fact exist, the seller can be held liable for intentional misrepresentation. A third possible response to a property condition question is that of "no representation." Here, the seller makes no claim to knowledge of whether a problem exists. With this answer, the seller is no longer liable for any disclosure relating to a particular feature, whether or not a defect is known.

Once the seller has signed the form and delivered it to the buyer, the buyer must acknowledge receipt and knowledge of the property condition disclosures, as well as the other provisions set forth on the form.

Licensee's role. The residential property re-seller must comply with the property condition disclosure requirement whether an agent is employed in the transaction or not. If an agent is involved in the transaction, the agent must disclose all material facts he or she knows or should reasonably know about the property, regardless of what the seller may have disclosed on the form.

Right of rescission. Sellers who fail to complete and deliver the property

condition disclosure statement to buyers in a timely fashion effectively give the buyer a subsequent right under certain conditions to rescind the sale contract and reclaim their deposits. The buyer must follow certain procedures and meet specific deadlines to effect the cancellation legitimately. The buyer's right to cancel persists until closing or occupancy, whichever comes first.

Disclosing material facts

Material fact defined. As explained in the chapter on agency, an agent has the duty to inform the client of all material facts, reports, and rumors that might affect the client's interests in the property transaction. A material fact is one that might affect the value or desirability of the property to a buyer if the buyer knew it. Material facts include

- the agent's opinion of the property's condition
- adverse facts about property condition, title defects, environmental hazards, and property defects

In recent years, the disclosure standard has been raised to require an agent to disclose items that a practicing agent should know, whether the agent actually had the knowledge or not, and regardless of whether the disclosure furthers or impedes the progress of the transaction.

Facts not considered to be material, and therefore not usually subject to required disclosure, include such items as property stigmatization (e.g., that a crime or death occurred on the property) and the presence of registered sex offenders in the neighborhood (in accordance with Megan's Law, federal legislation that requires convicted offenders to register with the state of residence; in some states, agents must provide registry information to buyers).

Agent liability. The agent may be held liable for failing to disclose a material fact if a court rules that the typical agent in that area would detect and recognize the adverse condition. There is no obligation to obtain or disclose information that is immaterial to the transaction, such as property stigmas.

An agent who sees a "red flag" issue, such as a potential structural or mechanical problem, should advise the seller to seek expert advice. Red flags can signal issues that significantly impact the value of the property and/or the cost of remediation. In addition to property condition per se, they may include such things as

- environmental concerns
- property anomalies, such as oversized or peculiarly shaped lots
- neighborhood issues of a specific type
- poor construction
- signs of flooding
- poor floorplan
- adjacent property features

The following exhibit is the first two pages of Florida's most recently revised SPDR (Seller's Property Disclosure – Residential) form (2025), which shows the level of detail expected in a seller's disclosure.

Seller's Property Disclosure – Residential

Notice to Licensee and Seller: Only the Seller should fill out this form.

Notice to Seller: Florida law[1] requires a **Seller** of a home to disclose to the **Buyer** all known facts that materially affect the value of the property being sold and that are not readily observable or known by the **Buyer**. This disclosure form is designed to help you comply with the law. However, this disclosure form may not address every significant issue that is unique to the Property. You should think about what you would want to know if you were buying the Property today; and if you need more space for additional information, comments, or explanations, check the Paragraph 12 checkbox and attach an addendum.

Notice to Buyer: The following representations are made by **Seller** and **not** by any real estate licensee. This disclosure is not a guaranty or warranty of any kind. It is not a substitute for any inspections, warranties, or professional advice you may wish to obtain. It is not a substitute for your own personal judgment and common sense. The following information is based only upon **Seller's** actual knowledge of the Property's condition. **Sellers** can disclose only what they actually know. **Seller** may not know about all material or significant items. You should have an independent, professional home inspection to verify the condition of the Property and determine the cost of repairs, if any. This disclosure is not a contract and is not intended to be a part of any contract for sale and purchase.

Seller makes the following disclosure regarding the property described as: ____________________
____________________ (the "Property")

The Property is ☐owner occupied ☐tenant occupied ☐unoccupied (**If unoccupied**, how long has it been since **Seller** occupied the Property? ____________

	Yes	No	Don't Know
1. Structures; Systems; Appliances			
(a) Are the structures including roofs; ceilings; walls; doors; windows; foundation; and pool, hot tub, and spa, if any, structurally sound and free of leaks?	☐	☐	☐
(b) Is seawall, if any, and dockage, if any, structurally sound?	☐	☐	☐
(c) Are existing major appliances and heating, cooling, mechanical, electrical, security, and sprinkler systems, in working condition, i.e., operating in the manner in which the item was designed to operate?	☐	☐	☐
(d) Does the Property have aluminum wiring other than the primary service line?	☐	☐	☐
(e) Are any of the appliances leased? If yes, which ones: ____________	☐	☐	☐
(f) If any answer to questions 1(a) – 1(c) is no, please explain: ____________			
2. Termites; Other Wood-Destroying Organisms; Pests			
(a) Are termites; other wood-destroying organisms, including fungi; or pests present on the Property or has the Property had any structural damage by them?	☐	☐	☐
(b) Has the Property been treated for termites; other wood-destroying organisms, including fungi; or pests?	☐	☐	☐
(c) If any answer to questions 2(a) - 2(b) is yes, please explain: ____________			
3. Water Intrusion; Drainage; Flooding			
(a) Has past or present water intrusion affected the Property?	☐	☐	☐
(b) Have past or present drainage or flooding problems affected the Property?	☐	☐	☐
(c) Is any of the Property located in a special flood hazard area?	☐	☐	☐
(d) Is any of the Property located seaward of the coastal construction control line?	☐	☐	☐
(e) Does your lender require flood insurance?	☐	☐	☐
(f) Do you have an elevation certificate? If yes, please attach a copy.	☐	☐	☐
(g) If any answer to questions 3(a) - 3(d) is yes, please explain: ____________			

[1] *Johnson v. Davis*, 480 So.2d 625 (Fla. 1985).

	Yes	No	Don't Know
4. Plumbing			
(a) What is your drinking water source? ☐public ☐private ☐well ☐other			
(b) Have you ever had a problem with the quality, supply, or flow of potable water?	☐	☐	☐
(c) Do you have a water treatment system? If yes, is it ☐owned ☐leased?	☐	☐	☐
(d) Do you have a ☐sewer or ☐septic system? If septic system, describe the location of each system: ______			
(e) Are any septic tanks, drain fields, or wells that are not currently being used located on the Property?	☐	☐	☐
(f) Are there or have there been any defects to the water system, septic system, drain fields or wells?	☐	☐	☐
(g) Have there been any plumbing leaks since you have owned the Property?	☐	☐	☐
(h) Are any polybutylene pipes on the Property?	☐	☐	☐
(i) If any answer to questions 4(b), 4(c), and 4(e) - 4(h) is yes, please explain: ______			
5. Roof and Roof-Related Items			
(a) To your knowledge, is the roof structurally sound and free of leaks?	☐	☐	☐
(b) The age of the roof is ______ years OR date installed ______			
(c) Has the roof ever leaked during your ownership?	☐	☐	☐
(d) To your knowledge, has there been any repair, restoration, replacement (indicate full or partial) or other work undertaken on the roof? If yes, please explain: ______	☐	☐	☐
(e) Are you aware of any defects to the roof, fascia, soffits, flashings or any other component of the roof system? If yes, please explain: ______	☐	☐	☐
6. Pools; Hot Tubs; Spas Note: Florida law requires swimming pools, hot tubs, and spas that received a certificate of completion on or after October 1, 2000, to have at least one safety feature as specified by Section 515.27, Florida Statutes.			
(a) If the Property has a swimming pool, hot tub, or spa that received a certificate of completion on or after October 1, 2000, indicate the existing safety feature(s): ☐enclosure that meets the pool barrier requirements ☐approved safety pool cover ☐required door and window exit alarms ☐required door locks ☐none			
(b) Has an in-ground pool on the Property been demolished and/or filled?	☐	☐	☐
7. Sinkholes Note: When an insurance claim for sinkhole damage has been made by the seller and paid by the insurer, Section 627.7073(2)(c), Florida Statutes, requires the seller to disclose to the buyer that a claim was paid and whether or not the full amount paid was used to repair the sinkhole damage.			
(a) Does past or present settling, soil movement, or sinkhole(s) affect the Property or adjacent properties?	☐	☐	☐
(b) Has any insurance claim for sinkhole damage been made? If yes, was the claim paid? ☐ yes ☐ no If the claim was paid, were all the proceeds used to repair the damage? ☐ yes ☐ no	☐	☐	☐
(c) If any answer to questions 7(a) - 7(b) is yes, please explain: ______			

Snapshot Review for Chapter 10

The following review summarizes the key rules and concepts from Chapter 10.

ESSENTIALS OF REAL ESTATE AGENCY

Historical Perspective

- agency law grows out of common law and statutory law
- essence of agency relationship: trust, confidence, mutual good faith

Agency Basics

- agency relationship based on trust, confidence, and good faith
- principal (client) hires agent (broker) to act on their behalf
- customer = third party not represented by the agent
- agency law derived from common law and statutory law

Types of Agency

- universal agency = broad authority through power of attorney
- general agency = ongoing authority within business activities
- special agency = authority for specific transaction only
- most real estate brokerage relationships are special agency

Creating and Terminating Agency

- created by written, oral, or implied agreement
- implied agency may arise from actions or conduct
- terminated by fulfillment, expiration, mutual agreement, or involuntary events
- involuntary termination causes: death, incapacity, agent's abandonment, property destruction, renunciation, breach, bankruptcy, license revocation

Duties Owed to The Transaction Parties

- fiduciary duties to the client: skill, care, and diligence, loyalty, obedience, confidentiality (survives termination of agency relationship), full disclosure of all material facts, accounting for funds, documents, and property
- duties owed to customers: honesty and fair dealing, reasonable care and skill, proper disclosure of material facts and hazards, avoid intentional or negligent misrepresentation
- principal's duties to agent: availability for decisions and direction, provide necessary information and documents, compensate agent if agreed duties are fulfilled

Brokerage Relationship Disclosure Act

- written disclosure required for single agent and no brokerage relationships
- applies mainly to residential property with four or fewer units
- transaction broker relationship presumed under Florida law

Nonrepresentation Relationships

- no fiduciary duties owed
- still requires honesty, fair dealing, disclosure of known material facts, and accounting

Single Agency Relationships

- agent represents either buyer or seller exclusively

- dual agency prohibited in Florida
- broker associates act as subagents of broker's client
- full fiduciary duties owed to client

Transaction Broker Relationships

- limited representation to both buyer and seller
- no undivided loyalty or fiduciary relationship
- duties include honesty, disclosure, accounting, and limited confidentiality
- allows brokerage to assist both parties in same transaction

Transitioning to Transaction Broker

- single agent may transition with written consent
- disclosure must include required statutory language and duties owed

Designated Sales Associate

- allowed in certain nonresidential transactions over $1 million
- broker designates separate associates to buyer and seller
- designated associates provide single-agent duties to assigned party

Documentation Requirements

- brokerage records retained minimum 5 years
- legal proceeding records retained at least 2 additional years if required

Residential Property Condition Disclosure Roles and Forms

- sellers of most residential properties must provide written disclosure
- disclosure addresses known defects and property conditions
- agents must disclose material facts they know or should know
- buyer may rescind contract if disclosure not timely delivered

Material Facts and Red Flags

- material facts affect value or desirability of property
- examples: structural defects, environmental hazards, flooding, title issues
- agents liable for failing to disclose known or reasonably discoverable defects
- stigmas and registered offender information generally not considered material factsTop of Form
- Bottom of Form

Chapter 10 Quiz: Brokerage Relationships and Disclosure Requirements

10.1 In an agency relationship, the party who hires the agent is the ______.

a. principal
b. customer
c. subagent
d. third party

10.2 A third party with whom an agent works but does not represent is the ______.

a. client
b. principal
c. fiduciary
d. customer

10.3 A licensee hired to handle one specific transaction, after which the relationship ends, is acting under ______.

a. universal agency
b. special (limited) agency
c. general agency
d. subagency

10.4 When the same brokerage represents both buyer and seller as fiduciaries in the same transaction, this is ______.

a. permitted as transaction brokerage
b. dual agency, which Florida prohibits
c. designated sales associate practice
d. required in all residential sales

10.5 The Brokerage Relationship Disclosure Act's written-disclosure requirements apply to ______.

a. all commercial leases
b. auctions only
c. residential sale transactions
d. new-home construction only

10.6 Florida law presumes that a licensee is operating as a ______ unless another relationship is established.

a. single agent
b. dual agent
c. designated sales associate
d. transaction broker

10.7 Which duty is owed by a single agent but NOT by a transaction broker?

a. loyalty
b. dealing honestly and fairly
c. accounting for all funds
d. using skill, care, and diligence

10.8 A single agent owes the client all of the following duties EXCEPT ______.

a. loyalty
b. confidentiality
c. obedience
d. limited confidentiality

10.9 In a transaction broker relationship, "limited confidentiality" means the licensee may NOT disclose ______.

a. the property's listed price
b. publicly recorded information
c. that the seller will accept less than the asking price
d. the square footage of the home

10.10 A licensee who has no brokerage relationship with a buyer or seller still owes the duty to ______.

a. be loyal to that party
b. disclose all known facts materially affecting value that are not readily observable
c. obey that party's instructions
d. maintain full confidentiality

10.11 The three duties in a no-brokerage-relationship are dealing honestly and fairly, accounting for all funds, and ______.

a. loyalty
b. disclosing known material facts not readily observable
c. obedience
d. full disclosure

10.12 A designated sales associate relationship is permitted only in ______.

a. residential transactions under $100,000
b. all residential sales
c. non-residential transactions where the buyer and seller each have assets of $1 million or more
d. transactions involving vacant land only

10.13 To use designated sales associates, the buyer and seller must each ______.

a. waive all disclosure rights
b. be represented by the same associate
c. agree to pay a double commission
d. sign a statement that their assets meet the $1 million requirement

10.14 A single agent who wishes to change to a transaction broker relationship during a transaction must ______.

a. obtain the customer's consent (Consent to Transition to Transaction Broker)
b. notify FREC in writing
c. cancel the listing agreement
d. wait until closing

10.15 The agent's duties to a customer (a party the agent does not represent) include ______.

a. loyalty and obedience
b. full confidentiality
c. honesty, fairness, and disclosure of known material facts
d. accounting to the customer for the client's funds

10.16 The seller's affirmative duty to disclose known defects that materially affect value and are not readily observable comes from ______.

a. the federal Fair Housing Act
b. the case of Johnson v. Davis
c. RESPA
d. the Statute of Frauds

10.17 An agent who observes a "red flag," such as a possible structural or mechanical problem, should ______.

a. ignore it unless asked
b. repair it personally
c. cancel the listing
d. advise the seller and recommend that the buyer investigate further

10.18 A licensee may enter into a listing agreement and be paid a commission ______.

a. even when there is no brokerage relationship with the customer
b. only as a single agent
c. only in non-residential transactions
d. only if the customer signs a single agent notice

10.19 Which is one of the three types of agency based on the scope of authority?

a. limited confidentiality
b. subrogation
c. universal agency
d. estoppel

10.20 The person the agent represents and owes fiduciary duties to is the ______.

a. customer
b. cooperating broker
c. appraiser
d. client (principal)

10.21 A transaction broker owes the customer the duty to ______.

a. be loyal to one party
b. deal honestly and fairly and use skill, care, and diligence
c. obey all instructions of the buyer
d. keep the transaction confidential from both parties

10.22 An agency relationship may be terminated by ______.

a. completion (performance) of the agency's purpose
b. the agent's preference alone at any time without cause
c. a red-flag disclosure
d. a CMA

CHAPTER 11: REAL ESTATE CONTRACTS

Contents

Learning Objectives

Upon completion of this chapter, you will be able to:

1. List and describe the essentials of a contract
2. Distinguish among formal, parol, bilateral, unilateral, implied, express, executory and executed contracts
3. Describe the various ways in which an offer is terminated
4. Describe the various methods of terminating a contract
5. Explain the remedies for breach of a contract
6. Describe the effect of the Statute of Frauds and the Statute of Limitations
7. Describe the elements of an option
8. Differentiate among the various types of listings
9. Explain and describe the various disclosures required in a real estate contract
10. Recognize what constitutes fraud
11. Recognize what constitutes culpable negligence
12. Distinguish among valid, void, voidable, and unenforceable contracts
13. Identify the requirements for a valid conveyance of real property
14. Explain how the Uniform Electronic Transactions Act (UETA) applies to electronic contracts and signatures
15. Describe the process of offer, counteroffer, and acceptance in forming a contract
16. Explain how a contract may be assigned and the effect of assignment on the parties
17. Describe who may prepare real estate contracts and the limits imposed by the unauthorized practice of law
18. Explain the agency foundations of a listing agreement and the relationship it creates between broker and principal
19. Identify the key clauses in an exclusive right to sell listing and an exclusive buyer agency agreement
20. Describe the essential components of a residential sales contract

Contract Essentials

Definition of a contract

A **contract** is an agreement between two or more parties who, in a "meeting of the minds," have pledged to perform or refrain from performing some act. A valid contract is legally enforceable because it meets the requirements of contract law. If a contract does not meet the requirements, it is invalid, and the parties to it cannot resort to a court to enforce its provisions.

Note that a contract is not a legal form or a prescribed set of words in a document, but rather the intangible agreement that was made in "the meeting of the minds" of the parties to the contract.

Real estate contracts are the legal agreements that underlie the transfer and financing of real estate, as well as the real estate brokerage business. Sale and lease contracts and option agreements are used to transfer real estate interests from one party to another. Mortgage contracts and promissory agreements are part of real estate financing. Listing and representation contracts establish client relationships and provide for compensation.

In order to work with real estate contracts, it is imperative to first grasp basic concepts that apply to all contracts in general. These concepts provide a foundation for understanding the specifics of particular types of real estate contracts.

Preparation of contracts

Unauthorized practice of law. Because real estate licensees must work with such contracts as listing agreements, buyer brokerage agreements, sale and purchase contracts, and option contracts as part of their normal course of business, they have received special dispensations to assist buyers and sellers with the drawing of these contracts to the extent that they may fill in the blanks on standardized forms prepared by attorneys.

The preparation of contracts and other legal instruments is the practice of law and the exclusive business of attorneys. Real estate licensees, unless they are also attorneys, can lose their licenses for preparing such documents. The offense is known as the unauthorized practice of law.

Brokers and associates may not draft contracts, but they may use standard promulgated forms and fill in the blanks.

As a rule, a broker or associate who completes real estate contracts is engaging in the unauthorized practice of law unless the broker is a party to the agreement, such as in a listing agreement or sales contract. Brokers and associates may not complete leases, mortgages, contracts for deed, or promissory notes to which they are not a party.

Licensees must be fully aware of what they are and are not legally allowed to do in preparing and interpreting contracts for clients. In addition to practicing law without a license, they expose themselves to lawsuits from clients who relied on a contract they believed was legally valid.

Legal status of contracts

In terms of validity and enforceability, a court may construe the legal status of a contract in one of four ways:

- valid
- valid but unenforceable

- void
- voidable

Valid. A valid contract is one that meets the legal requirements for validity. These requirements are explained in the next section.

A valid written contract is enforceable within a statutory time period. A valid oral contract is generally enforceable within a statutory period, except as noted below.

Valid but unenforceable. State laws declare that some contracts are enforceable only if they are in writing. These laws apply in particular to the transfer of interests in real estate. Thus, while an oral contract may meet the tests for validity, if it falls under the laws requiring a written contract, the parties will not have legal recourse to enforce performance. An oral long-term lease and an oral real estate sales contract are examples of contracts that may be valid but not enforceable.

Note that such contracts, if valid, remain so even though not enforceable. This means that if the parties fully execute and perform the contract, the outcome may not be altered.

Void. A void contract is an agreement that does not meet the tests for validity, and therefore is no contract at all. If a contract is void, neither party can enforce it.

For example, a contract that lacks consideration is void. Likewise, a contract to extort money from a business is void. Void contracts and instruments are also described as "null and void."

Voidable. A voidable contract is one that initially appears valid but is subject to rescission by a party to the contract who is deemed to have acted under some disability. Only the party that claims the disability may rescind the contract's legal effect.

For example, a party that was the victim of duress, coercion, or fraud in the creation of a contract and can prove it may disaffirm the contract. However, the disaffirmation must occur within a legal time frame for the act of rescission to be valid. Similarly, if the party that has cause to disaffirm the contract elects to perform it instead, the contract is no longer voidable but valid.

A voidable contract differs from a void contract in that the latter does not require an act of disaffirmation to render it unenforceable.

Criteria for validity A contract is valid only if it meets all of the following criteria.

Contract Validity Requirements

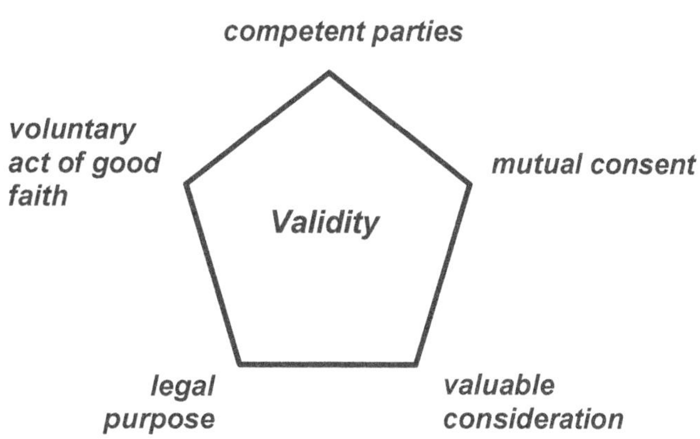

Competent parties. The parties to a contract must have the capacity to contract, and there must be at least two such parties. Thus, the owner of a tenancy for life cannot deed his interest to himself in the form of a fee simple, as this would involve only one party. Capacity to contract is determined by three factors:

- legal age
- mental competency
- legitimate authority

In Florida, a minor may contract, but the contract will be voidable and the minor can disaffirm the contract.

To be mentally competent, a party must have sufficient understanding of the import and consequences of a contract. Competency in this context is separate and distinct from sanity. Incompetent parties, or parties of "unsound mind," may not enter into enforceable contracts. The incompetency of a party may be ruled by a court of law or by other means. In some areas, convicted felons may be deemed incompetent, depending on the nature of the crime.

During the period of one's incompetency, a court may appoint a guardian who may act on the incompetent party's behalf with court approval.

If the contracting party is representing another person or business entity, the representative must have the *legal authority* to contract. If representing another person, the party must have a bona fide power of attorney. If the contracting party is representing a corporation, the person must have the appropriate power and approval to act, such as would be conferred in a duly executed resolution of the Board of Directors. If the contracting entity is a general partnership, any partner may validly contract on behalf of the partnership. In a limited partnership, only general partners may be parties to a contract.

Mutual consent. Mutual consent, also known as offer and acceptance and meeting of the minds, requires that a contract involve a clear and definite offer and an intentional, unqualified acceptance of the offer. In effect, the parties must agree to the terms without equivocation. A court may nullify a contract where the acceptance of terms by either party was partial, accidental, or vague.

Valuable consideration. A contract must involve a two-way exchange of valuable consideration as compensation for the other party's performance. The exchange of considerations must be two-way. The contract is not valid or enforceable if just one party provides consideration.

Valuable consideration can be something tangible, such as money, or something a party promises to do or not do. For example, a home builder may promise to build a house for a party as consideration for receiving money from the home buyer. Or, a landowner may agree not to sell a property as consideration for a developer's option money. Also, valuable consideration can be something intangible that a party must give up, such as a homeowner's occupancy of the house in exchange for rent. In effect, consideration is the price one party must pay to obtain performance from the other party.

Valuable consideration may be contrasted with good consideration, or "love and affection," which does not qualify as consideration in a valid contract. Good consideration is something of questionable value, such as a child's love for her mother. Good consideration disqualifies a contract because, while one's love or affection is certainly valuable to the other party, it is not something that is specifically offered in exchange for something else. Good consideration can, however, serve as a nominal consideration in transferring a real property interest as a gift.

In some cases, what is promised as valuable consideration must also be deemed to be sufficient consideration. Grossly insufficient consideration, such as $50,000 for a $2 million property, may invalidate a contract on the grounds that the agreement is a gift rather than a contract. In other cases where there is an extreme imbalance in the considerations exchanged, a contract may be invalidated as a violation of good faith bargaining.

Consideration

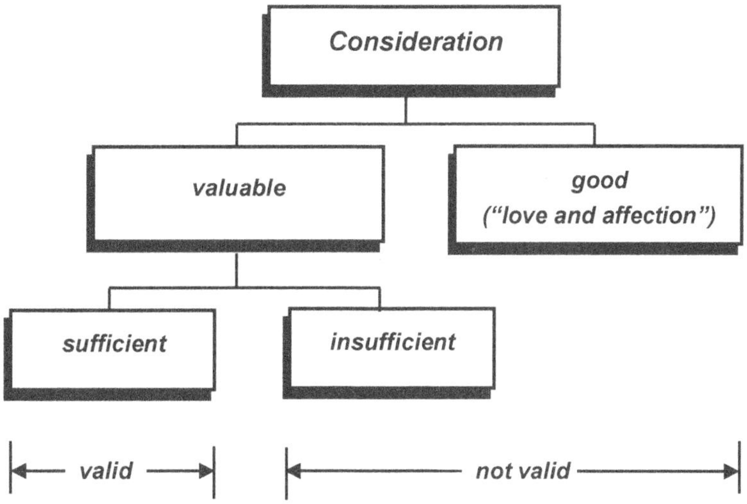

Legal purpose. The content, promise, or intent of a contract must be lawful. A contract that proposes an illegal act is void.

Voluntary, good faith act. The parties must enter into the contract in good faith, as a free and voluntary act. A contract is thus voidable if one party acted under duress, coercion, fraud, or misrepresentation.

For example, if a property seller induces a buyer to purchase a house based on assurances that the roof is new, the buyer may rescind the agreement if the roof turns out to be twenty years old and leaky.

Validity of a conveyance

contract In addition to satisfying the foregoing requirements, a contract that conveys an interest in real estate must:

- be in writing
- contain a legal description of the property
- be signed by one or more of the parties

A lease contract that has a term of one year or less is an exception. Such leases do not have to be in writing to be enforceable.

Enforcement limitations

Certain contracts that fail to meet the validity requirements are voidable if a damaged party takes appropriate action. The enforcement of voidable contracts, however, is limited by statutes of limitation. Certain other valid contracts may not be enforceable due to the statute of frauds.

Statute of limitations. The statute of limitations restricts the time period during which an injured party in a contract has the right to rescind or disaffirm the contract. A party to a voidable contract must act within the statutory period.

Statute of frauds. The statute of frauds requires that certain contracts be in writing to be enforceable. Real estate contracts that convey an interest in real property fall in this category, except that a lease of one year or less may be oral. All other contracts to buy, sell, exchange, or lease interests in real property must be in writing to be enforceable. In addition, listing agreements for a term longer than one year must be in writing.

The statute of frauds concerns the enforceability of a contract, not its validity. Once the parties to a valid oral contract have executed and performed it, even if the contract was unenforceable, a party cannot use the Statute of Frauds to rescind the contract.

For example, a broker and a seller have an oral agreement. Following the terms of the agreement, the broker finds a buyer, and the seller pays the commission. They have now executed the contract, and the seller cannot later compel the broker to return the commission under the Statute of Frauds.

UETA & electronic contracting

Contracting electronically through email and fax greatly facilitates the completion of transactions. Clients, lenders, title agents, inspectors, brokers, and other participants in a transaction can quickly share documentation and information. Electronic contracting is enabled by the Uniform Electronic Transactions Act (UETA) and the Electronic Signatures in Global and National Commerce Act (E-Sign), both federal laws. UETA, which has been incorporated into Florida law, provides that electronic records and signatures are legal and must be accepted. E-Sign makes contracts, records, and signatures legally enforceable, regardless of medium, even where UETA is not accepted.

Classifications of Contracts

Oral vs. written

A contract may be in writing or oral (parol). Certain oral contracts are valid and enforceable; others are not enforceable, even if valid. For example, Florida requires that listing agreements, sales contracts, option contracts, deeds and mortgage instruments, and leases exceeding one year be in writing to be enforceable.

Express vs. implied

An **express contract** is one in which all the terms and covenants of the agreement have been manifestly stated and agreed to by all parties, whether verbally or in writing.

An **implied contract** is an unstated or unintentional agreement that may be deemed to exist when the actions of any of the parties suggest the existence of an agreement.

A common example of an implied contract is an implied agency agreement. In implied agency, an agent who does not have a contract with a buyer performs acts on the buyer's behalf, such as negotiating a price that is less than the listing price. In so doing, the agent may have created an implied contract with the buyer, albeit unintentionally. If the buyer compensates the agent for the negotiating efforts, the existence of an implied agency agreement becomes even less disputable.

Bilateral vs. unilateral

A **bilateral contract** is one in which both parties promise to perform their respective parts of an agreement in exchange for performance by the other party.

An example of a bilateral contract is an exclusive listing: The broker promises to exercise due diligence in efforts to sell a property, and the seller promises to compensate the broker if and when the property sells.

In a **unilateral contract**, only one party promises to do something, provided the other party does something. The latter party is not obligated to perform any act, but the promising party must fulfill the promise if the other party performs.

An option is an example of a unilateral contract: in an option to buy, the party offering the option (optionor) promises to sell the property if the optionee exercises the option. While the potential buyer does not have to buy, the owner must sell if the option is exercised.

Executed vs. executory

An executed contract is one that has been fully performed and fulfilled: neither party bears any further obligation. A completed and expired lease contract is an executed contract: the landlord may repossess the premises, and the tenant has no further obligation to pay rent.

An executory contract is one in which performance is yet to be completed. A sales contract prior to closing is executory: while the parties have agreed to buy and sell, the buyer has yet to pay the seller and the seller has yet to deed the property to the buyer.

Contract Creation

Offer and acceptance

The mutual consent required for a valid contract is reached through the process of offer and acceptance: The offeror proposes contract terms in an offer to the offeree. If the offeree accepts all terms without amendment, the offer becomes a contract. The exact point at which the offer becomes a contract is when the offeree gives the offeror notice of the acceptance.

Offer, Counteroffer and Acceptance

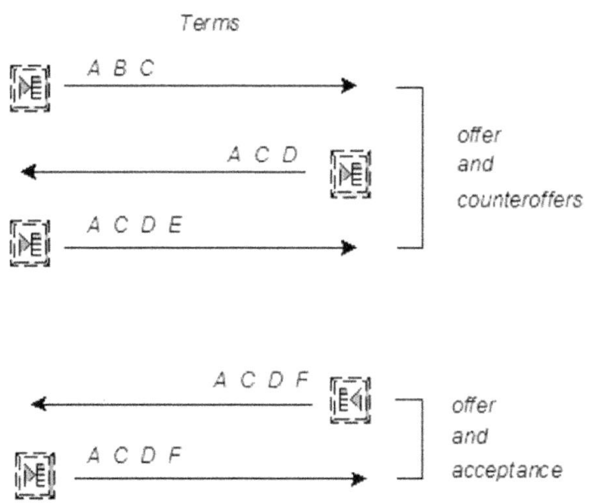

Offer. An offer expresses the offeror's intention to enter into a contract with an offeree to perform the terms of the agreement in exchange for the offeree's performance. In a real estate sale or lease contract, the offer must clearly state all intended terms in writing and be communicated to the offeree.

If an offer includes an expiration date and the phrase "time is of the essence," it expires at the specified time. In the absence of a stated time period, the offeree has a "reasonable" time to accept an offer.

Acceptance. An offer gives the offeree the power to accept. For an acceptance to be valid, the offeree must manifestly and unequivocally accept all terms of the offer without change, and so indicate by signing the offer, preferably with a date of signing. The acceptance must then be communicated to the offeror. If acceptance is communicated by mail, the offer is considered communicated as soon as it is placed in the mail.

Counteroffer

By changing any of the terms of an offer, the offeree creates a counteroffer, and the original offer is void. At this point, the offeree becomes the offeror, and the new offeree gains the right of acceptance. If accepted, the counteroffer becomes a valid contract provided all other requirements are met.

For example, a seller changes the expiration date of a buyer's offer by one day, signs the offer, and returns it to the buyer. The single amendment extinguishes the buyer's offer, and the buyer is no longer bound by any agreement. The seller's amended offer is a counteroffer, giving the buyer the right of acceptance. If the buyer accepts the counteroffer, the counteroffer becomes a binding contract.

Revocation of an offer

An offer may be revoked, or withdrawn, at any time before the offeree has communicated acceptance. The revocation extinguishes the offer and the offeree's right to accept it.

For example, a buyer has offered to purchase a house for the listed price. Three hours later, a family death radically changes the buyer's plans. She immediately calls the seller and revokes the offer, stating she is no longer interested in the house. Since the seller had not communicated acceptance of the offer to the buyer, the offer is legally cancelled.

If the offeree has paid consideration to the offeror to leave an offer open, and the offeror accepts, an option has been created that cancels the offeror's right to revoke the offer over the period of the option.

Termination of an offer

Any of the following actions or circumstances can terminate an offer:

- acceptance: the offeree accepts the offer, converting it to a contract
- rejection: the offeree rejects the offer
- revocation: the offeror withdraws the offer before acceptance
- lapse of time: the offer expires
- counteroffer: the offeree changes the offer
- death or insanity of either party

Assignment of a contract

A real estate contract that is not a personal contract for services can be assigned to another party unless the terms of the agreement specifically prohibit assignment.

Listing agreements, for example, are not assignable because they are personal service agreements between an agent and a principal. Sales contracts, however, are assignable because they involve the purchase of real property rather than personal services.

Contract Termination

Forms of contract termination

Termination of a contract, also called cancellation and discharge, may occur for any of the following causes.

Performance. A contract terminates when fully performed by the parties. It may also terminate for:

- partial performance, if the parties agree
- sufficient performance, if a court determines a party has sufficiently performed the contract, even though not to the full extent of every provision

Infeasibility. An otherwise valid contract can be canceled if it cannot be performed. Certain personal services contracts, for example, depend on the unique capabilities of a single person that cannot be substituted by someone else. If such a person dies or is sufficiently disabled, the contract is cancelable.

Mutual agreement. Parties to a contract can agree to terminate, or renounce, the contract. If the parties wish to create a new contract to replace the cancelled contract, they must comply with the validity requirements for the new contract. Such substitution is called novation.

Cooling-period rescission. Rescission is the act of nullifying a contract. In Florida, parties to certain contracts are allowed a statutory amount of time (usually three days) after entering into a contract, or "cooling period", to rescind the contract without cause. No reason needs to be stated for the cancellation, and the cancelling party incurs no liability for performance.

For example, consider the unsuspecting buyer of a lot in a new resort development. Such buyers are often the targets of hard-sell tactics, which lead to a completed sales contract and a deposit. The statutory cooling period allows the buyer to reconsider the investment in the absence of the persistent salesperson.

Revocation. Revocation is the cancellation of a contract by one party without the other party's consent. For example, a seller may revoke a listing to take the property off the market. While all parties have the power to revoke, they may not have a defensible right to do so. In the absence of justifiable grounds, a revocation may not relieve the revoking party of contract obligations.

For example, a seller who revokes a listing without grounds may be required to pay a commission if the broker found a buyer, or reimburse the broker's marketing expenses if no buyer was found.

Abandonment. Abandonment occurs when parties fail to perform contract obligations. This situation may allow the parties to cancel the contract.

Lapse of time. If a contract contains an expiration provision and a date, it automatically expires on that date.

Invalidity of contract. If a contract is void, it terminates without the need for disaffirmation. A voidable contract can be cancelled by operation of law or by rescission.

Breach of contract

A breach of contract is a failure to perform according to the terms of the agreement. Also called default, a breach of contract gives the damaged party the right to take legal action.

The damaged party may elect the following legal remedies:

- rescission
- forfeiture
- suit for damages
- suit for specific performance

Rescission. A damaged party may rescind the contract. This cancels the contract and returns the parties to their pre-contract position, including the refund of any funds already transferred.

Forfeiture. A forfeiture requires the breaching party to give up something under the terms of the contract. For example, a buyer who defaults on a sales contract may have to forfeit the earnest money deposit.

Suit for damages. A damaged party may sue for money damages in civil court. The suit must be initiated within the time period allowed by the statute of limitations. When a contract states the total amount due to a damaged party in the event of a breach, the compensation is known as **liquidated damages.** If the contract does not specify the amount, the damaged party may sue in court for **unliquidated damages**.

Suit for specific performance. A suit for specific performance seeks to compel the defaulting party to comply with the terms of the contract. Specific performance suits arise when it is difficult to determine damages due to the unique circumstances of the real property in question. The most common instance is a defaulted sale or lease contract in which the buyer or seller wants the court to compel the defaulting party to go through with the transaction, even when the defaulter would prefer to pay a damages award.

Listing Agreements

Foundations in agency law

A listing agreement, the document that puts an agent or broker in business, is a legally enforceable real estate agency agreement between a real estate broker and a client, authorizing the broker to perform a stated service for compensation. The unique characteristic of a listing agreement is that it is governed by both agency law and contract law.

The cornerstones of agency law in the context of a listing agreement are:

- definition of the roles of parties involved
- fiduciary duties of the agent
- agent's scope of authority

Parties. The principal parties to the contract are the listing broker and the client. The client may be a buyer, seller, landlord, or tenant in the proposed transaction. Legally, the broker is the client's agent. The principal party on the other side of the transaction is a customer or a potential customer, called a prospect. A broker or associate who assists the listing broker in finding a customer is an agent of the listing broker and a subagent of the client. A broker who represents the party on the other side of the transaction is an agent of that party, and not an agent of the listing broker.

Fiduciary duties. A listing agreement establishes an agency relationship between agent and client that commits the agent to the full complement of fiduciary duties to the client in fulfilling the agreement.

Scope of authority. Customarily, a listing is a special agency, or limited agency, agreement. Special agency limits the scope of the broker's authority to specific activities, generally those that generate customers and catalyze the transaction. A special agency agreement usually does not authorize a broker to obligate the client to a contract as a principal party unless the agreement expressly grants such authorization or the client has granted power of attorney to the broker. For example, a listing broker may not tell a buyer that the seller will accept an offer regardless of its terms. Telling the offeror that the offer is accepted would be an even more serious breach of the agreement.

Under agency law, a client is liable for actions a broker takes within the scope of authority granted by the listing agreement. A client is not liable for acts of the broker that go beyond the stated or implied scope of authority.

Thus, in the previous example, the seller would not be liable for the broker's statements that the offer would be accepted or had been accepted, because the broker lacked authority to make such statements. A broker who exceeds the scope of authority under the listing agreement risks forfeiting compensation and potentially incurring greater liabilities.

Types of listing agreements

A broker may represent any principal party of a transaction: seller, landlord, buyer, or tenant. An owner listing authorizes a broker to represent an owner or landlord. The three main types of owner listing agreements are the exclusive right-to-sell (or lease), exclusive agency, and open listing. Another type of listing, rarely used today but legal in Florida, is a net listing. The first three forms differ in how they state the conditions under which the broker will be paid. The net listing is a variation on how much the broker will be paid. A listing contract in Florida may be written, oral, or implied. If the term is longer than one year, it must be written.

Exclusive right-to-sell (or -lease). The exclusive right-to-sell, also called exclusive authorization-to-sell and, simply, the exclusive, is the most widely used owner agreement. Under the terms of this listing, a seller contracts exclusively with a single broker to procure a buyer or effect a sale transaction. If a buyer is procured during the listing period, the broker is entitled to a commission, regardless of who is the procuring cause. Thus, if anyone, the owner or another broker, sells the property, the owner must pay the listing broker the contracted commission.

The exclusive right-to-lease is a similar contract for a leasing transaction. Under the terms of this listing, the owner or landlord must pay the listing broker a commission if anyone procures a tenant for the named premises.

The exclusive listing gives the listing broker the greatest assurance of receiving compensation for marketing efforts.

An exclusive right-to-sell listing must have an expiration date if it is in writing.

Exclusive agency. An exclusive agency listing authorizes a single broker to sell the property and earn a commission, while giving the owner the right to sell the property without the broker's assistance, in which case no commission is owed. Thus, if any party other than the owner is procuring cause in a completed sale of the property, including another broker, the contracted broker has earned the commission. This arrangement may also be used in a leasing transaction: if any party other than the owner procures the tenant, the owner must compensate the listing broker.

A written exclusive agency listing must have an expiration date.

Open listing. An open listing is a *non-exclusive* authorization to sell or lease a property. The owner may offer such agreements to any number of brokers in the marketplace. With an open listing, the broker who is the first to perform under the listing terms is the sole party entitled to a commission. Performance usually consists of being the procuring cause in the finding of a ready, willing, and able customer. If the transaction occurs without a procuring broker, no commissions are payable.

Open listings are rare in residential brokerage. Brokers generally shy away from them because they offer no assurance of compensation for marketing efforts. In addition, open listings cause commission disputes. To avoid such disputes, a broker must register prospects with the owner to provide evidence of procuring cause if a transaction results.

A **buyer agency** or **tenant representation agreement** authorizes a broker to represent a buyer or tenant. The most commonly used form is an exclusive right-to-represent agreement, the equivalent of an exclusive right-to-sell. However, exclusive agency and open types of agreement may also be used to secure a relationship on this side of a transaction.

Buyer and tenant agency agreements create a fiduciary relationship with the buyer or tenant, just as seller listings create a fiduciary relationship with the seller. Generally, buyer and tenant representation agreements are subject to the same laws and regulations as those applying to owner listings. Thus:

> A representation agreement may be an exclusive, exclusive agency, or open listing. As with owner listings, the most widely used agreement is the exclusive. In this arrangement, the buyer agrees to work only with the buyer representative in procuring a property.

At the formation of the relationship, the buyer's agent has the duty to explain how buyer or tenant agency relationships work. This culminates in a signed agreement in which the principal understands and accepts these circumstances. During the listing term, the buyer or tenant agent's principal duties are to diligently locate a property that meets the principal's requirements.

Net listing. A net listing is one in which an owner sets a minimum acceptable amount to be received from the transaction and allows the broker to keep any amount received in excess as a commission, provided the broker has earned a commission under the other terms of the agreement. The owner's "net" may or may not account for closing costs.

For example, a seller requires $750,000 for a property. A broker sells the property for $830,000 and receives the difference of $80,000 in commission.

Net listings are generally regarded as unprofessional today. The argument against the net listing is that it creates a conflict of interest for the broker. It is in the broker's interest to encourage the owner to list at the lowest acceptable price, regardless of market value. Thus, the agent violates fiduciary duty by failing to place the client's interests above those of the agent.

Net listings are legal in Florida as long as the broker does not misrepresent the value of the property to the seller to the broker's advantage. For example, if a property's likely market value is $300,000, it would be a violation for a broker to lead the seller to believe the value is $275,000 for the purpose of retaining any selling amount over $275,000 instead of any selling amount over $300,000. To prevent this misrepresentation, the seller and the broker work together to determine a listing price. Then the broker retains any selling amount above the agreed-upon listing price minus any costs.

Listing			
Exclusive Right	$	Broker	IF customer is procured
Exclusive Agency	$	Broker	IF customer is procured and client does not procure
Open	$	Broker	IF broker procures customer
Net	$	Broker	IF customer is due commission, receives proceeds over seller's minimum
"Multiple Listing"	$	Broker	IF authority to enter listing in multiple listing service

Types of Listing

Transaction broker agreement. Recall from an earlier section that, in a transaction-broker relationship in Florida, the broker does not represent either party in a fiduciary capacity or as a single agent. Neither party has the right of the licensee's undivided loyalty. The transaction broker relationship is between the brokerage and the client. Florida law presumes that all licensees are operating as transaction brokers unless the broker and the customer have entered into a written single-agent or nonrepresentation agreement.

Multiple listing. A multiple listing is not a distinct listing contract but rather a provision in an exclusive listing authorizing the broker to publish the listing on a multiple listing service.

A multiple listing service (MLS) is an organization of member brokers who agree to cooperate in the sale of properties listed by other brokers. Members of the service agree to enter their exclusive listings into the listing distribution network so that every member is promptly informed of new listings as they come on the market. Historically, a listing broker also used the MLS to offer a portion of the commission to the broker who produced the buyer. As a result of the 2024 National Association of Realtors (NAR) antitrust settlement, whose practice changes took effect on August 17, 2024, offers of compensation to a cooperating broker may no longer be communicated through the MLS. Brokers continue to cooperate through the service to market and locate properties, but any compensation that a seller or listing broker chooses to offer a cooperating broker is now negotiated separately, outside the MLS.

Most consumers expect brokers to use a multiple listing service to market and locate properties. Working with an MLS, however, requires that the listing or representation agreement contain the necessary provisions to allow the licensee to place the listing into a multiple listing service and to ensure that all parties understand and agree to the relevant policies and procedures. The agreement must also state conspicuously that broker compensation is not set by law and is fully negotiable. In addition, an MLS participant who works with a buyer must enter into a written buyer brokerage agreement, disclosing how the licensee will be compensated, before showing the buyer a property.

The listing agreement used by members of a multiple listing service discloses relevant procedures and policies so that all principal parties to the agreement are aware of the pooling of the listing. A broker who works on a transaction listed in the MLS has all the duties and responsibilities inherent in agency law as the client's fiduciary agent. The settlement did not change these duties; the listing agreement continues to set forth the specific duties owed to the client.

Exclusive right to sell listing clauses

A written listing, particularly an exclusive, is a formal contract that includes the entirety of all agreements between the parties. If an agreement is left out, it is assumed not to exist. An included agreement is assumed to exist and is generally enforceable. If a written agreement contains mistakes, it is probably not valid or enforceable. For these reasons, a listing agreement needs to be accurate, error-free, and complete.

Different agreement types may include different required clauses. Generally, a written listing agreement requires at least the following information:

- names of all owners
- address or legal description of the listed property
- listing price
- expiration date
- commission terms
- authority granted

The following clause descriptions are found in a typical exclusive right-to-sell listing agreement.

Parties and authorization. The agreement should name all legal property owners or their duly authorized representatives as the client party. It must also name the broker.

An authorization clause sets forth the scope of the broker's authority, i.e., the type of listing. Note that the phrase "right-to-sell" is a misnomer. A broker cannot legally sell the property without proper power of attorney. The usual right is to effect a sale or find a buyer.

Real Property. A written listing agreement must include a property description. The real property description may include an address.

Fixtures. Typical agreements list what fixtures are included in the sale specifically, and "all other things attached or affixed to the property" generally. The seller must then enter which items are excluded from the sale.

Personal Property. The listing agreement should include all personal property to be included in the transaction and the listing price.

Listing price. A clause usually sets forth the gross price for the property and, if seller financing or assumption of the seller's loan is involved, the financing terms the owner will accept.

The listing price is the seller's asking price for the property. This may or may not be the price the seller ultimately accepts. The full listing price does not have to be obtained for the broker to earn a commission. The listing price clause may also state the seller's agreement to pay customary closing costs.

Listing term. In Florida, written listings must have a specific ending date. Failure to include a termination date in a written listing is grounds for revoking the real estate license. Any provision for renewal of the listing term should be very specific. Automatic renewals are illegal.

To protect the broker, some listings include a provision to extend the listing period if an expiration occurs while a sale contract is pending.

Agent's duties. This clause specifies the broker's responsibilities and authority to carry out certain activities. These typically include marketing activities, multiple listing service activities, property access and showings, authority to allow other parties access, permission to inspect existing mortgage financing documents, and authority to accept deposits. Commonly, the clause specifically bars the broker from executing any contract on behalf of the owner.

Broker's compensation. A clause will specify the broker's fee and the conditions that must be met for the fee to be earned. For instance, it may state that a commission is earned if a buyer is procured, a contract is executed, or the seller voluntarily transfers the property for any price during the listing period.

A fee clause usually provides for remedies in the event of default by the buyer or seller. In effect, if the seller breaches the listing without grounds after a buyer has been procured, the commission is payable. If the owner cannot sell the property for reasons beyond the owner's control, the owner is not liable for a commission. If the buyer breaches a sale contract, the seller typically claims the buyer's earnest money deposit as liquidated damages.

Procuring cause. Procuring cause is the compensation concept that identifies who has earned a commission or compensation as a result of his or her efforts in a given transaction. Specifically, procuring cause is attributable to the party who sets into motion a chain of events that leads uninterruptedly to a sale. Under the terms of certain listings, commissions are not generally payable unless the listing agent can claim to be the procuring cause.

Protection period. Many listings include a protection clause stating that, for a certain period after expiration, the owner is liable for the commission if the property sells to a party that the broker procured, unless the seller has since listed the property with another broker.

Multiple listing. This provision obtains the seller's consent to place the listing in a multiple listing service and authorizes the dissemination of information about the listing to members.

Cooperation with other agents. This clause requires the seller to agree or refuse to cooperate with subagents or buyer agents in selling the property, under what terms, and whether the seller agrees to compensate these parties. Recent agreements stipulate that subagents and buyer agents must disclose their relationships to the buyer upon initial contact and subsequently in writing. There may also be a warning to the seller not to disclose confidential information to a buyer broker insofar as this agent is required to disclose all relevant information to the buyer.

Nondiscrimination. Most exclusive listings contain an affirmation that the agent will conduct all affairs in compliance with state and federal fair housing and nondiscrimination laws.

Other disclosures by agent. In addition to agency, other disclosures may be included to cover any direct or indirect interest the broker has in the transaction and any special compensation the broker may be receiving from other parties connected to the transaction.

Seller's representations and promises. In this clause, the owner represents that he or she owns the property as stated in the listing and is legally capable of delivering a fee simple, marketable title. The clause may further require the owner to warrant that he or she

- is not represented by another party and will not list the property elsewhere during the listing period
- will not lease the property during the listing period without approval
- agrees to provide necessary information
- will refer all prospects directly to the broker without prior direct negotiation
- has reviewed a sample "Offer to Purchase and Sell" contract
- will make the property presentable and available for showing at reasonable times upon notice by agent

Seller's property condition disclosure. The listing form may require the seller to disclose the property's condition to prospective buyers. Florida law may allow buyers to cancel a sale contract if they have not received the seller's property condition disclosure before closing, occupancy, or other deadline. In addition, the listing may include among the seller's duties the requirement to complete and provide the agent with a Lead Paint Hazard addendum. A copy of the required notice to buyers may be attached to the listing agreement.

Seller's title and deed. A provision usually requires the owner to promise to deliver good and marketable title, title insurance, and to convey the property using a general warranty deed to a buyer. Without this covenant, the broker has no assurance that a transaction will occur, nor that he or she will be paid for procuring a buyer.

Flood hazard insurance. This clause requires the seller to disclose whether he or she is required to or presently maintains flood insurance on the property.

Limitation of liability. There is often a clause requiring the owner to indemnify the broker against liability arising from a casualty, loss, or the owner's misrepresentation during the listing period. In practice, liability and indemnification clauses do not necessarily absolve a broker from liability.

Escrow authorization. The seller authorizes escrow officers to disburse earned commission funds to the broker upon the broker's instructions.

IRS requirements; alien seller withholding. A clause may state that the seller will comply with IRS requirements for providing tax-related information. This ensures that an alien seller understands that the buyer must withhold a percentage of the sale price for the IRS.

Other listing provisions. An exclusive listing might also provide for:

- mediation: in the event of a dispute, the owner agrees to arbitrate differences before filing a lawsuit
- attorney fees: the losing party in a lawsuit must pay court costs and attorney fees
- acknowledgment: the owner acknowledges reading and understanding the agreement
- entire agreement: the listing cannot be changed without written agreement; the listing sets forth all agreements made
- binding effect: listing is binding and enforceable
- saving clause: if a portion of the agreement is invalid or unenforceable, the balance of the agreement remains valid as permitted by law

Notices to owner. Some listing agreements include notices to the seller concerning:

- fee negotiability: The broker's fee is the result of negotiations with the seller.
- fair housing laws: The broker and seller must comply with discrimination laws.
- keyboxes; security: The seller should take prudent measures to protect personal property and remove dangerous items that could cause injury.
- legal advice disclaimer: The broker cannot give legal advice.

Signatures. All owners and the broker must sign the listing and indicate the date of signing.

Exclusive buyer agency clauses

The exclusive buyer agency agreement is very similar to the exclusive right-to-sell agreement, the only significant differences being the agent's objectives and the fact that the principal is the buyer rather than the seller. The notable exception is how the agent is paid, as previously discussed.

The clauses, which are virtually identical to the exclusive right-to-sell, are:

- the identity of the principal and the agent's authorized activity
- the description of the property desired in terms of location, price, size, etc.
- the term of the agreement and its automatic termination
- the buyer's agreement to work exclusively through the agent
- the agent's duties to locate a suitable property according to the buyer's specifications
- the nondiscrimination clause
- signatures of the parties

The following clauses distinguish the buyer agency agreement from the exclusive right-to-sell agreement.

Buyer's representation of exclusivity. Here, the buyer affirms that he or she is not represented by another agent. In addition, the buyer acknowledges an understanding of the agency relationship.

Agent compensation. This clause sets forth how the agent is to be paid, whether by retainer or commission, who is to pay the commission, and what the buyer owes the agent in the event the seller does not participate in the agent's compensation. Second, the clause establishes the circumstances under which the agent has earned the commission. This includes finding a property during the agreement term or the buyer contracting to buy a property shown by the agent within a stipulated period of time following expiration. In addition, the clause provides that the agent will be paid if the buyer defaults on a sale contract.

Other buyers acknowledged. In this provision, the buyer acknowledges that the agent is working with other buyers who may be in competition for any property the buyer is shown by the agent.

Sales Contracts

Binding and enforceable. A real estate sale contract is a binding and enforceable agreement in which a buyer (the vendee) agrees to buy an identified parcel of real estate, and a seller (the vendor) agrees to sell it under certain terms and conditions. It is the document that is at the center of the transaction.

Three stages of real estate transfer. The conventional transfer of real estate ownership takes place in three stages. First, there is the negotiating period, during which buyers and sellers exchange offers to agree on all transfer terms that will appear in the sale contract. Second, once both parties have accepted all terms, the offer becomes a binding sale contract, and the transaction enters the pre-closing stage, during which each party makes arrangements to complete the sale according to the sale contract's terms. Third is the closing of the transaction, when the seller deeds title to the buyer, the buyer pays the purchase price, and all necessary documents are completed. At this stage, the sale contract has served its purpose and terminates.

Other names for the sale contract are *agreement of sale, contract for purchase, contract of purchase and sale, and earnest money contract.*

Legal characteristics

Executory contract. A sale contract is executory: the signatories have yet to perform their respective obligations and promises. Upon closing, the sale contract is fully performed and no longer exists as a binding agreement.

Signatures. All property owners should sign the sale contract. If the sellers are married, both spouses should sign to ensure they release their homestead, dower, and curtesy rights to the buyer at closing. Failure to do so does not invalidate the contract but can lead to encumbered title and legal disputes.

Enforceability criteria. To be enforceable, a sale contract must:

- be validly created (mutual consent, consideration, legal purpose, competent parties, voluntary act)
- be in writing
- identify the principal parties
- clearly identify the property, preferably by legal description
- contain a purchase price
- be signed by the principal parties

Written vs. oral form. A contract for the sale of real estate is enforceable only if it is in writing. Neither a buyer nor a seller can sue to compel the other to comply with an oral contract of sale, even if the contract is valid.

Assignment. Either party to a sale transaction may assign the sale contract to another party, subject to the provisions and conditions of the agreement.

Who may complete ? A broker or agent may assist the buyer and seller in completing an offer to purchase, provided the broker represents the client faithfully and does not charge a separate fee for the assistance. It is advisable for a broker to use a standard contract form promulgated by a state agency or real estate board, as such forms contain generally accepted language. This relieves the broker of the risk of creating new contract language that could be construed as the practice of law, for which the broker is not licensed.

Contract creation

Offer and acceptance. Full and unequivocal acceptance of an offer creates a contract of sale. Offer and acceptance may come from either buyer or seller. The offeree must accept the offer without making any changes whatsoever. A change terminates the offer and creates a new offer, or counteroffer. An offeror may revoke an offer for any reason prior to communication of acceptance by the offeree.

Equitable title. A sale contract gives the buyer an interest in the property that is called equitable title, or ownership in equity. If the seller defaults and the buyer can show good faith performance, the buyer can sue for specific performance, that is, to compel the seller to transfer legal title upon payment of the contract price.

Earnest money escrow

The buyer's earnest money deposit fulfills the consideration requirements for a valid sale contract. In addition, it provides the seller with potential compensation for damages if the buyer fails to perform. The amount of the deposit varies according to local custom. It should be noted that the earnest money deposit is not the only form of consideration that satisfies the requirement.

The sale contract provides the escrow instructions for handling and disbursing escrow funds. The earnest money is placed in a third-party trust account or escrow. A licensed escrow agent employed by a title company, financial institution, or brokerage company usually manages the escrow. An individual broker may also serve as the escrow agent.

The escrow holder acts as an impartial fiduciary for the buyer and seller. If the buyer performs under the sale contract, the deposit is applied to the purchase price.

Strict rules govern the handling of earnest money deposits, particularly when a broker serves as the escrow agent. For example, Florida law specifies when the broker must deposit the funds, how to account for them, and how to keep them separate from the broker's own funds.

Contract contingencies

A sale contract often includes contingencies. A contingency is a condition that must be met before the contract is enforceable.

The most common contingency concerns financing. A buyer makes an offer contingent on securing financing for the property on certain terms by a certain date. If the buyer is unable to secure the specified loan commitment by the deadline, the buyer may cancel the contract and recover the deposit. An appropriate and timely loan commitment eliminates the contingency, and the buyer must proceed with the purchase.

It is possible for both buyers and sellers to abuse contingencies in order to leave themselves a convenient way to cancel without defaulting. To avoid problems, the statement of a contingency should

- be explicit and clear
- have an expiration date
- expressly require diligence in the effort to fulfill the requirement

A contingency that is too broad, vague, or excessive in duration may invalidate the entire contract on the grounds of insufficiency of mutual agreement.

Restrictive covenants

Restrictive covenants are private limitations on the use of land, created in a deed or in a recorded declaration of covenants, conditions, and restrictions (CC&Rs) for a subdivision or association. They may limit such things as architectural style, building setbacks, fencing, signage, or commercial use, and they run with the land, binding later owners. Because they are private and separate from public zoning, a buyer should review the recorded covenants before closing, and the sale contract should make the sale subject to them.

Default

A sale contract is bilateral, since both parties promise to perform. As a result, either party may default by failing to perform. Note that a party's failure to meet a contingency does not constitute default, but rather entitles the parties to cancel the contract.

Buyer default. If a buyer fails to perform under the terms of a sale contract, the breach entitles the seller to seek damages in court. In most cases, the contract itself stipulates the seller's remedies. The usual remedy is forfeiture of the buyer's deposit as liquidated damages, provided the deposit is not grossly in excess of the seller's actual damages. It is also customary for the seller and broker to share the liquidated damages. The broker may not, however, receive liquidated damages in excess of the commission that would have been earned on the full listing price.

If the contract does not provide for liquidated damages, the seller may sue for damages, cancellation, or specific performance.

Seller default. If a seller defaults, the buyer may sue for specific performance, damages, or cancellation.

Division of a forfeited deposit. When a buyer defaults and the seller retains the earnest money as liquidated damages, the listing agreement governs how that forfeited deposit is divided. Under the typical Florida arrangement, the seller and the listing broker split the forfeited deposit equally, except that the broker's share may not exceed the commission the broker would have earned had the sale closed. Any excess goes to the seller.

Contract provisions

Sales contracts can vary significantly in length and detail. They also vary according to the type of sale transaction they describe. Multiple forms of the sales contract exist:

- Residential Contract of Sale
- Commercial Contract of Sale
- Foreclosure Contract of Sale
- Contract of Sale for New Construction
- Contract of Sale for Land
- Exchange Agreement

As the most common sales transaction is a residential sale, a Residential Contract of Sale is the type with which a licensee should first become familiar. A typical residential sale contract contains provisions of the following kind.

Parties, consideration, and property. One or more clauses will identify the parties, the property, and the basic consideration: the sale of the property in exchange for a purchase price.

There must be at least two parties to a sale contract: one cannot convey property to oneself. All parties must be identified, be of legal age, and have the capacity to contract.

The property clause also identifies fixtures and personal property included in the sale. Unless expressly excluded, items commonly construed as fixtures are included in the sale. Similarly, items commonly considered personal property are not included unless expressly included.

Legal description. A legal description must be sufficient for a competent surveyor to identify the property.

Price and terms. A clause states the final price and details how the purchase will occur. Of particular interest to the seller is the buyer's down payment, since the greater the buyer's equity, the more likely the buyer is to secure financing. In addition, a large deposit represents a buyer's commitment to complete the sale.

If seller financing is involved, the sale contract sets forth the terms of the arrangement: the amount and type of loan, the rate and term, and how the loan will be paid off.

It is important for all parties to verify that the buyer's earnest money deposit, down payment, loan proceeds, and other promised funds together equal the purchase price stated in the contract.

Loan approval. A financing contingency clause states the conditions under which the buyer can cancel the contract without default and receive a refund of the earnest money. If the buyer cannot secure the stated financing by the deadline, the parties may agree to extend the contingency by signing next to the changed dates.

Earnest money deposit. A clause specifies how the buyer will pay the earnest money. It may allow the buyer to pay it in installments. Such an option enables a buyer to hold on to the property briefly while obtaining the additional deposit funds. For example, a buyer who wants to buy a house makes an initial deposit of $200, followed in twenty-four hours by an additional $2,000. The sale contract includes the seller's acknowledgment of receipt of the deposit.

Escrow. An escrow clause provides for the custody and disbursement of the earnest money deposit and releases the escrow agent from certain liabilities in the performance of escrow duties.

Closing and possession dates. The contract states when title will transfer, as well as when the buyer will take physical possession. Customarily, possession occurs on the date when the deed is recorded, unless the buyer has agreed to other arrangements.

The closing clause generally describes what must take place at closing to avoid default. A seller must provide clear and marketable title. A buyer must produce purchase funds. Failure to complete any pre-closing requirements stated in the sale contract is a default and grounds for the aggrieved party to seek recourse.

Conveyed interest; type of deed. One or more provisions will state what type of deed the seller will use to convey the property, and what conditions the deed will be subject to. Common "subject to" conditions include easements, association memberships, encumbrances, mortgages, liens, and special assessments. Typically, the seller conveys a fee simple interest by means of a general warranty deed.

Title evidence. The seller covenants to produce the best possible evidence of property ownership. This is commonly in the form of title insurance.

Closing costs. The contract identifies the closing costs each party will pay. Customarily, the seller pays title and property-related costs, and the buyer pays financing-related costs. Annual costs such as taxes and insurance are prorated between the parties. Note that who pays any particular closing cost is negotiable.

Damage and destruction. A clause stipulates the obligations of the parties in case the property is damaged or destroyed. The parties may negotiate alternatives, including the seller's obligation to repair, the buyer's obligation to buy if repairs are made, and the option for either party to cancel.

Default. A default clause identifies remedies for default. Generally, a buyer may sue for damages, specific performance, or cancellation. A seller may do likewise or claim the earnest money as liquidated damages.

Broker's representation and commission. The broker discloses the applicable agency relationships in the transaction and identifies the party responsible for paying the brokerage commission.

Seller's representations. The seller warrants that there will be no liens on the property that cannot be settled and extinguished at closing. In addition, the seller warrants that all representations are true; if they are found to be otherwise, the buyer may cancel the contract and reclaim the deposit.

A sales contract may include numerous additional clauses, depending on the complexity of the transaction. The following are some common additional provisions.

Inspections. The parties agree to inspections and remedial action based on findings.

Owner's association disclosure. The seller discloses the existence of an association and the obligations it imposes.

Survey. The parties agree to a survey to satisfy financing requirements.

Environmental hazards. The seller notifies the buyer that there may be hazards that could affect the use and value of the property.

Compliance with laws. The seller warrants that there are no undisclosed building code or zoning violations.

Due-on-sale clause. The parties state their understanding that loans that survive the closing may be called due by the lender. Both parties agree to hold the other party harmless for the consequences of an acceleration.

Seller financing disclosure. The parties agree to comply with applicable state and local disclosure laws concerning seller financing.

Rental property; tenants' rights. The buyer acknowledges the rights of tenants following closing.

FHA or VA financing condition. A contingency allows the buyer to cancel the contract if the price exceeds the FHA or VA estimates of the property's value.

Flood plain; flood insurance. Seller discloses that the property is in a floodplain and that the buyer must carry flood insurance if the buyer uses certain lenders for financing.

Condominium assessments. Seller discloses assessments the owner must pay.

Foreign seller withholding. The seller acknowledges that the buyer must withhold 15% of the purchase price at closing if the seller is a foreign person or entity and forward the withheld amount to the Internal Revenue Service. Certain limitations and exemptions apply.

Tax-deferred exchange. For income properties only, the buyer and seller disclose their intentions to participate in an exchange and agree to cooperate in completing necessary procedures.

Merger of agreements. Buyer and seller state that there are no other agreements

between the parties that are not expressed in the contract.

Notices. The parties agree on how they will give notice to each other and what they will consider to be delivery of notice.

Time is of the essence. The parties agree that they can amend dates and deadlines only if they both give written approval.

Fax transmission. The parties agree to accept facsimile transmission of the offer, provided receipt is acknowledged and original copies of the contract are subsequently delivered.

Survival. The parties remain liable for the truthfulness of their representations and warranties after the closing.

Dispute resolution. The parties agree to resolve disputes through arbitration rather than court proceedings.

C.L.U.E. Report. CLUE (Comprehensive Loss Underwriting Exchange) is a claims history database used by insurance companies in underwriting or rating insurance policies. A CLUE Home Seller's Disclosure Report shows a five-year insurance loss history for a specific property. Among other things, it describes the types of any losses and the amounts paid. Many home buyers now require sellers to provide a CLUE Report (which only the property owner or an insurer can order) as a contingency appended to the purchase offer. A report showing a loss from water damage and mold, for instance, might lead a buyer to decide against making an offer because of the potential difficulty of obtaining insurance. A report showing no insurance loss within the previous five years, on the other hand, is an indication that the availability and pricing of homeowner's insurance will not present an obstacle to the purchase transaction, and also that the property has not experienced significant damage or repair during that time period.

Addenda. Addenda to the sale contract become binding components of the overall agreement. The most common addendum is the seller's property condition disclosure. The following are examples of other potential addenda:

- agency disclosure
- asbestos / hazardous materials
- liquidated damages
- radon disclosure
- flood plain disclosure
- tenant's lease

Required disclosures

To ensure that a seller complies with all Florida disclosure requirements when selling a property, Florida Realtors® provides the Sellers Real Property Disclosure form. The form allows the buyer to evaluate the property in detail prior to signing a purchase contract. The following are disclosures required by Florida laws:

Radon. This is the easiest hazard to detect and mitigate. It is an odorless, colorless, tasteless, and radioactive gas that is created in the ground where uranium and radium exist. Prolonged exposure to radon can cause lung cancer. It can enter the home through any cracks, gaps, or cavities, including crawl spaces and openings around pipes. A radon test can easily detect it, so home inspections should include this test.

Florida statute requires real estate professionals to disclose the dangers of radon gas in writing and include the following required language:

> RADON GAS: Radon is a naturally occurring radioactive gas that, when it has accumulated in a building in sufficient quantities, may present health risks to persons who are exposed to it over time. Levels of radon that exceed federal and state guidelines have been found in buildings in Florida. Additional information regarding radon and radon testing may be obtained from your county health department.

Energy efficiency disclosure. The Florida Building Energy-Efficiency Rating Act establishes a statewide, uniform energy-efficiency rating system for new and existing residential, public, and commercial buildings. The Act requires sellers to provide an information brochure to the buyer before or at the time the buyer executes a purchase contract.

The brochure lets the buyer know there is an option for an energy-efficiency rating on the building and includes information about the class of the building as well as how to analyze the building's energy-efficiency rating, methods for improving the building's rating, and a notice to residential buyers that the rating may qualify them for an energy-efficient mortgage from a lender.

Lead-based paint. This hazard cannot be absorbed through the skin, but it becomes dangerous when it is ingested or inhaled. It can be found in most homes built before 1978 and may be present in the air, drinking water, food, contaminated soil, deteriorating paint, and paint dust. Children are particularly susceptible because they may ingest paint chips, allowing lead to enter their bloodstream. Homebuyers and renters must receive the EPA-HUD-US Consumer Product Safety Commission's booklet, "Protect Your Family from Lead in Your Home," and must be informed if lead-based paint is present in the home. Buyers may have a risk assessment performed prior to purchasing the home.

Homeowners' association. Florida law requires owners of real property subject to a homeowners association to disclose this fact to potential purchasers before executing a contract. The form of the disclosure must be substantially in the form identified in the statute. The statute mandates disclosure of mandatory HOA membership and the associated assessments and fees. Failure to provide this disclosure can result in the sale being voided.

A typical HOA disclosure package also includes

- declarations
- articles of incorporation
- bylaws
- articles of organization
- operating agreements
- rules and regulations
- party wall agreements
- minutes of annual owners' meeting
- minutes of directors' or managers' meetings
- financial documents: balance sheet, income and expenditures, budget, reserve study, unpaid assessments, audit report, list of fees and charges
- list of insurance policies
- list of assessments by unit type

The seller is responsible for making the disclosures, but the buyer must exercise due diligence in reading and understanding them. The agent's responsibility is to make sure the disclosures are made.

Homeowners' association reforms. The 2024 Legislature substantially amended the Homeowners' Association Act (Chapter 720). Among the changes a licensee should know:

- directors and community association managers of many associations must now complete educational requirements
- associations must follow stricter financial-reporting and recordkeeping rules, and an association of 100 or more parcels must post its governing documents and other records on a website or make them available through an application
- fining and suspension procedures are tighter, requiring notice and a hearing before an independent committee
- homeowners gained new protections, for example regarding the parking of personal and work vehicles, garbage containers, holiday decorations, and vegetable gardens or clotheslines not visible from the front of the property
- certain misconduct by officers, directors, or managers, such as accepting kickbacks or concealing records, can now be a criminal offense

Separate 2024 laws require associations to give members copies of the rules and covenants and to adopt hurricane-protection specifications, which the association may not unreasonably deny. These reforms increase the governance and transparency duties of an association, which a buyer will want to evaluate when reviewing association records before purchase.

Condominium disclosures. Florida law regulates condominium disclosures as well, requiring that sellers provide specific condominium documents to buyers:

- Declaration of Condominium
- Articles of Incorporation
- Bylaws

- most recent financial information
- frequently asked questions and answers sheet

The buyer has a 3-day statutory right of rescission upon receipt of the required documents.

Condominium building-safety disclosures. After the 2021 collapse of the Champlain Towers South condominium in Surfside, the Legislature enacted a series of building-safety reforms, beginning with Senate Bill 4-D in 2022, that affect the sale of older condominium and cooperative units. Two requirements are central.

Milestone inspection. A condominium or cooperative building that is three or more habitable stories in height must undergo a milestone structural inspection by a licensed engineer or architect when it reaches 30 years of age, or 25 years if it is within three miles of the coast and the local enforcement agency requires it, and every 10 years after that. The first phase is a visual inspection; a second, more detailed phase is required if substantial structural deterioration is found.

Structural Integrity Reserve Study (SIRS). The same buildings must complete a SIRS at least every 10 years. The study determines how much the association must reserve to maintain major components such as the roof, load-bearing walls, fireproofing, plumbing, electrical systems, waterproofing, exterior painting, and windows. Under the reforms, the association may no longer vote to waive or reduce reserves for these structural components, a significant change from prior law.

Because these documents reveal the physical and financial condition of the building, a buyer of a resale unit should receive the milestone inspection report and the SIRS along with the other condominium documents. A licensee should be prepared to explain that older coastal buildings may face large reserve contributions or special assessments as a result of these requirements, which can affect both affordability and insurability.

Flood insurance. The Natural Hazards Disclosure law requires sellers to disclose whether the property is located in a flood zone and whether flood insurance is required. While there is no mandated language for the disclosure, it should notify the buyer that a mortgage lender may require flood insurance and that the National Flood Insurance Program provides flood insurance at premiums based on the risk of flooding at the property's location. It should also state that the buyer should not rely on the premiums paid by the seller as an indication of the premiums the buyer will pay.

Flood disclosure. Effective October 1, 2024, Section 689.302, Florida Statutes, requires the seller of residential real property to give the buyer a separate written FLOOD DISCLOSURE at or before the time the sales contract is signed. This requirement is in addition to the flood-zone and flood-insurance notices described above. On the form, the seller must disclose whether the seller has ever filed a flood-damage insurance claim on the property, including a claim with the National Flood Insurance Program, and whether the seller has ever received federal flood assistance, such as FEMA disaster assistance, for the property. The form also carries a disclaimer reminding the buyer that a standard homeowner's policy generally does not cover flood loss and that the buyer should consider obtaining separate flood insurance. The statute defines flooding broadly to include the overflow of inland or tidal waters, the rapid accumulation of runoff or surface water from any source, and sustained standing water caused by rainfall. Because the disclosure must be delivered before the contract is executed, the licensee should make sure the seller completes and provides the form early in the transaction. Like the Johnson v. Davis duty, this statute is another narrowing of Florida's traditional caveat emptor rule for residential sales.

Property tax. Florida Statute 689.261 requires the inclusion of a property tax disclosure summary with the standard disclosure form, either inserted into the contract or provided as a separate document. Statute mandates the language:

> *Buyers should not rely on the seller's current property taxes as the amount of property taxes that the buyer may be obligated to pay in the year subsequent to purchase. A change of ownership or property improvements triggers reassessments of the property that could result in higher property taxes. If you have any questions concerning valuation, contact the county property appraiser's office for information.*

Building code violation. In Florida, if a property owner has been cited for a code violation and sells the property before the citation is settled in court, the owner must disclose the citation in writing to the buyer and provide the buyer a copy of all related materials, notify the new owner of the requirement to comply with the code, and notify the code enforcement official of the property transfer.

Known hazardous substances on the property. Florida requires the seller to disclose any known environmental contamination or hazards on the property, such as an underground fuel or heating oil tank that is known to have leaked.

Transfer Disclosure Statement (TDS) – Florida law requires sellers to provide buyers a written statement disclosing items such as appliances, structural defects and modifications, possible easements, certain neighborhood problems, and other material facts that may impact the buyer's decision to close the transaction.

Inundation zones. If the property is near and below a dam, the seller should disclose that it is subject to potential flooding in the event of a dam failure.

Very high fire hazard severity zones. A Florida seller must also disclose whether the property is in an area where property owners may be required to perform specific fire-prevention maintenance.

Wildland fire areas. The seller must disclose whether the property is in an area where the state is responsible for fire suppression.

Coastal property. If the property is located near the coast, Florida statute requires disclosure of potential coastal erosion and that the property is subject to federal, state, and local construction limitations. An affidavit or survey must be provided indicating the location of the coastal construction control line.

Community Development District disclosure. Florida statute requires that each contract for the initial sale of a parcel of land or a residential unit within a community development district include the following disclosure immediately above the buyer's signature in a boldface type larger and more conspicuous than the rest of the contract text:

> *The (name of district) community development district may impose and levy taxes or assessments, or both taxes and assessments, on this property. These taxes and assessments pay the construction, operation, and maintenance costs of certain public facilities and services of the district and are set annually by the governing board of the district. These taxes and assessments are in addition to county and other local governmental taxes and assessments and all other taxes and assessments provided for by law.*

Megan's Law. Purchase contracts and leases are required to include notice that a sex offender database is available for public review to learn about the proximity of registered sex offenders.

HIV/AIDS. Under Florida Statute § 689.25, the fact that a prior occupant of a property was infected with HIV or diagnosed with AIDS is considered **nonmaterial** to the value of the property. Thus, sellers and licensees are not required to disclose it, and any failure to do so cannot form the basis of a cause of action. (Similar rules surround information such as whether a death occurred on the property and whether a person was suspected or convicted of a crime.) This statute is supported by Florida Statute Chapter 760, which prohibits discrimination based on handicap (disability). HIV/AIDS is classified federally and in Florida as a disability, making it unlawful to refuse to sell, rent, or otherwise discriminate in housing because of that disability.

If a buyer asks about health-related issues of previous occupants, licensees and sellers should simply rely on the statutory language noting that such information is not material under Florida law.

Foreign Ownership Restrictions

Since July 1, 2023, Chapter 692, Florida Statutes (created by Senate Bill 264), has restricted certain foreign buyers, called foreign principals, from acquiring Florida real property. A foreign principal is generally a government, entity, or individual connected with one of seven foreign countries of concern: the People's Republic of China, Russia, Iran, North Korea, Cuba, the Maduro regime in Venezuela, and Syria. The law sets three levels of restriction:

- foreign principals from any of the seven countries may not acquire agricultural land
- foreign principals from the seven countries may not acquire real property on or within 10 miles of a military installation or a critical infrastructure facility, such as a power plant, water treatment plant, seaport, or airport
- with narrow exceptions, persons domiciled in China who are not United States citizens or lawful permanent residents, the Chinese government, and entities based in China may not acquire any Florida real property

Limited exceptions exist. A person who holds a current non-tourist visa, or asylum documentation, may buy one residential property of up to two acres that is not within five miles of a military installation. Interests lawfully held before July 1, 2023, may be kept but must be registered with the state, and property acquired by inheritance, through enforcement of a lien, or to collect a debt must generally be sold within three years.

Because the restriction applies to the buyer, the law requires the buyer to sign an affidavit at or before closing stating that the buyer is not a prohibited foreign principal, or that the purchase otherwise complies with Chapter 692. FREC adopted the required form affidavits, one for a natural person and one for an entity, in Rule 61J2-10.200, F.A.C., effective January 17, 2024. A licensee should make sure the affidavit is obtained, because a knowing sale to a prohibited buyer can carry civil penalties and, under the China-specific provisions, criminal penalties.

These ownership restrictions are separate from FIRPTA. FIRPTA is a federal tax rule that requires a buyer to withhold part of the purchase price when the seller is a foreign person; it does not limit who may own property. Chapter 692, by contrast, limits the right of certain foreign buyers to acquire property in the first place. Chapter 692 has been challenged in federal court but remains in effect and enforceable as of this writing.

Material defects affecting value

For many years, the rule governing property sales was caveat emptor, known as "let the buyer beware." The gist of this rule was that the seller had no obligation to disclose any defects in the property that would affect its value, no matter how serious the defect might be. If the buyer asked, the seller could not lie, but if the buyer didn't ask, the seller didn't tell.

Johnson v. Davis. This practice changed in 1985 because of the Johnson v. Davis case, in which the Florida Supreme Court ruled that "where the seller of a home knows of facts materially affecting the value of the property [that] are not readily observable and are not known to the buyer, the seller is under a duty to disclose them to the buyer." Sellers must now disclose the defect or provide the following statement:

"Seller knows of no facts materially affecting the value of the Real Property which are not readily observable and which have not been disclosed to Buyer."

This disclosure is known as the Johnson v. Davis duty to disclose.

As a result of this case, buyers of residential property are not required to prove fraud or negligence when they are seeking relief for damages resulting from the seller's failure to disclose defects. Buyers need only prove that the seller knew of a latent, material defect and failed to disclose it, and thus, the buyer sustained damages. Latent defects are those that are not visible, obvious, or readily observable. Buyers are not obligated to search for latent defects. The Johnson v. Davis case concluded that "one should not be able to stand behind the impervious shield of caveat emptor and take advantage of another's ignorance."

"As is" provision. Standard purchase contracts include terms requiring sellers to make certain types of repairs to the property up to a specified dollar amount. However, "As Is" contracts allow the buyer to inspect the property without any repair obligations on the seller. During the 15-day inspection period, if the buyer does not agree with the seller's decision not to repair any discovered defects, the buyer can cancel the contract without penalty. A buyer who signs the "As is" contract is waiving any claims against the seller and the seller's agent for any defects that existed at closing but were not discovered until after closing.

However, the "As is" contract is not exempt from the Johnson v. Davis disclosure requirement. Not only must the seller disclose any known defect, but he or she must include additional language in the contract stating that, other than the duty to disclose, the seller "extends and intends no warranty and makes no representation of any type, either express or implied, as to the physical condition or history of the property."

Rayner vs. Wise. As an example of how an "as is" contract is impacted by disclosure requirements, consider the case of Rayner v. Wise.

Rayner entered into a purchase contract for a home listed by Wise Realty. The agreement required the sellers to provide a termite inspection report disclosing any termite damage. An inspection by a local firm revealed visible termite damage and wet rot, but neither the listing agent nor the seller disclosed this. In fact, Wise Realty requested that a representative from Seminole Gator Exterminator (Noegel) provide a letter stating there was no active infestation.

After taking possession, Rayner discovered extensive undisclosed termite damage. He sued Wise Realty and Noegel for fraudulent misrepresentation. A lower court held that because the purchase contract was "as is," no fraud took place. The District Court of Appeal of Florida reversed that finding, stating that "as is" clauses do not bar claims for fraudulent nondisclosure of material facts.

Licensee's duty to disclose. The seller's duty established in Johnson v. Davis is matched by the licensee's own duty to disclose. As explained in Chapter 10, a licensee must disclose all known facts that materially affect the value of the property and are not readily observable to the buyer, and Florida holds the licensee to what a reasonable, practicing licensee should know, not merely what he or she actually knows. In the contract setting, this means a licensee cannot rely on the seller's silence, or on an "as is" clause, to avoid disclosing a known material defect.

A material fact is one that would affect a buyer's decision, or the property's value or desirability, if known. In a transaction these commonly include adverse conditions of the property, title defects, and known environmental hazards. When a licensee observes a "red flag," such as a sign of a structural, mechanical, or environmental problem, or an unusual feature such as an oddly shaped or non-conforming lot, the licensee should advise the seller to obtain an expert evaluation rather than guess at its significance. Chapter 10 lists the categories of material facts and red flags in full. By contrast, the nonmaterial facts described next, such as property stigmas, generally need not be disclosed.

Stigmatized property disclosure. The agent may be held liable for failing to disclose a material fact if a court rules that the typical agent in that area would detect and recognize the adverse condition. Note, however, that there is no obligation to obtain or disclose information that is immaterial to the transaction, such as property stigmas. Common stigmas include homes previously occupied by residents who had been afflicted with AIDS or HIV, or that a given property is alleged to be haunted.

Other Contracts

Options: essential characteristics

An option-to-buy is an enforceable contract in which a potential seller, the **optionor,** grants a potential buyer, the **optionee**, the right to purchase a property before a stated time for a stated price and terms. In exchange for the right of option, the optionee pays the optionor valuable consideration.

For example, a buyer wants to purchase a property for $1,500,000, but needs to sell a boat to raise the down payment. The boat will take two or three months to sell. To accommodate the buyer, the seller offers the buyer an option to purchase the property at any time before midnight on the day that is ninety days from the date of signing the option. The buyer pays the seller $10,000 for the option. If the buyer exercises the option, the seller will apply the $10,000 toward the earnest money deposit and subsequent down payment. If the optionee lets the option expire, the seller keeps the $10,000. Both parties agree to the arrangement by completing a sale contract as an addendum to the option, then executing the option agreement itself.

An option-to-buy places the optionee under no obligation to purchase the property. However, the seller must perform under the contract terms if the buyer exercises the option. An option is thus a unilateral agreement. Exercise of the option creates a bilateral sale contract, binding both parties to perform. An unused option terminates at the expiration date.

An optionee can use an option to prevent the sale of a property to another party while seeking to raise funds for the purchase. A renter with a lease option-to-buy can accumulate down payment funds while paying rent to the landlord. For example, an owner may lease a condominium to a tenant with an option to buy. If the tenant exercises the option, the landlord agrees to apply $500 of the monthly rent paid before the option date toward the purchase price. The tenant pays the landlord the nominal sum of $1,000 for the option.

Options can also facilitate the acquisition of commercial property. The option period gives a buyer time to investigate zoning, space planning, building permits, environmental impacts, and other feasibility issues before the purchase, without losing the property to another party in the meantime.

Contract requirements. To be valid and enforceable, an option-to-buy must:

- include actual, non-refundable consideration

  The option must require the optionee to pay a specific consideration that is separate from the purchase price. The consideration cannot be refunded if the option is not exercised. If the option is exercised, the consideration may be applied to the purchase price. If the option is a lease option, portions of the rent may qualify as separate consideration.

- include price and terms of the sale

  The price and terms of the potential transaction must be clearly expressed and cannot change over the option period. It is customary for the parties to complete and attach a sale contract to the option to satisfy this requirement.

- have an expiration date

The option must automatically expire at the end of a specific period.

- be in writing

  Because a potential transfer of real estate is involved, Florida's statute of frauds requires that an option be in writing.
- include a legal description
- meet general contract validity requirements

  The basics include competent parties, the optionor's promise to perform, and the optionor's signature. Note that it is not necessary for the optionee to sign the option.

Common provisions of options. Beyond the required elements, it is common for an option to include provisions covering:

- how to deliver notice of election

  A clause clarifies how to make the option election, exactly when the election must be completed, and any additional terms required, such as an earnest money deposit.
- forfeiture terms

  A clause provides that the optionor is entitled to the consideration upon expiration of the option term.
- property and title condition warranties

  The optionor warrants that the property will be maintained in a certain condition, and that title will be marketable and insurable.
- how option consideration will be credited

  A clause states how the optionor will apply the option consideration toward the purchase price.

Right of first refusal

A right of first refusal gives its holder the first opportunity to buy or lease a property if the owner later decides to sell or lease it. Unlike an option, which lets the holder buy at a set price during a set period whether or not the owner wants to sell, a right of first refusal is triggered only when the owner receives an offer the owner is willing to accept; the holder may then match that offer's price and terms or step aside and let the third party proceed. Rights of first refusal are common in leases, condominiums, and co-ownership arrangements.

Lease purchases

A lease purchase is a transaction in which a tenant leases a property for a specified period of time with a contractual obligation to purchase the property at the end of the lease. The lease purchase is NOT the same as a lease option, in which the tenant has the option but no obligation to purchase.

Generally, the process takes this form:

- tenant and owner enter into a standard lease agreement
- at the same time, the tenant and owner enter into a purchase agreement that sets the future price and terms

- the tenant often pays an upfront fee or additional consideration, which may be credited toward the purchase price
- depending on the lease agreement terms, a portion of the lease payments may or may not be applied toward the down payment
- at the end of the lease term or at the time specified, the tenant is required to obtain financing and complete the purchase

Contracts for deed A contract for deed (land contract, installment sale contract, conditional sales contract, agreement for deed) allows the buyer of a property to defer payment of some or all of the purchase price over a specified period. During the period, the seller holds legal title while the buyer holds equitable title. The buyer takes possession of the property, makes payments of principal and interest to the seller, and maintains the property. At the end of the period, the buyer pays the seller the remaining purchase price, and the seller conveys legal title to the buyer.

A contract for deed serves several purposes for a seller. First, it facilitates a sale that might otherwise be impossible. Second, it may give the seller certain tax benefits. Since the seller is not liable for capital gains tax until the purchase price is received, the installment sale lowers the seller's tax liability in the year of the sale. There may also be a reduction in closing costs. Disadvantages for the seller include the buyer creating encumbrances during the contract or causing disputes and litigation over it.

For the buyer, the contract for deed enables a purchase when adequate credit and funds for a down payment and loan qualification may be lacking. Disadvantages for the buyer include: the seller may not be able to deliver marketable title at the end of the contract period, but the buyer must make payments nevertheless; or the seller may cloud the title with liens; or the seller may not have applied the buyer’s payments to the seller’s necessary loan payments.

Snapshot Review for Chapter 11

The following review summarizes the key rules and concepts from Chapter 11.

CONTRACT ESSENTIALS

- contract = legally enforceable agreement between parties
- requires: competent parties, mutual consent, consideration, legal purpose, voluntary good-faith act
- contracts conveying real estate interests must generally be in writing, include legal description, be signed
- oral contracts may be valid but unenforceable under the Statute of Frauds
- licensees may fill in blanks on approved forms but may not draft legal documents
- electronic contracts and signatures are enforceable under UETA and E-Sign laws

Classifications of Contracts

- express = stated verbally or in writing
- implied = created by actions/conduct
- bilateral = both parties promise performance
- unilateral = one party promises if another acts (option contract)
- executory = obligations remain
- executed = fully performed
- contract legal status: valid (meets criteria); void (does not meet criteria); voidable (can be voided); valid but unenforceable

Offer and Acceptance

- valid acceptance must exactly match offer terms
- changing any term creates a counteroffer
- offer may be revoked before acceptance is communicated
- "time is of the essence" creates strict deadlines

Contract Termination

- performance
- mutual agreement (novation)
- rescission
- abandonment
- expiration of time
- breach of contract

Remedies for Breach

- rescission
- forfeiture of deposit
- forfeited deposit usually split equally between seller and listing broker; broker's share capped at the commission
- suit for damages
- specific performance

Listing Agreements

- agreement between broker and client for brokerage services
- governed by agency law and contract law
- written listings in Florida must include expiration date
- automatic renewals prohibited

Types of Listings

- exclusive right-to-sell: broker earns commission regardless of who finds buyer
- exclusive agency: owner may sell without commission owed
- open listing: only procuring broker earns commission
- net listing: broker keeps amount above seller's minimum; legal but discouraged

Important Listing Clauses

- parties and property description
- listing price
- commission terms
- broker authority and duties
- protection period
- MLS authorization
- seller disclosures
- signatures of all owners

Sales Contracts

- binding agreement between buyer (vendee) and seller (vendor)
- must include parties, property description, purchase price, signatures
- earnest money serves as consideration and is held in escrow
- financing contingency allows buyer to cancel if financing cannot be obtained
- buyer default may result in forfeiture of earnest money
- seller default may result in damages or specific performance

Common Contract Provisions

- closing and possession dates
- title evidence
- closing costs
- inspections and surveys
- default remedies
- flood zone and HOA disclosures
- right of first refusal: holder's first chance to buy or lease if the owner decides to sell or lease
- restrictive covenants: private deed or CC&R use limits that run with the land

Required Disclosures

- Florida requires disclosure of:
- radon gas
- lead-based paint (pre-1978 homes)
- homeowners' association membership
- condominium documents

- flood hazards and insurance requirements
- property tax reassessment warning
- known environmental hazards
- coastal property conditions
- community development district assessments
- residential flood disclosure (s. 689.302): prior flood-damage claims and federal flood assistance, given before the contract
- condominium resale: milestone inspection report and structural integrity reserve study (SIRS) for buildings three or more stories
- homeowners' association reforms (Chapter 720): expanded governance, financial reporting, and records access

Foreign Ownership Restrictions

- Chapter 692 (SB 264): foreign principals from seven countries of concern restricted from acquiring Florida real property
- broadest ban applies to buyers domiciled in China; narrow exception for one home up to two acres not within five miles of a military installation
- buyer signs affidavit at or before closing (FREC Rule 61J2-10.200); separate from FIRPTA tax withholding

Property Disclosure Duty

- caveat emptor (buyer beware) once governed home sales
- Johnson v. Davis (1985): seller must disclose known defects that materially affect value and are not readily observable
- the licensee shares the seller's duty to disclose known material facts
- an 'as is' clause does not waive the Johnson v. Davis disclosure duty
- stigmatized-property conditions may still require disclosure

Chapter 11 Quiz: Real Estate Contracts

11.1 A contract is best defined as ______.

a. an agreement between parties that is enforceable by law
b. any written document signed by two people
c. a listing form approved by FREC
d. a verbal promise that carries no obligation

11.2 Which is a required element of a valid contract?

a. a notary's seal
b. valuable consideration
c. a recorded deed
d. a real estate license

11.3 For a contract to be valid, competent parties must be ______.

a. licensed real estate professionals
b. Florida residents
c. of legal age and sound mind
d. represented by attorneys

11.4 "Love and affection" offered in place of something of value is ______.

a. valuable consideration
b. legal purpose
c. an executed contract
d. good consideration that does not satisfy a valid contract

11.5 A contract formed for an illegal purpose is ______.

a. void
b. voidable
c. valid but unenforceable
d. implied

11.6 Under the Statute of Frauds, a contract for the sale of real estate generally must be ______.

a. notarized
b. in writing to be enforceable
c. recorded within 10 days
d. approved by FREC

11.7 A contract in which all terms are explicitly stated and agreed to is a(n) ______.

a. implied contract
b. unilateral contract
c. express contract
d. voidable contract

11.8 A contract created by the parties' conduct rather than stated words is a(n) ______.

a. express contract
b. executed contract
c. void contract
d. implied contract

11.9 A contract in which both parties promise to perform, such as a sales contract, is ______.

a. bilateral
b. unilateral
c. executed
d. void

11.10 An option to buy is an example of a ______ contract, because only one party is obligated.

a. bilateral
b. unilateral
c. executed
d. voidable

11.11 A contract fully performed by both parties is ______.

a. executory
b. voidable
c. executed
d. unenforceable

11.12 A sales contract that has been signed but not yet closed is ______.

a. executed
b. void
c. unilateral
d. executory

11.13 A contract that fails the tests of validity and is no contract at all is ______.

a. void
b. voidable
c. valid
d. executory

11.14 A contract one party may cancel because of fraud, duress, or coercion is ______.

a. void
b. voidable
c. executed
d. unenforceable

11.15 Acceptance of an offer that exactly matches its terms creates ______.

a. a counteroffer
b. an option
c. mutual consent (a meeting of the minds)
d. a void contract

11.16 When an offeree changes a term of an offer and returns it, the result is ______.

a. immediate acceptance
b. an executed contract
c. a unilateral contract
d. a counteroffer that voids the original offer

11.17 An offer may be revoked by the offeror ______.

a. at any time before the offeree communicates acceptance
b. only after acceptance
c. only with FREC approval
d. never once it is made

11.18 Under Florida's adoption of UETA, contracts and signatures created electronically are ______.

a. never enforceable
b. enforceable
c. valid only for leases
d. valid only if notarized

11.19 A real estate contract that is not a personal service contract may be assigned ______.

a. only with FREC approval
b. never
c. unless the agreement specifically prohibits assignment
d. only after closing

11.20 Substituting a new contract or party for an existing one, with the parties' agreement, is ______.

a. rescission
b. assignment
c. forfeiture
d. novation

11.21 Rescission of a contract ______.

a. cancels the contract and returns the parties to their pre-contract position
b. compels the breaching party to perform
c. transfers the contract to a third party
d. awards money damages

11.22 A suit for specific performance seeks to ______.

a. recover money damages
b. compel the defaulting party to comply with the contract's terms
c. cancel the contract
d. assign the contract

11.23 When a buyer defaults, the seller's usual contract remedy is ______.

a. specific performance by the buyer
b. a new listing agreement
c. forfeiture of the buyer's earnest money deposit as liquidated damages
d. rescission with a full refund to the buyer

11.24 If a seller defaults, the buyer may sue for ______.

a. forfeiture of the deposit
b. a commission
c. a counteroffer
d. specific performance, damages, or cancellation

11.25 Under an exclusive right-to-sell listing, the broker earns a commission ______.

a. regardless of who procures the buyer during the listing period
b. only if the broker personally finds the buyer
c. only if the seller approves the buyer
d. only in a net listing

11.26 Under an open listing, a commission is owed ______.

a. to every broker in the MLS
b. only to the broker who procures the buyer
c. to no one
d. regardless of who sells the property

11.27 In a net listing, the broker's compensation is ______.

a. a fixed percentage set by FREC
b. always 6%
c. any amount received above the seller's stated net price
d. paid by the buyer

11.28 Florida requires that a written listing agreement ______.

a. be recorded in the county
b. renew automatically
c. be notarized
d. include a definite expiration date

11.29 In a sales contract, the buyer is the ______ and the seller is the ______.

a. vendee; vendor
b. vendor; vendee
c. optionor; optionee
d. mortgagee; mortgagor

11.30 A financing contingency allows the buyer to ______.

a. extend the closing indefinitely
b. cancel the contract and recover the deposit if the specified loan is not obtained
c. avoid paying earnest money
d. assign the contract to the lender

11.31 In an option-to-buy, the optionee ______.

a. is obligated to purchase the property
b. must be a licensed broker
c. has the right, but not the obligation, to purchase the property
d. automatically owns the property

11.32 Under a contract for deed, until the buyer completes all payments, ______.

a. the buyer holds legal title
b. neither party has any interest
c. the broker holds title in escrow
d. the seller retains legal title while the buyer holds equitable title

CHAPTER 12:
FINANCING REAL ESTATE

Contents

- **Mortgage Concepts and Practices**
- **Common Mortgage Characteristics**
- **The Primary Mortgage Market**
- **The Secondary Mortgage Market**
- **Mortgage Foreclosure**
- **Residential Loan Underwriting**
- **Types of Mortgages and Sources of Financing**
- **Fair Credit and Lending Laws**
- **Mortgage Fraud**

Learning Objectives

Upon completion of this chapter, you will be able to:

1. Distinguish between a mortgage and a note and list the essential elements of each
2. Describe Florida's statutory foreclosure process
3. Identify mortgage priorities and the concept of subordination
4. Identify the characteristics of a conventional mortgage and calculate a mortgage payment on a new loan using financial tables and/or a financial calculator
5. Identify the provisions of FHA-insured mortgage loans and Veterans Affairs (VA) loans and calculate the maximum loan amount and required investment for an FHA residential mortgage loan
6. Explain the calculation of the interest rate on an adjustable rate mortgage (ARM) and describe the features of other types of mortgages.
7. Identify the characteristics of purchase money, participation, blanket, and package mortgages
8. Describe the types of discrimination prohibited by the Equal Credit Opportunity Act (ECOA) and identify the provisions of the Truth-in-Lending Act and Regulation Z
9. Identify the provisions of the Consumer Financial Protection Bureau of closing requirements regarding the loan estimate
10. Calculate the minimum qualifying ratios for conventional and FHA mortgages and estimate the approximate yield to the lender based on the number of points charged
11. Explain the relationship among down payment, loan-to-value ratio, and borrower equity
12. Describe the purpose of discount points and origination fees and their effect on loan cost and yield
13. Explain the purpose of an escrow impound account in a mortgage loan
14. Identify the primary sources of home financing and the role of mortgage loan originators
15. Describe the purpose of the secondary mortgage market and the roles of Fannie Mae, Ginnie Mae, and Freddie Mac

16. Identify the characteristics of seller financing
17. Describe the residential loan underwriting process and the factors a lender evaluates
18. Identify common mortgage clauses, including acceleration, defeasance, due-on-sale, and prepayment provisions
19. Explain the difference between lien-theory and title-theory states and its effect on the rights of the mortgagor and mortgagee
20. Recognize the common types of mortgage fraud and the licensee responsibility to avoid them

Mortgage Concepts and Practices

Mortgage law

Hypothecation. It is common to use borrowed money to purchase real estate. When a borrower gives a note promising to repay the borrowed money and executes a mortgage on the real estate for which the money is being borrowed as security, the financing method is called mortgage financing. The term "mortgage financing" also applies to real estate loans secured by a deed of trust. The process of securing a loan by pledging a property without giving up ownership of the property is called **hypothecation**.

Lien theory vs. title theory. States differ in their interpretation of who owns mortgaged property. Those that regard the mortgage as a lien held by the mortgagee (lender) against the property owned by the mortgagor (borrower) are called **lien-theory** states. Those that regard the mortgage document as a conveyance of ownership from the mortgagor to the mortgagee are called **title-theory** states. Some states interpret ownership of mortgaged property from a point of view that combines aspects of both title and lien theory. Florida is considered a lien-theory state.

Loan instruments A valid mortgage or trust deed financing arrangement requires

- a note as evidence of the debt
- the mortgage or trust deed as evidence of the collateral pledge

Promissory note. In addition to executing a mortgage or trust deed, the borrower signs a promissory note for the amount borrowed. The amount of the loan is typically the difference between the purchase price and the down payment. A promissory note creates a personal liability for the borrower to repay the loan.

A borrower who executes a promissory note is the maker or payer of the note. The lender is the payee. To be properly executed, all parties who have an interest in the property should sign the note. The note sets forth:

- the loan amount
- the term of the loan
- the method and timing of repayment
- the interest rate to be paid
- the borrower's promise to pay

The note may also state that it is payable to the bearer, if used with a deed of trust, or to the mortgagee, if used with a mortgage. Other items in the mortgage document or deed of trust may be repeated in the promissory note, especially:

- the right to prepay the loan balance
- charges for late payment
- conditions for default
- notifications and cures for default
- other charges

A promissory note is a **negotiable instrument**, which means the payee may assign it to a third party. The assignee would then have the right to receive the borrower's periodic payments.

Fannie Mae / Freddie Mac Uniform Florida Fixed-Rate Note. This is a Florida-adapted standardized note form that was created and adopted through the joint efforts of the country's largest secondary mortgage market purchasers and traders. The Uniform Florida Fixed-rate Note contains all the necessary provisions for ready-acceptability as a marketable financial instrument. To view the form, see https://singlefamily.fanniemae.com/media/11241/display .

The essential characteristics and contents of this note are as follows:

- interest rate is fixed and remains constant over the life of the loan
- the debt amount (principal plus interest); (monthly) repayment method; loan term; default and late payment provisions to protect lender

Mortgage instrument. A mortgage is a legal document stating the pledge of the borrower to the lender. The mortgage document pledges the borrower's ownership interest in the real estate in question as collateral against performance of the debt obligation in a process referred to as **hypothecation**.

A borrower who executes a mortgage is a **mortgagor**. The lender named in the mortgage is the **mortgagee**. In a trust deed, the borrower is the **trustor** and the lender is **beneficiary**. The mortgage or trust document identifies the property being given as security, giving both its legal description and mailing address. The document contains much of the same information as the note, including:

- the debt amount
- the term of the loan
- method and timing of payments

The document does not usually provide details about the payment amount, interest rate, or charges.

Satisfaction of mortgage. The release clause, also known as a **defeasance** clause, may specify that the mortgagee will execute a **satisfaction of mortgage** (also known as **release of mortgage** and **mortgage discharge**) to the mortgagor. In the case of a deed of trust, the lender as beneficiary requests the trustee to execute a **release deed** or **deed of reconveyance** to the borrower as trustor. The release deed or satisfaction should be recorded as necessary in county records to show that the mortgagee/trustee has extinguished all liens against the property.

Flow of a Mortgage Transaction

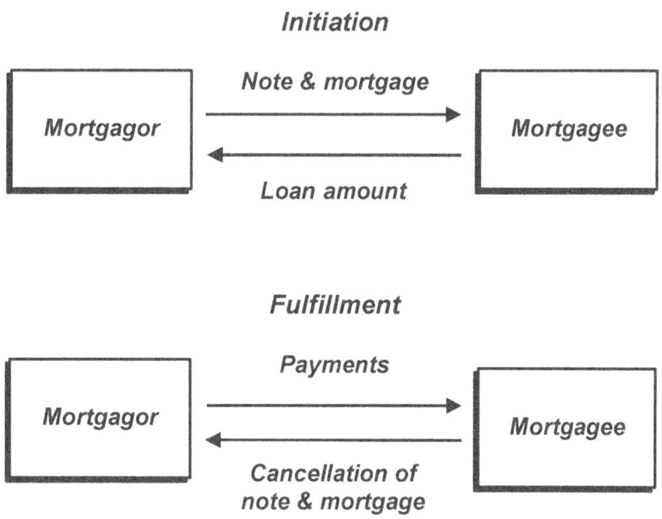

Mortgage priority

First mortgages vs. junior mortgages. Lien priority determines the order of the liens' claims on the security underlying the debt. The highest ranking lien is first to receive proceeds from the foreclosed and liquidated security. The lien with lowest priority is last in line. The owner receives any sale proceeds that remain after all lienors receive their due.

Lien priority is of paramount concern to the creditor, since it establishes the level of risk in recovering loaned assets in the event of default. Date of recording determines priority. The rule is: *the earlier the recording date of the lien, the higher its priority.*

Subordination agreements. A lienor can change the priority of a lien by voluntarily agreeing to subordinate, or lower, the lien's position in the hierarchy. This change is often necessary when a mortgage lender will not originate a mortgage loan unless it is senior to all other junior liens on the property. The lender may require the borrower to obtain agreements from other lien holders to subordinate their liens to the new mortgage.

Essential legal provisions of mortgages: primary provisions

Promise to repay. The borrower must make timely payments according to the terms of the note.

Taxes and property insurance. Unless waived by the lender or prohibited by law, the borrower must make monthly payments to cover taxes and property, or hazard, insurance. If applicable, the borrower must also pay flood insurance and mortgage insurance installments.

Periodic payments of taxes and insurance are held in a reserve fund called the escrow account. The Real Estate Settlement Procedures Act (RESPA) limits the amount of funds that the lender can require and hold for this purpose.

The borrower's monthly payment to the lender for principal and interest is called the P&I payment (principal and interest). The amount, which also includes the escrow payment, is called PITI (principal, interest, taxes, insurance).

Maintenance and covenant of good repair (occupancy, preservation, maintenance, and protection of the property). The borrower must take and maintain occupancy of the property as the borrower's principal residence according to the lender's requirements. The borrower must not use or neglect the property in such a way as to impair the lender's lien on the property. This could include using the property for illegal purposes, creating hazardous waste on the property, or destroying the improvements.

Other mortgage provisions

Prepayment. The borrower may pay off the loan, in whole or in part, before loan maturity and without penalty. In Florida, this provision is assumed to be true unless a clause specifically states otherwise.

Right to reinstate. If the lender holds the borrower in default under the terms of the mortgage and proceeds to enforce its rights under the document, such as by foreclosing, the borrower has the right to reinstate his or her interest by performing certain actions. This usually means paying overdue mortgage payments and any other expenses the lender may have incurred in protecting its rights. The clause, also known as a redemption clause, gives the borrower a period of time to satisfy obligations and prevent the lender from forcing a sale of the property.

Due on sale. If the borrower sells or transfers its interest in the property without the lender's approval, the lender may demand immediate and full repayment of the loan balance. This is an alienation clause, also known as a due-on-sale clause and a call clause. It allows the lender to prevent the assumption of the mortgage by a buyer if the borrower sells the property.

Release (defeasance). The lender agrees to release the mortgage or trust document to the borrower when the borrower has paid off the loan and all other sums secured by the document. The release deed or satisfaction should be recorded as necessary in county records to show that the mortgagee/trustee has extinguished all liens against the property.

Application of payments. The amount of each payment is applied to various items in order of priority. Unless local law provides otherwise, this order is: 1) prepayment charges; 2) escrow; 3) interest; 4) principal; 5) late charges.

Charges and Liens. The borrower is liable for paying any charges, liens, or other expenses that may have priority over the mortgage or trust instrument.

Hazard or Property Insurance. The borrower must keep the property insured as the lender requires. Insurance proceeds, in case of a claim, are applied first to restoring the property, or, if that is not feasible, to payment of the debt.

Protection of Lender's Rights in the Property. The lender may take actions it believes are necessary to protect its rights in the property if the borrower's actions threaten them. The costs of these actions would be charged to the borrower, and become part of the monthly payment.

Mortgage Insurance. The lender may require the borrower to obtain private mortgage insurance, or PMI. Mortgage insurance protects the lender against loss of a portion of the loan (typically 20-25%) in case of borrower default. Private mortgage insurance generally applies to loans that are not backed by the Federal Housing Administration (FHA) or Veterans Administration (VA) and that have a down payment of less than 20% of the property value.

Inspection. With proper notice, the lender may inspect the property if there is reasonable cause to fear damage to its lien.

Condemnation. If the property is condemned or taken by eminent domain, the lender declares a claim on any resulting proceeds.

Borrower Not Released; Forbearance by Lender Not a Waiver. The lender reserves the right to take future action against the borrower for default, even if the lender decides not to take immediate action. If the lender agrees to change the terms of the loan, it does not release the borrower from the original liability.

Common Mortgage Characteristics

Principal

The capital amount borrowed, on which interest payments are calculated, is the original loan principal. In an amortizing loan, part of the principal is repaid periodically along with interest, so that the principal balance decreases over the life of the loan. At any point during the life of a mortgage loan, the remaining unpaid principal is called the **loan balance**, or **remaining balance**.

Down payment

The difference between the purchase price of a property and the amount financed by a loan is the amount of cash the buyer must produce at the time of purchase. This amount is the down payment. The cash amount pledged and escrowed at the time of the offer is applied toward the down payment at closing.

Loan-to-value ratio & equity

Lenders usually lend only a portion of a property's value as a protection against loss. The relationship of the loan amount to the property value, expressed as a percentage, is called the loan-to-value ratio, or LTV. If the lender's loan-to-value ratio is 80%, the lender will lend only $80,000 per $100,000 of a home's appraised value. The difference between the property value and the borrower's indebtedness is referred to as the buyer's equity. If the LTV on a loan is 80%, then the equity is 100% - 80%, or 20%. At any given time following loan origination, the buyer's equity is the (current market value minus the loan balance).

Interest

Interest is a charge for the use of the lender's money. Interest may be paid in advance at the beginning of the payment period, or in arrears at the end of the payment period, according to the terms of the note. Mortgage interest is most commonly paid in arrears. The **interest rate** is a percentage applied to the principal to determine the amount of interest due. The rate may be fixed for the term of the loan, or it may be variable, according to the terms of the note. A loan with a fixed interest rate is called a fixed-rate loan; a loan with a variable interest rate is commonly called an adjustable-rate loan.

Because the interest rate on a mortgage loan does not reflect the full cost of the loan to the borrower, federal law requires a lender on a residential property to compute and disclose an **Annual Percentage Rate (APR)** that includes other finance charges in addition to the basic interest rate in the calculation.

Florida has laws against **usury**, which is the charging of excessive interest rates on loans. The laws prescribe maximum rates that can be charged on loans of varying amounts.

Servicing

Loan servicing involves collecting and keeping records of loan payments and providing documentation of the loan to the borrower. The originating lender may provide the servicing and charge a percentage of the loan amount for the service, or it may pass the responsibility to another lender or financial services entity.

Escrow account

Mortgage lenders usually require borrowers to pay property taxes and hazard insurance in monthly instalments of 1/12 of the annual amount. These periodic payments are held in a reserve fund called the escrow account and paid out to the appropriate party as due . The Real Estate Settlement Procedures Act (RESPA) limits the amount of funds that the lender can require and hold for this purpose.

The borrower's monthly payment to the lender for principal and interest is called the P&I payment (principal and interest). The amount, which also includes the escrow payment, is called PITI (principal, interest, taxes, insurance).

Discount points

From the point of view of a lender or investor, the amount loaned in a mortgage loan is the lender's capital investment, and the interest paid by the borrower is the return earned by the invested capital. It is often the case that a lender needs to earn a greater return than the interest rate alone provides. For example, a lender may require a higher yield on a low-interest VA loan, which has an interest rate cap. In such a case, the lender charges up-front discount points to cover the difference between the loan's interest rate and the required return. This effectively increases the loan's yield for the lender.

A discount point is one percent of the loan amount. Thus, one point on a $100,000 loan equals $1,000. The lender charges this as prepaid interest at closing by funding only the face amount of the loan minus the discount points. The borrower, however, must repay the full loan amount, along with interest calculated on the full amount.

The value of one discount point to a lender is usually estimated to be equivalent to raising the interest rate on the loan by 1/8%. Thus, a lender must charge 8 points to raise the yield by 1%. If a lender needs to earn 7% on a loan offered at 6.5%, the number of points necessary would be figured as follows:

7.0% - 6.5% = .5%

.5% x 8 (points per 1%) = 4 points

On a loan of $1,000,000, the 4 points would cost the borrower:

1,000,000 x .04 = $40,000.

The borrower would effectively receive $960,000 from the lender and owe principal and interest on a $1,000,000 loan. For tax reasons, it is usually advisable for the borrower to receive the full loan amount from the lender and pay the points in a check that is separate from that used for other closing costs. As prepaid interest, points paid in this way may be deductible on the borrower's income tax return for the year of the purchase. The borrower should seek the advice of a tax consultant concerning this matter.

Origination fee

Lenders often charge borrowers a loan origination fee to cover the costs of processing the loan application and obtaining supporting information, such as credit reports. The fee is most often in the range of 1-2% of the loan amount.

Take-out commitment

A take-out commitment offers to make a loan that will "take out" another lender's loan, i.e., pay it off and replace it. The take-out loan is most often used to retire a construction loan. The take-out lender agrees to pay off the short-term construction loan by issuing a long-term permanent loan.

Term

The loan term is the period of time over which the loan must be repaid. A "30-year loan" is a loan whose balance must be fully repaid at the end of 30 years. A "five-year balloon loan" is a loan whose balance must be paid off at the end of five years, although its payments may be calculated on a term of another length, such as fifteen or thirty years. Such a loan is also sometimes described as a 30-year loan with a five-year "call."

Payments

The loan term, loan amount, and interest rate combine to determine the periodic payment amount. When these three quantities are known, it is possible to identify the periodic payment from a mortgage table or with a financial calculator. Mortgage payments are usually made monthly. On an amortizing loan, a portion of the payment goes toward repaying the loan balance in advance, and the remainder goes toward paying interest in arrears.

For example, Mary and Jerry King borrow $400,000 to finance the purchase of a home. The loan has a 30-year term at an interest rate of 5% and is amortizing. The monthly payment for this loan will be $2,147. For the first payment at the end of the month, the Kings owe interest on $400,000 for that month. At 5%, this amounts to $1,666.67. Since their payment is $2,147 and the interest charge is $1,666.67, the $480.33 difference is applied to an advance principal payment. The following month, the Kings will pay interest on the new, smaller loan balance of $399,519.67 ($400,000.00 – 480.33).

If a borrower pays more than the scheduled payment amount, the excess is credited toward principal repayment, reducing the principal balance by that amount. The required minimum payment amount remains constant for the life of the loan, but the loan term can be reduced through this method, thereby reducing the total amount of interest paid over the life of the loan.

Assignment of mortgages

The holder of rights and interests in a property can usually transfer them to another by contract. This right of assignment generally holds true of mortgages. The assignee takes on primary liability, and the assignor remains secondarily liable for any contractual duties unless a novation agreement relieves the assignor of responsibility.

In the case of a mortgaged property, the mortgage instrument and the promissory note are transferred by means of an assignment of mortgage, but it is the assignment of the promissory note that actually conveys to the assignee the rights to the mortgaged property. The original mortgagor now must make loan payments to the assignee.

Estoppel. The assignor of the mortgage provides to the party who purchases the assigned mortgage a **certificate of estoppel** that states the loan balance, the rate of interest, and the most recent date of payment to ensure that no contrary claims about these factors can be made later.

The Primary Mortgage Market

The mortgage market

Mortgage loans provide borrowers with funds to purchase real estate. Money for mortgages primarily comes from cash savings of individuals, the government, and businesses. This money may become available through the process of **intermediation**, in which funds on deposit with financial institutions are loaned out to borrowers, or **disintermediation**, in which the owners of the savings invest their money directly by making loans or other investments. Government actions and investor activities affect the supply of money for mortgage loans and encourage or discourage the market for mortgage loans as an investment.

Supply and demand for money. Money is a limited commodity subject to the effects of supply and demand. The federal government's monetary policy controls the supply of money in order to achieve the country's economic goals. An excessive supply of money usually causes interest rates to fall and consumer prices to rise. Conversely, an excessive demand for money, such as for mortgage loans, causes interest rates to rise and prices to fall. Regulation of the money supply addresses these fluctuations to control and limit wide swings in the supply-and-demand cycle. These efforts, in turn, help to buffer the economy from severe inflationary or recessionary trends.

Regulating the money supply. The Federal Reserve System regulates the money supply by means of three methods:

- selling or re-purchasing government securities, primarily Treasury bills
- changing the reserve requirement for member banks. The reserve is a percentage of depositors' funds that banks and other regulated financial institutions may not lend out.
- changing the interest rate, or discount rate that the system charges member institutions for borrowing funds from the Federal Reserve System central banks

When the Federal Reserve sells Treasury bills, the money paid for the securities is removed from the economy's money supply. Conversely, when it repurchases Treasury bills, the cash paid out to investors puts money back into the economy.

The second control, regulating reserve requirements, effectively restricts how much money banks can put into the economy through the disbursement of loans. When the Federal Reserve raises reserve requirements, banks have less money to lend, decreasing the money supply. When the Fed lowers reserve requirements, banks have more money to lend, increasing the money supply.

The third control, and perhaps the most effective, is the regulation of the discount rate that member banks must pay to borrow money. If the discount rate goes up, it becomes more cost-prohibitive to borrow. Therefore, the money supply tightens. If the discount rate is lowered, banks have an incentive to borrow more money to lend to customers.

Primary sources of home financing

Primary mortgage market. The primary mortgage market consists of lenders who originate mortgage loans directly to borrowers. Primary mortgage market lenders include:

- savings and loans: residential mortgages and home equity loans; conventional, FHA, and VA loans

- commercial banks: construction loans; conventional, FHA, and VA loans
- mutual savings banks: residential and home improvement loans; conventional, FHA, and VA loans
- life insurance companies: commercial loans, especially for apartment, office, retail, and industrial properties
- mortgage bankers: mortgage loan originations; FHA and VA loans
- credit unions: residential and home improvement loans; conventional, FHA, and VA loans

Mortgage brokers. Mortgage brokers are also part of the primary mortgage market, even though they do not lend to customers directly. Rather, they are instrumental in procuring borrowers for primary mortgage lenders.

The primary lender assumes the initial risk of the long-term investment in the mortgage loan. Primary lenders sometimes also service the loan until it is paid off. Servicing loans entails collecting the borrower's periodic payments, maintaining and disbursing funds in escrow accounts for taxes and insurance, supervising the borrower's performance, and releasing the mortgage on repayment. In many cases, primary lenders employ mortgage servicing companies, which service loans for a fee.

Portfolio lenders. A primary mortgage market lender may or may not sell its loans into the secondary market. Many lenders originate loans for the purpose of retaining the investments in their own loan portfolio. These loans are referred to as portfolio loans, and lenders originating loans for their own portfolio are called portfolio lenders. Portfolio lenders are less restricted by the standards and forms imposed on other lenders by secondary market organizations. In retaining their portfolio loans, portfolio lenders may vary underwriting criteria and hold independent standards for down payment requirements and the condition of the collateral.

Mortgage loan originators

Mortgage loan originators (MLOs) work for banks, credit unions, and savings and loan institutions, receiving and processing mortgage loan applications, negotiating loan terms and conditions, and selling existing mortgage loans to investors. An MLO license is necessary in Florida and requires a prescribed number of hours of education and passing of a test. The Secure and Fair Enforcement for Mortgage Licensing Act (SAFE Act) sets minimum standards for MLO licensing and registration. The Nationwide Mortgage Licensing System (NMLS) is the provider and registrar of MLO licenses.

Seller financing

The seller may provide some or all of the financing for the buyer's purchase. Some of the most common methods of seller financing are purchase money mortgages, including the wraparound, and the contract for deed.

Purchase money mortgage. With a purchase money mortgage, the borrower gives a mortgage and note to the seller to finance some or all of the purchase price of the property. The seller in this case is said to "take back" a note, or to "carry paper," on the property. Purchase money mortgages may be either senior or junior liens.

Wraparound. In a wraparound loan arrangement, the seller receives a junior mortgage from the buyer and uses the buyer's payments to make the payments on the original first mortgage. A wraparound enables the buyer to obtain financing with a minimum cash investment. It also potentially enables the seller to profit from any difference between a lower interest rate on the senior loan and a higher rate on the wraparound loan. A wraparound is possible only if the senior mortgagee allows it.

Contract for deed. Under a contract for deed arrangement, the seller retains title, and the buyer receives possession and equitable title while making payments under the terms of the contract. The seller conveys title when the contract has been fully performed.

The Secondary Mortgage Market

Lenders, investors, and government agencies that buy loans already originated by someone else, or originate loans indirectly through someone else, constitute the secondary mortgage market.

Secondary mortgage market organizations include:

- Federal National Mortgage Association (FNMA, or Fannie Mae)
- Federal Home Loan Mortgage Corporation (FHLMC, or Freddie Mac)
- Government National Mortgage Association (GNMA, or Ginnie Mae)
- investment firms that assemble loans into packages and sell securities based on the pooled mortgages
- life insurance companies
- pension funds
- primary market institutions that also invest as secondary lenders

Cycle of mortgage money flow

Secondary mortgage market organizations buy pools of mortgages from primary lenders and sell securities backed by these pooled mortgages to investors. By selling securities, the secondary market brings investor money into the mortgage market. By purchasing loans from primary lenders, the secondary market returns funds to them, thereby enabling them to originate more mortgage loans.

The Mortgage Money Flow

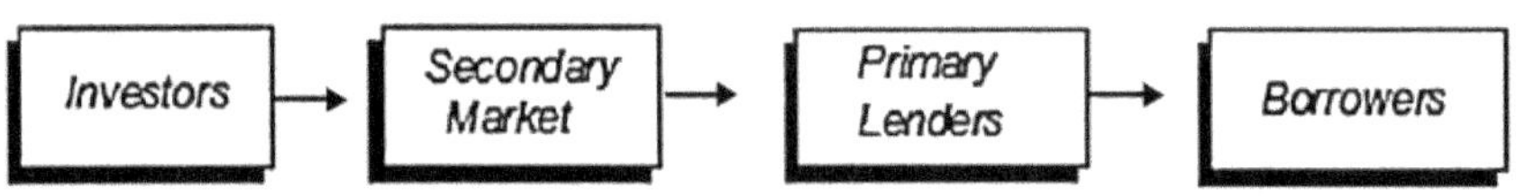

Primary lenders profit from selling loans to the secondary market. The secondary market acquires a profitable long-term investment without underwriting, originating, or servicing the loans. Secondary market organizations customarily hire primary lenders or loan servicing companies to service mortgage pools.

Secondary market loan requirements. The secondary market only buys loans that meet established requirements for collateral quality, borrower, and documentation. Since many primary lenders intend to sell their loans to the secondary market, the qualification standards of the secondary market limit and effectively control the kind of loans the primary lender will originate.

As major players in the secondary market, the Federal National Mortgage Association (FNMA, "Fannie Mae"), Government National Mortgage Association (GNMA, "Ginnie Mae), and Federal Home Loan Mortgage Corporation (FHLMC, "Freddie Mac") tend to set the standards for the primary market.

FNMA, or Fannie Mae

The Federal National Mortgage Association (FNMA, or Fannie Mae) is a government-sponsored enterprise, originally organized as a privately-owned corporation. As a secondary market player, it:

- buys conventional, FHA-backed, and VA-backed loans
- gives banks mortgage-backed securities in exchange for blocks of mortgages
- offers lenders firm loan purchase commitments, provided they conform to Fannie Mae's lending standards
- sells bonds and mortgage-backed securities
- guarantees payment of interest and principal on mortgage-backed securities

Standardized note forms for Florida. The Fannie Mae / Freddie Mac Uniform Florida Fixed Rate Note for single-family properties can be reviewed via the following link: https://singlefamily.fammiemae.com/media/11241/display

Conforming and non-conforming loans. Loans that meet the guidelines of Fannie Mae are called conforming loans. Those that do not are, by the same token, called non-conforming loans.

GNMA, or Ginnie Mae

GNMA, or Ginnie Mae, is a division of the Department of Housing and Urban Development. Its purpose is to administer special assistance programs and to help Fannie Mae in its secondary market activities. Specifically, GNMA

- guarantees payment on FNMA high-risk, low-yield mortgages and absorbs the difference in yield between the mortgages and market rates
- guarantees privately generated securities backed by pools of VA-and FHA-guaranteed loans

FHLMC, or Freddie Mac

The **Federal Home Loan Mortgage Corporation** (FHLMC), or Freddie Mac, is a government-sponsored enterprise, originally chartered as a corporation in 1970. As a secondary market player, FHLMC buys mortgages and pools them, selling bonds backed by the mortgages in the open market. Freddie Mac guarantees performance on FHLMC mortgages.

A federal conservator, the Federal Housing Finance Authority (FHFA), now operates Fannie Mae and Freddie Mac as conservators with the U.S. Treasury a majority owner of both organizations.

Mortgage Foreclosure

Lien enforcement

All liens can be enforced by the sale or other transfer of title of the secured property, whether by court action, operation of law, or through powers granted in the original loan agreement. The enforcement proceedings are referred to as foreclosure.

State law governs the foreclosure process. Broadly, a statutory or court-ordered sale enforces a general lien, including a judgment lien. A lawsuit or loan provision authorizing the sale or direct transfer of the attached property enforces a specific lien, such as a mortgage. Real estate tax liens are enforced through tax foreclosure sales, or tax sales.

The defaulting borrower may also offer the lender a deed in lieu of foreclosure to avoid the foreclosure process, but the lender does not have to accept it. Finally, there is the option of a short sale, which also avoids foreclosure but must be agreed to by the lender and borrower.

Foreclosure

Three types of foreclosure processes enforce mortgage liens:

- judicial foreclosure
- non-judicial foreclosure
- strict foreclosure

Foreclosure Processes

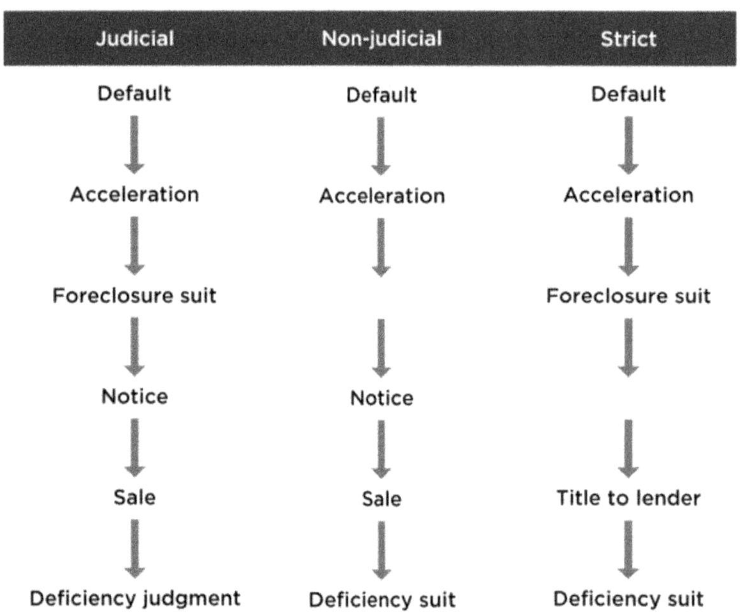

Judicial foreclosure. Judicial foreclosure occurs in states (such as Florida) that use a two-party mortgage document (borrower and lender) that does not contain a "power of sale" provision. Lacking this provision, a lender must file a **foreclosure suit** and undertake a court proceeding to enforce the lien.

- **acceleration and filing**

  If a borrower has failed to meet loan obligations despite proper notice and applicable grace periods, the lender can accelerate the loan or declare that the loan balance and all other sums due on the loan are immediately payable.

  If the borrower does not pay off the loan in full, the lender then files a foreclosure suit, naming the borrower as defendant. The suit asks the court to:

  - terminate the defendant's interests in the property
  - order the property sold publicly to the highest bidder
  - order the proceeds applied to the debt

- **lis pendens**

  In the foreclosure suit, a lis pendens gives public notice that the mortgaged property may soon have a judgment issued against it. This notice enables other lienholders to join in the suit against the defendant.

- **writ of execution**

  If the defendant fails to meet the demands of the suit during a prescribed period, the court orders the termination of interests of any and all parties in the property, and orders the property to be sold. The court's writ of execution authorizes an official, such as the county sheriff, to seize and sell the foreclosed property.

- **public sale and sale proceeds**

  After public notice of the sale, the property is auctioned to the highest bidder. The new owner receives title free and clear of all previous liens, whether the lienholders have been paid or not. Proceeds from the sale are applied to the payment of liens in order of priority. After payment of real estate taxes, lienholders' claims, and sale costs, any remaining funds are paid to the mortgagor (borrower).

- **deficiency judgment**

  If the sale does not yield sufficient funds to cover the amounts owed, the mortgagee may seek a deficiency judgment from the court. This enables the lender to attach and foreclose a judgment lien on other real or personal property the borrower owns.

- **right of redemption**

  The borrower's right of redemption, also called the equity of redemption, is the right to reclaim a property that has been foreclosed upon by paying the amounts owed to creditors, including interest and costs. Redemption is possible within a redemption period. Florida allows redemption at any time until the foreclosure sale concludes.

Non-judicial foreclosure. When there is a "power of sale" provision in the mortgage or trust deed, a non-judicial foreclosure can force the sale of the liened property without a foreclosure suit. The "power of sale" clause, in effect, enables the mortgagee to order a public sale without a court decree.

- **foreclosure process**

On default, the foreclosing mortgagee records and delivers notice to the borrower and other lienholders. After the proper period, a "notice of sale" is published, the sale is conducted, and all liens are extinguished. The highest bidder then receives unencumbered title to the property.

- **deficiency suit**

  The lender does not obtain a deficiency judgment or lien in a non-judicial foreclosure action. The lender instead must file a new deficiency suit against the borrower.
- **reinstatement and redemption**

  During the notice of default and notice of sale periods, the borrower may pay the lender and terminate the proceedings. Reinstatement and redemption rights in Florida end with the conclusion of the foreclosure sale. There is no right of redemption in non-judicial foreclosure.

Strict foreclosure. Strict foreclosure is a court proceeding that gives the lender title directly by court order, rather than providing cash proceeds from a public sale.

On default, the lender gives the borrower official notice. After a prescribed period, the lender files suit in court, whereupon the court establishes a period within which the defaulting party must repay the amounts owed. If the defaulter does not repay the funds, the court orders the transfer of full, legal title to the lender.

Deed in lieu of foreclosure

A defaulting borrower facing foreclosure may avoid court actions and costs by voluntarily deeding the property to the mortgagee. This is accomplished through a deed-in-lieu of foreclosure, which transfers legal title to the lienholder. The transfer, however, does not terminate any existing liens on the property, and not all lenders will accept this course of action.

Short sale

A **short sale** occurs when a property owner owes more than the property's resale value and loan payoff and agrees to let the lender sell it in exchange for release from the lien. The lender may or may not agree to accept the deficient price as satisfaction and may require the seller to pay the deficiency by way of a deficiency judgment. There may also be tax consequences for the seller. To avoid the deficiency, the seller must ensure that the agreements include a full release of the underlying debt and a statement that it has been fully satisfied.

After retaking the property through foreclosure or a short sale, the property becomes "bank-owned," also known as REO (real estate owned). **Forbearance** or a **loan modification** allows the borrower to avoid legal action and keep the property under a new agreement with the lender.

The parties to a short sale are the buyer and seller. The lender is a third-party contingency who must approve the sale. The process is generally as follows.

Short sale procedure

1. The borrower or borrower's agents contact the lender to discuss the short sale option.
2. If willing, the lender sets the required terms of the short sale.
3. The real estate agent provides the lender with a Broker's Price Opinion (BPO).

4. The agent lists the property for sale at the price that will cover the mortgage.
5. The agent places a note in the Multiple Listing Service (MLS) stating that the lender will consider a short sale.
6. A buyer submits an offer.
7. The owner agrees to the contract
8. The lender approves the short sale.
9. The transaction closes.
10. Lender's action to recover deficiency may ensue.

Residential Loan Underwriting

Overview

To qualify for a mortgage loan, a borrower must meet the lender's qualifications in terms of income, debt, cash, and net worth. In addition, a borrower must demonstrate sufficient creditworthiness to be an acceptable risk.

Borrower requirements. The lender must rely on eight types of information to determine that the borrower has the ability to repay the loan:

- current income or assets (excluding the value of the mortgaged property)
- current employment status
- credit history
- monthly payment for the mortgage
- monthly payments being made on other loans on the same property
- monthly payments for other mortgage-related expenses
- other debts
- monthly debt payments compared to monthly income (debt-to-income ratio)

The lender cannot use a temporarily low rate (introductory or "teaser" rate) to determine qualification. For an adjustable-rate mortgage (ARM), the highest rate

the borrower might have to pay is generally to be used.

The "ability to repay" requirements are relaxed in certain circumstances where the borrower is attempting to refinance from a riskier loan (such as an interest-only loan) to a less risky one (such as a fixed-rate mortgage loan.

Qualified Mortgage. A Qualified Mortgage is one that meets the "ability-to-repay" requirements, has certain required features, and is not allowed to have others. There are exceptions to these rules for certain kinds of small lenders. Issuing a Qualified Mortgage gives the lender certain legal protections in case the borrower fails to repay the loan.

Loan application process

The process of initiating a mortgage loan begins when a borrower completes a loan application and submits it to a lender for evaluation by the lender's underwriters.

Forms. Most lenders use some version of the "Uniform Residential Loan Application" promulgated by Fannie Mae. This form requests the borrower to provide information about the property and the borrower. The standard form includes the loan amount requested, based on an estimate of the purchase, refinance, or other underlying transaction.

Information required by the lender. The application must include supporting documentation for the information indicated in the following exhibit.

Property and Borrower Information

Property information	age & year built original cost	year acquired current loan balance
Borrower information	age employment history assets	education monthly income & expenses debts
Supporting documentation	appraisal report purchase contract	credit report income and employment verification

Completion. The application must be complete for the lender to consider it. The form must be signed and dated by the applicant(s) and delivered to the lending institution. The **application process begins** when the lender receives the completed application package from the applicant. Federal law requires the lender to accept all applications and to give applicants notice of the disposition of their applications. If the lender denies the loan application because of fraudulent information on the application form, the borrower has no claim to a refund of the application fee.

Loan underwriting

Loan underwriting is the process of assessing the lender's risk in giving a loan. Mortgage underwriting includes:

- evaluating the borrower's ability to repay the loan
- appraising the value of the property offered as security
- determining the terms of the loan

Risk. A lender undertakes a number of risks in lending money. The principal risks are that the borrower will default on repayment of the loan and that the borrower will damage the value of the property as security. In addition, the lender runs the risk that, in the event of a foreclosure, the sales proceeds from the property will be insufficient to cover the lender's loss.

Qualification. A lender assesses risks by examining, or qualifying, both borrower and property. In qualifying a borrower, an underwriter weighs the ability of the borrower to repay the loan. This requires an analysis of whether the borrower's income, cash resources, creditworthiness, net worth, and employment stability meet the lender's standards.

In qualifying a property, an underwriter assesses the ability of the property value to cover potential losses. In this evaluation, a lender requires that the appraised value of the property be more than adequate to cover the contemplated loan and

costs. To protect further against loss, a lender will usually lend only a portion of the property's value. The relationship of the loan amount to the property value, expressed as a percentage, is called the **loan-to-value ratio, or LTV**. If the lender's loan-to-value ratio is 80%, the lender will lend only $320,000 on a home appraised at $400,000. The difference between what the lender will lend and what the borrower must pay for the property is the amount the borrower must provide in cash as a down payment.

Even if borrower and property qualify, a lender may, under certain circumstances, seek further protection against risk by requiring the borrower to obtain private mortgage insurance. This is frequently the case with loans requiring a relatively small down payment, leading to a high loan-to-value ratio.

Qualifying the buyer

Credit evaluation and credit scoring. A lender must obtain a written credit report on any applicant who submits a completed loan application. The credit report will contain the applicant's history regarding:

- outstanding debts
- payment behavior (timeliness, collection problems)
- legal information of public record (lawsuits, judgments, bankruptcies, divorces, foreclosures, garnishments, repossessions, defaults)

Problems with payment behavior and legal actions are likely to cause a lender to deny the application, unless the applicant can provide an acceptable explanation of mitigating and temporary circumstances that caused the problem.

If a lender denies a loan on the basis of a credit report, the lender must disclose in writing that the applicant is entitled to a statement of reason from any creditor responsible for the negative report.

Since 1995, the Federal Home Loan Mortgage Corporation and the Federal National Mortgage Association have been encouraging lenders to use credit scoring to evaluate loan applicants. **Credit scoring** is a computer-based method of assigning a numerical value to an applicant's credit. The credit score is a statistical prediction of a borrower's likelihood of defaulting on a loan.

Qualifying ratios. Lenders want to be assured that the borrower has adequate means to make all necessary periodic payments on the loan, in addition to other housing expenses and debts, such as credit card payments and car payments. Most lenders use two ratios to estimate an applicant's ability to fulfill a loan obligation: an *income ratio,* or *housing expense ratio*, and a *debt ratio*, or *housing plus debt ratio, or total obligations ratio*. They also consider the stability of an applicant's income. Please note that the income and debt ratios in the discussion below do not necessarily reflect the latest ratios used by FHA, VA, or other lenders. Check for updates on the websites of those agencies.

- **income ratio**

  The income ratio, or housing expense ratio, establishes borrowing capacity by limiting the percentage of gross income a borrower may spend on housing costs. Housing costs include principal, interest, taxes, and homeowner's insurance, and may include monthly assessments, mortgage insurance, and utilities. The income ratio formula is:

  Income Ratio

  $$\frac{monthly\ housing\ expense}{monthly\ GROSS\ income} = income\ ratio$$

  To identify the maximum monthly housing expense an income ratio allows, modify the formula as follows:

  monthly gross income x income ratio = monthly housing expense

Most conventional lenders require that this ratio be no greater than 25-28%. In other words, a borrower's total housing expenses cannot exceed 28% of gross income. For an FHA-backed loan, the ratio is 31%. VA-guaranteed loans do not use this qualifying ratio.

For example, if a couple has a combined monthly gross income of $12,000, and a lender's maximum income ratio is 28%, the couple's monthly housing expense cannot exceed $3,360:

$12,000 x 28% = $3,360

- **debt ratio**

  The debt ratio considers all monthly obligations in the income ratio, plus any additional monthly payments the applicant must make on other debts. The lender will specifically review minimum monthly payments due on revolving credit and other consumer loans. The debt ratio formula is:

Debt Ratio

$$\frac{\textit{monthly housing expense} + \textit{monthly debt obligations}}{\textit{monthly GROSS income}} = \textit{debt ratio}$$

To identify the housing expenses plus the debt a debt ratio allows, modify the formula as follows:

monthly gross income x debt ratio = monthly housing expense + monthly debt obligations

Most conventional lenders require this debt-to-income ratio to be no greater than 36%. For an FHA-backed loan, the debt ratio may not exceed 43%. The VA uses 41% and a variable "residual income" calculation. The FHA and VA include in the debt figure any obligation costing more than $100 per month and any debt with a remaining term exceeding six months.

Using the 36% debt ratio, the couple whose monthly income is $12,000 will be allowed to have monthly housing and debt obligations of $4,320:

$12,000 gross income x 36% = $4,320 expenses and debt

VA-guaranteed loans also require a borrower to meet certain qualifications based on net income after paying federal, state, and Social Security taxes, as well as housing maintenance and utility expenses. Residual income requirements vary by family size, loan amount, and geographic region.

Income stability. A lender looks beyond income and debt ratios to assess an applicant's income stability. Important factors are:

- how long the applicant has been employed at the present job
- how frequently and for what reasons the applicant has changed jobs in the past
- how likely secondary income, such as bonuses and overtime, is to continue on a regular basis
- how educational level, training and skills, age, and type of occupation may affect the continuation of the present income level in the future.

Cash qualification. Since a lender advances only a portion of the purchase price of a property, according to the lender's loan-to-value ratio, the lender will verify that a borrower has the cash resources to make the required down payment. If some of a borrower's down payment cash comes as a gift from a relative or friend, a lender may require a gift letter from the donor stating the amount of the gift and that there is no requirement to repay it. On the other hand, if someone is lending an applicant a portion of the down payment with a repayment provision, the lender will consider this another debt obligation and adjust the debt ratio accordingly. This can lower the amount a lender is willing to lend.

Net worth. An applicant's net worth shows a lender the depth of the applicant's cash reserves, the value and liquidity of assets, and the extent to which assets exceed liabilities. These facts are important to a lender as an indication of the applicant's ability to sustain debt payment in the event of loss of employment.

Underwriting decision and commitment

When a lender's underwriters have qualified an applicant, and the lender has decided to offer the loan, the lender gives the applicant a written notice of the agreement to lend under specific terms. This written promise is the **loan commitment.** The commitment may take a number of common forms, including a firm commitment, a lock-in commitment, a conditional commitment, and a take-out commitment.

A **firm commitment** is a straightforward offer to make a specific loan at a specific interest rate for a specific term. This kind of commitment is the one most commonly offered to home buyers.

A **"lock-in" commitment** is an offer to lend a specific amount for a specific term at a specific interest rate, but the interest rate is subject to an expiration date, for instance, sixty days. This guarantees that the lender will not raise the interest rate during the application and closing periods. The borrower may have to pay points or some other charge for the lock-in.

A **conditional commitment** offers to make a loan if certain provisions are met. This kind of commitment generally applies to construction loans. A typical condition for funding the loan is completion of a development phase.

A **take-out commitment** is an offer to make a loan that will "take out" another lender's loan, i.e., pay it off and replace it. The take-out loan is most often used to retire a construction loan. The take-out lender agrees to pay off the short-term construction loan by issuing a long-term permanent loan.

Automated Underwriting

Use of automated underwriting. Automated underwriting systems (AUS) are computer-based programs used by lenders to evaluate a borrower's creditworthiness and risk level. These systems analyze data such as credit scores, income, assets, ratios, and loan characteristics to determine whether a loan should be approved, referred for further review, or denied. These systems are used primarily in residential mortgage lending to streamline loan approvals and ensure compliance with secondary mortgage market guidelines.

Benefits. Multiple benefits are associated with using AUS for loan processing. Loan decisions are generated quickly, often within minutes. All applications are evaluated using standardized criteria, reducing subjective judgment. The systems are more efficient than manual underwriting, and the volume of paperwork may be reduced because the process is electronic. The systems use statistical modeling and large datasets to evaluate default risk, and the speed and efficiency of an AUS reduces operational costs for lenders, which, in theory at least, may translate into lower borrower costs.

Detriments. On the flip side, using an AUS limits lenders' flexibility. Unique or nontraditional borrowers may not fit standard algorithms. As with all systems, accurate input is required for accurate output. AUS processing may not account for all compensating factors that a skilled underwriter might recognize. Although these systems are designed to be neutral, algorithm-based systems can still reflect systemic patterns present in historical data, and lenders may rely heavily or exclusively on AUS findings without sufficient independent review.

Types of Mortgages and Sources of Financing

Conventional mortgages

A **conventional mortgage** loan is a permanent, long-term loan that is not FHA-insured or VA-guaranteed. Market rates usually determine the loan's interest rate.

Down payment and LTV. Because there is no insurance or guarantee from a government agency, the risk to a lender is greater for a conventional loan than for a non-conventional loan. This risk may be reflected in higher interest rates and stricter down payment and income qualification requirements. However, this is not always the case.

The loan-to-value (LTV) ratio is often lower on conventional loans than on those backed by the government, which means the down payment is higher. At the same time, conventional loans allow greater flexibility in fees, rates, and terms than do insured and guaranteed loans.

Private mortgage insurance , or PMI. Because conventional loans with a down payment of less than 20% of the property value carry higher risk, lenders often require borrowers to obtain private mortgage insurance (PMI). Mortgage insurance protects the lender against loss of a portion of the loan amount in the event of borrower default. PMI can be paid as a lump sum, annually, or monthly. When the borrower has achieved 20 percent equity in the property (the loan balance falls to 80% of the home's original value), the lender or servicer must terminate the PMI requirement on the borrower's written request.

Common mortgage types

Variations in the structure of interest rates, terms, payments, and principal repayment produce a number of commonly recognized mortgage loan types. Among these are the following.

Amortizing loan. Amortization is the gradual repayment of principal and interest over the term of the loan. The borrower's periodic payments to the lender include a portion for interest and a portion for principal. In a fully amortizing mortgage, the principal balance is zero at the end of the term. In a partially amortizing loan, the payments are not sufficient to retire the debt. At the end of the loan term, there is still a principal balance to be paid off.

Negatively amortized loan. Negative amortization causes the loan balance to increase over the term. This occurs if the borrower's periodic payment is insufficient to cover the interest owed for the period. The lender adds the amount of unpaid interest to the borrower's loan balance. Temporary negative amortization occurs on graduated payment loans and may occur on an adjustable-rate mortgage.

Adjustable and fixed-rate loans. Loans may have fixed or variable rates of interest over the loan term. Adjustable-rate mortgages (ARMs) allow the lender to change the interest rate at specified intervals and by a specified amount. Federal regulations place limits on incremental interest rate increases and on the total amount by which the rate may be increased over the loan term.

Components and mechanics of ARMs. There are numerous forms of adjustable rate loans, each with variations of the quantifications and limits on any or all of the following variables: the index, the margin, the adjustment interval, interest rate caps, and whether the loan may amortize negatively.

- **index** – this is a benchmark financial indicator that fluctuates based on market conditions, which is used to determine changes in the interest rate after any fixed initial periods

- **margin** – this is a fixed number of percentage points added to a fluctuating interest rate index to determine the new interest rate after the initial fixed period ends; new interest rate = index rate + the margin
- **adjustment interval** – this is how often an interest rate is adjusted, which can be quarterly, annually, every 5 years, etc.
- **interest rate caps-** caps set upward or downward limits on how much an interest rate can increase or decrease; caps serve to minimize the potential damage or windfall that unlimited adjustments can create
- **payment caps** – this cap limits how much a payment can increase or decrease; some payment caps allow a borrower to actually pay less than what is owed at a given interest rate level; the lender then adds the unpaid amounts to the loan balance, which then begins to accrue more interest expense; here, the loan balance increases due to the deficient payment
- **negative amortization** – this is a loan with an increasing principal balance despite regular payments being made; usually, there are caps on how much balances can increase; this situation is remedied by requiring a balloon payment, or retiring the loan altogether

Conforming v. non-conforming loans

Conforming loans. A conforming loan is a mortgage that meets the underwriting standards and loan limits established by Fannie Mae and Freddie Mac. Because these two organizations are the primary purchasers of mortgages from lenders, loans written by those lenders must conform to the stated standards in order to be eligible for sale. These loans have the following characteristics:

- fall within annual loan limits set by the Federal Housing Finance Agency (FHFA)
- meet specific credit, income, DTI, and documentation guidelines
- require full income and asset verification
- typically offer lower interest rates because they carry less risk and are easily resold

Non-conforming loans. A non-conforming loan does not meet Fannie Mae or Freddie Mac guidelines and therefore cannot be sold to the standard secondary mortgage market. This can happen for several reasons:

- The loan is considered a jumbo loan because it exceeds conforming loan limits.
- The borrower does not meet the standard credit or DTI guidelines.
- The borrower is self-employed or has other non-traditional income.
- The property type is unique and is therefore considered nonstandard collateral.

Lenders who fund non-conforming loans will most likely keep them in their own loan portfolios or sell them to private investors.

Custom mortgages

Partially amortized. A loan with a balance at the end of the term is a partially amortized, or balloon, loan. The monthly payments of principal and interest are not enough to fully repay the loan amount. A final payment (the balloon payment) is necessary to retire the loan. Florida requires a mortgage with such a loan to be clearly identified on the face of the mortgage, with the balloon payment amount specified.

Bi-weekly. If a loan is amortized as for a regular loan with 12 monthly payments per year, but payments are scheduled twice per month (biweekly) instead of once, the result is that the equivalent of an extra monthly payment is made each year. This is because there are 52 weeks in a year, which means 26 biweekly payments, which equals 13 months. With this arrangement, the borrower pays off the loan more quickly and saves substantial interest.

Package loans. A package loan finances the purchase of real estate and personal property. For example, a package loan might finance a furnished condominium, complete with all fixtures and decor.

Home equity loans. The ostensible purpose of this type of loan is to obtain funds for home improvement. Structurally, the home equity loan is a junior mortgage secured by the homeowner's equity. For some lenders, the maximum home equity loan amount is based on the difference between the property's appraised value and the lender's maximum loan-to-value ratio, including all existing mortgage loans. Thus, if a home is appraised at $500,000 and the lender's maximum LTV is 80%, the lender will lend a total of $400,000. If the owner's existing mortgage balance is $325,000, the owner would qualify for a $75,000 home equity loan.

Purchase money. With a purchase money mortgage, the borrower gives a mortgage and note to the seller to finance some or all of the purchase price of the property. The seller in this case is said to "take back" a note, or to "carry paper," on the property. Purchase money mortgages may be either senior or junior liens.

Reverse annuity. In a reverse annuity mortgage, a homeowner pledges the equity in the home as security for a loan that is paid out in regular monthly amounts over the term of the loan. The homeowner can convert equity into cash without losing ownership or possession.

Other types of custom loans

Senior and junior loans. When there are multiple loans on a single property, liens are prioritized by order of the mortgages. The first, or senior, loan generally has priority over any subsequent loans. Second loans are riskier than first loans because the senior lender is satisfied first in the event of default. Therefore, interest rates on second mortgages are generally higher than on first mortgages.

Fixed and graduated payment loans. Loans may have variable payments over the term or a single fixed payment. With a graduated payment mortgage, the payments at the beginning of the loan term are insufficient to fully amortize the loan, and unpaid interest is added to the principal balance. Payments are later adjusted to fully amortize the loan's increased balance over the remaining loan term.

Interest-only loan. In an interest-only loan, periodic payments over the loan term apply only to interest owed, not to principal. At the end of the term, the full balance must be paid off in a lump-sum, "balloon" payment. Since these loans have no periodic principal payments, their monthly payments are smaller than those of amortizing loans for the same amount at the same interest rate.

Buydown loan. A buydown loan involves prepaying interest on a loan. The prepayment effectively lowers the interest rate and the borrower's periodic payments. Buydowns typically occur when a builder wants to market a new development to a buyer who cannot quite qualify for the loan at market rates. By "buying down" a borrower's mortgage, a builder enables the borrower to obtain the loan. The builder may then pass the costs of the buydown to the buyer through a higher purchase price.

Construction loan. A construction loan finances the construction of improvements. This type of loan is paid out by the lender in installments linked to stages of the construction process. The loan is usually interest-only, and the borrower makes periodic payments based on the amount disbursed so far. As short-term, high-risk financing, the interest rates are usually higher than those for long-term financing. The borrower is expected to find permanent ("take out") financing elsewhere to pay off the temporary loan when construction is complete.

Bridge loan. A bridge, or gap, loan is used to cover a gap in financing between short-term construction financing and long-term permanent financing. For instance, a developer may have difficulty finding a long-term lender to take out the construction loan. However, as the construction loan is expensive and must be paid off as soon as possible, the developer may find an interim lender who will pay off the construction loan but not agree to a long-term loan.

Participation loan. In a participation loan, the lender participates in the income and/or equity of the property, in return for giving the borrower more favorable loan terms than would otherwise be justified. For instance, the borrower makes smaller periodic payments than the interest rate and loan amount require, and the lender makes up the difference by receiving some of the property's income. This type of loan usually involves an income property.

Permanent (take-out) loan. A permanent loan is a long-term loan that "takes out" a construction or short-term lender. The long-term lender pays off the balance on the construction loan when the project is completed, leaving the borrower with a long-term loan under more favorable terms than the construction loan offered.

Blanket. A blanket mortgage is secured by more than one property, such as multiple parcels of real estate in a development.

Sale-and-leaseback. In a sale-and-leaseback, an owner that occupies a commercial property sells it to an investor and simultaneously leases it back under a long-term lease, continuing to operate from the same location. The arrangement converts the owner's equity into cash that can be reinvested in the business, removes the real estate from the company's balance sheet, and lets the former owner deduct the lease payments as a business expense. The investor-buyer becomes the landlord and obtains a property with a built-in, creditworthy tenant.

Government-insured loans (FHA loans)

Purpose of FHA loans. The Federal Housing Administration (FHA) is an agency of the Department of Housing and Urban Development (HUD). It does not lend money, but insures permanent long-term loans made by others. The lender must be approved by the FHA, and the borrower must meet certain FHA qualifications. In addition, the property used to secure the loan must meet FHA standards. The FHA insures that the lender will not suffer significant loss in the case of borrower default. To provide this security, FHA insures the loan and charges the borrower an insurance premium. FHA loans typically have a higher loan-to-value ratio than conventional loans, allowing borrowers to make a smaller down payment.

FHA loan characteristics

The basic FHA-insured loan program is the **Title II, Section 203(b)** program for loans on one- to four-family residential properties. Among the features of this program are the following.

Qualifying ratios. FHA lenders use two ratios, the income ratio (also called the housing expense ratio, or HER) and the debt ratio (also called the total obligations ratio, or TOR), to assess a borrower's ability to repay a loan. These ratios are discussed in detail in a later section.

FHA mortgage insurance. The FHA determines how much mortgage insurance must be provided and charges the borrower an appropriate mortgage insurance premium (MIP). The initial premium is payable at closing (called an up-front mortgage insurance premium, UFMIP). Further annual premiums are charged monthly. The amount of the premium varies according to the loan term and the applicable loan-to-value ratio.

Lending source. The FHA does not make or process loans. It approves lenders, who then make loans according to FHA parameters.

Direct endorsement. Under the FHA direct endorsement program, HUD authorizes approved lenders to underwrite and approve FHA-insured loans on their own, reviewing the appraisal, the borrower's credit, and the property without submitting the file to HUD for prior approval. The lender certifies that the loan meets FHA requirements, and HUD then insures it. The program greatly speeds FHA loan processing while leaving HUD responsible for insuring the loan.

Borrower default. The FHA reimburses the lender for losses due to default by the borrower, including costs of foreclosure.

Appraisal. The property must be appraised by an FHA-approved appraiser. The property must also meet the FHA's standards for type and quality of construction, neighborhood quality, and other features.

Maximum loan amount. The FHA has set maximum loan amounts for over 80 regions. Borrowers within a region are limited to the loan ceiling amount in effect for the region. In addition, the maximum loan amount is restricted by the loan-to-value ratios in effect. The maximum FHA-backed loan a borrower can obtain will be the lesser of the regional ceiling amount or the amount dictated by the loan-to-value standard. Calculations are based on the lesser of the sale price or the appraised value.

Down payment requirement. The minimum down payment for an FHA-backed loan is based on the lower of the appraised value or the sales price. The present requirement for single-family residential loans is 3.5%.

Maximum loan term. Thirty years is the maximum length of the repayment period.

Prepayment privilege. The borrower has the right to pay off the loan at any time without penalty, provided the lender is given prior notice. The lender may charge up to 30 days' interest if the borrower provides less than 30 days' notice.

Assumability. FHA-backed loans on owner-occupied properties are assumable if the buyer is qualified. Lenders and borrowers should check with FHA for current requirements.

Interest rate. The lender and borrower negotiate the interest rate on an FHA- backed loan without any involvement by FHA.

Points, fees , and costs. The lender may charge discount points, a loan origination fee, and other such charges. These may be paid by the buyer or the seller. However, if the seller pays more than a specified percentage of the costs normally paid by a buyer, the FHA may regard these as sales concessions and lower the sales price on which the loan insurance amount is based.

In addition to Section 203(b) loan programs, FHA offers insurance coverage for other loan products. These include:

- home improvement loans
- subsidized loans for low- and middle-income families
- loans for condominiums
- loans for multi-family projects
- graduated-payment loans
- adjustable-rate loans

VA-guaranteed Loans

The loan guarantee. The Veterans Administration (Department of Veterans Affairs) offers loan guarantees to qualified veterans. The VA, like the FHA, does not lend money except in certain areas where other financing is not generally available. Instead, the VA partially guarantees permanent long-term loans originated by VA-approved lenders on properties that meet VA standards. The VA's guarantee enables lenders to issue loans with higher loan-to-value ratios than would otherwise be possible. The interest rate on a VA-guaranteed loan is usually lower than that on a conventional loan. The borrower does not pay any premium for the loan guarantee, but does pay a VA funding fee at closing.

VA loans: key characteristics

Qualifications. VA –guaranteed loans are available to veterans, their surviving spouse if not remarried, and persons on active duty.

Eligibility. Eligibility requirements vary depending on length of service and other circumstances. Prospective borrowers should consult the VA website https://www.va.gov/housing-assistance/home-loans/eligibility/ to learn how to acquire a Certificate of Eligibility to present to lenders.

Lending source. VA-approved lenders make most VA-guaranteed loans, although the VA can make direct loans where approved lenders are not available. The lender and the borrower negotiate interest rate, points, and closing costs.

Property eligibility. VA-guaranteed loans are issued for financing, refinancing, or construction of residential properties of one- to four-dwelling units, provided the borrower resides in one of the units.

Qualifying ratios. The VA uses a debt ratio (total obligations ratio, or TOR) and calculations adjusted for regional incomes to qualify a borrower. This process is described in more detail in a later section.

Borrower default. The VA reimburses the lender for losses up to the guaranteed amount if the proceeds from a foreclosure sale fail to cover the loan balance.

Appraisal. The property must be appraised by a VA-approved appraiser. The VA issues a Certificate of Reasonable Value, which establishes a maximum value for the VA-guaranteed portion of the loan. The property must meet certain VA specifications.

Down payment requirement. The VA usually requires no down payment, although the lender may require one.

Maximum loan amount (entitlement). The VA does not cap the loan amount, but it does limit the liability it can assume, which usually influences the amount an institution will lend. The amount a qualified veteran with full entitlement can borrow without making a down payment determines the practical loan limits. This amount varies by county. The basic entitlement available to each eligible veteran is $36,000. Lenders will generally lend a maximum of 4 times that amount without a down payment if the veteran is fully qualified and the property appraises for the asking price.

A veteran must apply for a Certificate of Eligibility to find out how much the VA will guarantee in a particular situation.

Maximum loan term. The maximum loan term for one- to four-family residences is 30 years. For loans secured by farms, the maximum loan term is 40 years.

Prepayment privilege. The loan may be paid off early without penalty.

Assumability. VA loans are assumable with lender approval. Usually, the person assuming the loan must have VA eligibility, and the assumption may have to be approved by the VA.

Interest rate. Lender and borrower negotiate the interest rate for all VA-insured loans.

Points, fees , and costs. The lender may charge discount points, origination fees, and other reasonable costs. These may be paid by the seller (with some limits) or the buyer, but may not be financed. The VA funding fee, however, may be included in the loan amount. The funding fee is a percentage of the loan amount, which varies based on the type of loan, military category, whether the loan is a first-time loan, and whether there is a down payment.

Other VA programs. In addition to insuring loans to veterans, the VA may insure loans for lenders who set up a special account with the VA. The VA may also actually lend money directly when an eligible veteran cannot find other mortgage money locally.

Rural Housing Services Administration Loan

A Rural Housing Service (RHS) loan, commonly known as a USDA loan, is a government-backed mortgage designed to help low- to moderate-income borrowers purchase homes in eligible "rural" areas. The program is administered by the United States Department of Agriculture. Note that "rural" generally means an area that has a population of 35,000 or fewer. These areas are defined not only by population but also by urbanization and the extent of urban amenities. Small towns, villages, and some suburban areas on the outskirts of major metropolitan regions may qualify if they meet USDA criteria.

Small towns, villages, and some suburban areas on the outskirts of major metropolitan regions may qualify if they meet USDA criteria.

Other qualification criteria are as follows:

- borrower household income must fall within USDA limits for the county
- generally limited to low- to moderate-income households (typically up to 115% of area median income
- no statutory limits, but most lenders require a credit score of at least 640 for streamlined approval
- borrowers must demonstrate stable employment and sufficient income
- typical DTI ratios around 29% housing and 41% total debt
- property must be a single-family residence (including some condos or manufactured homes) used as borrower's primary residence
- borrower must be a U.S. citizen, U.S. non-citizen national, or qualified alien

Borrowers are not required to have a down payment, but they must pay both an upfront and an ongoing guarantee fee.

Financing Mortgaged Property

When a buyer pays cash for a property at closing, any existing mortgage on the property is paid off from the sale proceeds, and the seller's interests are transferred to the buyer. The cash may be entirely the buyer's, or some of it may be the proceeds of a new mortgage loan undertaken by the buyer. However, there are other ways for the buyer to purchase a mortgaged property, namely:

- subject to the existing mortgage
- with a wraparound mortgage
- by assumption of the existing mortgage
- by contract for deed

Purchasing "Subject to" property

In buying a property subject to the existing mortgage, the buyer takes title and makes loan payments to the mortgagee (lender), while the seller (original mortgagor) remains personally responsible for the loan payments. In the event of a default, the lender can foreclose and sue the seller (not the buyer) for any deficiency if the sale proceeds do not satisfy the debt.

Purchase money mortgages

With a purchase money mortgage, the borrower gives a mortgage and note to the seller to finance some or all of the purchase price of the property. The seller in this case is said to "take back" a note, or to "carry paper," on the property. Purchase money mortgages may be either senior or junior liens.

Wraparounds

In a wraparound loan arrangement, the seller receives a junior mortgage from the buyer, and uses the buyer's payments to make the payments on the original first mortgage. A wraparound enables the buyer to obtain financing

with a minimum cash investment. It also potentially enables the seller to profit from any difference between a lower interest rate on the senior loan and a higher rate on the wraparound loan. A wraparound is possible only if the senior mortgagee allows it.

Assumptions

With a mortgage assumption, the buyer acquires title to a mortgaged property and, signing a new promissory note with the lender, takes on personal responsibility for the terms and payments of the mortgage. The buyer is now primarily liable, but the original mortgagor remains secondarily liable under the original promissory note. Thus, if the buyer defaults, the lender can sue both the buyer and the seller for any deficiency in the proceeds of a foreclosure sale to satisfy the debt. A novation agreement, signed by seller, buyer, and lender, can relieve the seller of any further liability after the sale.

Contracts for deed

A contract for deed (land contract, installment sale contract, conditional sales contract, agreement for deed) allows the buyer of a property to defer payment of some or all of the purchase price over a specified period. During the period, the seller holds legal title while the buyer holds equitable title. The buyer takes possession of the property, makes payments of principal and interest to the seller, and maintains the property. At the end of the period, the buyer pays the seller the remainder of the full purchase price, and the seller conveys legal title to the buyer.

A contract for deed serves several purposes for a seller. First, it facilitates a sale that might otherwise be impossible. Second, it may give the seller certain tax benefits. Since the seller is not liable for capital gains tax until the purchase price is received, the installment sale lowers the seller's tax liability in the year of the sale. There may also be a reduction in closing costs. Disadvantages for the seller include: the buyer might create encumbrances during the contract or cause disputes and litigation over the contract.

For the buyer, the contract for deed makes possible a purchase where adequate credit and funds for a down payment and loan qualification may be lacking. Disadvantages for the buyer include: the seller may not be able to deliver marketable title at the end of the contract period, but the buyer must make payments nevertheless; or the seller may cloud the title with liens; or the seller may not have applied the buyer's payments to the seller's necessary loan payments.

Land development and construction loans

Land development loans overview. A land development loan is named for its purpose, to help finance the construction of infrastructure improvements to a tract of land. These would include streets, curbs, sewers, surveys, and landscaping.

Construction loans overview. Construction loans help finance improvements on a specific site within a larger development. Such improvements would include the building, driveways, landscaping, and related work. Here, increments of the total loan amount are disbursed as improvements are completed. Interest is charged on these loan portions as they are disbursed to the buyer. When improvements are complete, the borrower obtains permanent financing, and the construction loan is paid off.

Blanket loans. A blanket loan is one where the developer hypothecates other properties as collateral for additional financing. The blanket loan is retired when the hypothecated property – typically lots – is sold to buyers. In simpler terms, it is the developer's way of stair-stepping the completion of a development – the developer uses completed lots as collateral for financing new, surveyed lots. The cycle is completed when a buyer purchases the collateralized lot with its completed infrastructure improvements, and the developer uses the funds to pay off the outstanding balance on the blanket loan and/or finance new lots.

Takeout commitment. The take-out commitment is a pledge to grant a longer-term, "permanent" loan on given portions of completed construction in the development, if not for the entire development itself. The prime example here is where a permanent lender pledges to give a homebuyer a long-term loan for a completed new home. The homebuyer gets the takeout loan and pays off all accumulated construction debt on the property. The takeout commitment facilitates obtaining the construction financing in the first place, since the construction lender knows he or she will be able to complete the development cycle.

Buydowns. Buydowns are a form of developer assistance that help buyers qualify for a given loan. In a buydown, the borrower prepays portions of the interest up front to the lender. This effectively lowers the interest rate for the borrower, who now achieves a more affordable financing situation for the loan underwriters. Now the qualifying ratios may be met since the payments are more affordable. The rate reduction is typically for the initial loan period.

Fair Credit and Lending Laws

Equal Credit Opportunity Act (ECOA)

The Equal Credit Opportunity Act (ECOA) requires a lender to evaluate a loan applicant based on the applicant's own income and credit rating, unless the applicant requests that the lender consider another person's income and credit rating in the application. In addition, ECOA has prohibited a number of practices in mortgage loan underwriting. Accordingly, a lender may not:

- discount or disregard income from part-time work, a spouse, child support, alimony, or separate maintenance. Further, the loan officer may not ask whether any of the applicant's income is derived from these sources.
- assume that income for a certain type of person will be reduced because of an employment interruption due to childbearing or childraising. The loan officer may not ask about the applicant's plans or behavior concerning childbearing or birth control.

- refuse a loan solely on the basis that the security is located in a certain geographical area.
- ask applicants any question about their age, sex, religion, race, or national origin, except as the law may require.
- require a spouse to sign any document unless the spouse's income is to be included in the qualifying income, or unless the spouse agrees to become contractually obligated, or the state requires the signature for some purpose, such as clearing clouded title.

If a lender denies a loan request or offers a loan under terms different from those requested by the applicant, the lender must give the applicant written notice stating specific reasons for the action.

Borrower requirements. The lender must rely on eight types of information to determine that the borrower has the ability to repay the loan:

- current income or assets (excluding the value of the mortgaged property)
- current employment status
- credit history
- monthly payment for the mortgage
- monthly payments for other loans on the same property
- monthly payments for other mortgage-related expenses
- other debts
- monthly debt payments compared to monthly income (debt-to-income ratio)

The lender cannot use a temporarily low rate (introductory or "teaser" rate) to determine qualification. For an adjustable-rate mortgage (ARM), the highest rate

the borrower might have to pay is generally to be used.

The "ability to repay" requirements are relaxed in certain circumstances when the borrower is attempting to refinance from a riskier loan (such as an interest-only loan) to a less risky one (such as a fixed-rate mortgage).

Qualified Mortgage. A Qualified Mortgage is one that meets the "ability-to-repay" requirements, has certain required features, and is not allowed to have others. There are exceptions to these rules for certain kinds of small lenders. Issuing a Qualified Mortgage provides the lender with certain legal protections if the borrower fails to repay the loan.

Consumer Credit Protection Act

The Consumer Credit Protection Act (CCPA) is a comprehensive federal law comprising several specific acts relating to consumer credit and indebtedness. Among the most relevant acts for real estate licensees are the Truth in Lending Act and the Equal Credit Opportunity Act. These acts are discussed below.

Truth-in-Lending and Regulation Z

The Consumer Credit Protection Act, enacted in 1969 and since amended by the Truth-in-Lending Simplification and Reform Act, is implemented by the Federal Reserve's **Regulation Z.** Regulation Z applies to all loans secured by a residence. It does not apply to commercial loans or to agricultural loans over $25,000. Its provisions cover the disclosure of costs, the right to rescind the credit transaction, advertising credit offers, and penalties for non-compliance with the act.

The Dodd-Frank Wall Street Reform and Consumer Protection Act of 2010 (Dodd-Frank Act) established the Consumer Financial Protection Bureau (CFPB). to protect consumers by carrying out federal consumer financial laws. The CFPB consolidates most Federal consumer financial protection authority in one place, including enforcement of RESPA, ECOA, and the Truth in Lending Act.

Disclosure of costs. Under Regulation Z, a lender must disclose all finance charges as well as the true Annual Percentage Rate (APR) in advance of closing. A lender does not have to show the total interest payable over the loan term or include in the finance charges settlement costs such as appraisal, title, credit report, survey, or legal work fees. Disclosure must be distinctly presented in writing.

Rescission. A borrower has a limited right to cancel the credit transaction, usually within three days of completion. The right of rescission does not apply to "residential mortgage transactions," that is, to mortgage loans used to finance the purchase or construction of the borrower's primary residence.

Advertising. Any type of advertising to offer credit is subject to the requirements of full disclosure if it includes:

- a down payment percentage or amount
- an installment payment amount
- a specific amount for a finance charge
- a specific number of payments
- a specific repayment period
- a statement that there is no charge for credit

If any of these items appear in the advertising, the lender must disclose the down payment amount or percentage, repayment terms, the APR, and whether the rate can be increased after consummation of the loan.

Noncompliance. Willful violation of Regulation Z is punishable by up to a year in prison and/or a fine of up to $5,000. Other violations may be punished by requiring payment of court costs, attorneys' fees, damages, and a fine of up to $1,000.

Real Estate Settlement Procedures Act (RESPA)

RESPA is a federal law that aims to standardize settlement practices and ensure that buyers understand settlement costs. RESPA applies to purchases of residential real estate (one- to four-family homes) to be financed by "federally related" first mortgage loans. Federally related loans include:

- VA- and FHA-backed loans
- other government-backed or -assisted loans
- loans that are intended to be sold to FNMA, FHLMC, GNMA, or other government-controlled secondary market institutions
- loans made by lenders who originate more than one million dollars per year in residential loans.

In addition to mandating settlement procedures, RESPA prohibits lenders from paying kickbacks or unearned fees to parties who may have helped them obtain the borrower's business. This would include, for example, a fee paid to a real estate agent for referring a borrower to the lender.

To inform and educate borrowers, RESPA requires lenders to provide a loan applicant with a **loan information booklet** and a **loan estimate**. The booklet, produced by the Consumer Financial Protection Bureau, explains RESPA provisions, general settlement costs, and the required **Closing Disclosure** form. The lender must provide the estimate of closing costs within three days following the borrower's application.

Disclosures. The Consumer Financial Protection Bureau (CFPB) requires lenders to use two specific forms to disclose settlement costs to the buyer. A lender must provide a Loan Estimate (H-24) within three days of receiving the loan application and allow the buyer to see the Closing Disclosure (H-25) three days before loan consummation. A lender must also provide a buyer with a copy of the information booklet, "Your Home Loan Toolkit," concerning mortgage loans, closing costs, and closing procedures. The disclosures specify:

- settlement charges
- title charges
- recording and transfer fees
- reserve deposits required
- tax and insurance escrow deposits required
- any other fees or charges
- total closing costs

The disclosure forms vary, depending on loan type. The costs in the Closing Disclosure must match those in the Loan Estimate within certain standards.

Mortgage Fraud

Mortgage fraud is a crime that involves an intentional misstatement, misrepresentation, or omission of information that a lender or underwriter relies on in making, buying, or insuring a mortgage loan secured by real property. Possible perpetrators include borrowers, loan officers, real estate agents, appraisers, attorneys, escrow and title officers, and others. Offenders may be prosecuted in both federal and state courts.

Common types of mortgage fraud

Common examples of mortgage fraud include the following.

Applications. There are many ways for a loan application to be fraudulent. For example, a borrower may attempt to obtain a loan on a property intended for investment at a low interest rate by fraudulently stating that the borrower will occupy the property as a residence. In another context, the borrower may overstate income, understate liabilities, or make a false claim about employment to qualify for a loan.

Appraisals. An appraised value may be overstated or understated. Overstating may enable the borrower to obtain more money from the lender, possibly to share with the seller or an agent. Understating may allow a buyer to obtain a property at an artificially low price.

Multiple loans. A borrower may obtain more than one loan on the same property, creating unknown liabilities for lenders with junior mortgages and requiring all lenders to engage in litigation.

Lien stacking. Perpetrators may record multiple deeds of trust or assignment documents on the same property in a short period of time so that the liens won't be discovered in a title search. In this way, multiple lenders may be induced to make loans on the same property.

Identity theft. A person using a stolen identity may obtain a loan and abscond with the proceeds without making any payments to the lender. The person whose identity has been stolen may be left liable.

Straw borrowers. The credit information of an individual who is not the true buyer may be used to obtain a loan where the actual buyer would not qualify.

Loans. A buyer with poor credit may be qualified for a loan without being required to provide documentation of employment, income, assets, or indebtedness. When the borrower cannot repay the loan, the lender takes the collateral and profits from the fees and down payment.

Red flags

Inflated appraisals, inflated contract prices, missing or incomplete documentation, recent ownership changes, loan anomalies, and other irregularities may indicate that mortgage fraud is in progress. Associates should take note and report concerns to their brokers.

Mortgage fraud is a felony in Florida. The felony is one of the third degree if loan documents show a loan amount under $100,000, and second degree if it is greater. Florida's mortgage fraud statute can be viewed at http://www.leg.state.fl.us/statutes/index.cfm?App_mode=Display_Statute&URL=0800-0899/0817/Sections/0817.545.html .

Snapshot Review for Chapter 12

The following review summarizes the key rules and concepts from Chapter 12.

MORTGAGE CONCEPTS

Mortgage Basics

- mortgage financing = borrower signs note and mortgage as security for loan
- hypothecation = pledging property without giving up ownership
- Florida is a lien-theory state
- mortgagor = borrower; mortgagee = lender

Loan Instruments

- promissory note = evidence of debt and promise to repay
- mortgage = security instrument pledging property as collateral
- note includes loan amount, repayment terms, interest rate, default provisions
- satisfaction of mortgage releases lien when debt is paid
- a mortgage may be assigned to another holder; an estoppel certificate verifies the unpaid balance

Mortgage Priority

- recording date determines lien priority
- first mortgage has highest priority
- junior liens paid after senior liens
- subordination agreements change lien priority voluntarily

Mortgage Clauses

- PITI = principal, interest, taxes, insurance
- escrow account holds tax and insurance payments
- due-on-sale clause allows lender to demand payoff upon transfer
- defeasance clause releases mortgage when loan satisfied
- right of reinstatement allows borrower to cure default

COMMON MORTGAGE CHARACTERISTICS

Loan Components

- principal = original amount borrowed
- down payment = purchase price minus loan amount
- LTV ratio compares loan amount to property value
- equity = value minus debt

Interest and Payments

- fixed-rate loans maintain same rate for term
- adjustable-rate loans (ARMs) allow periodic rate changes
- APR reflects total borrowing cost beyond interest rate
- amortized payments reduce both interest and principal over time

Fees and Accounts

- escrow accounts pay taxes and insurance
- discount points = prepaid interest charged at closing

- origination fee covers lender processing costs
- PMI generally required for conventional loans above 80% LTV

PRIMARY AND SECONDARY MORTGAGE MARKETS

Primary Mortgage Market

- lenders originate loans directly to borrowers
- includes banks, savings associations, mortgage bankers, credit unions
- mortgage brokers connect borrowers with lenders
- portfolio lenders retain loans instead of selling them

Secondary Mortgage Market

- secondary market buys existing mortgage loans
- increases available mortgage funds and liquidity
- FNMA (Fannie Mae), GNMA (Ginnie Mae), FHLMC (Freddie Mac) major participants
- conforming loans meet secondary market standards

Mortgage Loan Originators

- MLOs process applications and negotiate loan terms
- SAFE Act establishes licensing standards
- NMLS maintains registration and licensing system

Mortgage Foreclosure

- foreclosure enforces lender's lien after borrower default
- Florida primarily uses judicial foreclosure
- acceleration clause makes full balance immediately due

Judicial Foreclosure Process

- lender files foreclosure lawsuit
- lis pendens gives public notice of pending action
- property sold at public auction
- deficiency judgment possible if proceeds insufficient
- borrower retains right of redemption until sale concludes

Alternatives to Foreclosure

- deed in lieu transfers title voluntarily to lender
- short sale allows lender-approved sale below loan balance
- loan modification or forbearance may avoid foreclosure

Residential Loan Underwriting

- lender evaluates borrower and property risk
- considers income, debts, credit, employment, assets, and cash reserves
- appraisal confirms collateral value
- Qualified Mortgage rules address ability-to-repay standards

Buyer Qualification

- income ratio measures housing expense against gross income
- debt ratio measures total obligations against income
- lenders review credit reports and credit scores

- stable employment and sufficient cash reserves improve approval chances

Loan Commitments

- firm commitment = straightforward approval
- lock-in commitment guarantees interest rate for set period
- conditional commitment requires certain conditions be met
- automated underwriting systems (AUS) speed loan evaluation

TYPES OF MORTGAGES

Conventional and Government Loans

- conventional loans are not FHA-insured or VA-guaranteed
- FHA insures loans made by approved lenders
- VA guarantees loans for eligible veterans
- FHA loans allow lower down payments and higher LTVs
- FHA direct endorsement lets approved lenders underwrite and approve FHA loans without prior HUD review

Common Mortgage Types

- amortized, partially amortized, and balloon loans
- fixed-rate and adjustable-rate mortgages
- interest-only and graduated-payment loans
- construction, bridge, blanket, and home equity loans
- reverse annuity mortgage converts equity into income
- sale-and-leaseback: owner sells then leases back, freeing equity while keeping occupancy

Fair Credit and Lending Laws

- Equal Credit Opportunity Act (ECOA): the lender must judge an applicant on his or her own income and creditworthiness, and may not discriminate by age, sex, religion, race, or national origin
- ECOA bars refusing a loan based on the property's geographic area, and requires the lender to state the reasons for a denial or for different terms
- ability-to-repay rule: the lender verifies income, employment, credit history, debts, and the debt-to-income ratio; a temporary teaser rate cannot be used to qualify the borrower
- a Qualified Mortgage meets the ability-to-repay standard and includes required loan features
- Truth-in-Lending Act and Regulation Z: the lender must disclose all finance charges and the true Annual Percentage Rate (APR)
- the borrower has a limited three-day right of rescission on certain credit transactions
- advertising that states specific credit terms triggers full Regulation Z disclosure
- the Dodd-Frank Act created the Consumer Financial Protection Bureau (CFPB)
- RESPA standardizes settlement practices, requires a loan information booklet and Loan Estimate, and prohibits kickbacks and unearned fees
- the CFPB requires the Loan Estimate and Closing Disclosure, which must match within allowed tolerances

Mortgage Fraud

- mortgage fraud is an intentional misstatement, misrepresentation, or omission that a lender relies on to fund a loan

- common types: fraudulent applications, inflated or understated appraisals, multiple loans on the same property, and lien stacking
- identity theft: a stolen identity is used to obtain a loan and abscond with the proceeds
- straw borrowers: another person's credit is used to qualify while the true buyer remains hidden
- red flags: inflated appraisals or contract prices, missing or incomplete documentation, recent ownership changes, and loan anomalies
- mortgage fraud is a felony in Florida

Chapter 12 Quiz: Financing Real Estate

12.1 A promissory note is ______.

a. the borrower's written promise to repay the loan
b. the document that pledges the property as security
c. a government insurance policy
d. the lender's guarantee to fund

12.2 The mortgage instrument functions to ______.

a. transfer ownership to the lender
b. pledge the property as security for the loan
c. set the interest rate
d. insure the lender against default

12.3 Pledging property as security for a loan without giving up possession is called ______.

a. subordination
b. novation
c. hypothecation
d. defeasance

12.4 In a mortgage, the borrower is the ______.

a. mortgagee
b. vendee
c. trustee
d. mortgagor

12.5 Florida is classified as a ______.

a. lien-theory state
b. title-theory state
c. deed-of-trust state
d. community-property state

12.6 When a loan is fully paid, the lender records a ______ to clear the lien.

a. deed in lieu
b. satisfaction of mortgage
c. subordination agreement
d. promissory note

12.7 When two mortgages exist on a property, priority is generally determined by ______.

a. the size of each loan
b. the borrower's preference
c. the date each was recorded
d. the interest rate

12.8 The clause that lets a lender demand the entire balance upon default is the ______.

a. prepayment clause
b. defeasance clause
c. subordination clause
d. acceleration clause

12.9 A due-on-sale (alienation) clause allows the lender to ______.

a. demand full repayment if the borrower transfers the property without approval
b. raise the interest rate annually
c. waive the down payment
d. release part of the collateral

12.10 In Florida, unless a clause states otherwise, a borrower may pay off a loan early ______.

a. only with a penalty
b. without a prepayment penalty
c. only after five years
d. only with lender consent

12.11 The clause providing that the lender will release its lien once the debt is paid is the ______.

a. acceleration clause
b. escalation clause
c. defeasance (release) clause
d. alienation clause

12.12 An agreement in which a lien holder allows its loan to move to a lower priority is a ______.

a. satisfaction
b. novation
c. reconveyance
d. subordination clause

12.13 The loan-to-value (LTV) ratio expresses the relationship between ______.

a. the loan amount and the property's value
b. the interest rate and the term
c. taxes and insurance
d. income and debt

12.14 A homeowner's equity is ______.

a. the total of all mortgage payments made
b. the property's value minus the debt owed against it
c. the original purchase price
d. the annual property tax

12.15 One discount point equals ______ of the loan amount.

a. 10 percent
b. 5 percent
c. 1 percent
d. one-half percent

12.16 A loan origination fee is charged by the lender to ______.

a. insure the loan
b. lower the interest rate
c. pay the appraiser
d. cover the cost of processing the loan

12.17 Private mortgage insurance (PMI) ______.

a. protects the lender against loss when the down payment is small
b. protects the borrower if he or she loses a job
c. is required on all VA loans
d. pays the property taxes

12.18 Lenders often collect monthly amounts for taxes and insurance in a(n) ______.

a. discount account
b. escrow (impound) account
c. sinking fund
d. reserve for depreciation

12.19 The market in which loans are originated directly with borrowers is the ______.

a. secondary mortgage market
b. bond market
c. primary mortgage market
d. money market

12.20 Fannie Mae (FNMA) operates primarily in the ______.

a. primary mortgage market
b. insurance market
c. construction lending market
d. secondary mortgage market

12.21 Which entity is a government-owned corporation that guarantees securities backed by pools of FHA and VA loans?

a. Ginnie Mae (GNMA)
b. Fannie Mae (FNMA)
c. Freddie Mac (FHLMC)
d. the Federal Reserve

12.22 Freddie Mac (FHLMC) is best described as a ______.

a. federal insurance agency
b. government-sponsored enterprise in the secondary market
c. primary lender
d. title insurer

12.23 Florida enforces mortgage liens through ______.

a. strict foreclosure
b. nonjudicial power-of-sale foreclosure
c. judicial foreclosure
d. self-help repossession

12.24 A borrower who conveys the property to the lender to avoid foreclosure is offering a ______.

a. short sale
b. satisfaction
c. subordination
d. deed in lieu of foreclosure

12.25 A short sale occurs when ______.

a. the lender agrees to accept less than the balance owed on the loan
b. the property sells within 30 days
c. the borrower prepays the loan
d. the lender forecloses in under 90 days

12.26 The housing expense (income) ratio limits the percentage of ______ a borrower may spend on housing.

a. net income
b. gross income
c. take-home pay
d. the loan amount

12.27 The total obligations (debt) ratio considers the borrower's housing expense plus ______.

a. property taxes only
b. utilities
c. other recurring debt payments
d. the down payment

12.28 A conventional mortgage is one that is ______.

a. insured by the FHA
b. guaranteed by the VA
c. issued only by the government
d. not insured or guaranteed by a government agency

12.29 A loan that meets Fannie Mae and Freddie Mac guidelines is called a ______.

a. conforming loan
b. subprime loan
c. jumbo loan
d. package loan

12.30 An FHA loan is ______.

a. guaranteed by the Department of Veterans Affairs
b. insured by the Federal Housing Administration
c. funded directly by the federal government
d. available only to first-time buyers

12.31 A VA-guaranteed loan is available to ______.

a. any borrower with good credit
b. low-income borrowers only
c. eligible veterans and service members
d. investors buying rental property

12.32 A purchase money mortgage is a form of ______.

a. government insurance
b. construction lending
c. secondary-market security
d. seller financing

12.33 When a buyer takes title "subject to" the existing mortgage, ______.

a. the seller remains personally liable on the original loan
b. the buyer formally assumes the loan and releases the seller
c. the loan is automatically paid off
d. the lender must approve the down payment

12.34 The Equal Credit Opportunity Act (ECOA) prohibits ______.

a. prepayment of loans
b. discrimination against credit applicants based on protected characteristics
c. charging discount points
d. the sale of loans into the secondary market

12.35 The Truth-in-Lending Act and Regulation Z require lenders to disclose ______.

a. the seller's net proceeds
b. the appraised value
c. the annual percentage rate (APR) and finance charges
d. the property's zoning

CHAPTER 13: CLOSING REAL ESTATE TRANSACTIONS

Contents

- **Preliminary Steps to Closing**
- **The Closing Event**
- **Real Estate Settlement Procedures Act**
- **Financial Settlement of the Transaction**
- **State Transfer Taxes**
- **Other Charges**
- **Closing Disclosure Statement**
- **Closing Cost Itemization: Case Illustration**

Learning Objectives

Upon completion of this chapter, you will be able to:

1. Describe the preliminary steps to closing a transaction
2. Describe the objective of a pre-closing inspection
3. Identify the provisions of the Consumer Financial Protection Bureau of Closing Requirement
4. as they relate to the Closing Disclosure
5. Identify RESPA prohibitions
6. Identify IRS reporting provisions concerning foreign investors
7. Describe the various sections of the Closing Disclosure
8. Prorate property taxes, mortgage interest and prepaid rent
9. Understand Closing Disclosure
10. Describe the closing process, including the transfer of title and the transfer of purchase funds
11. Explain the escrow closing procedure and the role of the closing agent
12. Identify the broker role and responsibilities in the closing process
13. Identify the RESPA disclosure requirements, including the Loan Estimate and the information booklet, and the timing of each
14. Explain how debits and credits are used to settle a real estate transaction
15. Calculate the Florida documentary stamp taxes on deeds and notes and the intangible tax on mortgages
16. Identify the other closing charges, including title insurance, document preparation, and the municipal lien search

Preliminary Steps to Closing

Contracting and escrow

Fully executed purchase contract. Whether the contract is a standard form, such as the FAR/BAR "As Is" contract, or a custom agreement, it contains the terms and conditions governing the transaction. It sets forth the duties and obligations of each party, including giving the buyer a specified timeframe to inspect the property. The contract should be reviewed and renegotiated until both parties are satisfied enough to sign it. The contract is enforceable only when it is fully executed.

Earnest money and other funds. After the execution of the contract (typically within three days), the buyer provides earnest money to the licensee as a good-faith deposit. The licensee must turn the money over to his or her broker by the end of the next business day after receiving it. The broker must then deposit the earnest money into an escrow account within 3 business days of the date the licensee received it.

The escrow account may be the broker's own, or it may be with a title company or an attorney. The earnest money will remain in the escrow account until the transaction is completed (closing), at which time it will be transferred to the appropriate party. If the purchase contract requires any additional funds from the buyer before closing, those funds must be tracked and deposited into the escrow account as specified in the contract.

The pre-closing period

Loan application and approval. A buyer who plans to finance the home purchase must obtain a mortgage loan before completing the purchase. Buyers may obtain pre-approval for a loan before finding a home, so they know the maximum amount they qualify for. Pre-approval also speeds up the closing process by eliminating any additional wait time for loan approval. If the buyer has not been pre-approved, he or she must apply for and obtain loan approval. The buyer may also want to lock in the loan's interest rate in advance so there are no rate increases during the loan approval and transaction closing processes.

Most transactions allow for the contract to be contingent upon the buyer's obtaining conventional or FHA financing for the purchase. Since loan approval is typically a contingency in the purchase contract, the seller should be notified once approval is obtained.

Contingencies. The purchase contract usually includes contingencies. Typical contingencies include the following:

- the buyer's financing
- the buyer's home and pest inspections
- the seller's disclosure of all known material facts that can affect the home's value
- the seller's completion of any agreed-upon repairs unless the contract is an "as is" agreement
- the buyer's right to cancel the contract based on the results of the inspections

The contract will address whether the contingencies are subject to active or passive approval. If they are to be actively approved, the contract must also include the dates by which the contingencies must be met and removed. If approval of the contingencies is to be passive, they will be considered approved if the buyer does not actively disapprove them.

Appraisal. The lender will order a property appraisal to ensure the property's value is sufficient to cover the mortgage loan if the buyer defaults. The buyer will also be interested in the appraisal to determine if the selling price is in line with the property's actual value. The buyer has a right to receive a copy of the appraisal at least three business days before the scheduled closing.

Title search and insurance. A title search verifies property ownership and uncovers any missing deeds and/or title clouds. The search is performed in the county where the property is located. Any issues found are the seller's responsibility to correct. To protect against unknown title issues that may arise in the future, both the lender and the buyer need separate title insurance policies.

Inspections. One of the most important steps in a real estate transaction is having the buyer inspect the property to ensure it is in saleable condition. This is especially important in a state as hot and humid as Florida, since the climate poses many risks to properties. The property inspection will check the structure and all systems on the property, including plumbing, electrical, and HVAC. Even with "As Is" contracts, property inspections are important to determine what issues, if any, the property has.

A pest inspection (separate from a property inspection) is especially critical in Florida, where wood-destroying organisms (WDO), such as termites and carpenter ants, are a real threat. Inspectors issue a WDO report and provide copies to the buyer, lender, and title company. Contingencies in the contract should include available actions if this inspection uncovers infestation or damage.

Required repairs. Unless the contract specifies the sale is "As Is," contingencies should include repairs, payment, or a lowered sale price for any issues found in either inspection. Once the repairs are completed, the work should be inspected to ensure they were completed and done properly. Then this contingency can be removed.

Survey. Like inspections and title searches, a survey is crucial for confirming the suitability and representation of the property. Both title companies and lenders require surveys. Buyers should also require one, as a survey will confirm whether the property boundaries match the publicly recorded legal description and whether there are any major encroachments on the property.

Buyer hazard insurance. Lenders require a property hazard insurance policy to be in place prior to closing. In Florida, insurance policies for flood and windstorm coverage are also particularly important, and lenders will require them depending on the property's location (such as in a coastal or low-lying flood area). Property insurance rates are set by the company offering coverage, but standard flood coverage is a national program, so those rates are set by FEMA.

Final preparations

Final walkthrough. Before closing, the buyer and the buyer's agent should perform a walkthrough of the property to make sure the seller or tenant has vacated the property. They should also check for the removal of any furnishings and appliances not included in the sale, and for the completion of any previously agreed-upon repairs. This is the point to confirm that all related contingencies have been removed.

Review of closing documents. Several vital closing documents must be signed and executed before the closing is finalized. These include the warranty deed, bill of sale, closing disclosure, a closing statement, loan documents such as the note and mortgage, and title clearing documents. Some of these documents are prepared by the title company or the attorney, and others by the lender.

Both the seller and the buyer need to review all of the documents they will be signing. While real estate licensees are not attorneys, they should be familiar with closing documents, be able to explain them to their clients, and make any necessary (and legal) changes or corrections. They should review the closing disclosure with their clients the day before the scheduled closing and plan to attend the actual closing.

Additional buyer funds. Before closing, the buyer may need to deposit additional funds into escrow. As the original earnest money is generally applied to the down payment, various additional payments may be required at different times before closing. For example, the lender may require the buyer to deposit funds in an escrow account to pay for the property's insurance and taxes, protecting the lender's collateral.

Just before escrow closes, both the buyer and the seller receive a closing statement from the escrow officer that lists the purchase price, all expenses associated with the purchase, and how those expenses will be allocated between the buyer and the seller. Many of the fees listed on the closing statement will have already been paid. However, the final closing statement has the credits and debits, which are paid out of escrow on behalf of the party being debited. Both the buyer and the seller will want to review the closing statement to ensure everything is in order. The seller will also want assurance that the buyer has the funds to close the transaction.

Earnest money transfer. In accordance with Florida license law, if the broker has held the earnest money in his or her own escrow account, the broker must account for and deliver all appropriate funds, deposits, payments, abstract of title, mortgage, conveyance, lease, and associated documents to the closing agent and/or other designated entitled individuals. When closing is imminent, and the lender has approved the loan, the closing agent will prepare to transfer the earnest money deposit, the additional buyer proceeds, and the mortgage loan funds to the seller.

The Closing Event

The setting

The closing event is the culmination of the real estate transaction. During this event, the buyer pays the purchase price and receives title to the property. At the same time, the buyer completes financing arrangements, and the buyer and seller pay all required taxes, fees, and charges.

Customary practices. There are several customary procedures and practices for conducting real estate closings in Florida. For example, it is common for sellers to pay for the documentary stamp tax on the deed and for buyers to pay the documentary stamp tax on the note. See "Rules of thumb" later in this section for more examples.

Time. The sale contract sets the closing date, usually within sixty days of signing. The time between signing and closing is expected to be sufficient to remove any contingencies, such as the buyer obtaining financing, completing inspections, and correcting identified physical defects. Failure of either buyer or seller to perform pre-closing actions specified in the contract can delay or terminate the transaction. If the contract includes a statement that "time is of the essence," all parties agree to meet the time limitations exactly as stated. If both parties consent, however, they can reschedule the closing date.

Location. Closings occur at various locations, such as the title company's office, the lender, the escrow agent, one of the attorneys, the broker, or the county recorder. The sale contract specifies the location.

Parties at closing. The primary parties at the closing are normally the buyer, seller, and a closing agent or escrow officer. Other parties who might be present include the title officer, attorneys, brokers or agents, and the lender's representative. It is not actually necessary for any of these parties to attend the meeting. The closing agent can complete the transaction, provided all documents have been duly executed in advance.

The closing process

The closing process consists of the buyer and seller verifying that each has fulfilled the terms of the sale contract. If they have, then the mortgage loan, if any, is closed; all expenses are apportioned and paid; the consideration is exchanged for the title; final documents are signed; and arrangements are made to record the transaction according to local laws.

The Closing Process

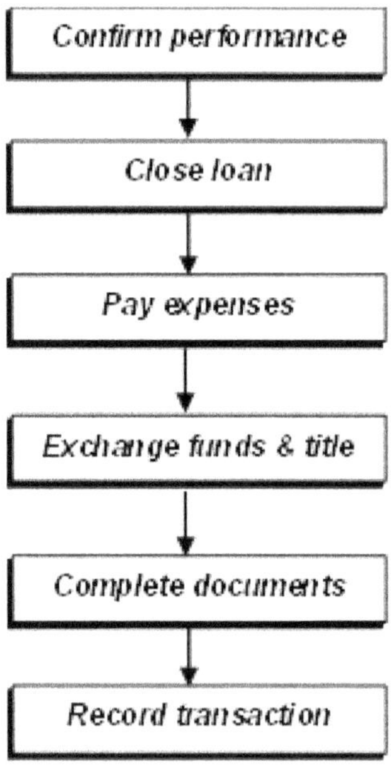

Transfer of title

The seller must provide evidence of marketable title, such as a commitment for title insurance from a title insurer. Before making a title commitment, a title company conducts a title search to identify any liens, encumbrances, restrictions, conditions, or easements affecting the title.

If there are any encumbrances or liens that damage the title, the seller is expected to remove these prior to the date specified in the contract. The most common title cloud is an unpaid lien.

The seller may also be asked to execute an affidavit of title stating that, since the date of the original title search, the seller has incurred no new liens, judgments, unpaid bills for repairs or improvements, no unrecorded deeds or contracts, no bankruptcies or divorces that would affect title, or any other defects the seller is aware of.

The purchaser, purchaser's lender, or title company may require a survey to verify the location and size of the property. The survey also identifies any easements, encroachments, or flood plain hazards.

The buyer should inspect the property to ensure it is in the condition the seller states, and that any repairs or other required actions have been performed. A final inspection, called a buyer's walk-through, should be conducted as close to the closing date as possible.

If the seller's mortgage lien(s) are to be satisfied at closing, the lender will provide a **payoff statement**, also called an **offset statement**, specifying the amount of unpaid principal and any interest due as of the closing date, plus fees that will be due the lender and any credits or penalties that may apply. The holder of a note secured by a trust deed will provide a similar statement, called a **beneficiary statement**, to show any unpaid balance. Even if the buyer is assuming the seller's mortgage, the buyer will want to know the exact unpaid balance as of the closing date.

Finally, the seller produces and/or deposits with the escrow agent the deed that conveys the property to the buyer.

Transfer of purchase funds

The buyer usually produces and/or deposits with the escrow agent the following:

- earnest money
- loan funds and documents
- any other cash needed to complete the purchase

Escrow procedures

If the closing occurs "in escrow" rather than face-to-face, the principal parties deposit funds and documents with the appointed escrow agent, and the escrow agent disburses funds and releases documents to the appropriate parties when all the conditions of the escrow have been met. If, for any reason, the transaction cannot be completed, for instance, if the buyer refuses the title as it is offered, or the buyer fails to produce the necessary cash, the escrow instructions usually provide a mechanism for reconveying title to the seller and funds to the buyer. In such a case, both parties return to their original status as if no sale had occurred.

Lender closing requirements

A lender is concerned about the quality of the collateral a borrower provides in exchange for the mortgage loan. The collateral would be endangered by defects in the title, by liens that would take precedence over the mortgage lien, such as a tax lien, and by physical damage to the property that is not repaired. Consequently, the lender typically requires a survey, a property inspection, hazard insurance, a title insurance policy, a reserve account for taxes and insurance, and possibly, private mortgage insurance. In some cases, the lender may also require a certificate of occupancy verifying that any new construction performed complies with local building codes.

Broker's role

A broker usually continues to provide service between the signing of the sale contract and the closing by arranging pre-closing activities such as inspections, surveys, appraisals, and repairs, and generally taking steps to ensure the closing can proceed as scheduled.

A broker may conduct proceedings at the closing meeting, or may have no further role in the transaction after the sale contract is signed, depending on local practices and the transaction in question. In Florida, proceedings are conducted by a closing officer, but the broker or associate is expected to be able to explain and verify entries on the closing documents and to attend the closing with the buyer and seller. The broker or associate is also responsible for delivering the escrow check to the closing.

Finally, if the seller of the property is a non-resident alien, U.S. law may require the broker to withhold and transmit to the Internal Revenue Service a portion of the sale proceeds to cover the alien seller's income tax liability. There are also special reporting requirements when the transaction involves a non-resident alien.

Foreign-principal affidavit at closing. As discussed in Chapter 11, Chapter 692, Florida Statutes, requires the buyer of Florida real property to sign an affidavit, at or before closing, attesting that the buyer is not a prohibited foreign principal or that the purchase otherwise complies with the law. The closing agent ordinarily collects this affidavit along with the other closing documents. This state requirement is separate from the federal FIRPTA withholding that applies when the seller is a foreign person.

Real Estate Settlement Procedures Act

The **Real Estate Settlement Procedures Act** (RESPA) is a consumer protection statute enacted in 1974. Its purpose is to clarify settlement costs and eliminate kickbacks and fees that increase them. RESPA specifies certain closing procedures when a purchase:

- involves a residential property, including one- to four-family residences, cooperatives, and condominiums;
- involves a first or second mortgage lien; and
- is being financed by a "federally-related" mortgage loan, which includes loans made by a federally-insured lender; loans insured or guaranteed by the VA or FHA, loans administered by HUD, and loans intended to be sold to FNMA, FHLMC, or GNMA.

RESPA regulations do not apply to transactions that are otherwise financed, except in the case of an assumption in which the terms of the assumed loan are modified or the lender's charges for the assumption exceed $50.

RESPA is directed at lenders and settlement companies, but licensees should be familiar with requirements and changes implemented as of January, 2014. The Dodd-Frank Act of 2010 granted rule-making authority under RESPA to the Consumer Financial Protection Bureau (CFPB) and generally granted the CFPB authority to supervise and enforce compliance with RESPA and its implementing regulations.

In 2013, the CFPB made substantive and technical changes to the existing regulations. Substantive changes included modifying the servicing transfer notice requirements and implementing new procedures and notice requirements for borrowers' error-resolution requests and information requests. The amendments also included new provisions related to escrow payments, force-placed insurance, general servicing policies, procedures, and requirements, early intervention, continuity of contact, loss mitigation, and the relation of RESPA's servicing provisions to state law. These RESPA amendments went into effect on January 10, 2014.

TRID

Effective October 3, 2015, a TILA/RESPA Integrated Disclosure Rule (TRID) integrates the disclosure requirements of RESPA and Truth-in-Lending, replacing the old Good Faith Estimate form and HUD-1 Uniform Settlement Statement with a new Loan Estimate form and Closing Disclosure form, respectively.

Information booklet

A lender subject to RESPA must give loan applicants the CFPB booklet, "Your Home Loan Toolkit," within three days of receiving a loan application. This booklet describes loans, closing costs, and the Closing Disclosure form.

Loan Estimate

A lender must give the applicant, at the time of application or within three business days of application, a Loan Estimate (H-24) of likely settlement costs. This estimate is usually based on comparable transactions completed in the area. The terms stated in the Closing Disclosure must agree with those of the Loan Estimate within certain limits.

Mortgage servicing disclosure

The lender must disclose to the buyer whether it intends to service the loan or convey it to another lender for servicing. This disclosure must also include information on how the buyer can resolve complaints.

Closing Disclosure

Under CFPB rules, a lender must use the Closing Disclosure (H-25) to disclose settlement costs to the buyer. This form covers all costs the buyer must pay at closing, whether to the lender or to other parties. Use of this form enforces RESPA's prohibitions against a lender's requiring a buyer to deposit an excessive amount in the tax and insurance escrow account or to use a particular title company for title insurance. The consumer must receive the completed form not later than three business days before closing, and has the right to inspect a revised form one business day before closing. A description and example of this form are provided later in this section.

Disclosures after settlement

Loan servicers must provide borrowers with an annual escrow statement that summarizes all inflows and outflows in the prior 12-month period. The statement must also disclose shortfalls or overages in the account and how the discrepancies will be resolved.

Limits on escrow accounts

Section 10 of RESPA limits the amounts lenders can require borrowers to place in escrow for purposes of paying taxes, hazard insurance, and other property-related expenses. The limitation applies to initial deposits and deposits made over the loan's term.

Referral fees and kickbacks

RESPA prohibits the payment of fees as part of a real estate settlement when no services are actually rendered. This prohibition includes referral fees for such services as title searches, title insurance, mortgage loans, appraisals, credit reports, inspections, surveys, and legal services.

Business relationships and affiliations among real estate firms, mortgage brokers, title insurance firms, and other such companies that are involved in a transaction are permitted, provided the relationships are disclosed in writing to the consumer, the consumer is free to go elsewhere for the relevant service, and the companies do not exchange fees for referrals.

Financial Settlement of the Transaction

Settlement process

The process of settlement consists of five basic steps:

1. Identify selling terms and closing costs.
2. Determine non-prorated debits and credits.
3. Determine prorated debits and credits.
4. Complete the closing statement.
5. Disburse funds.

Selling terms and closing costs

Selling terms include the price of the property, the buyer's deposit and down payment, and the terms and amounts of the buyer's financing. Closing costs are final expenses that the buyer or seller must pay at closing to complete the transaction. The sale contract identifies all selling terms and who pays which costs. The apportionment of expenses is subject to negotiation and, in the absence of a specific agreement, is determined by custom. Closing costs include such items as brokerage fees, mortgage-related fees, title-related expenses, and real estate taxes.

Florida customary cost allocation. Which party pays each charge is ultimately negotiable, but Florida follows well-settled customs that shape the settlement figures. The seller customarily pays the documentary stamp tax on the deed and, in most counties, the owner's title insurance policy; the buyer customarily pays the documentary stamp tax on the promissory note, the intangible tax on a new mortgage, the lender's title policy, and recording fees. (These Florida transfer taxes are detailed in the transfer-tax discussion in this chapter.) Because several of these customs vary by county, a licensee should confirm local practice and reflect it in the closing statement and prorations.

Debits and credits The closing statement accounts for the debits and credits of the buyer and seller to settle and complete the transaction. A debit is an amount that one party must pay at closing or has already paid prior to closing. A credit is an amount that a party must receive at closing or that has already been received.

The excess of the buyer's debits over the buyer's credits is the amount the buyer must bring to the closing. The excess of the seller's credits over the seller's debits is the amount the seller will receive at closing.

An individual expense item that one party owes to a party unrelated to the transaction, such as an attorney or the state, is treated as a debit to that party only. An income or expense item that affects both parties is apportioned, or prorated, to each party to reflect the proper amount that each owes or should receive. A prorated item is treated as a debit to one party and a credit to the other party for the same amount.

Prorated items Non-prorated items. Non-prorated items are costs incurred by one party only. Items not prorated include those listed in the next exhibit.

Non-Prorated Items

Buyer usually pays	Seller usually pays
Mortgage recording fees	Stamp tax on deed
Documentary stamp tax	Title insurance
Intangible tax on mortgage	Brokerage fee

Buyer usually pays	Seller usually pays
Mortgage-related fees: appraisal, credit, survey, loan origination	Inspection fees Title-related expenses
Impound reserves: insurance, taxes	Attorney fees
Attorney fees	

Prorated items. Many of the items to be settled at the closing are partly the responsibility of the buyer and partly of the seller. Some are expenses the seller has paid in advance, for which the buyer owes the seller part of the expense. Some are income items that the seller received in advance, and the seller owes the buyer a portion of those amounts. Others are items the buyer will have to pay in arrears, and the seller owes the buyer part of the expense. The method of dividing financial responsibility for such items is proration. With a prorated item, there is always a debit to one party and a corresponding credit to the other party for the same amount.

Items paid in advance. At closing, the seller has paid some items in advance that cover a period beyond the closing date. In effect, the seller has prepaid some of the buyer's expenses, and the buyer must reimburse the seller. Heating oil and natural gas are typical items. By the same token, the seller of a rental property may have received rent or rental deposits in advance, and must reimburse the buyer for the part that belongs to the buyer.

For an expense the seller paid in advance, *the buyer receives a debit, and the seller receives a credit.*

For income the seller received in advance, *the buyer receives a credit and the seller receives a debit.*

Items paid in arrears. At closing, the seller has incurred certain expenses that have not been billed or paid and that the buyer will have to pay later. A typical item is real estate taxes.

For an item the buyer will pay in arrears, *the buyer receives a credit, and the seller receives a debit.*

Items Paid in Arrears and Advance

	arrears	advance
real estate taxes	x	
mortgage interest	x	
rents received by seller		x
utilities	x	

Computing prorations

The primary methods of calculating prorations are the 360/30-day method, which computes prorations based on a 360-day year and 30-day month, and the 365-day method, which computes prorations based on a 365-day year. The 360/30-day method is commonly used for prorating mortgage interest. Either method may be used for real estate taxes, depending on local practice.

It is customary in Florida that the seller owns the property up to midnight of the day before the closing date unless stated otherwise in the contract. Thus, the closing day is apportioned to the buyer in computing prorations. If not specified in the contract, the prorating method will follow local custom.

12-month / 30-day method. The 12-month/30-day method determines an average daily rate of payment for an item, prorated over a 30-day month and a 360-day year. The method consists of the following steps for annual and monthly items.

Annual items

1. Identify the total amount to be prorated.
2. Divide this amount by 12 to obtain an average monthly rate.
3. Divide the monthly rate by 30 to obtain an average daily rate.
4. Multiply the monthly amount times the seller's number of months of ownership in the year of the sale up to the month of closing. For the month of closing, multiply the seller's number of days of ownership times the daily amount and add the result to the previous result. The final result is the seller's pro rata share of this item.
5. The buyer's pro rata share of an item is the total amount less the seller's pro rata share.

Monthly items

1. Identify the total amount to be prorated.
2. Divide this amount by 30 to obtain the average daily amount.
3. Multiply the daily amount times the seller's number of days of ownership. The result is the seller's pro rata share of this item.
4. The buyer's pro rata share of an item is the total amount less the seller's pro rata share.

Prorating Annual Item: Real Estate Tax

12-month/30-day Method

A sale transaction on a single-family house closes on March 2. County taxes for the previous year, to be paid in arrears, amount to $1,730. The seller owns the house through the day of closing. What are the seller's and buyer's prorated shares of this item?

Total amount due:		=	**$ 1,730.00**
Monthly amount:	1,730 ÷ 12	=	$ 144.17
Daily amount:	144.17 ÷ 30	=	$ 4.81
Seller's share:	144.17 x 2 mo.	=	$ 288.34
	4.81 x 2 days	=	$ 9.62
	288.34 + 9.62	=	$ 297.96
Buyer's share	1,730 - 297.96	=	$ 1,432.04

Closing statement entries. The seller will be charged for the seller's share of the proration. $297.96 will be debited to the seller and credited to the buyer, as the buyer must pay the seller's share when the tax bill is received.

Prorating Monthly Item: Rent Received

12-month/30-day Method

The house in the previous example was rented during the listing and selling period for $1800 per month. Rent for March was paid to the seller on March 1. What is the buyer's prorated share of this rent? The day of closing, March 2, belongs to the seller.

Total received:		=	**$ 1,800.00**
Daily amount:	1800 ÷ 30	=	$ 60.00
Seller's share:	60.00 x 2 days	=	$ 120.00
Buyer's share	1800.00 – 120.00	=	$ 1,680.00

Closing statement entries. The seller will be charged for the buyer's share of the proration: $1,680.00 will be debited to the seller's account and credited to the buyer's account because the seller has received rent that belongs to the new owner after closing.

365-day method

The 365-day method uses the actual number of days in the calendar. The steps in the calculation are the same for annual and monthly prorations. The steps are:

1. Identify the total annual or monthly amount to be prorated.
2. For an annual proration, divide the total amount by 365 to obtain a daily amount (366 in a Leap Year). For a monthly proration, divide the total amount by the actual number of days in the month to obtain the daily amount.
3. Multiply the daily amount times the seller's number of days of ownership. The result is the seller's pro rata share of the item.
4. The buyer's pro rata share of an item is the total amount less the seller's pro rata share.

The seller in the previous example has a $1,730 tax bill, paid annually in arrears on December 31. Closing is on March 2, and the seller owns the day of closing. What is the seller's prorated share of this item?

Total amount due:		=	**$ 1,730.00**
Daily amount:	1730 ÷ 365	=	$ 4.74
Seller's share:	61 days x 4.75	=	$ 289.14
Buyer's share:	1730 - 289.14	=	$1,440.86

Closing statement entries. The seller will be charged for the seller's share of the proration; an amount of $289.14 will be debited to the seller's account and credited to the buyer's account because the buyer will have paid the seller's share of the tax bill in arrears.

State Transfer Taxes

State documentary stamp tax on deeds

Transfer tax, or **documentary stamp tax** as it is referred to in Florida, is a tax imposed by states, counties, and cities on the transfer of the title of property from one person or entity to another within the jurisdiction. It is based on a percentage of the property's sale price, and it is due at closing or by the time the deed is recorded. Some jurisdictions in Florida mandate who is to pay the tax. The common practice is for the seller to pay the tax, but local market conditions influence who pays and allow for negotiations. For example, in a seller's market, the seller is in a position to negotiate for the buyer to pay, while a buyer's market puts the onus on the seller to pay.

Regardless of the market, sellers are mandated by law to deliver a recordable deed, which requires that the stamp tax has been paid. Consequently, if the seller is not able to convince the buyer to pay the tax, the seller will be responsible for paying it to be able to deliver the recordable deed. The party responsible for paying the tax would have been negotiated prior to closing, so the tax will show as a debit on that person's column on the closing statement.

Because the tax is a revenue source for local governments, tax rates are periodically raised when needed for the city or county's budgetary expenses. Currently, the rate is $0.70 (70 cents) per $100 of the sale price throughout Florida. However, in Miami-Dade County, the rate is $0.60 (60 cents) per $100 of the sale price for single-family homes, with an additional surtax of $0.45 (45 cents) per $100 for other residential dwellings, such as townhouses.

To illustrate, if the sale price of a single-family home in Broward County is $300,000, or 3,000 of the $100 tax units, the procedure is: multiply the total tax units by the $0.70 tax rate. The documentary stamp tax on this sale would be $2,100.

In Miami-Dade County, the same home with the same sale price would still have 3,000 tax units. Multiply those units by the $0.60 Miami-Dade tax rate, and the documentary stamp tax on this single-family home sale would be $1,800.

On another note, if the $300,000 sale had concerned condominiums in each of the two counties, in Broward County (or any other Florida county except Miami-Dade), the tax units, rate, and documentary stamp tax would be the same as for the single-family home: $2,100.

In Miami-Dade County, the tax units, rate, and documentary stamp tax would also be the same as for the single-family home: $1,800. However, the 3,000 tax units would also be multiplied by the additional $0.45 surtax rate, resulting in $1,350. That amount would then be added to the $1,800, resulting in $3,150 due for the stamp tax.

Exemptions. Florida property transfer tax exemptions include the following transfers:

- for no consideration (as a gift)
- between spouses with no consideration and no existing mortgage
- between ex-spouses within 1 year of the divorce
- through a will
- through a partition deed
- by the U.S. government or between government agencies
- by eminent domain
- from a nonprofit organization to a state agency

State documentary stamp tax on notes

Intangible tax is calculated on the loan amount identified on the promissory note. The promissory note is the document that creates and explains the debt, shows the loan amount, and details how the loan will be repaid. Florida statute imposes a one-time nonrecurring tax of 2 mills ($0.002) on each dollar of a mortgage loan or other lien against the property. It may be easier to figure the tax as $0.20 (20 cents) per $100 or $2 per $1,000 of the total loan amount. The intangible tax is due at loan closing and is recorded as a debit to the buyer on the closing statement.

The intangible tax works as follows. These taxes are not based on the location of the property within the state, nor do they differentiate between single-family homes and other residential dwellings. They are determined by the loan amount, not the property's value. So, let's go back to that $300,000 home sale.

Let's say the buyer placed an offer for the full $300,000 and paid a cash down payment of $50,000. He then financed the remaining $250,000, which equals 250 $1,000 tax units. Multiplying 250 tax units by the $2 tax rate results in an intangible tax of $500.

State intangible tax on mortgages

In addition to the documentary stamp tax charged on the sale of property, Florida statute also imposes a documentary stamp tax on mortgages and liens against property within the state. The tax rate is $0.35 (35 cents) per $100 of the total owed, in accordance with the promissory note. The tax is paid by the buyer/borrower and is due at closing.

To illustrate, let's go back to the $300,000 home sale. Again, location within Florida is irrelevant. Again, let's say the buyer paid the $50,000 down payment in cash and financed the remainder of the sale price. Divide the financed $250,000 by 100 to determine the 2,500 tax units. Then multiply the 2,500 tax units by the $0.35 tax rate. The tax owed on this note is $875 and will show as a debit for the buyer on the closing statement.

Other Charges

Document preparation

It is customary for the person who has to sign a document to pay the cost of preparing it. Thus, the seller pays for preparing the deed, and the buyer pays for preparing the mortgage and note. Each item will appear as a debit to the paying party on the closing disclosure, with no corresponding credit to the other party.

Recording

The party who wants a document recorded customarily is the one who pays the fee for recording it. Thus, the buyer pays for recording the deed, even though the seller paid for preparing it. Again, the fee will appear as a debit to the paying party on the closing disclosure.

Broker's commission

The listing or representation agreement establishes who pays commissions, but it is common that the person who employs the broker is the one who pays. The commission is a debit to the paying party on the closing disclosure.

Title insurance

There are fees and charges for title-related items such as providing a title abstract or an opinion of title. There are also costs associated with the purchase of a lender's title insurance policy and an owner's title insurance policy. The question of who pays these charges is open to negotiation.

Municipal lien search

In addition to the title search, a Florida closing typically includes a municipal lien search. This search, ordered from the local government or a search service, uncovers obligations that may not appear in the official recorded records but can still attach to the property, such as code-enforcement liens, unpaid water, sewer, and solid-waste charges, special assessments, and open or expired building permits. Because these unrecorded municipal claims can pass to the new owner, the buyer or closing agent obtains the search before closing so the items can be resolved or prorated.

Closing Disclosure Statement

Forms and procedures

As mentioned earlier, the TILA/RESPA Integrated Disclosures (TRID) rule mandates forms and procedures in the closing process. These are as follows.

- Lenders must give the consumer a copy of the **booklet**, "Your Home Loan Toolkit," **at the time** of loan application.
- Lenders must deliver or mail the **Loan Estimate** (Form H-24) to the consumer **no later than the third business day** after receiving a loan application. (A "business day" in this context is any day on which the lender's offices are open for business. An "application" exists when the consumer has provided the lender or mortgage broker six pieces of information: name, income, Social Security number, property address, estimated property value, and loan amount sought.
- Lenders must provide the **Closing Disclosure** (Form H-25) to the consumer **at least three business days** before consummation of the loan. (A "business day" in this context is any calendar day except a Sunday or the day on which a legal public holiday is observed. "Consummation" refers to the day on which the borrower becomes indebted to the creditor; this may or may not correspond to the day of closing the transaction.)

Good faith

Creditors are responsible for ensuring that the figures stated in the Loan Estimate are made in good faith and consistent with the best information reasonably available to the creditor at the time they are disclosed.

Good faith is measured by calculating the difference between the estimated charges originally provided in the Loan Estimate and the actual charges paid by or imposed on the consumer in the Closing Disclosure.

Generally, if the charge paid by or imposed on the consumer exceeds the amount originally disclosed on the Loan Estimate it is not in good faith, regardless of whether the creditor later discovers a technical error, miscalculation, or underestimation of a charge, although there are exceptions.

Types of charges

For certain costs or terms, creditors are permitted to charge consumers more than the amount disclosed on the Loan Estimate without any tolerance limitation.

These charges are:

- prepaid interest; property insurance premiums; amounts placed into an escrow, impound, reserve, or similar account
- charges for services required by the creditor if the creditor permits the consumer to shop and the consumer selects a third-party service provider not on the creditor's written list of service providers

- charges paid to third-party service providers for services not required by the creditor (may be paid to affiliates of the creditor)

However, creditors may only charge consumers more than the amount disclosed when the original estimated charge, or lack of an estimated charge for a particular service, was based on the best information reasonably available to the creditor at the time the disclosure was provided.

Charges for third-party services and recording fees paid by or imposed on the consumer are grouped together and subject to a 10% cumulative tolerance ("10% tolerance" charges). This means the creditor may charge the consumer more than the amount disclosed on the Loan Estimate for any of these charges so long as the total sum of the charges added together does not exceed the sum of all such charges disclosed on the Loan Estimate by more than 10%.

For all other charges ("zero tolerance" charges), creditors are not permitted to charge consumers more than the amount disclosed on the Loan Estimate under any circumstances other than changed circumstances that permit a revised Loan Estimate.

If the amounts paid by the consumer at closing exceed the amounts disclosed on the Loan Estimate beyond the applicable tolerance threshold, the creditor must refund the excess to the consumer no later than 60 calendar days after consummation.

Applicable transactions

The Integrated Disclosures rule applies to most closed-end consumer mortgages. It does not apply to:

- home equity lines of credit (HELOCs)
- reverse mortgages
- mortgages secured by a mobile home or by a dwelling that is not attached to real property (i.e., land)
- loans made by persons who are not considered "creditors" by virtue of the fact that they make five or fewer mortgages in a year.

However, certain types of loans that used to be subject to TILA but not RESPA are now subject to the TILA-RESPA rule's integrated disclosure requirements, including:

- construction-only loans
- loans secured by vacant land or by 25 or more acres
- credit extended to certain trusts for tax or estate planning

Guides and detailed information about the current TILA-RESPA rule can be found on the Consumer Financial Protection Bureau (CFPB) website at https://www.consumerfinance.gov/policy-compliance/guidance/tila-respa-disclosure-rule/

The H-25 Closing Disclosure form

The H-25 Closing Disclosure form consists of five pages. Pages 1, 4, and 5 vary, depending on the loan type. To illustrate the form, we use a sample disclosure for a 30-year fixed rate loan that is presented on the CFPB website.

Page 1 has four sections: general information, Loan Terms, Projected Payments, and Costs at Closing.

General information. This section has three columns:

- Closing information –issue date, closing date, disbursement date, settlement agent, file number, property address, and sale price
- Transaction information – names and addresses for borrower, seller, and lender
- Loan information – loan term, loan purpose, product type, loan type, and loan ID number

Loan Terms. This section states the loan amount, interest rate, and monthly principal and interest payment, and indicates whether any of those amounts can increase after closing. It also gives specifics of any prepayment penalty or balloon payment.

Projected Payment. This section displays the borrower's payment for principal and interest and mortgage insurance, an estimated escrow payment, and the total estimated monthly mortgage payment for years 1-7 and 8-30 of the loan term. It also provides an estimate of monthly tax, insurance, and assessment payments and indicates whether the payments will be held in escrow.

Costs at Closing. The last section of page 1 shows the borrowers' total closing costs (brought forward from page 2) and the total amount of cash the buyer needs to close (brought forward from page 3).

Page 2 details the closing costs. There are two sections divided into four columns:

- Description of the costs: loan costs and other costs
- Costs paid by the borrower – "at closing" or "before closing"
- Costs paid by the seller – "at closing" or "before closing"
- Costs paid by others (in the example, someone other than buyer or seller pays for the appraisal)

Loan Costs. The first section deals with the loan costs:

A. Origination charges, such as points, application fee, and underwriting fee
B. Charges for services the borrower did not shop for - items the lender requires, such as appraisals and credit reports
C. Services the borrower did shop for - items the borrower orders on his own, such as pest inspections, survey fees, and title insurance
D. The total of A, B, and C above

Other Costs. The second section deals with additional transaction-related costs:

E. Taxes and other government fees, such as recording fees and transfer taxes
F. Prepaid items, such as homeowner's insurance, mortgage insurance, prepaid interest, and property taxes to be paid before the first scheduled loan payment
G. Initial escrow payment at closing – an amount the borrower will pay the lender each month to be held in escrow until due, typically for insurance premiums and tax instalments
H. Other costs not covered elsewhere on the disclosure, such as items as association fees, home warranty fees, home inspection fees, real estate commission, and prorated items
I. The total of the costs of E, F, G, and H above
J. The total borrower-paid closing costs from D + I above. This total is carried to the bottom of page 1 as "Costs at Closing – Closing Costs."

Page 3 has two sections, one for calculating cash to close, the other for summarizing the transactions of the borrower and seller.

Calculating Cash to Close. The first section compares the final costs of the loan with the lender's original Loan Estimate. This calculation considers costs paid before closing, down payment, deposits, seller credits, adjustments, and other credits. The last line of the calculation is "Cash to close," the amount the borrower needs to produce at closing.

When an amount has changed, the creditor must indicate where the consumer can find the amounts that have changed on the Loan Estimate. For example, if the Seller Credit amount changed, the creditor can indicate that the consumer should "See Seller Credits in Section L." When the increase in Total Closing Costs exceeds the legal limits, the creditor must disclose this fact and the dollar amount of the excess in the "Did this change?" column. A statement directing the consumer to the Lender Credit on page 2 must also be included if the creditor owes a credit to the consumer at closing for the excess amount.

Summaries of Transactions. The second section of page 3 is divided into two columns (or subsections), one to summarize the borrower's transaction and the other for the seller's transaction. The borrower's column includes:

K. amounts due from the borrower at closing, including the sale price and adjustments for items paid by the seller in advance.

L. amounts already paid by or on behalf of the borrower at closing, such as deposit, loan amount, loan assumptions, seller credits, other credits, and adjustments for items unpaid by the seller, such as taxes and assessments.

The calculation at the bottom of the left column subtracts the totals already paid by the borrower (line L) from the total due from the borrower (line K) to derive the Cash to Close due from the borrower at closing. This figure is the same as that at the bottom of page 1 under "Costs at Closing – Cash to Close."

The seller's column of the Summaries section includes:

M. amounts due to the seller at closing, including the sale price of the property and adjustments for items paid by the seller in advance.

N. amounts due from the seller at closing, such as closing costs the seller will pay, payoff of first or second mortgages, seller credit, and adjustments for items unpaid by the seller, such as taxes and assessments.

The calculation at the bottom of the right column subtracts the total due from the seller (line N) from the total due to the seller (line M) to derive the Cash to Seller, which is the amount the seller will receive at closing.

Page 4 provides additional Loan Disclosures:

- Assumption –whether the lender will allow a loan assumption on a future transfer
- Demand feature –whether the lender can require early repayment
- Late payment – the fee the lender will charge for a late payment
- Negative amortization –whether the loan is negatively amortized, which increases loan amount and diminishes the borrower's equity over the term
- Partial payments –whether the lender accepts partial payments and applies them to the loan
- Security interest –identifies the property securing the loan
- Escrow account – itemizes what is included in the escrow account and states the monthly escrow payment

Page 5 provides additional calculations, disclosures, and contact information:

- Loan Calculations –the total amount of all payments on the loan, the dollar amount of the finance charges over the life of the loan, the amount financed, the annual percentage rate (APR), and the total interest percentage (TIP)

- Other Disclosures –other important information for the borrower, including the right to a copy of the appraisal report and an indication of whether the borrower is protected against liability for the unpaid balance in the event of a foreclosure
- Contact Information –names, addresses, license numbers, contact names, email addresses, and phone numbers for persons involved in the transaction.
- Confirm Receipt –the borrowers' signatures confirming receipt of the Closing Disclosure document. Signing the document does not indicate acceptance of the loan.

Sample H-25 Closing Disclosure, Page 1

Closing Disclosure

This form is a statement of final loan terms and closing costs. Compare this document with your Loan Estimate.

Closing Information		Transaction Information		Loan Information	
Date Issued	4/15/2013	**Borrower**	Michael Jones and Mary Stone	**Loan Term**	30 years
Closing Date	4/15/2013		123 Anywhere Street	**Purpose**	Purchase
Disbursement Date	4/15/2013		Anytown, ST 12345	**Product**	Fixed Rate
Settlement Agent	Epsilon Title Co.	**Seller**	Steve Cole and Amy Doe		
File #	12-3456		321 Somewhere Drive	**Loan Type**	☒ Conventional ☐ FHA
Property	456 Somewhere Ave		Anytown, ST 12345		☐ VA ☐ ______
	Anytown, ST 12345	**Lender**	Ficus Bank	**Loan ID #**	123456789
Sale Price	$180,000			**MIC #**	000654321

Loan Terms		Can this amount increase after closing?
Loan Amount	$162,000	NO
Interest Rate	3.875%	NO
Monthly Principal & Interest *See Projected Payments below for your Estimated Total Monthly Payment*	$761.78	NO
		Does the loan have these features?
Prepayment Penalty		YES • **As high as $3,240** if you pay off the loan during the first 2 years
Balloon Payment		NO

Projected Payments		
Payment Calculation	**Years 1-7**	**Years 8-30**
Principal & Interest	$761.78	$761.78
Mortgage Insurance	+ 82.35	+ —
Estimated Escrow *Amount can increase over time*	+ 206.13	+ 206.13
Estimated Total Monthly Payment	$1,050.26	$967.91

		This estimate includes	**In escrow?**
Estimated Taxes, Insurance & Assessments *Amount can increase over time* *See page 4 for details*	$356.13 a month	☒ Property Taxes	YES
		☒ Homeowner's Insurance	YES
		☒ Other: Homeowner's Association Dues	NO
		See Escrow Account on page 4 for details. You must pay for other property costs separately.	

Costs at Closing		
Closing Costs	$9,712.10	Includes $4,694.05 in Loan Costs + $5,018.05 in Other Costs – $0 in Lender Credits. *See page 2 for details.*
Cash to Close	$14,147.26	Includes Closing Costs. *See Calculating Cash to Close on page 3 for details.*

Sample H-25 Closing Disclosure, Page 2

Closing Cost Details

Loan Costs	Borrower-Paid At Closing	Borrower-Paid Before Closing	Seller-Paid At Closing	Seller-Paid Before Closing	Paid by Others
A. Origination Charges	**$1,802.00**				
01 0.25 % of Loan Amount (Points)	$405.00				
02 Application Fee	$300.00				
03 Underwriting Fee	$1,097.00				
04					
05					
06					
07					
08					
B. Services Borrower Did Not Shop For	**$236.55**				
01 Appraisal Fee to John Smith Appraisers Inc.					$405.00
02 Credit Report Fee to Information Inc.		$29.80			
03 Flood Determination Fee to Info Co.	$20.00				
04 Flood Monitoring Fee to Info Co.	$31.75				
05 Tax Monitoring Fee to Info Co.	$75.00				
06 Tax Status Research Fee to Info Co.	$80.00				
07					
08					
09					
10					
C. Services Borrower Did Shop For	**$2,655.50**				
01 Pest Inspection Fee to Pests Co.	$120.50				
02 Survey Fee to Surveys Co.	$85.00				
03 Title – Insurance Binder to Epsilon Title Co.	$650.00				
04 Title – Lender's Title Insurance to Epsilon Title Co.	$500.00				
05 Title – Settlement Agent Fee to Epsilon Title Co.	$500.00				
06 Title – Title Search to Epsilon Title Co.	$800.00				
07					
08					
D. TOTAL LOAN COSTS (Borrower-Paid)	**$4,694.05**				
Loan Costs Subtotals (A + B + C)	$4,664.25	$29.80			

Other Costs	Borrower-Paid At Closing	Borrower-Paid Before Closing	Seller-Paid At Closing	Seller-Paid Before Closing	Paid by Others
E. Taxes and Other Government Fees	**$85.00**				
01 Recording Fees Deed: $40.00 Mortgage: $45.00	$85.00				
02 Transfer Tax to Any State			$950.00		
F. Prepaids	**$2,120.80**				
01 Homeowner's Insurance Premium (12 mo.) to Insurance Co.	$1,209.96				
02 Mortgage Insurance Premium (mo.)					
03 Prepaid Interest ($17.44 per day from 4/15/13 to 5/1/13)	$279.04				
04 Property Taxes (6 mo.) to Any County USA	$631.80				
05					
G. Initial Escrow Payment at Closing	**$412.25**				
01 Homeowner's Insurance $100.83 per month for 2 mo.	$201.66				
02 Mortgage Insurance per month for mo.					
03 Property Taxes $105.30 per month for 2 mo.	$210.60				
04					
05					
06					
07					
08 Aggregate Adjustment	– 0.01				
H. Other	**$2,400.00**				
01 HOA Capital Contribution to HOA Acre Inc.	$500.00				
02 HOA Processing Fee to HOA Acre Inc.	$150.00				
03 Home Inspection Fee to Engineers Inc.	$750.00			$750.00	
04 Home Warranty Fee to XYZ Warranty Inc.			$450.00		
05 Real Estate Commission to Alpha Real Estate Broker			$5,700.00		
06 Real Estate Commission to Omega Real Estate Broker			$5,700.00		
07 Title – Owner's Title Insurance (optional) to Epsilon Title Co.	$1,000.00				
08					
I. TOTAL OTHER COSTS (Borrower-Paid)	**$5,018.05**				
Other Costs Subtotals (E + F + G + H)	$5,018.05				
J. TOTAL CLOSING COSTS (Borrower-Paid)	**$9,712.10**				
Closing Costs Subtotals (D + I)	$9,682.30	$29.80	$12,800.00	$750.00	$405.00
Lender Credits					

CLOSING DISCLOSURE — PAGE 2 OF 5 • LOAN ID # 123456789

Sample H-25 Closing Disclosure, Page 3

Calculating Cash to Close Use this table to see what has changed from your Loan Estimate.

	Loan Estimate	Final	Did this change?
Total Closing Costs (J)	$8,054.00	$9,712.10	**YES** • See **Total Loan Costs (D)** and **Total Other Costs (I)**
Closing Costs Paid Before Closing	$0	– $29.80	**YES** • You paid these Closing Costs **before closing**
Closing Costs Financed (Paid from your Loan Amount)	$0	$0	**NO**
Down Payment/Funds from Borrower	$18,000.00	$18,000.00	**NO**
Deposit	– $10,000.00	– $10,000.00	**NO**
Funds for Borrower	$0	$0	**NO**
Seller Credits	$0	– $2,500.00	**YES** • See Seller Credits in **Section L**
Adjustments and Other Credits	$0	– $1,035.04	**YES** • See details in **Sections K and L**
Cash to Close	$16,054.00	$14,147.26	

Summaries of Transactions Use this table to see a summary of your transaction.

BORROWER'S TRANSACTION

K. Due from Borrower at Closing		**$189,762.30**
01 Sale Price of Property		$180,000.00
02 Sale Price of Any Personal Property Included in Sale		
03 Closing Costs Paid at Closing (J)		$9,682.30
04		
Adjustments		
05		
06		
07		
Adjustments for Items Paid by Seller in Advance		
08 City/Town Taxes	to	
09 County Taxes	to	
10 Assessments	to	
11 HOA Dues	4/15/13 to 4/30/13	$80.00
12		
13		
14		
15		
L. Paid Already by or on Behalf of Borrower at Closing		**$175,615.04**
01 Deposit		$10,000.00
02 Loan Amount		$162,000.00
03 Existing Loan(s) Assumed or Taken Subject to		
04		
05 Seller Credit		$2,500.00
Other Credits		
06 Rebate from Epsilon Title Co.		$750.00
07		
Adjustments		
08		
09		
10		
11		
Adjustments for Items Unpaid by Seller		
12 City/Town Taxes	1/1/13 to 4/14/13	$365.04
13 County Taxes	to	
14 Assessments	to	
15		
16		
17		
CALCULATION		
Total Due from Borrower at Closing (K)		$189,762.30
Total Paid Already by or on Behalf of Borrower at Closing (L)		– $175,615.04
Cash to Close ☒ From ☐ To Borrower		**$14,147.26**

SELLER'S TRANSACTION

M. Due to Seller at Closing		**$180,080.00**
01 Sale Price of Property		$180,000.00
02 Sale Price of Any Personal Property Included in Sale		
03		
04		
05		
06		
07		
08		
Adjustments for Items Paid by Seller in Advance		
09 City/Town Taxes	to	
10 County Taxes	to	
11 Assessments	to	
12 HOA Dues	4/15/13 to 4/30/13	$80.00
13		
14		
15		
16		
N. Due from Seller at Closing		**$115,665.04**
01 Excess Deposit		
02 Closing Costs Paid at Closing (J)		$12,800.00
03 Existing Loan(s) Assumed or Taken Subject to		
04 Payoff of First Mortgage Loan		$100,000.00
05 Payoff of Second Mortgage Loan		
06		
07		
08 Seller Credit		$2,500.00
09		
10		
11		
12		
13		
Adjustments for Items Unpaid by Seller		
14 City/Town Taxes	1/1/13 to 4/14/13	$365.04
15 County Taxes	to	
16 Assessments	to	
17		
18		
19		
CALCULATION		
Total Due to Seller at Closing (M)		$180,080.00
Total Due from Seller at Closing (N)		– $115,665.04
Cash ☐ From ☒ To Seller		**$64,414.96**

CLOSING DISCLOSURE PAGE 3 OF 5 • LOAN ID # 123456789

Sample H-25 Closing Disclosure, Page 4

Additional Information About This Loan

Loan Disclosures

Assumption
If you sell or transfer this property to another person, your lender
☐ will allow, under certain conditions, this person to assume this loan on the original terms.
☒ will not allow assumption of this loan on the original terms.

Demand Feature
Your loan
☐ has a demand feature, which permits your lender to require early repayment of the loan. You should review your note for details.
☒ does not have a demand feature.

Late Payment
If your payment is more than *15* days late, your lender will charge a late fee of *5% of the monthly principal and interest payment.*

Negative Amortization (Increase in Loan Amount)
Under your loan terms, you
☐ are scheduled to make monthly payments that do not pay all of the interest due that month. As a result, your loan amount will increase (negatively amortize), and your loan amount will likely become larger than your original loan amount. Increases in your loan amount lower the equity you have in this property.
☐ may have monthly payments that do not pay all of the interest due that month. If you do, your loan amount will increase (negatively amortize), and, as a result, your loan amount may become larger than your original loan amount. Increases in your loan amount lower the equity you have in this property.
☒ do not have a negative amortization feature.

Partial Payments
Your lender
☒ may accept payments that are less than the full amount due (partial payments) and apply them to your loan.
☐ may hold them in a separate account until you pay the rest of the payment, and then apply the full payment to your loan.
☐ does not accept any partial payments.
If this loan is sold, your new lender may have a different policy.

Security Interest
You are granting a security interest in
456 Somewhere Ave., Anytown, ST 12345

You may lose this property if you do not make your payments or satisfy other obligations for this loan.

Escrow Account
For now, your loan
☒ will have an escrow account (also called an "impound" or "trust" account) to pay the property costs listed below. Without an escrow account, you would pay them directly, possibly in one or two large payments a year. Your lender may be liable for penalties and interest for failing to make a payment.

Escrow		
Escrowed Property Costs over Year 1	$2,473.56	Estimated total amount over year 1 for your escrowed property costs: *Homeowner's Insurance* *Property Taxes*
Non-Escrowed Property Costs over Year 1	$1,800.00	Estimated total amount over year 1 for your non-escrowed property costs: *Homeowner's Association Dues* You may have other property costs.
Initial Escrow Payment	$412.25	A cushion for the escrow account you pay at closing. See Section G on page 2.
Monthly Escrow Payment	$206.13	The amount included in your total monthly payment.

☐ will not have an escrow account because ☐ you declined it ☐ your lender does not offer one. You must directly pay your property costs, such as taxes and homeowner's insurance. Contact your lender to ask if your loan can have an escrow account.

No Escrow		
Estimated Property Costs over Year 1		Estimated total amount over year 1. You must pay these costs directly, possibly in one or two large payments a year.
Escrow Waiver Fee		

In the future,
Your property costs may change and, as a result, your escrow payment may change. You may be able to cancel your escrow account, but if you do, you must pay your property costs directly. If you fail to pay your property taxes, your state or local government may (1) impose fines and penalties or (2) place a tax lien on this property. If you fail to pay any of your property costs, your lender may (1) add the amounts to your loan balance, (2) add an escrow account to your loan, or (3) require you to pay for property insurance that the lender buys on your behalf, which likely would cost more and provide fewer benefits than what you could buy on your own.

Sample H-25 Closing Disclosure, Page 5

Loan Calculations

Total of Payments. Total you will have paid after you make all payments of principal, interest, mortgage insurance, and loan costs, as scheduled.	$285,803.36
Finance Charge. The dollar amount the loan will cost you.	$118,830.27
Amount Financed. The loan amount available after paying your upfront finance charge.	$162,000.00
Annual Percentage Rate (APR). Your costs over the loan term expressed as a rate. This is not your interest rate.	4.174%
Total Interest Percentage (TIP). The total amount of interest that you will pay over the loan term as a percentage of your loan amount.	69.46%

Questions? If you have questions about the loan terms or costs on this form, use the contact information below. To get more information or make a complaint, contact the Consumer Financial Protection Bureau at **www.consumerfinance.gov/mortgage-closing**

Other Disclosures

Appraisal
If the property was appraised for your loan, your lender is required to give you a copy at no additional cost at least 3 days before closing. If you have not yet received it, please contact your lender at the information listed below.

Contract Details
See your note and security instrument for information about
- what happens if you fail to make your payments,
- what is a default on the loan,
- situations in which your lender can require early repayment of the loan, and
- the rules for making payments before they are due.

Liability after Foreclosure
If your lender forecloses on this property and the foreclosure does not cover the amount of unpaid balance on this loan,

☒ state law may protect you from liability for the unpaid balance. If you refinance or take on any additional debt on this property, you may lose this protection and have to pay any debt remaining even after foreclosure. You may want to consult a lawyer for more information.

☐ state law does not protect you from liability for the unpaid balance.

Refinance
Refinancing this loan will depend on your future financial situation, the property value, and market conditions. You may not be able to refinance this loan.

Tax Deductions
If you borrow more than this property is worth, the interest on the loan amount above this property's fair market value is not deductible from your federal income taxes. You should consult a tax advisor for more information.

Contact Information

	Lender	Mortgage Broker	Real Estate Broker (B)	Real Estate Broker (S)	Settlement Agent
Name	Ficus Bank		Omega Real Estate Broker Inc.	Alpha Real Estate Broker Co.	Epsilon Title Co.
Address	4321 Random Blvd. Somecity, ST 12340		789 Local Lane Sometown, ST 12345	987 Suburb Ct. Someplace, ST 12340	123 Commerce Pl. Somecity, ST 12344
NMLS ID					
ST License ID			Z765416	Z61456	Z61616
Contact	Joe Smith		Samuel Green	Joseph Cain	Sarah Arnold
Contact NMLS ID	12345				
Contact ST License ID			P16415	P51461	PT1234
Email	joesmith@ficusbank.com		sam@omegare.biz	joe@alphare.biz	sarah@epsilontitle.com
Phone	123-456-7890		123-555-1717	321-555-7171	987-555-4321

Confirm Receipt

By signing, you are only confirming that you have received this form. You do not have to accept this loan because you have signed or received this form.

Applicant Signature Date Co-Applicant Signature Date

CLOSING DISCLOSURE PAGE 5 OF 5 • LOAN ID # 123456789

Closing Cost Itemization: Case Illustration

The Closing Disclosure summarizes the financial settlement of a transaction. At closing, the closing agent generally provides a statement to the buyer and/or seller detailing receipts and disbursements from relevant escrow accounts to which the buyer and/or seller contributed funds as part of the transaction. The following illustration shows how some of these cost components are calculated and allocated in a sample transaction.

Selling terms and closing costs

Lawrence and Sandy Binder have accepted an offer on their house located at 928 Elm Street, Littleburg. The buyers, Bill and Dillis Waite, offered $450,000, with earnest money of $70,000 and the remaining $380,000 of the purchase price to come from a new conventional loan from Scepter Mortgage Company. The loan is for 30 years at 5.5% interest, with a monthly principal plus interest payment of $2,158. The lender is charging 1.5 points and a 1% origination fee. Closing is set to occur at Alta Title Company at 4 p.m. on May 10 of the current (non-leap) year.

The Binders have an agreement to pay a broker's commission of 6% to Littleburg Realty. Their unpaid mortgage loan balance as of May 1 will be $184,000. Their monthly interest payments are $613.00. The annual interest rate is 4%. The previous year's county taxes, amounting to $2,572, have been paid by the seller in arrears. The current year's taxes, not yet billed or paid, are assumed to be the same as the previous year's. The parties agree to prorate using the 365-day method, and that the day of closing belongs to the seller. The relevant facts and costs, and who pays them according to the terms of the sale contract, are summarized below.

Selling terms

Sale price:	$450,000
Deposit/downpayment	$70,000
Loan amount	$380,000

Seller-paid Costs

Commissions:	6% of sale price (.06)
Real estate taxes:	$2,572, to be prorated
Title insurance:	$900 owner's coverage
Seller's attorney:	$1,500
Record Release Deed:	$25
Survey:	$550
Transfer stamps	
state:	$162
county:	$162
Seller's loan payoff:	$184,000 + 10 days' prorated May interest @ $613/month

Buyer- paid Costs

Sale price:	$450,000 ($70,000 earnest money already deposited by buyer)
Appraisal fee:	$400 already paid by buyer
Credit report:	$50 already paid by buyer
Closing fee:	$350
Recording fees:	$55
Title insurance:	$250 for lender's coverage
Buyer's attorney:	$1,200
Pest inspection:	$100
Buyer's loan:	$380,000; 30-year fixed @ 5.5% (.055) points: 1.5% of loan amount (.015) origination fee: 1.0% of loan amount (.01)

Hazard insurance:	$2,400/year
Real estate taxes:	$2,572.00, to be prorated
Tax and insurance escrow:	8 months' taxes, 4 months' insurance
Prepaid interest:	from day after closing to end of month

Prorations and charges

According to the summarized sale contract, the only cost to be prorated and shared between seller and buyer is the real estate tax. Other costs to be computed are the broker's commission, the seller's unpaid mortgage interest, the buyer's loan fees and points, the buyer's tax and insurance escrows, and the buyer's prepaid mortgage interest.

Commission. The commission paid by the seller is:

$450,000 x 6% = $27,000.00

At closing, this amount will be charged, or debited, to the seller.

Real estate taxes. Using the 365-day method, the daily amount is $2,572 ÷ 365, or $7.05 (rounded). The total number of days is the number of days in January, February, March, and April, plus 10 days in May, or (31+28+31+30+10), or 130 days. At closing, the seller's share of $916.50 is charged to the seller and the buyer is credited with the same amount.

Total amount due:		=	$	2,572.00
Daily amount:	2,572 ÷ 365	=	$	7.05
Seller's share	7.051 x 130	=	$	916.50
Buyer's share:	2,572 – 916.50	=	$	1,655.50

Seller's unpaid mortgage interest. Since mortgage interest is paid in arrears, the seller owes the lender for the interest not yet charged for the ten days of the month of closing. This amount is therefore debited to the seller.

Daily amount:	613 ÷ 31 days	=	$	19.77
Seller's charge:	19.77 x 10 days	=	$	197.70

Buyer's loan origination and points. The buyer's debits for loan fees and points are:

Fee:	380,000 x 1%	=	$	3,800
Points:	380,000 x 1.5%	=	$	5,700

Buyer's escrow. The lender requires the buyer to establish an escrow account to cover eight months of real estate taxes and four months of hazard insurance. The debits charged to the buyer are therefore:

Taxes:

Annual amount:		=	$	2,572.00
Monthly amount:	2,572 ÷ 12	=	$	214.33
Amount due:	214.33 x 8 mo.	=	$	1,714.64

Insurance:

Annual amount:		=	$	2400.00
Monthly amount:	2400 ÷ 12	=	$	200.00
Amount due:	200 x 4 mo.	=	$	800.00

Prepaid interest. The lender requires the buyer (borrower) to pay, in advance, the interest on the loan amount disbursed at closing to cover the 21 days of the closing month that would be due in arrears later. Note that the lender is not charging the borrower for interest for the day of closing. The buyer's first mortgage payment, which will cover the month of June, will not be due until July 1. Charged to buyer:

Monthly amount:	380K x 5.5% ÷ 12	=	$	1741.67
Daily amount:	1,741.67 ÷ 31	=	$	56.18
Total prepaid interest	56.18 x 21 days	=	$	1179.78

Snapshot Review for Chapter 13

The following review summarizes the key rules and concepts from Chapter 13.

PRELIMINARY STEPS TO CLOSING

Contract and Escrow

- fully executed contract required before closing process begins
- earnest money deposited according to escrow requirements
- financing, inspection, appraisal, title, and repair contingencies addressed before closing

Pre-closing Activities

- loan approval and appraisal completed
- title search and title insurance obtained
- municipal lien search uncovers unrecorded code, utility, and special-assessment liens
- property, pest, and survey inspections conducted
- hazard insurance secured if required by lender

Final Preparations

- buyer conducts final walkthrough
- closing documents reviewed
- additional buyer funds deposited if necessary
- foreign-principal affidavit collected at or before closing (Chapter 692); separate from FIRPTA withholding

Closing

- purpose: buyer receives title; seller receives proceeds; loan, taxes, fees, and expenses settled
- key participants: buyer and seller; closing agent/escrow officer; lenders, attorneys, brokers, title company (as applicable)
- broker responsibilities: coordinate inspections and repairs, review closing documents with clients, deliver escrow funds and attend closing

RESPA

- protects consumers during settlement process
- requires disclosure of settlement costs
- prohibits kickbacks and referral fees

TRID Requirements

- Loan Estimate delivered within 3 business days of application
- Closing Disclosure delivered at least 3 business days before closing

Financial Settlement

- debits: amount owed; credit: amount received
- closing statement balances all charges and payments
- prorated items: property taxes, mortgage interest, rent, utilities
- proration methods: 360-day method; 365-day method

Florida Transfer Taxes

- seller typically pays documentary stamp tax on deed

- buyer typically pays: documentary stamp tax on note, intangible tax on mortgage, loan and recording fees

Closing Disclosure (CD)

- purpose: final accounting of transaction costs; required under TRID
- major sections: loan terms, closing costs, cash to close, transaction summary, loan disclosures

Good Faith Requirement

- closing costs compared to loan estimate; certain fees subject to tolerance limits

Chapter 13 Quiz: Closing Real Estate Transactions

13.1 The primary purpose of a real estate closing is to ______.

a. transfer title to the buyer and disburse funds to the seller
b. determine the property's market value
c. record the listing agreement
d. set the interest rate on the loan

13.2 A title search is performed before closing to ______.

a. estimate the closing costs
b. confirm the seller can convey marketable title
c. calculate the documentary stamp tax
d. schedule the walk-through

13.3 The neutral third party who conducts the closing, holds the funds, and disburses them is the ______.

a. listing broker
b. appraiser
c. closing (settlement) agent
d. mortgage loan originator

13.4 The buyer's final walk-through before closing is intended to ______.

a. renegotiate the price
b. order the appraisal
c. sign the deed
d. verify the property's condition before title transfers

13.5 The Real Estate Settlement Procedures Act (RESPA) was enacted to ______.

a. clarify settlement costs and eliminate kickbacks
b. set maximum interest rates
c. license closing agents
d. establish property tax rates

13.6 RESPA prohibits ______.

a. the use of escrow accounts
b. referral fees and kickbacks among settlement service providers
c. seller financing
d. title insurance

13.7 Under TRID, a lender must give the applicant a Loan Estimate ______.

a. at the closing table
b. within 30 days of closing
c. within three business days of the loan application
d. only if the buyer requests it

13.8 The Closing Disclosure is a form that ______.

a. lists the comparable sales
b. transfers title to the buyer
c. sets the listing price
d. itemizes the final loan terms and closing costs for the borrower

13.9 TRID integrated the disclosure requirements of RESPA and ______.

a. the Truth-in-Lending Act
b. the Fair Housing Act
c. the Statute of Frauds
d. the Bulk Sales Act

13.10 On a closing statement, a debit is ______.

a. money the party receives at closing
b. an amount a party owes or must pay at closing
c. the broker's commission only
d. always split equally

13.11 The purchase price appears as a ______.

a. credit to the buyer and a debit to the seller
b. debit to both parties
c. debit to the buyer and a credit to the seller
d. credit to both parties

13.12 The buyer's earnest money deposit appears on the closing statement as a ______.

a. debit to the seller
b. debit to the buyer
c. credit to the seller
d. credit to the buyer

13.13 The brokerage commission is customarily a ______.

a. debit to the seller
b. credit to the seller
c. debit to the buyer
d. credit to the buyer

13.14 The payoff of the seller's existing mortgage is a ______.

a. credit to the seller
b. debit to the seller
c. credit to the buyer
d. debit to the buyer

13.15 A non-prorated item is one that ______.

a. is always split 50/50
b. is paid by the lender
c. is charged entirely to one party
d. is never shown on the closing statement

13.16 Proration at closing is the process of ______.

a. calculating the sale price
b. paying off the mortgage
c. recording the deed
d. dividing continuing expenses between buyer and seller as of the closing date

13.17 In Florida, real estate property taxes are paid ______.

a. in arrears
b. in advance
c. at the time of listing
d. only at closing

13.18 Because Florida taxes are paid in arrears, the tax proration at closing is typically a ______.

a. debit to the buyer and a credit to the seller
b. credit to the buyer and a debit to the seller
c. debit to both parties
d. non-prorated item

13.19 The two common proration methods are the 365-day method and the ______.

a. 90-day method
b. 180-day method
c. 360-day (30-day-month) method
d. 400-day method

13.20 Annual property taxes on a home are $3,600. As of the closing date, the seller has owned the property for exactly six months of the current tax year. Using the 30-day-month method, the seller's prorated share of the taxes is ______.

a. $600
b. $900
c. $3,600
d. $1,800

13.21 A tenant paid the full $900 monthly rent at the beginning of the month. The sale closes with exactly 10 days remaining in a 30-day month. The seller must credit the buyer approximately ______ for the unearned rent.

a. $300
b. $90
c. $600
d. $900

13.22 The Florida documentary stamp tax on a deed, customarily paid by the seller, is ______.

a. $0.35 per $100 of the loan
b. $0.70 per $100 of the sale price
c. $2 per $1,000 of the loan
d. $1.00 per $100 of the sale price

13.23 A single-family home outside Miami-Dade County sells for $300,000. The documentary stamp tax on the deed, at $0.70 per $100 of the price, is ______.

a. $210
b. $1,050
c. $2,100
d. $3,000

13.24 The documentary stamp tax on a promissory note, customarily paid by the buyer, is ______.

a. $0.70 per $100 of the sale price
b. $2 per $1,000 of the loan
c. $1.00 per $100 of the loan
d. $0.35 per $100 of the loan amount

13.25 A buyer finances $250,000 with a new mortgage. The Florida intangible tax on the mortgage, at $2 per $1,000, is ______.

a. $500
b. $875
c. $250
d. $5,000

13.26 An owner's title insurance policy ______.

a. protects the lender only
b. protects the buyer against defects in the title
c. guarantees the property's value
d. replaces the need for a deed

13.27 A Florida closing typically includes a municipal lien search to ______.

a. determine the sale price
b. appraise the property
c. uncover unrecorded code-enforcement and utility liens
d. calculate the commission

13.28 A seller sells her home for $300,000. She pays off a $150,000 mortgage balance, a 6% brokerage commission, and $2,100 in documentary stamp taxes on the deed. Ignoring other costs, her approximate net proceeds are ______.

a. $150,000
b. $132,000
c. $147,900
d. $129,900

CHAPTER 14: FEDERAL INCOME TAX LAWS

Contents

Learning Objectives

Upon completion of this chapter, you will be able to:

1. Identify the major features of the 2018 Tax Cuts and Jobs Act
2. Describe the income tax treatment for principal and second homes regarding real estate property taxes, mortgage interest deductions, and prepayment penalties
3. Describe the requirements for mortgage interest deductions and understand the requirements for deducting points
4. Explain the features for first-time homebuyers regarding the IRA deduction for the down payment and related expenses
5. Identify the special rules for tax deductions on vacation homes
6. Identify the special rules that apply for persons who deduct expenses for a home office
7. Identify the tax incentives for low-income housing
8. Identify the requirements for excluding tax on the gain on sale of a principal home
9. Itemize the steps required to calculate net operating income, before-tax cash flow, after-tax cash flow, and net taxable income from the operations of an investment property and describe the process used to allocate the acquisition costs of a property between land and improvements
10. Calculate after-tax cash flow; taxable income for an investment property; and the depreciation (cost recovery) for residential and nonresidential investment property
11. Distinguish between passive and non-passive income and list four principal tax classifications of real property
12. Describe the IRS tax treatment regarding the sale of investment property, including determination and taxing of gain or loss, short-term gain vs. long-term gain, and after-tax reversion
13. Describe the advantages of the installment sale method and like-kind exchanges, including a Section 1031 Exchange

2025 Big Beautiful Bill

Changes overview

The One Big Beautiful Bill Act (OBBBA) is a federal statute signed into law on July 4, 2025. The bill includes tax and spending policies at the core of the Trump administration's agenda. This act represents one of the most significant updates to the U.S. tax code since 2017.

One of the core provisions of the OBBBA is a permanent extension of tax cuts implemented in 2017. The act introduces new deductions and incentives, restructures credits and investment programs, and reduces or eliminates certain clean energy incentives.

The following is a brief discussion of three major changes in the act that impact the real estate industry.

Bonus depreciation

The act reinstates and makes permanent 100% bonus depreciation for qualifying property. This allows investors to deduct the full cost of certain assets in the first year rather than over time.

Tax deductions

The OBBBA made permanent the 20% Qualified Business Income (QBI) deduction for pass-through entities. It relaxes business interest deduction rules.

Incentives and credits

In addition to the previous changes, this act expands the Low-Income Housing Tax Credit, makes permanent certain Opportunity Zones, while implementing stricter qualification rules, and phases out or reduces clean energy tax incentives.

Industry impact

Overall, this act is intended to increase investment activity by encouraging property acquisitions, development projects, and capital improvements. It improves cash flow for investors through faster deductions and lower taxable income. Finally, it incentivizes great housing development by expanding affordable housing credits and Opportunity Zones.

Thus, in general, it creates a more favorable financial environment for real estate investors and developers while introducing strategic planning considerations around timing, property type, and tax optimization.

However, the act may slow sustainable building projects and increase long-term operating costs for some developments.

2018 Tax Cuts and Jobs Act

Standard deduction

No Florida income tax. One point of context frames this entire chapter: Florida imposes no state personal income tax, and its constitution prohibits one. Every deduction, exclusion, and gain discussed here is therefore a matter of federal income tax only. A Florida homeowner or investor who sells at a gain may owe federal capital-gains tax, but no separate Florida income tax on the sale, and the federal deductions described below produce no parallel state benefit, because there is no Florida income-tax return on which to claim them.

The 2018 Tax Cuts and Jobs Act (TCJA) nearly doubled the standard deduction for individual taxpayers. The impact of this was a drastic reduction in the number of taxpayers who itemize. The increased standard deduction eliminated the direct tax benefits of owning a home (direct deduction of mortgage interest and related expenses), though individuals whose deductions exceed the standard deduction may still itemize.

Reduction of state, local tax deduction

This act capped deductions for state and local taxes paid at a combined $10,000. The cap disproportionality affected higher-income taxpayers and residents of high-tax states, with supporters claiming the law made the tax system less skewed toward wealthier households and shifted benefits toward broader tax relief for the majority of taxpayers.

Cap on home interest deduction

The TCJA reduced the mortgage interest deduction cap from $1M to $750,000 for loans funded after December 15, 2017. Again, the goal was to benefit a broader spectrum of the taxpayer base while reducing benefits to the wealthy.

Interest on home equity loans

Under this act, interest on home equity loans and HELOCs is no longer deductible unless the funds are used to buy, build, or substantially improve the home securing the loan. This discourages using home equity for consumer spending while also reducing the flexibility of using home equity as a tax-advantaged borrowing tool.

Income Tax Treatment – Principal Home

Real estate property taxes

Taxpayers who are able to itemize may deduct real estate property taxes (limited by the $40,000 SALT cap).

Mortgage interest Deduction

Itemizers may deduct mortgage interest on acquisition debt of up to $750,000 for purchases after December 15, 2017, or $1M for purchases made prior to that date.

Points. Points paid to obtain a mortgage are a form of prepaid interest and may be deductible. Points paid to buy or improve a taxpayer's principal residence are generally deductible in full in the year paid, provided they meet IRS conditions and reflect the customary practice in the area. Points paid to refinance a mortgage, by contrast, generally must be deducted ratably over the life of the new loan rather than all at once.

Prepayment Penalties

While few of today's mortgage loans include a prepayment penalty, borrowers whose loans do include such a penalty may be able to deduct the prepayment penalty as "additional interest" if their mortgage interest is otherwise deductible. The deduction is taken in the year paid if the taxpayer itemizes deductions. This applies to primary residences and some second homes, subject to limits on acquisition debt.

Capital gains Exclusion

One of the primary tax benefits of home ownership is the exclusion of a certain amount of capital gains on the sale of a primary residence. This benefit will be addressed more fully in the next section.

Other benefits

Other benefits to home ownership exist. Some employer-provided housing can be excluded from taxable income if it meets IRS requirements. Business owners may be able to deduct home office expenses for portions of the home used regularly and exclusively for business. Owners may be able to deduct casualty losses if damage occurs as a result of a federally declared disaster.

Taxation of Vacation Homes

Taxation of vacation homes

A primary factor in the taxation of vacation homes is how much the home is used by the owner during a year.

If the property is rented for 14 or fewer days during a year (referred to as the 14-day rule), the rental income is not taxable. However, owners may not deduct rental expenses for this period, though mortgage interest and property taxes may still be deducted if the owner itemizes deductions.

Most properties are considered mixed-use vacation homes because they are rented for more than 15 days a year and their personal use exceeds the IRS threshold. The home is considered a residence if personal use exceeds 14 days or 10% of the rental days, whichever is greater. All rental income is taxable, and expenses must be allocated between personal and rental use. Rental deductions cannot exceed rental income, and losses generally cannot offset other income. Excess expenses can be carried forward.

If a home is used as a rental with little to no personal use (below the 14-day/10% threshold), it is treated as a regular rental property. Owners can deduct all ordinary and necessary expenses and depreciate the property. Losses may be deductible (subject to passive activity rules).

Taxation of the Home Office

Taxation of the home office

Self-employed individuals, even those who simply have a side business, may be able to take some deductions for the use of an area in the home for an office. This treatment is NOT available to W2 employees who work from home.

The area must be used only for business. A desk in an occupied bedroom, for example, does not meet the requirements. Even occasional personal use disqualifies it. In addition, the use must be consistent and ongoing.

The office must be for a business purpose and serve as the principal place of business, a place to meet clients or customers, or a separate structure used for business.

Those eligible for this deduction may deduct a proportionate share of mortgage interest or rent, property taxes, utilities, insurance, and maintenance/repairs. For example, in a 2,000-square-foot home with an office that is 200 square feet, the eligible proportion of expenses would be 10%.

A second potential method of calculating the deduction is to take a $ 5-per-square-foot deduction (up to 300 s.f.), with a maximum deduction of $1,500.

The deduction cannot exceed business income, nor can it create or increase a loss. Excess amounts may be carried forward if using the actual expense method.

Sale of Principal Residence

Exclusion of gain on sale or exchange

Particularly in a market such as the one we've seen over the past several years, real estate value appreciation has gifted many homeowners with substantial equity in their homes. Homeowners can exclude a significant portion of the gain on the sale of a primary residence ($250,000 for single filers, $500,000 for married taxpayers filing jointly).

Gains over these limitations are taxable, and the exclusion may be taken only once every two years. Owners must have used the property as a primary residence for at least two of the past five years at the time of sale.

Partial exclusion of gain. A taxpayer who does not meet the two-year ownership-and-use test, or who has used the exclusion within the prior two years, may still claim a partial exclusion if the sale is due to a change in place of employment, health reasons, or other unforeseen circumstances. The partial exclusion is prorated based on the portion of the two-year requirement the taxpayer actually met.

Reporting requirements to IRS

Generally, if any gain on the sale of the residence is fully excludable and the owner meets the ownership and use tests, the sale does not have to be reported on the homeowner's tax return. However, many accountants do report it on Form 8949 and show the exclusion adjustment.

If a 1099-S is issued to report the gross proceeds, which is typical in the sale of a property that was not a primary residence, or if the gain exceeds the exclusion limits, the sale must be reported to the IRS.

Investment Property Taxation

Determination of net taxable income

Investment property income is usually reported on Schedule E. Gross income includes rental income, advance rent, and security deposits (if retained at the end of a lease). From these proceeds, taxpayers can deduct mortgage interest, property taxes, insurance, repairs and maintenance, property management fees, owner-paid utilities, and depreciation. This calculation results in net income or loss.

Depreciation is a key deduction: residential property depreciates over 27.5 years, and commercial property depreciates over 39 years. Note that only the building is depreciated. Land does not depreciate.

Losses may be limited by passive activity rules. Generally, rental losses are passive and can only offset passive income. However, up to $25,000 may offset ordinary income if the property owner actively participates in the investment.

Taxes from operations

Net income is taxed as ordinary income, subject to the taxpayer's regular income tax rate (not capital gains rates). Net losses may be deductible (subject to limits or carried forward to subsequent years.

Derivation of capital gain/loss

A capital gain or loss on the sale of investment property occurs only on the sale of the property. The gain or loss is calculated by determining the amount realized (sale price less selling expenses). Then the adjusted basis is calculated (original purchase price plus capital improvements less depreciation taken. The gain or loss is computed by subtracting the adjusted basis from the amount realized from the sale.

Capital gain taxation

Capital gains tax is computed in two steps. The portion of the gain attributable to depreciation can be taxed at up to 25%. The remaining gain (if the property was held for more than one year) may be taxed at 0%, 15%, or 20%, depending on income level.

Higher-income taxpayers may also be required to pay a 3.6% net investment income tax.

Estimating tax liability

Investment property owners can estimate annual tax liability by multiplying net rental income by the ordinary tax rate.

Upon sale, owners can estimate potential capital gains tax by first determining the amount of depreciation taken and multiplying it by up to 25%. The remaining gain is then multiplied by the taxpayer's tax rate (0%, 15%, or 20%).

Methods of Deferring Taxes Upon Disposition

Installment sales – basic mechanics

One method of reducing capital gains tax in a given year is to sell the property on an installment contract. Any gain is realized when payments are received, rather than on the total sale price. This smooths taxable income over time and may reduce exposure to higher tax brackets and NIIT.

Note that depreciation recapture is taxed in the year of the sale.

Like-kind exchange essentials

A like-kind exchange, also called a 1031 exchange, is the most important tax deferral strategy for investment real estate. Note that this strategy is not available for a primary residence and that it only defers taxes. It does not lessen, decrease, or eliminate taxes.

To implement a 1031 exchange, investors must comply with strict IRS timelines and purchase requirements, as follows:

- The exchange must be for a like-kind property (real estate), though the IRS defines this with a broad brush.
- The current property is sold to a buyer. Typically, the contract must identify that the transaction is a 1031-exchange.
- At closing, all proceeds must go to a qualified intermediary (QI). Any proceeds the seller touches become taxable.
- A 45-day identification period begins upon the closing date of the original property. Generally, buyers must identify, in writing, up to three potential replacement properties within 45 calendar days. Some variations exist. For example, the buyer can identify any number of properties as long as the total value is less than or equal to 200% of the sold property.
- The taxpayer must close on the replacement property(ies) within 180 days from the closing on the relinquished property.
- At closing, the QI transfers proceeds from the relinquished property sale to the closing agent to the application to the new property.

If proceeds from the relinquished property are greater than the purchase price of the new property, the excess is considered "boot" and is taxable. Any mortgage reduced or paid off from the proceeds of a relinquished property is also considered "boot" and is therefore taxable. To avoid this tax issue, investors must ensure the new property has at least as much debt as the relinquished property and purchase a property of equal or greater value than the relinquished property. As an alternative, the investor may replace some or all of the debt with cash.

Snapshot Review for Chapter 14

The following review summarizes the key rules and concepts from Chapter 14.

2025 Big Beautiful Bill

- permanent 100% bonus depreciation
- permanent 20% Qualified Business Income (QBI) deduction
- expanded Low-Income Housing Tax Credit
- expanded Opportunity Zone incentives

2018 Tax Cuts and Jobs Act

- increased standard deduction
- SALT deduction capped at $10,000
- mortgage interest deduction limited to qualifying acquisition debt
- home equity interest deductible only when used to buy, build, or improve the property

PRINCIPAL RESIDENCE

Tax Benefits

- property tax and mortgage interest deductions for qualifying taxpayers
- Florida imposes no state personal income tax; only federal income tax applies to these gains and deductions
- certain prepayment penalties deductible as interest
- points on a home purchase generally deductible in full the year paid; refinance points deducted over the loan's life

Capital Gain Exclusion

- $250,000 exclusion (single)
- $500,000 exclusion (married filing jointly)
- ownership and occupancy required for 2 of previous 5 years
- partial exclusion available for an early sale due to a job change, health, or unforeseen circumstances

Vacation Homes

- rent 14 days or less: rental income not taxable

Mixed-use Property

- personal and rental use combined
- income taxable; deductions limited

Rental Property

- minimal personal use
- expenses and depreciation deductible

Home Office

- requirements: exclusive and regular business use, principal place of business or client meeting area
- deduction methods: actual expense method; simplified method ($5 per sq. ft.; maximum $1,500)

Investment Property Taxation

- deductible expenses: mortgage interest, property taxes, insurance, repairs and maintenance, property management fees, depreciation
- depreciation: residential: 27.5 years; commercial: 39 years; land not depreciable

Capital Gains

- capital gain = amount realized − adjusted basis
- depreciation recapture taxed separately
- long-term gains taxed at preferential rates

Tax Deferral Strategies

- installment sale: gain recognized as payments received
- 1031 exchange: investment property only; qualified intermediary required; 45-day identification period; 180-day closing period
- boot: cash or debt relief received; taxable to investor

Chapter 14 Quiz: Federal Income Tax Laws

14.1 Which of the following statements best describes one major impact of the 2025 One Big Beautiful Bill on real estate investors?

a. It eliminates all depreciation deductions for investment property.
b. It discourages capital improvements by increasing taxable income.
c. It encourages investment activity through faster deductions and lower taxable income.
d. It removes all affordable housing incentives.

14.2 Under the OBBBA, what change was made to bonus depreciation?

a. Bonus depreciation was reduced to 50% for qualifying assets.
b. Bonus depreciation was eliminated for commercial property.
c. Bonus depreciation was temporarily suspended through 2030.
d. Bonus depreciation was reinstated and made permanent at 100%.

14.3 Which provision of the 2018 Tax Cuts and Jobs Act (TCJA) reduced the number of taxpayers who itemize deductions?

a. The increase in Opportunity Zone incentives
b. The reduction in mortgage interest rates
c. The near doubling of the standard deduction
d. The elimination of depreciation deductions

14.4 The TCJA capped deductions for state and local taxes at a combined total of ______.

a. $25,000
b. $750,000
c. $1 million
d. $10,000

14.5 Mortgage interest on acquisition debts for homes purchased after December 15, 2017, is generally deductible on balances up to which of the following?

a. $500,000
b. $1 million
c. $750,000
d. $250,000

14.6 How is a vacation home rented for 14 or fewer days during the year treated for federal income tax purposes?

a. The rental income is fully taxable.
b. The owner may deduct unlimited rental losses.
c. The rental income is not taxable.
d. The property automatically becomes commercial property.

14.7 Which taxpayer is most likely to qualify for the home office deduction?

a. A self-employed individual with a regularly used exclusive business area
b. A W-2 employee working remotely for convenience
c. Any homeowner with internet access
d. A renter who occasionally answers work emails at home

14.8 A vacation property is considered a residence for tax purposes when personal use exceeds which of the following?

a. 30 days regardless of rental activity
b. 14 days or 10% of rental days, whichever is greater
c. 10 days in any calendar year
d. 50% of the total occupancy period

14.9 Residential income property is generally depreciated over how many years?

a. 15
b. 27.5
c. 30
d. 39.5

14.10 Which statement correctly describes a requirement of a 1031 like-kind exchange?

a. Replacement property must be identified within 45 days after closing on the relinquished property
b. The seller may temporarily keep the proceeds before investing them.
c. The exchange may be used for a taxpayer's principal residence.
d. The replacement property must be located in the same state.

14.11 To qualify for the capital-gains exclusion on a primary residence, the owner generally must have used the home as a primary residence for at least ______.

a. two of the last five years
b. the entire time they owned it
c. at least ten years
d. one of the last three years

14.12 Nonresidential (commercial) real property is depreciated over ______.

a. 27.5 years
b. 39 years
c. 15 years
d. 45 years

14.13 For depreciation purposes, which part of a real estate investment may NOT be depreciated?

a. the building
b. the roof
c. the land
d. the improvements

14.14 A Section 1031 like-kind exchange allows an investor to ______.

a. avoid paying any tax ever
b. depreciate the land
c. exclude rental income
d. defer capital-gains tax on the exchanged property

14.15 A capital gain on investment real estate is generally recognized ______.

a. only when the property is sold
b. every year the property is held
c. at the time of purchase
d. only if the property is refinanced

PART IV: SPECIALTIES

CHAPTER 15:
INVESTMENT REAL ESTATE

Contents

Learning Objectives

Upon completion of this chapter, you will be able to:

1. Distinguish among the different types of real estate investments
2. Identify the advantages and disadvantages of investing in real estate
3. Distinguish among the various types of risk
4. Explain the importance of investment analysis
5. Explain how leverage affects the return on a real estate investment
6. Describe how taxable income and cost recovery depreciation apply to investment real estate
7. Explain how gain on the sale of investment property is taxed and how the principal residence exclusion applies
8. Calculate net operating income, pre-tax cash flow, and after-tax cash flow for an income property
9. Identify common measures of investment performance
10. Describe how to match an investment property to an investor financial qualifications, objectives, and time horizon
11. Distinguish among the common commercial lease types and between usable and rentable square footage

Investment Fundamentals

Characteristics of an investment

The idea of investment is simple: take something of value and put it to work in some way to increase its value over time. With any investment, one wants the original investment to grow, without losing it. This idea is called **conservation of capital**. Unfortunately, no investment is truly secure. External conditions change, and the investment itself can change. Even if you do nothing with it, its value does not remain constant.

Risk versus return. The general rule in investing is that the safer the investment, the slower it gains in value. The more you want it to gain, and the more quickly, the more you must risk losing it. How much do you want to earn, and how much are you willing to risk to earn it? The reward from investing directly corresponds to the degree of risk.

Management. Another aspect of investment is the amount of attention you must pay to it to make it work. You can deposit cash in a passbook account and forget about it. You can use your cash to buy a business and run it yourself to grow and earn from it. How much do you want to be involved in managing your investment?

Liquidity. The issue of exchangeability is an important one in investment. How easy is it to recover your invested resource without loss and exchange it for another one you want? If there is a ready market for the type of resource you have, other people want to buy and sell it for themselves, your investment is liquid.

Rewards

The basic aim of financial investment is to increase one's wealth, adding value to what one has. This can occur in several ways.

Income. An investment can generate income on a periodic basis. You may consume this cash, spending it on goods and services that, once used, have no further value. Or you may use the cash to invest in another asset.

Appreciation. Your invested asset may gain value over time due to increased market demand. When you sell or exchange it for something else you prefer, you get more than you originally put into the investment.

Leverage. You may pledge the value of your resource to borrow funds in order to make an investment that is larger than your own resource permits you to do directly. The small resource is used as a lever to make a larger investment, thereby increasing your opportunity to benefit from income, appreciation, and other rewards of investing.

Tax benefits. Some investments are treated under tax laws that enable investors to reduce or defer the tax owed. Tax dollars you don't have to pay are dollars you have available for other uses, such as consumption or further investment.

Risks

Investment risks arise from a variety of general sources, including the market, business operations, the value of money, and changes in interest rates.

Market risk. Changes in the demand for your invested resource may cause your investment to lose value and to become illiquid.

Business risk. Changes in the operation of a business with which your investment is connected may reduce or eliminate the income- and appreciation- earning capacity of your investment.

Purchasing power risk. Changes in the value of money as an exchange medium, such as through inflation, may decrease the practical value of your invested resource.

Financial risk. Changes in financial markets, particularly in interest rates, may reduce the value of your investment by making it less desirable to others and by making it more expensive for you to maintain.

Types of investments

Four of the most important types of investment are investments in money, equity, debt, and real estate.

Money investments. A money investment is one in which the basic form of the investment remains money. Examples are: deposit accounts, certificates of deposit, money funds, and annuities. The basic reward from a money investment is interest. Money investments are relatively safe, with correspondingly conservative rates of return.

Debt investments. A debt investment is one in which an investor buys a debt instrument. Examples are bonds, notes, mortgages, and bond mutual funds. The basic reward is interest. Debt investments are usually riskier than money investments and less risky than stocks or real estate.

Equity investments. An equity investment is one in which an investor purchases an ownership interest in a business. Examples are stocks and stock mutual funds. The basic rewards come in the form of dividends and share price appreciation. Equity investments are generally riskier than money and debt investments.

Real estate investments. A real estate investment is one in which an investor *buys real estate for its investment benefits rather than primarily for its utility*. It may have the features of both an equity and a debt investment, depending on the type of real estate involved and numerous other factors, such as the type of

interest one owns. A real estate investor may invest in an income-producing property or a non-income-producing property.

- **non-income property**
  a residential property used as the investor's primary residence. The basic reward, beyond the enjoyment of use, comes in the form of appreciation. There may also be tax benefits, depending on how the purchase is financed.
- **income property**
  a property owned specifically for the investment rewards it offers. Examples are multi-family residential properties, retail stores, industrial properties, and office buildings. Rewards come in any or all of the forms mentioned earlier: income, appreciation, leverage, and tax advantages.

Real Estate as an Investment

Real estate investments participate in the general risks and rewards of all investments. However, real estate investments are often complex. They are also distinguished by their lack of liquidity and by the amount of management they require. In addition, each investor has specific aims and circumstances that affect the viability of any particular real estate investment for that individual. Licensees who lack expertise in real estate investment analysis should refer potential investors to a competent advisor. Nevertheless, a licensee should be familiar with the basics of real estate as an investment.

Risk and reward

Capital invested in real estate is always subject to the full range of risks: market changes, income shortfalls, negative leverage, tax law changes, and poor overall returns.

Market demand for a specific type of property can decline. For example, retailers in a business district may vacate stores to obtain better space in a new shopping center. Market downturns leave the income property investor with an unmarketable property or one that can only be re-leased at a loss of some portion of the original investment. Thus, the expected reward from income or appreciation may never be obtained.

Another risk of the investment property is the cost of development or operation. If start-up or operating costs exceed rental income, the owner must dip into additional capital to maintain the investment until income increases. If income does not rise, or if costs do not decline, the investor can simply run out of money.

Leverage is a constant risk in real estate investment. If the property fails to generate sufficient revenue, the costs of borrowed money can bankrupt the owner, just as development and operating costs can. Investors often overlook the fact that leverage only works when the yield on the investment exceeds the costs of borrowed funds.

Tax law is an ongoing risk in long-term real estate investment. If the investor's tax circumstances or the tax laws change, the investor may end up paying more capital gains and income taxes than planned, undermining the investment's return. An investor needs to carefully consider the value of such potential tax benefits as deductions for mortgage interest, tax losses, deferred gains, exemptions, and tax credits for certain types of real estate investment.

Another consideration is opportunity cost. Opportunity cost is the return that an investor could earn on capital invested with minimal risk. If the real estate investment, with all its attendant risk, cannot yield a greater return than an

investment elsewhere involving less risk, then the opportunity cost is too high for the real estate investment. Despite all the risks, real estate remains a popular investment because, historically, the rewards have outweighed the risks. Real estate has proven to be relatively resistant to adverse inflationary trends that have hurt money, debt, and stock investments. In addition, real estate has proven to be a viable investment in view of the economy's continued expansion over the last fifty years.

Illiquidity

Compared with other classes of investment, real estate is relatively illiquid. Even in the case of liquidating a single-family residence, one can expect a marketing period of at least several months in most markets. In addition, it takes time for the buyer to obtain financing and to complete all the other phases of closing the transaction. Commercial and investment properties can take much longer, depending on market conditions, leases, construction, permitting, and a host of other factors. The investor who is in a hurry to dispose of such an investment can expect to receive a lower sales price than may be ideal. Compare this with the ease of drawing money out of a bank account or selling a stock.

Management requirements

Real estate tends to require a high degree of investor involvement in the management of the investment. Even raw land requires some degree of maintenance to preserve its value: drainage, fencing, payment of taxes, and periodic inspection, to name a few tasks. Improved properties often require extensive management, including repairs, maintenance, onsite leasing, tenant relations, security, and fiscal management.

Taxation of Real Estate Investments

Real estate investments are taxed on the income they produce and on the increase in value, or gain, when the investment is sold. These forms of taxation are distinct from the ad valorem taxation of real estate.

Taxable Income

Taxable income from investment real estate is the gross income received minus any expenses, deductions or exclusions that current tax law allows. Taxable income from real estate is added to the investor's other income and taxed at the investor's marginal tax rate. The "Investment Analysis of an Income Property" section below gives details.

Cost recovery

Cost recovery, or **depreciation**, allows the owner of income property to deduct a portion of the property's value from gross income each year over the life of the asset. The "life of the asset" and the deductible portion are defined by law. In theory, the owner recovers the full cost of the investment if it is held to the end of the asset's economic life as defined by the Internal Revenue Service. At the time of selling the asset, the accumulated cost recovery is subtracted from the investment's original value as part of determining the taxable capital gain.

Cost recovery is allowed only for income properties and that portion of a non-income property that is used to produce income. It applies only to improvements. Land cannot be depreciated. The part of a property that can be depreciated is called the **depreciable basis**.

Depreciation schedules. Residential rental properties are depreciated over a period of 27.5 years. The basic annual deduction for such property is 3.636%, with adjustments for the month of the taxable year in which the property was placed in service. Non-residential income properties placed in service after 1994 are depreciated over a period of 39 years (basic annual percentage is 2.564%). The proper method of depreciation should be determined in consultation with a qualified tax advisor.

Gain on sale

When real estate, whether non-income or income, is sold, a taxable event occurs. If the sale proceeds exceed the original cost of the investment, subject to some adjustments, there is a **capital gain** that is subject to tax. If the sales proceeds are less than the original cost with adjustments, there is a **capital loss.**

An investor can sometimes defer the reporting of gain or loss, and, hence, taxation of gain, by participating in an exchange of like-kind assets. The legislation that deals with like-kind exchanges is contained in Section 1031 of the IRS code. These tax-deferred exchanges are sometimes called **Section 1031 exchanges** and **Starker exchanges**, named for an investor who won a case against the IRS.

To qualify under Section 1031, there must have been a legitimate exchange of the assets involved. The property being transferred must have been held for productive use in a trade or business or held as an investment and must be exchanged for property that will also be used in a trade or business or be held as an investment. Tax on gain is deferred until the investment or business property is sold and not exchanged.

Interest

Mortgage interest incurred by loans to buy, build, or materially improve a primary or secondary residence is deductible from gross income. The interest on a home equity loan may be deducted only if the loan is used to "buy, build or substantially improve" the home that secures the loan. Principal payments on a loan are not deductible.

For income properties that are held as investments, interest on debts incurred to finance the investment is deductible as investment interest up to the amount of net income received from the property.

Residential Investment Analysis

Investment analysis examines the economic performance of an investment. The analysis includes costs, income, taxation, appreciation, and return.

A property acquired and used as a primary residence is an example of a non-income property. If a portion of a residence is used for business (i.e., a home office), this portion only may be treated as an income property for tax purposes. Since, by definition, a non-income property does not generate income, its value as an investment must come from one or more of the other sources: appreciation, leverage, or tax benefits.

Appreciation

Appreciation is the increase in value of an asset over time. A simple way to estimate appreciation on a primary residence is to subtract the price originally paid from the estimated current market value:

Current value - original price = total appreciation

For example, if a house was bought for $300,000 and its estimated market value now is $400,000, it has appreciated by $100,000.

Original price:	**$300,000**
Current market value:	$400,000
Total appreciation:	$100,000

Total appreciation can be stated as a percentage increase over the original price by dividing the estimated total appreciation by the original price.

The house in the last example has appreciated by 33%:

$$\frac{(Total\ appreciation)}{Original\ price} = \%\ appreciated$$

$$\frac{100{,}000}{300{,}000} = 33\%$$

To estimate the percentage of annual appreciation, divide the percent appreciated by the number of years the house has been owned:

$$\frac{\%\ total\ appreciation}{years\ owned} = \%\ appreciation\ per\ year$$

If the house in the previous example has been owned for three years, the annual appreciation has been 11%.

$$\frac{33\%}{3\ years} = 11\%\ appreciation\ per\ year$$

Deductibles

The primary tax benefit available to the owner of a non-income property is the annual deduction for mortgage interest. The portion of annual mortgage payments that goes to repay principal must be subtracted to determine the amount paid for interest. Principal repayment is not deductible. Furthermore, depreciation is not allowed for non-income properties.

Tax liability

The seller of a principal residence may owe tax on capital gain that results from the sale. The IRS defines gain on the sale of a home as amount realized from the sale minus the adjusted basis of the home sold.

Amount realized. The amount realized, also known as net proceeds from sale, is expressed by the formula:

	sale price
-	costs of sale
	amount realized

The sale price is the total amount the seller receives for the home. This includes money, notes, mortgages or other debts the buyer assumes as part of the sale.

Costs of sale include brokerage commissions, relevant advertising, legal fees, seller-paid points and other closing costs. Certain fixing-up expenses, as discussed further below, can be deducted from the amount realized to derive an **adjusted sale price** for the purpose of postponing taxation on gain.

For example, Larry and Mary sold their home for $350,000. Their selling costs, including the commission they paid Broker Betty and amounts paid to inspectors, a surveyor, and the title company, amounted to ten percent of the selling price, or $35,000. The amount they realized from the sale was therefore $315,000.

Adjusted basis. Basis is a measurement of how much is invested in the property for tax purposes. Assuming that the property was acquired through purchase, the beginning basis is the cost of acquiring the property. Cost includes cash and debt obligations, and such other settlement costs as legal and recording fees, abstract fees, surveys, charges for installing utilities, transfer taxes, title insurance, and any other amounts the buyer pays for the seller.

The beginning basis is increased or decreased by certain types of expenditures made while the property is owned. Basis is increased by the cost of capital improvements made to the property. Assessments for local improvements such as roads and sidewalks also increase the basis. Examples of capital improvements are: putting on an addition, paving a driveway, replacing a roof, adding central air conditioning, and rewiring the home.

Basis is decreased by any amounts the owner received for such things as easements.

The basic formula for **adjusted basis** is:

	Beginning basis
+	Capital improvements
-	Exclusions, credits, or other amounts received
	Adjusted basis

For example, Mary and Larry originally paid $200,000 for their home. They spent an additional $10,000 on a new central heating and cooling unit. Their adjusted basis at the time of selling it is therefore $210,000.

Gain on sale. The gain on sale of a primary residence is represented by the basic formula:

	Amount realized (net sales proceeds)
-	Adjusted basis
	Gain on sale

Gain on sale, if it does not qualify for an exclusion under current tax law, is taxable.

Gain on Sale

	Selling price of old home	$350,000
-	Selling costs	35,000
=	Amount realized	315,000
	Beginning basis of old home	200,000
+	Capital improvements	10,000
=	Adjusted basis of old home	210,000
	Amount realized	315,000
-	Adjusted basis	210,000
=	Gain on sale	105,000

In the case of Mary and Larry, their capital gain was $315,000 - $210,000, or $105,000. They will owe tax on this amount in the year of the sale unless they qualify for the exclusion described below.

Gains tax exclusion

Tax law provides an exclusion of $250,000 for an individual taxpayer and $500,000 for married taxpayers filing jointly. The exclusion of gain from sale of a residence can be claimed *every two years,* provided the taxpayer

- owned the property for at least two years during the five years preceding the date of sale;
- used the property as principal residence for a total of two years during that five-year period;
- has waited two years since the last use of the exclusion for any sale.

Losses are not deductible, and there is no carry-over of any unused portion of the exclusion. Postponed gains from a previous home sale under the earlier rollover rules reduce the basis of the current home if that home was a qualifying replacement home under the old rule.

Income Property Investment Analysis

Income properties are those that are held primarily for the generation of income. In addition to commercial and investment properties such as office buildings, this category includes residential rental properties. An important difference between income and non-income properties is that deductions for depreciation are allowed on income properties. Income properties, like non-income properties, generate a gain (or loss) on sale, and they also create an annual income stream. The annual income streams are determined on both a pre-tax and after-tax basis in order to determine the productivity of the investment.

Pre-tax cash flow

Cash flow is the difference between the amount of actual cash flowing into the investment as revenue and out of the investment for expenses, debt service, and all other items. Cash flow concerns cash items only, and therefore excludes depreciation, which is not a cash expense Pre-tax cash flow, or cash flow before taxation, is calculated as follows:

	Potential rental income
-	<u>Vacancy and collection loss</u>
=	Effective rental income
+	<u>Other income</u>
=	Gross operating income (GOI)
-	Operating expenses
-	<u>Reserves</u>
=	Net operating income (NOI)
-	<u>Debt service</u>
=	Pre-tax cash flow

Potential rental income is the annual amount that would be realized if the property is fully leased or rented at the scheduled rate. **Vacancy and collection loss** is rental income lost because of vacancies or tenants' failure to pay rent. **Effective rental income** is the potential income adjusted for these losses. To that is added any **other income** the property generates, such as from laundry or parking charges, to obtain **gross operating income**. **Operating expenses** paid by the landlord include such items as utilities and maintenance. These are deducted from gross operating income. Some owners also set aside a cash **reserve** each year to build up a fund for capital replacements in the future, for example, to replace a roof or a furnace. Cash reserves are <u>not</u> deductible for tax purposes until spent as deductible repairs or maintenance. The remainder is **net operating income (NOI)**. When the annual amount paid for **debt service**, including principal and interest, is subtracted, the remainder is the **pre-tax cash flow**.

For instance, a small office building of 3,500 square feet rents at $20 per square foot. If fully rented, the annual rental income would be $70,000. Historically, the property averages $4,200 in vacancy and collection losses. Equipment rental will provide an additional $2,000 per year in income. The owner will have to pay operating expenses amounting to ten dollars per square foot, or $35,000 per year. The owner sets aside one dollar per square foot, or $3,500 per year, for reserves. The owner financed the purchase of the building with a loan that requires annual debt service in the amount of $20,000. The pre-tax cash flow for the building is illustrated in the following exhibit.

Pre-tax Cash Flow

	Potential rental income	$70,000
-	Vacancy and collection loss	4,200
=	Effective rental income	65,800
+	Other income	2,000
=	Gross operating income (GOI)	67,800
-	Operating expenses	35,000
-	Reserves	3,500
=	Net operating income (NOI)	29,300
-	Debt service	20,000
=	Pre-tax cash flow	9,300

Tax liability

The owner's tax liability on taxable income from the property is based on taxable income rather than cash flow. Taxable income and tax liability are calculated as follows:

	Net operating income (NOI)
+	Reserves
-	Interest expense
-	Cost recovery expense
=	Taxable income
x	Tax rate
=	Tax liability

Taxable income is net operating income minus all allowable deductions. Cost recovery expenses are deductible, while allowances for reserves and payments on loan principal are not. Thus, since reserves were deducted from gross operating income to determine NOI, this amount must be added back in. As only the interest portion of debt service is deductible, the principal amount must be removed from the debt service payments and the interest expense deducted from NOI. Taxable income, multiplied by the owner's marginal tax bracket, gives the **tax liability**.

Note on tax rate: when a rental property is owned as an individual or by way of a pass-through entity (partnership, LLC treated as a partnership for tax purposes, or S corporation), its net income is taxed at the individual's personal marginal income tax rate. The next exhibit shows the tax liability for the previous example using an individual rate of 24%.

Tax Liability

	Net operating income (NOI)	29,300
+	Reserves	3,500
-	Interest expense	10,000
-	Cost recovery expense	22,000
=	taxable income	800
x	tax rate (24%)	.24
=	tax liability	192

After-tax cash flow

After-tax cash flow is the amount of income from the property that actually goes into the owner's pocket after income tax is paid. It is figured as:

	Pre-tax cash flow
-	Tax liability
=	After-tax cash flow

The after-tax cash flow for the sample property is illustrated in the following exhibit.

	Pre-tax cash flow	9,300
-	Tax liability	192
=	After-tax cash flow	9,108

Investment performance

Investors measure the investment performance of an income property in many different ways, depending on their needs. A few of the common measures are:

$$\frac{\text{Net operating income}}{\text{price}} = \text{return on investment (ROI)}$$

$$\frac{\text{cash flow}}{\text{cash invested}} = \text{cash-on-cash return (C on C)}$$

$$\frac{\text{cash flow}}{\text{equity}} = \text{return on equity (ROE)}$$

The annual cash-flow statement above is the property's pro forma, which investors usually extend over the full holding period. Applying the following ratios to that pro forma lets properties of different sizes and prices be compared on common terms. The measures below assume the sample building sold for $300,000, financed with a $225,000 loan (75 percent loan-to-value), leaving $75,000 of invested equity.

Capitalization rate. NOI divided by value ($29,300 ÷ $300,000 = 9.8 percent) measures the unleveraged return and is used both to compare properties and to estimate value from income.

Cash-on-cash return (equity dividend rate). Pre-tax cash flow divided by equity invested ($9,300 ÷ $75,000 = 12.4 percent) is the first-year return on the actual cash the investor put in.

Debt service coverage ratio (DSCR). NOI divided by annual debt service ($29,300 ÷ $20,000 = 1.47) shows how comfortably income covers the loan payment. Lenders commonly require at least 1.20 to 1.25.

Operating expense ratio. Operating expenses divided by gross operating income ($35,000 ÷ $67,800 = 51.6 percent) indicates how much of the income is consumed by operations; an unusually high ratio can signal inefficiency or an aging property.

Break-even ratio. Operating expenses plus debt service divided by gross operating income ($55,000 ÷ $67,800 = 81.1 percent) is the occupancy level at which income just covers expenses and debt. The lower the ratio, the more cushion against vacancy.

Loan-to-value and loan constant. Loan-to-value is the loan divided by value ($225,000 ÷ $300,000 = 75 percent) and declines as the loan amortizes. The loan constant is annual debt service divided by the original loan amount ($20,000 ÷ $225,000 = 8.9 percent); comparing it to the capitalization rate reveals whether leverage is positive (cap rate above the constant) or negative.

Per-square-foot measures. Expenses per square foot ($10), price per square foot ($85.71), and rent per square foot ($20) normalize properties of different sizes for quick comparison.

Net present value and discounted cash flow. Over a holding period, an investment produces a series of annual cash flows plus a reversion, the net proceeds when the property is sold. Discounted cash flow analysis restates each future amount at its present value using the investor's required rate of return, then sums them. Net present value is that sum minus the initial investment: a positive NPV means the property beats the required return, and a negative NPV means it falls short.

Internal rate of return. The internal rate of return is the discount rate at which net present value equals zero, in effect the annual rate the investment actually earns once the timing of every cash flow and the reversion is taken into account. NPV expresses results in dollars at a chosen discount rate, while IRR expresses them as a percentage; because each assumes a different reinvestment rate, the two can rank competing investments differently. Both can be calculated before or after tax, and the after-tax figures often matter most in real estate, where depreciation and financing can make after-tax returns differ sharply from pre-tax returns.

Sensitivity analysis. Because every projection rests on assumptions, an investor tests how the return changes when key variables, such as rent, vacancy, operating expenses, the exit capitalization rate, or the interest rate, move against the forecast. A worst-case scenario reveals whether the investment still meets the investor's minimum return and whether the debt-service-coverage and break-even ratios stay within safe limits for that property type, which is the heart of basic risk analysis.

Matching Properties with Investor Needs

User vs. investor property

Buyers shopping for investment properties focus on different characteristics than buyers shopping for a primary residence.

Buyers interested in property for personal use focus on lifestyle factors (schools, commute, aesthetics, and emotional appeal). Financial return is secondary, often limited to appreciation and tax benefits.

Investment buyers focus on a property's ability to generate income, appreciation, or both. These buyers evaluate properties on metrics such as potential cash flow, cap rates, internal rate of return (IRR), and return on investment (ROI). Decisions should be made based on data (rent potential, expenses, market trends, and exit strategy), not emotions.

Critical location rules of thumb

Location remains the most influential factor in real estate performance. While the process differs from one investor (and property type) to another, there are some general rules of thumb.

- the "path of progress rule" reflects the wisdom of investing where growth is expanding
- proximity to major employers, hospitals, universities, or business hubs supports rental demand
- easy access to highways, public transit, and commercial centers enhances desirability
- stable neighborhoods with low crime, good schools, and maintained properties correlate with stable or rising values
- supply and demand impacts appreciation and rent growth

Geographical/service area definition

Investors must define where they are willing and able to operate.

Local vs. remote investing. An analysis of local vs. remote investing is critical and must consider the benefits of investing locally (market familiarity and easier property management). Remote investors rely more heavily on property managers and data analysis.

Service area considerations. Those considering remote investments must analyze the availability of reliable property management services, contractor and maintenance networks, and local regulations regarding zoning, rental controls, and landlord/tenant laws.

Market segmentation. Other factors, particularly in residential investments, include choosing between urban, suburban, and rural areas and selecting property class. (Class A = luxury housing, Class B = middle market, and Class C = workforce housing.)

Financial Qualification

Before matching properties, investors must clearly define their financial capacity. How much capital is available? Reserves (should be 3 – 12 months of expenses)?

Financing ability. What about financing ability, including credit scores, debt-to-income ratio, and available loan types?

Return requirements. What return requirements were identified in the planning stages (minimum acceptable cash-on-cash return and target cap rate or IRR)?

Risk tolerance. What is the investor's risk tolerance? Some investors are more conservative and prefer stable, lower-yield assets. Some investors are more aggressive and may pursue value-add or redevelopment opportunities.

Duration matching

Another critical factor investors face is duration matching. The property strategy must align with how long the investor plans to hold the asset.

Short-term. A short-term investment is considered 1-3 years. For example, fix-and-flip investors focus on getting in and getting out. These investors focus on forced appreciation achieved through improvements or modifications to the property or its operations (such as better management practices). These investors are quite sensitive to market timing and transaction costs.

Medium-term. A 3- to 7-year term is considered a medium-term investment. These investors focus on value-add or moderate appreciation plays. A value-add strategy may involve buying an underperforming or outdated property and improving it through 1) renovations, 2) better management, such as raising below-market rents or reducing vacancies, or 3) operational fixes such as cutting expenses and improving tenant quality. The result is higher income, which typically translates into greater value.

A moderate appreciation play strategy relies more on market growth over time, with limited active changes by the investor. These investors generally buy a property in a stable or growing area and hold it while property values gradually rise and rents increase due to market influences. Using this strategy allows the market to create the appreciation.

Long-term. Investments intended to play out over a period of seven years or more are considered long-term investments. This may be referred to as a buy-and-hold strategy. The emphasis is on cash flow, amortization, and long-term appreciation.

Bottom line. Effective matching occurs when all five elements (property type, location, geographic scope, financial structure, and holding period) align with the investor's needs, constraints, and goals.

Commercial Leasing Essentials

Commercial real estate language

Commercial leasing is fundamentally about allocating space, risk, and cost between landlord and tenant. Unlike residential leases, nearly every term is negotiable and expressed in industry-specific language.

Lease types. In a **gross (or full-service)** lease, the tenant pays a specified rental amount, and the landlord covers most operating expenses (taxes, insurance, and maintenance).

A **net lease** requires the tenant to pay a base rent plus some or all of the related operating expenses. With a single net (N) lease, the tenant pays the property taxes. Under a double-net (NN) lease, the tenant is responsible for taxes and insurance. Under a triple-net (NNN) lease, the tenant pays for taxes, insurance, and maintenance. This is the most common type of net lease.

A percentage lease requires tenants to pay a specified amount of base rent plus a percentage of the tenant's business revenue. This type of lease is common in the retail arena.

Terminology. Understanding various terms related to commercial leasing will deepen your understanding of the field as a whole.

Rent and financial terms vocabulary:

- base rent – minimum rent paid before additional charges
- additional rent – operating expenses passed through to the tenant
- operating expenses – taxes, insurance, utilities, maintenance
- CAM (common area maintenance) – costs for shared areas such as lobbies, parking lots, and landscaping
- escalations – scheduled rent increases, either fixed or tied to inflation
- expense stop – landlord pays expenses up to a base year; tenant pays increases beyond that

Space and use vocabulary:

- demised premises – the space leased exclusively to the tenant
- use clause – defines what the tenant is allowed to do in the space
- exclusive use clause – prevents landlord from leasing nearby space to competitors
- co-tenancy clause – tenant's obligations may depend on other tenants (common in retail centers)

Risk and legal vocabulary:

- term – lease length
- options – rights to renew, expand, or terminate
- assignment/subletting – tenant's ability to transfer the lease
- default – failure to meet lease obligations
- personal guarantee – owner personally backs the lease if the business fails

Usable vs. rentable space

This is one of the most important, and often most misunderstood, concepts in commercial leasing.

- usable square footage (USF) – the actual space the tenant occupies and uses, including offices, storage, private areas
- rentable square footage (RSF) – USF plus a proportionate share of the common areas, including lobbies, hallways, restrooms, elevators
- load factor – refers to the percentage added to USF to calculate RSF (RSF = USF × (1 + Load Factor)

The load factor is calculated based on the ratio of common area to tenant-usable space. The building type impacts the load factor. Office buildings typically use a load factor of 10–25%; high-rise office towers are typically higher, while retail strips are typically lower. Industrial spaces use the lowest load factor.

Note that the load factor can change due to renovations, re-measurements, or simple lease-allowed recalculations.

Rent determination and tenant costs

Gross leasable area. Gross leasable area (GLA) is the total floor area designed for a tenant's exclusive use and on which rent is charged, including basements and mezzanines but excluding common areas. It is the standard rent basis in retail leasing, where rent and percentage-rent thresholds are quoted per square foot of GLA. GLA differs from rentable square footage, which adds a share of building common areas to the tenant's usable space.

Percentage rent and break point. A percentage lease, common in retail, requires the tenant to pay a base rent plus a percentage of gross sales above a stated threshold called the break point. The natural break point is found by dividing the annual base rent by the percentage rate. For example, a store with $60,000 of annual base rent and a 6 percent overage rate has a natural break point of $1,000,000 ($60,000 ÷ 0.06); the tenant pays 6 percent of all sales above $1,000,000 as additional percentage rent. A lease may also set an artificial break point higher or lower than the natural one by negotiation. Percentage leases require the lease to define gross sales precisely and to give the landlord the right to audit the tenant's sales records.

Rent concessions. A rent concession is an inducement a landlord offers to attract or retain a tenant, such as a period of free or abated rent, a reduced rent for part of the term, or a moving allowance. Concessions lower the tenant's effective rent below the face (quoted) rent, so an investor analyzing a property must look past the stated rent roll to the concessions actually granted.

Expense stops and caps. An expense stop limits the landlord's exposure to rising operating costs: the landlord pays operating expenses up to a base-year amount, and the tenant pays its share of any increase above that stop. An expense cap works in the tenant's favor, limiting the amount of expense increase that can be passed through in a given year. Expenses passed from landlord to tenant under these provisions are called pass-throughs.

Tenant improvement allowances. A tenant improvement (TI) allowance is a dollar amount, usually stated per square foot, that the landlord contributes toward customizing the space for the tenant. When a tenant wants improvements costing more than the allowance, the landlord may finance the excess and recover it as additional rent amortized over the lease term with interest. For example, if the landlord funds $25,000 of improvements beyond the allowance and amortizes it over a five-year lease at 9 percent, the tenant's rent increases by about $519 per month, or roughly $6,228 per year, for the term.

Structural components synopses

Recognizing building components helps clarify who pays for what, a critical issue in commercial leases.

Core building components. Structural elements are typically the landlord's responsibility. These elements include the foundation, structural walls, roof structure, and load-bearing systems.

Building systems. Responsibility for building systems depends on the lease type. In a gross lease, the landlord usually pays for these systems. In a triple-net lease, the tenant often pays a proportionate share. These systems include the HVAC, electrical, plumbing, and elevator systems.

Interior. This is generally the tenant's space. The tenant is responsible for walls, flooring, ceilings, fixtures and finishes, and interior lighting.

Common areas. Typically borne by the landlord, common-area costs may be passed on to tenants through CAM charges. These areas include the lobby, parking lots, landscaping, and shared hallways.

Financing and lease priority

Interest computation. The way interest is calculated affects the true cost of a loan. With simple interest, interest is charged only on the outstanding principal balance, which declines as the loan amortizes; this is the standard method for mortgages. With add-on interest, interest is computed on the entire original principal for the full term, added to principal, and the total divided into equal payments. Because the borrower pays interest on the full amount even as the balance falls, add-on interest produces an effective (nominal) rate well above the quoted rate and is far more costly than simple interest.

Reducing annual debt service. An investor can lower the annual debt service on a property in several ways: lengthening the amortization term, using an interest-only or balloon structure, making a larger down payment to reduce the loan amount, buying down the interest rate with points, or refinancing when rates fall. Each lowers the payment but carries a trade-off, such as more total interest, a future balloon, or more equity tied up in the property.

Recourse vs. non-recourse. A recourse loan allows the lender, on default, to pursue the borrower's other assets beyond the pledged property for any deficiency. A non-recourse loan limits the lender to the property itself; the borrower is not personally liable for a shortfall. Non-recourse terms favor the borrower and are common in larger commercial financing, though lenders usually require carve-outs that restore personal liability for fraud, waste, or unauthorized transfers.

Legal priority of leases and mortgages. When a property is leased and mortgaged, priority generally follows recording order. A lease signed and recorded before a mortgage is superior to it, so the tenant's rights survive a foreclosure of that mortgage. A lease entered after the mortgage is subordinate, and a foreclosure can extinguish it. Lenders frequently require a subordination, non-disturbance, and attornment

(SNDA) agreement, under which the tenant subordinates its lease to the mortgage in exchange for the lender's promise not to disturb the tenant's possession as long as the tenant performs.

Estoppel certificates. Before closing a purchase or loan, a buyer or lender typically requires an estoppel certificate from each tenant. In it, the tenant confirms the key lease terms, the rent and deposit, and that the landlord is not in default. Once signed, the tenant is estopped from later asserting facts that contradict the certificate, giving the buyer or lender reliable confirmation of the income stream it is acquiring or financing.

Snapshot Review for Chapter 15

The following review summarizes the key rules and concepts from Chapter 15.

INVESTMENT FUNDAMENTALS

Characteristics of Investment

- goal: conservation of capital while increasing wealth over time
- every investment involves a balance of risk, return, liquidity, and management requirements
- rewards: income, appreciation, leverage, and tax benefits
- risks: market changes, business risk, inflation, interest-rate changes, poor investment performance
- major investment types: money investments, debt investments, equity investments, and real estate investments

Real Estate as an Investment

- advantages: potential for income, appreciation, leverage, and favorable tax treatment; historically provides some protection against inflation
- challenges: relatively illiquid compared to stocks and savings accounts; often requires significant management and ongoing oversight; subject to market, financing, operating, and tax-law risks

Taxation of Real Estate Investments

- taxable income: investment property income taxed after allowable deductions

Cost Recovery (Depreciation)

- residential rental property depreciated over 27.5 years
- nonresidential property depreciated over 39 years
- land cannot be depreciated

Gain on Sale

- sale may create a taxable capital gain or loss
- a Section 1031 exchange may defer taxation on qualifying investment property

Interest Deductions

- qualified mortgage interest may be deductible
- interest on investment-property financing is generally deductible subject to IRS rules

INVESTMENT ANALYSIS

Residence as an Investment

- value is derived primarily from appreciation, leverage, tax benefits, and capital-gain exclusions.
- gain exclusion: up to $250,000 for single taxpayers and $500,000 for married taxpayers filing jointly.
- income property analysis: key measures include net operating income (NOI), pre-tax cash flow, tax liability, and after-tax cash flow

Matching Properties with Investor Needs

- key considerations: property type, location, geographic service area, financial capacity, and investment objectives should align with the investor's goals

Investment Time Horizons

- short-term (1–3 years): typically fix-and-flip strategies
- medium-term (3–7 years): value-add and moderate appreciation strategies
- long-term (7+ years): buy-and-hold focus on cash flow, amortization, and appreciation

Investment Performance

- capitalization rate = NOI ÷ value; cash-on-cash (equity dividend rate) = pre-tax cash flow ÷ equity
- debt service coverage ratio = NOI ÷ debt service; lenders typically want at least 1.20 to 1.25
- operating expense ratio = operating expenses ÷ gross operating income
- break-even ratio = (operating expenses + debt service) ÷ gross operating income
- loan-to-value = loan ÷ value; loan constant = annual debt service ÷ loan amount
- NPV = present value of the cash flows less the investment; IRR = the rate at which NPV equals zero
- sensitivity analysis tests returns under worst-case assumptions

COMMERCIAL LEASING PRIMER

Common Lease Types

- gross lease: tenant pays fixed rent; landlord pays most operating expenses
- net lease: tenant pays rent plus some operating expenses. variations include single net (taxes), double net (taxes and insurance), and triple net (taxes, insurance, and maintenance)
- percentage lease: tenant pays base rent plus a percentage of business sales

Important Terminology

- base rent: minimum rent paid before additional charges
- common area maintenance (CAM): tenant's share of costs for common areas
- escalation clause: provides for future rent increases
- use clause: limits how the tenant may use the property
- assignment/subletting: transfer of lease rights to another party
- usable square footage (USF): space occupied exclusively by the tenant
- rentable square footage (RSF): usable space plus a share of common areas
- load factor: percentage added to USF to determine RSF
- gross leasable area (GLA): tenant's exclusive floor area; the retail rent basis
- percentage rent: paid on sales above the break point (base rent ÷ percentage rate)
- rent concession: free or reduced rent or allowances that lower effective rent
- expense stop or cap: limits operating-cost increases passed through to the tenant
- tenant improvement (TI) allowance: landlord build-out contribution; excess financed as additional rent

Building Responsibilities

- structural components – generally the landlord's responsibility
- interior improvements – generally the tenant's responsibility
- common area expenses – often passed through to tenants as CAM charges

Financing and Lease Priority

- recourse loan: lender may pursue the borrower's other assets; non-recourse is limited to the property

- lease priority: a lease predating a mortgage survives foreclosure; a later lease can be extinguished
- SNDA: tenant subordinates to the mortgage in exchange for non-disturbance of possession
- estoppel certificate: tenant confirms lease terms for a buyer or lender to rely on
- add-on interest: charged on the full original principal; costlier than simple interest

Chapter 15 Quiz: Investment Real Estate

15.1 The return on an investment is best described as ______.

a. the income or profit the investor receives
b. the total cost of the property
c. the amount of the mortgage
d. the property's assessed value

15.2 Using borrowed funds to acquire an investment larger than one's own resources allow is called ______.

a. liquidity
b. leverage
c. depreciation
d. amortization

15.3 Compared with stocks, real estate is generally considered ______.

a. more liquid
b. risk-free
c. relatively illiquid
d. exempt from taxation

15.4 Compared with many other investments, direct ownership of real estate typically requires ______.

a. no capital
b. no risk
c. instant resale
d. active, hands-on management

15.5 Real estate is often viewed as a good ______.

a. hedge against inflation
b. source of immediate liquidity
c. tax-free investment
d. management-free asset

15.6 Taxable income from an investment property is generally the gross income minus ______.

a. the mortgage principal
b. allowable expenses, deductions, and exclusions
c. the purchase price
d. the down payment

15.7 Cost recovery (depreciation) allows the owner of income property to ______.

a. increase the property's basis
b. avoid all capital gains
c. deduct a portion of the property's value each year
d. defer the mortgage payments

15.8 Cost-recovery deductions are allowed ______.

a. on a personal residence
b. on vacant land
c. on the land portion of any property
d. only for income-producing property

15.9 Cost recovery (depreciation) on an investment property applies to ______.

a. the improvements (building), not the land
b. the land, not the building
c. both the land and the building
d. the outstanding loan balance

15.10 A residential rental building (excluding land) has a depreciable basis of $275,000. Its annual cost-recovery deduction is approximately ______.

a. $27,500
b. $10,000
c. $5,000
d. $2,750

15.11 On the sale of a primary residence, the tax law allows a gain exclusion of ______.

a. $100,000 for any taxpayer
b. no exclusion
c. $250,000 for a single filer and $500,000 for married filing jointly
d. $500,000 for any taxpayer

15.12 Net operating income (NOI) is calculated as effective rental income minus ______.

a. debt service
b. depreciation
c. income taxes
d. operating expenses

15.13 A rental property produces effective rental income of $100,000 and has operating expenses of $40,000. Its net operating income is ______.

a. $60,000
b. $40,000
c. $140,000
d. $100,000

15.14 Pre-tax cash flow equals net operating income minus ______.

a. operating expenses
b. annual debt service
c. vacancy loss
d. depreciation

15.15 A property's net operating income is $60,000 and its annual debt service is $45,000. The pre-tax cash flow is ______.

a. $105,000
b. $60,000
c. $15,000
d. $45,000

15.16 After-tax cash flow is pre-tax cash flow minus ______.

a. operating expenses
b. debt service
c. depreciation
d. the investor's tax liability

15.17 In an income projection, vacancy and collection loss is ______.

a. subtracted from potential rental income
b. added to effective income
c. ignored
d. the same as debt service

15.18 Which of the following is an operating expense used in calculating NOI?

a. the mortgage principal and interest
b. property management and maintenance costs
c. depreciation
d. income taxes

15.19 When calculating NOI, which item is NOT deducted?

a. property taxes
b. insurance
c. debt service (mortgage payments)
d. management fees

15.20 A property purchased primarily for the owner's own occupancy or business use rather than for income is a ______.

a. a triple-net property
b. a leveraged property
c. a speculative property
d. a user property

15.21 Matching an investor's holding period to the appropriate property is known as ______.

a. duration (time-horizon) matching
b. leverage
c. reconciliation
d. cost recovery

15.22 Matching an investor to a suitable property requires the broker to evaluate the investor's ______.

a. loan pre-approval only
b. financial qualifications and investment objectives
c. personal hobbies
d. political affiliation

15.23 In a gross lease, operating expenses such as taxes and insurance are typically paid by ______.

a. the tenant
b. the mortgage lender
c. the landlord
d. the local government

15.24 A net lease requires the tenant to pay base rent plus ______.

a. a percentage of gross sales
b. nothing else
c. the landlord's mortgage
d. some or all of the property's operating expenses

15.25 Under a triple-net (NNN) lease, the tenant pays the property's ______.

a. taxes, insurance, and maintenance
b. mortgage principal
c. income taxes
d. depreciation

15.26 A percentage lease, common in retail, requires the tenant to pay ______.

a. only a flat annual fee
b. base rent plus a percentage of business revenue
c. the landlord's income tax
d. no rent at all

15.27 Usable square footage (USF) refers to ______.

a. the total area of the building
b. the common areas only
c. the actual space the tenant occupies and uses
d. the parking lot

15.28 Rentable square footage (RSF) equals usable square footage plus ______.

a. the mortgage amount
b. the depreciation
c. nothing
d. a proportionate share of the common areas

15.29 The load factor is ______.

a. the percentage added to usable space to arrive at rentable space
b. the interest rate on the loan
c. the vacancy rate
d. the depreciation rate

15.30 A tenant's usable space is 1,000 square feet, and the building's load factor is 15%. The rentable square footage is ______.

a. 850
b. 1,150
c. 1,015
d. 1,500

CHAPTER 16:
ZONING, PLANNING AND ENVIRONMENTAL CONTROLS

Contents

Learning Objectives

Upon completion of this chapter, you will be able to:

1. Describe the major provisions of Florida's Community Planning Act and explain the purpose of the concurrency provision
2. Explain the purpose of the concurrency provision
3. Distinguish among a variance, special exception, and a nonconforming use
4. Describe the characteristics of a planned unit development
5. Distinguish between zoning and subdivision regulations
6. Explain the goals of public land use control and the role of police power
7. Describe the purpose of a master plan and the required elements of a comprehensive plan
8. Identify the purpose of building codes and describe how the Live Local Act affects local land use and affordable housing
9. Describe the National Flood Insurance Program NFIP and the flood zone requirements affecting Florida properties

Planning and Zoning

While the Constitution guarantees the right of individual ownership of real estate, it does not guarantee the uncontrolled sale, use, and development of real estate. As American history demonstrates, unregulated use of real estate has the potential to cause significant damage to property values and the environment. Moreover, amid this century's explosive urban growth, it has become clear that regulating land use is necessary to preserve the community's interests, safety, and welfare.

Without a central authority to exert control, land use tends to be chaotic. For example, rapid growth can outpace the support capabilities of basic municipal services such as sewers, power, water, schools, roads, and communications. On an aesthetic level, communities need controls to keep certain commercial and industrial land uses out of residential areas to prevent property values from being undermined by pollution, noise, and traffic congestion.

Goals of land use control

Over time, public and private control of land use has come to focus on certain core purposes. These are:

- preservation of property values
- promotion of the highest and best use of property
- balance between individual property rights and the public good, i.e., its health, safety, and welfare
- control of growth to remain within infrastructure capabilities
- incorporation of community consensus into regulatory and planning activities

Optimal management of real property use must balance the interests of the individual with those of the surrounding community. While maintaining the value of an individual estate is important, the owner must recognize that unregulated use and development can jeopardize not only the owner's estate but also neighboring properties. Similarly, the community must keep in mind the effects of government actions on individual property values, since local government is largely supported by property taxes.

Public Land Use Control

A community achieves its land usage goals through a three-phase process, as the exhibit illustrates:

- development of a master plan for the jurisdiction
- administration of the plan by a municipal, county, or regional planning commission
- implementation of the plan through public control of zoning, building codes, permits, and other measures

Municipal, county, and regional authorities develop comprehensive land use plans for a particular community with the input of property owners. A planning commission manages the master plan and enforces it by exercising its power to establish zones, control building permits, and create building codes.

In addition to public land use planning and control, some private entities, such as subdivision associations, can impose additional land use standards on owners within their legal jurisdiction. Private controls are primarily implemented by deed restrictions.

The master plan

Public land use planning incorporates long-term use strategies and growth policies in a **land use plan,** or **master plan.** In Florida, the process of land use planning begins when the state legislature enacts laws requiring all counties and municipalities to adopt a land use plan. The land use plan must not only reflect the needs of the local area, but also conform to state and federal environmental laws and the plans of regional and state planning agencies. The state enforces its planning mandates by giving state agencies the power to approve county and local plans.

The master plan, therefore, fuses state and regional land use laws with local land use objectives that correspond to the municipality's social and economic conditions. The completed plan becomes the overall guideline for creating and enforcing zones, building codes, and development requirements.

Planning objectives

The primary objectives of a master plan are generally to control and accommodate social and economic growth.

Amount of growth. A master plan sets specific guidelines on how much growth the jurisdiction will allow. While all communities desire a certain degree of growth, too much growth can overwhelm services and infrastructure.

To formulate a growth strategy, a plan initially forecasts growth trends, then estimates how well the municipality can keep pace with the growth forecast. The outcome is a policy position that limits building permits and development projects to desired growth parameters. A growth plan considers:

- nature, location, and extent of permitted uses
- availability of sanitation facilities
- adequacy of drainage, waste collection, and potable water systems
- adequacy of utilities companies
- adequacy and patterns of thoroughfares
- housing availability
- conservation of natural resources
- adequacy of recreational facilities
- ability and willingness of the community to absorb new taxes, bond issues, and assessments

Growth patterns. In addition to the quantity of growth, a master plan also defines what type of growth will occur and where. Major considerations are:

- the type of enterprises and developments to allow
- residential density and commercial intensity
- effects of industrial and commercial land uses on residential and public sectors, i.e., where to allow such uses
- effect of new developments on traffic patterns and thoroughfares
- effects on the environment and environmental quality (air, water, soil, noise, visual aspects)
- effect on natural resources that support the community
- code specifications for specific construction projects

Accommodating demand. As the master plan sets forth guidelines for how much growth will be allowed, it must also make plans for accommodating expanding or contracting demand for services and infrastructure. The plan must identify:

- facilities requirements for local government

- new construction requirements for streets, schools, and social services facilities such as libraries, civic centers, etc.
- new construction required to provide power, water and sewer services

Plan development

In response to land use objectives, community attitudes, and conclusions drawn from research, the planning personnel formulate their plan. In the course of planning, they analyze

- population and demographic trends
- economic trends
- existing land use
- existing support facilities
- traffic patterns

Planning management

Public land use management takes place within county and municipal **planning departments**. These departments are responsible for:

- long-term implementation of the master plan
- creating rules and restrictions that support plans and policies
- enforcing and administering land use regulations on an everyday basis

The planning commission. In most jurisdictions, a planning commission or board comprised of officials appointed by the government's legislative entity handles the planning function.

The commission oversees the operations of the department's professional planning staff and support personnel. In addition, the commission makes recommendations to elected officials concerning land use policy and policy administration.

Commission authority and duties. The planning commission is responsible for:

- approving site plans and subdivision plans
- approving building permits
- ruling on zoning issues
- controlling signage

Commission support staff. After the planning commission proposes policies and sets goals and standards, the Commission's support staff carries out the collection and analysis of land use information necessary to develop the comprehensive plan.

Florida's Growth Policy and Community Planning Act (CPA)

Chapter 163 F. S. growth policy

Florida's Growth Policy and Community Planning Act recognizes and promotes the beneficial impact that strong urban centers have on local and state economies and resources and, thus, urges respective governments to revitalize urban centers by providing adequate infrastructure, human services, safe neighborhoods, educational facilities, and economic development.

The Act refers to this effort as infill development and redevelopment, wherein public services such as water, transportation, schools, etc., are already in place prior to capital improvements in areas that suffer from pervasive poverty and unemployment with substandard properties.

Florida's Community Planning Act was established to strengthen the power of local governments in establishing comprehensive planning programs for future development; in encouraging appropriate use of land, water, and resources in the interest of the public; and in overcoming current and future problems caused by land use and development.

The intent of the Act was to have local governments concentrate on community land use and growth for the protection of public health, safety, and general welfare, while the state government concentrates on protecting state resources and facilities.

The Act protects the traditional economic base of Florida, i.e., agriculture, tourism, and military presence, and encourages economic diversification, workforce development, and community planning. The Act also protects private property and the rights of private property owners.

Department of Economic Opportunity

The Department of Community Affairs (DCA), which monitored housing and commercial development in Florida, was abolished in 2011. The DCA was originally established to prevent sprawl and congestion. In its stead, the ***Department of Economic Opportunity (DEO)*** was created, and the power to make development decisions was relegated to local governments, thereby diminishing state oversight. The DEO supervises funds used to incentivize businesses to come to Florida.

Required elements of a comprehensive plan

A comprehensive plan must be implemented by adopting sufficient land use control ordinances and capital improvement programs. The plan must contain the following required elements.

Future land use. The plan must designate the proposed future distribution and location of residential, commercial, industrial, agricultural, recreational, conservation, education, public facilities, and other categories of land use. The plan must also include the standards for control and distribution of population densities and building intensities.

Traffic circulation. The plan must include a transportation element to plan for a multimodal transportation system with emphasis on public transportation systems. The transportation element must address traffic circulation to include the types, locations, and extent of existing and proposed major thoroughfares and transportation routes, and maps showing the existing and proposed system features. An airport plan may be incorporated into the master plan.

Conservation of natural resources. A conservation element must be included in the plan for the conservation, use, and protection of air, water, water recharge areas, wetlands, water wells, marshes, soils, beaches, shores, flood plains, rivers, lakes, forests, wildlife, marine habitat, minerals, and other resources.

Recreation. The plan is also to include an element for a comprehensive system of public and private sites for recreation to include natural reservations, parks and playgrounds, parkways, beaches, open spaces, waterways, and other recreation facilities.

Housing. A mandated housing element must include principles, guidelines, standards, and strategies for providing housing for all current and future residents, the elimination of substandard dwelling conditions, the improvement of existing housing, sites for future housing, relocation housing, and affordable housing.

Coastal zone protection where relevant. Another element of the plan is for coastal management to maintain and restore the quality of the coastal zone environment, preserve populations of wildlife and marine life, protect coastal zone resources, and manage coastal zone development.

Intergovernmental coordination. An intergovernmental coordination element must be included that shows the relationships and states principles and guidelines to be used in coordinating the comprehensive plan with 1) plans from local government units that do not have regulatory authority over land use, 2) comprehensive plans of adjacent municipalities and areas, and 3) the state comprehensive plan. The comprehensive plan must show consideration for plans of these other entities.

Utilities. An element for sanitary sewer, solid waste, drainage, potable water, and natural groundwater aquifer recharge must also be included in the plan to indicate means for providing protection for these facilities in the area.

Concurrency. Concurrency is a set of land use regulations that local governments within Florida adopt to assure that new development does not exceed the local government's ability to handle it. The local government needs to have enough infrastructure capacity to support any proposed development.

Regulations require the governments to meet concurrency requirements for sanitary sewer, solid waste, drainage, and potable water by the time a certificate of occupancy is issued for the development. Parks and recreation, schools, and transportation facilities no longer fall under the state's concurrency requirements. They and other non-mandatory public facilities may, however, fall under a local government's concurrency requirements if the local government's plan provides the principles, guidelines, standards, and strategies for applying the concurrency to the facility.

Optional elements may include historical, scenic preservation, economic, and public buildings.

Public Land Use Control

At the state level, the legislature enacts laws that control and restrict land use, particularly from an environmental perspective. At the local level, county and city governments control land use through the authority known as **police power**. The most common expressions of police power are county and municipal **zoning**. Other examples of public land use control are:

- subdivision regulations
- building codes
- eminent domain
- environmental restrictions
- development requirements

Governments also have the right to **own** real property for public use and welfare. In exercising its ownership rights, a municipality may **annex** property adjacent to its existing property or purchase other tracts of land through conventional transfers. Where necessary, it may force property owners to sell their property through the power of **eminent domain**.

Zoning

Zoning is the primary tool by which cities and counties regulate land use and implement their respective master plans. The Constitution grants the states the legal authority to regulate, and the states delegate the authority to counties and municipalities through legislation called **enabling acts**.

The zoning ordinance. The vehicle for zoning a city or county is the zoning ordinance, a regulation enacted by the local government. The intent of zoning ordinances is to specify land usage for every parcel within the jurisdiction. In some areas, state laws permit zoning ordinances to apply to areas immediately beyond the legal boundaries of the city or county.

Zoning ordinances implement the master plan by regulating **density, land use intensity, aesthetics,** and **highest and best use.** Ordinances typically address:

- the nature of land use-- office, commercial, residential, etc.
- size and configuration of a building site, including setbacks, sidewalk requirements, parking requirements, and access
- site development procedures
- construction and design methods and materials, including height restrictions, building-to-site area ratios, and architectural styles
- use of space within the building
- signage

Ordinance validity. Local planners do not have unlimited authority to do whatever they want. Their zoning ordinances must be clear in import, apply to all parties equally, and promote health, safety, and welfare of the community in a reasonable manner.

Building permits. Local governments enforce zoning ordinances by issuing building permits to those who want to improve, repair, or refurbish a property. To receive a permit, the project must comply with all relevant ordinances and codes. Further zoning enforcement is achieved through periodic inspections.

Types of zones. One of the primary applications of zoning power is the separation of residential properties from commercial and industrial uses. Proper design of land use in this manner preserves the aesthetics and value of neighborhoods and promotes the success of commercial enterprises through intelligently located zones.

Six common types of zones and their respective priorities are as follows.

- residential
- commercial
- industrial
- agricultural
- public
- planned unit development (PUD)

Residential. Residential zoning restricts land use to private, non-commercial dwellings. Sub-zones in this category further stipulate the types of residences allowed, whether single-family, multi-unit complexes, condominiums, publicly subsidized housing, or other forms of housing.

Residential zoning regulates:

- density, by limiting the number and size of dwelling units and lots in an area
- values and aesthetics, by limiting the type of residences allowed. Some areas adopt buffer zones to separate residential areas from commercial and industrial zones.

Commercial. Commercial zoning regulates the location of office and retail land usage. Some commercial zones allow combinations of office and retail uses on a single site. Sub-zones in this category may limit the type of retail or office activity permitted, for example, a department store versus a strip center.

Commercial zoning regulates:

- intensity of usage, by limiting the area of store or office per site area. Intensity regulation is further achieved by minimum parking requirements, setbacks, and building height restrictions.

Industrial. Industrial zoning regulates:

- intensity of usage
- type of industrial activity
- environmental consequences

A municipality may not allow some industrial zones, such as heavy industrial, at all. The industrial park is a relatively recent concept in industrial zoning.

Agricultural. Agricultural zoning restricts land use to farming, ranching, and other agricultural enterprises.

Public. Public zoning restricts land use to public services and recreation. Parks, post offices, government buildings, schools, and libraries are examples of uses allowed in a public zone.

Planned Unit Development (PUD). planned unit development zoning restricts use to the development of whole tracts that are designed to use space efficiently and maximize open space. A PUD zone may be for residential, commercial, or industrial uses, or combinations thereof.

Community Development District (CDD). A community development district is a special-purpose unit of local government, authorized by Chapter 190, Florida Statutes, that a developer can establish to finance, build, and maintain the infrastructure of a large planned community. The district issues tax-exempt bonds to fund roads, water and sewer systems, drainage, and recreational amenities, then repays the bonds through assessments levied on the properties within the district. A CDD is governed by a board of supervisors, elected at first by the landowner-developer and over time by the resident property owners. Because buyers in a CDD pay annual assessments in addition to ordinary property taxes, Florida law requires that this obligation be disclosed before a sale closes, as discussed in Chapter 11. Unlike a PUD, which is a zoning classification governing land use, a CDD is a financing and management entity governing infrastructure.

Zoning administration

Florida's Community Planning Act. In Florida, local zoning and land-use decisions operate within the framework of the Community Planning Act (Chapter 163, Part II, Florida Statutes). The Act requires each county and municipality to adopt a comprehensive plan governing future growth and requires that zoning ordinances and individual land-use decisions be consistent with that plan. The variances, special exceptions, and rezonings described here are therefore granted by local boards under state-mandated procedures and must conform to the local comprehensive plan; a decision inconsistent with the plan can be challenged. This framework is what ties Florida's local zoning administration to statewide growth-management policy.

Zoning Board of Adjustment. A county or local board, usually called the zoning board of adjustment or zoning appeals board, administers zoning ordinances. The board rules on interpretations of zoning ordinances as they apply to specific land use cases presented by property owners in the jurisdiction. In effect, the zoning board is a court of appeals for owners and developers who desire to use land in a manner that is not entirely consistent with existing ordinances.

The board conducts hearings of specific cases and renders official decisions regarding the land use based on evidence presented.

A zoning board generally deals with such issues and appeals as:

- nonconforming use
- variance
- special exception or conditional use permit
- zoning amendment

If the board rejects an appeal, the party may appeal the ruling further in a court of law.

Nonconforming use. A nonconforming use is one that clearly differs from current zoning. Usually, nonconforming uses result when a zoning change leaves existing properties in violation of the new ordinance. This type of nonconforming use is a legal nonconforming use. A board usually treats this kind of situation by allowing it to continue for any of the following periods:

- indefinitely
- until the structures are torn down
- only while the same use continues, or
- until the property is sold

For instance, a motel is situated in a residential area that no longer allows commercial activity. The zoning board rules that the motel may continue to operate until it is sold, destroyed, or used for any other commercial purpose.

An **illegal nonconforming use** is one that conflicts with ordinances that were in place before the use commenced. For instance, if the motel in the previous example is sold, and the new owner continues to operate the property as a motel, the motel is now an illegal, nonconforming use.

Variance. A zoning variance allows a use that differs from the applicable ordinance for a variety of justifiable reasons, including that:

- compliance will cause unreasonable hardship
- the use will not change the essential character of the area
- the use does not conflict with the general intent of the ordinance

For example, an owner mistakenly violates a setback requirement by two feet. His house is already constructed, and complying with the full setback now would be extremely expensive, if not impossible.

The zoning board grants a variance on the grounds that compliance would cause an unreasonable hardship.

A grant of a zoning variance may be unconditional, or it may require conditions to be fulfilled, such as removing the violation after a certain time.

Special exception. A special exception grant authorizes a use that is not consistent with the zoning ordinance in a literal sense, yet is clearly beneficial or essential to the public welfare and does not materially impair other uses in the zone.

A possible example is an old house in a residential zone adjacent to a retail zone. The zoning board might grant a special exception to a local group that proposes to renovate the house and convert it to a local museum, which is a retail use, since the community stands to benefit from the museum.

Amendment. A current or potential property owner may petition the zoning board for an outright change in the zoning of a particular property. For example, a property zoned for agricultural use has been idle for years. A major employer desires to develop the property for a local distribution facility, which would create numerous jobs, and petitions for an amendment. The board changes the zoning from agricultural to light industrial to permit the development. Since a change in zoning can have significant economic and social impact, an appeal for an amendment is a difficult process that often involves public hearings.

Subdivision regulation

In addition to complying with zoning ordinances, a developer of multiple properties in a subdivision must meet requirements for subdivisions.

Subdivision plat approval. The developer submits a plat of subdivision containing surveyed plat maps and comprehensive building specifications. The plat, as a minimum, shows that the plan complies with local zoning and building ordinances. The project can commence only after the relevant authority has approved the plat.

Subdivision requirements typically regulate:

- location, grading, alignment, surfacing, street width, highways
- sewers and water mains
- lot and block dimensions
- building and setback lines
- public use dedications
- utility easements
- ground percolation
- environmental impact report
- zoned density

Concurrency. Florida has adopted policies that require developers, especially of subdivisions, to take responsibility for the impact of their projects on the local infrastructure by taking corrective action. Concurrency is a policy that requires the developer to make accommodations concurrently with the development of the project itself, not afterward. For example, if a project will create a traffic overload in an area, the developer may have to widen the road while constructing the project.

FHA requirements. In addition to local regulation, subdivisions must meet FHA (Federal Housing Authority) requirements to qualify for FHA financing insurance. The FHA sets standards similar to local ordinances to ensure an adequate level of construction quality, aesthetics, and infrastructure services.

Subdividing and development of land. Subdividing is the division of a single parcel of raw land into smaller lots, blocks, and streets for sale or development. The party who does this, the subdivider, prepares and records the subdivision plat described above; a developer then installs the infrastructure the lots require, such as roads, drainage, and water and sewer lines. Florida regulates this activity both to ensure orderly growth and to guarantee that new development pays for its share of the public facilities it makes necessary.

Dedication. As a condition of plat approval, a developer is usually required to dedicate land or improvements to the local government for public use. Common dedications include the streets, sidewalks, drainage easements, utility easements, and sometimes park or school sites within the subdivision. Once the dedication is accepted, the property becomes public, and the government assumes responsibility for maintaining it.

Impact fees. An impact fee is a one-time charge a local government imposes on new development to help pay for the off-site capital improvements the development will burden, such as roads, schools, parks, water and sewer capacity, and police and fire facilities. Because the fee shifts the cost of growth from existing taxpayers to those creating the new demand, Florida law requires that an impact fee be based on the most recent and localized data, bear a reasonable connection to the need the development creates and the benefit it receives, and be earmarked for that purpose. The Florida Impact Fee Act also limits how often and how steeply local governments may raise these fees.

Building codes

Building codes allow the county and municipality to protect the public against the hazards of unregulated construction. Building codes establish standards for virtually every aspect of a construction project, including off-site improvements such as streets, curbs, gutters, drainage systems, and on-site improvements such as the building itself.

The Florida Building Commission developed the Florida Building Code after Hurricane Andrew revealed the need for more robust codes throughout the state. The statewide Code governs the design, construction, erection, alteration, modification, repair, and demolition of public and private buildings, structures, and facilities in the state. Separate books are available for plumbing, residential, energy conservation, hurricane zone test protocols, building, accessibility, existing building, fuel gas, and mechanical codes. The Code is updated every 3 years and often amended annually.

The Code now includes risk categories for building types based on three wind speed maps. Because Florida coastal areas encounter higher wind speed storms, those areas must meet the higher wind load requirements. The Code defines those areas and provides options for meeting the building code requirements through initial construction and upgrades to existing structures.

Building permits. Florida statute mandates that anyone who plans to construct, enlarge, alter, repair, move, demolish, or change the occupancy of a building or structure or perform any work that is regulated by the Florida Building Code must first obtain the required permit. Depending on the work to be done, one project may require multiple permits. For example, renovating a structure may require a general building permit but may also require an electrical and/or plumbing permit.

Florida permits usually require drawn plans of the work to be done and proof of the property's ownership. Again, depending on the work to be done, the permit may also require proof of insurance and/or proof of current licenses for any contractors or other professionals performing the work. New construction will also require a Florida energy code compliance certificate. Submission of the work plans will also allow the city or county building department to determine if the work will comply with wind load requirements.

Building inspections. During building construction or renovation, work completed will need to be inspected for code compliance and correctness. When an inspection is required for a particular phase of construction, work may not continue or resume until the inspector signs off on that phase. Inspections are typically required several times during a build or renovation. When the project is completed, a final inspection is required so that a certificate of occupancy can be issued and the property can be approved for occupancy and use.

R-value. An R-value is a measurement of the effectiveness of insulation and its resistance to heat flow. The higher the R-value, the higher the resistance, or the better the energy efficiency. City and county building and energy codes specify the minimum R-value required for the building envelope that is defined as the parts of the structure that separate the outdoor environment from the interior environment, or the roof, walls, and floors.

The Live Local Act

The Live Local Act (Senate Bill 102, 2023, as later amended) is a statewide affordable-housing law that significantly limits local control over certain residential development. Its most important features for real estate practice are:

Zoning preemption. In areas zoned for commercial, industrial, or mixed use, a local government must administratively approve a qualifying multifamily or mixed-use development, without a rezoning or public hearing, if at least 40 percent of the units are reserved as affordable for at least 30 years. The local government generally may not apply its usual density, height, or use limits to these projects, subject to safeguards that protect adjacent single-family neighborhoods.

Rent-control preemption. The Act reinforces Florida's prohibition on local rent control.

Tax incentives and funding. The Act provides property-tax exemptions for qualifying affordable units and funds state housing programs and down-payment assistance.

The Live Local Act is a leading example of state preemption overriding local home rule in land-use regulation. Because a qualifying project bypasses the normal rezoning and hearing process, a licensee working with developers, or with owners near a proposed project, should understand when the Act applies. Its zoning preemptions are scheduled to expire on October 1, 2033.

Flood Zones

The National Flood Insurance Act of 1968 created the Federal Insurance Administration and made flood insurance available for the first time. The Act also led to the creation of the National Flood Insurance Program, whose goals were to provide flood insurance for structures and their contents that are located in communities with minimal floodplain management standards and to establish insurance rates for structures located in identified flood hazard areas.

The Flood Disaster Protection Act of 1973 amended the NFIP by making the purchase of flood insurance mandatory for the protection of property located in Special Flood Hazard Areas.

National Flood Insurance Program (NFIP)

Qualifying for NFIP. The Federal Emergency Management Agency (FEMA) administers the NFIP and has established requirements communities must meet to participate in the program. The communities must agree to adopt and enforce regulations that reduce flood risks. Homeowners, renters, and business owners may obtain flood loss insurance through insurance agencies if the subject property is located in a community that participates in the program.

NFIP criteria for "Special Flood Hazard Areas" (SFHA). FEMA has identified flood zones throughout the U.S. and shows those areas on their Flood Insurance Rate Maps (FIRM), including the categories of flood risk for each area: low-risk, moderate-risk, and high-risk.

Any high-risk area is also identified as a special flood hazard area, which is defined as an area with a 1% chance of flooding in any year. That does not mean the area will flood every year; rather, it means there is a 1% statistical possibility of flooding every year. The 1% annual chance flood is also referred to as the base flood or 100-year flood. This is of special interest to mortgage lenders because that means there is a 1 in 4 chance of flooding during a 30-year mortgage. Thus, mortgage lenders holding loans on property located in a SFHA typically require the homeowner to carry flood insurance on the property.

SFHAs are identified as either A zones (SFHA floodplain areas) or V zones (SFHA coastal land area).

Development within SFHAs restrictions. Before beginning development within a SFHA, a developer must obtain a permit to ensure the project will meet the NFIP requirements and local community ordinances. Requirements vary based on the actual zone where the property is located and the type of structure being built.

Because V zones have higher flood risks, structures in those areas must be anchored to withstand the force of waves, high winds, and erosion and to prevent collapse and/or movement. Development sites are to be graded to prevent waterflow from entering into ground floor structures. Structures built on slopes must have drainage paths to guide waterflow away from the structures.

Development within SFHAs must not obstruct the natural flow of flood waters. For example, removing sand from beaches removes the natural barrier built up over years and exposes inland areas to increased flood risks. These standards protect residents and property from flooding, and they preserve floodplains as a natural means of flood control.

Residential structure requirements

Residential structures in the SFHA's V zone must have the lowest floor above the "Base Flood Elevation" or have an open foundation (often referred to as pilings or stilts) to allow water flooding the area to flow under the structure without causing damage.

Nonresidential structure requirements

Nonresidential structures in the SFHA's V zone must have the lowest floor above the Base Flood Elevation, be water-tight below the Base Flood Elevation, or have an open foundation.

Proportion of NFIP purchasers in Florida

It has been estimated that approximately 15% of American homeowners have flood insurance policies. However, due to hurricane-related flooding in recent years, approximately 35–40% of those policyholders are Floridians. Even Texas, South Carolina, and Louisiana, which are also flood-prone, do not come close to that number of policyholders.

Environmental and Special Land-Use Controls

Beyond zoning, planning, and flood regulation, several federal and state programs govern how environmentally sensitive land may be developed and how subdivided land may be sold across state lines.

The Clean Water Act and wetlands. Wetlands, such as marshes, swamps, and bogs, are protected because they filter water, store floodwater, and provide wildlife habitat. The federal Water Pollution Control Act, commonly called the Clean Water Act, makes it unlawful to deposit dredged or fill material into wetlands or other waters of the United States without a permit. Under Section 404 of the Act, the U.S. Army Corps of Engineers administers this permitting process, often jointly with Florida's environmental agencies. A developer who plans to build on or near wetlands must obtain the necessary federal and state permits before disturbing them.

Coastal Zone Management and the CCCL. The federal Coastal Zone Management Act encourages coastal states to protect their coastal resources, including wetlands, beaches, dunes, and barrier islands. Florida carries out this purpose in part through the Coastal Construction Control Line (CCCL) program under Section 161.053, Florida Statutes. The CCCL marks the landward limit of the area subject to severe fluctuation from a major coastal storm. Construction seaward of the line requires a special permit from the Florida Department of Environmental Protection, which reviews the project for its effect on the beach-dune system, storm protection, and neighboring property.

The Interstate Land Sales Full Disclosure Act. This federal law protects buyers of subdivided land sold across state lines, a response to past abuses in marketing remote lots sight-unseen. A developer who offers a covered subdivision must register it with the federal government and give each prospective purchaser a Property Report disclosing the essential facts about the land, such as access, utilities, title, and restrictions. A buyer who does not receive the Property Report before signing may have the right to rescind the contract, and certain misrepresentations create additional remedies. The law contains numerous exemptions, including for smaller subdivisions and for parcels that meet specified improvement conditions.

Developments of regional impact. A development of regional impact (DRI) is a project that, because of its size, character, or location, would substantially affect the health, safety, or welfare of citizens in more than one county. Historically, such a project underwent an additional review by a regional planning council before approval, to address effects like traffic, water use, and environmental impact that crossed local boundaries. Florida has since folded most of that review into the state coordinated review process for comprehensive-plan amendments, so a separate DRI review is now required only in limited circumstances; the underlying principle, that very large projects receive scrutiny beyond the single jurisdiction hosting them, remains part of the state's growth-management framework.

Snapshot Review for Chapter 16

The following review summarizes the key rules and concepts from Chapter 16.

PLANNING AND ZONING

Goals of Land Use Control

- preserve property values; promote highest and best use
- protect public health, safety, and welfare
- control growth within infrastructure capabilities
- balance private property rights and community interests

The Master Plan

- long-term guide for land use, growth, development, and infrastructure
- combines local objectives with state and regional requirements

Planning Objectives

- control amount and location of growth
- address housing, transportation, utilities, and environmental concerns
- accommodate future service and infrastructure needs

Planning Management

- planning commission administers land-use policies
- approves plans, permits, zoning matters, and development proposals

Florida's Growth Policy And Community Planning Act

- Chapter 163, F.S.
- promotes comprehensive planning and responsible growth
- encourages infill development and redevelopment
- protects private property rights while promoting public welfare

Department of Economic Opportunity (DEO)

- shifts greater development authority to local governments
- oversees programs encouraging economic growth

Required Plan Elements

- future land use
- transportation and traffic circulation
- housing and recreation
- conservation of natural resources
- utilities and intergovernmental coordination
- concurrency – infrastructure must be available to support new development; applies to sewer, solid waste, drainage, and potable water systems

PUBLIC LAND USE CONTROL

Zoning

- primary tool used to implement the master plan
- regulates land use, density, building size, setbacks, and development standards

- common zones: residential, commercial, industrial, agricultural, public, and PUD

Planned Unit Development (PUD)
- designed for efficient land use and increased open space
- may combine residential, commercial, or industrial uses

Community Development District (CDD)
- special-purpose local government (Chapter 190) that finances community infrastructure
- issues bonds repaid by assessments on district properties; CDD fees disclosed before sale
- a financing and management entity, unlike a PUD, which is a zoning classification

Zoning Administration
- Zoning Board of Adjustment hears appeals and interpretations
- nonconforming use: lawful use existing before zoning change
- variance: exception granted because of hardship
- special exception: use allowed because it benefits the public
- amendment: rezoning or change in zoning classification

Subdivision Regulation
- subdivision plat must be approved before development
- regulates streets, utilities, easements, density, and environmental impacts
- must satisfy FHA requirements for insured financing
- subdivider divides raw land into lots and blocks under the recorded plat
- dedication: streets, easements, and sites conveyed to the public as a condition of approval
- impact fees: one-time charges funding off-site infrastructure needed by new development

Florida Building Code
- governs construction, alteration, repair, and demolition
- includes wind-load requirements and coastal building standards

Permits and Inspections
- permits required for most construction and renovation projects
- inspections required throughout construction process
- final inspection required before certificate of occupancy issued

R-value
- measure of insulation effectiveness and resistance to heat flow

The Live Local Act
- Live Local Act (SB 102): state preemption of local zoning, density, and height for qualifying affordable housing
- requires 40 percent affordable units for 30 years in commercial, industrial, or mixed-use zones; administrative approval without rezoning
- also preempts local rent control; zoning preemptions sunset October 1, 2033

Flood Zones
- National Flood Insurance Program (NFIP): administered by FEMA; provides flood insurance in participating communities; Special Flood Hazard Areas (SFHAs) have a 1% annual flood risk

- development requirements: special permits required within SFHAs; development may not obstruct natural flood-water flow

Structure Requirements

- residential: lowest floor above base flood elevation or open foundation
- nonresidential: elevated, watertight, or open-foundation construction

Environmental and Special Controls

- Clean Water Act: Section 404 permit (U.S. Army Corps) to dredge or fill wetlands
- Coastal Zone Management Act protects wetlands, beaches, dunes, and barrier islands
- Coastal Construction Control Line (CCCL, s. 161.053): DEP permit to build seaward of the line
- Interstate Land Sales Full Disclosure Act: registration plus a Property Report to buyers
- development of regional impact (DRI): large project affecting more than one county

Chapter 16 Quiz: Zoning, Planning, and Environmental Controls

16.1 Which statement best explains the purpose of land use control?

a. It guarantees unlimited property development rights.
b. It eliminates the need for municipal infrastructure planning.
c. It helps protect property values, public welfare, and environmental quality.
d. It prevents all residential growth within municipalities.

16.2 Which one of the following is a major goal of land use control?

a. Eliminate all zoning ordinances.
b. Balance individual property rights with the public good.
c. Prohibit private ownership of real estate.
d. Transfer all planning authority to the federal government.

16.3 Communities generally achieve their land use goals through a three-phase process that includes development of a master plan, implementation through zoning and permits, and which of the following?

a. Elimination of infrastructure standards
b. Privatization of municipal services
c. Administration by a planning commission
d. Mandatory annexation of nearby communities

16.4 What is the primary purpose of a master plan?

a. Regulate only agricultural land use.
b. Provide guidelines for long-term growth and land use.
c. Replace all building codes within a municipality.
d. Establish mortgage lending standards.

16.5 Which factor would most likely be considered when formulating a community growth strategy?

a. The color preferences of homeowners
b. Federal income tax rates
c. The number of private insurance carriers
d. Availability of sanitation facilities and utilities

16.6 A master plan's growth pattern objectives typically address which of the following?

a. Stock market activity
b. Traffic patterns and environmental impacts
c. Federal banking regulations
d. Mortgage interest deductions

16.7 Planning personnel commonly analyze population trends, economic trends, and traffic patterns during which of the following activities?

a. Subdivision plat recording
b. Building code enforcement
c. Plan development
d. Eminent domain proceedings

16.8 In most jurisdictions, the planning commission is responsible for which of these tasks?

a. Approving site plans and ruling on zoning issues
b. Issuing title insurance policies
c. Collecting property taxes
d. Establishing federal environmental laws

16.9 Florida's Growth Policy and Community Planning Act encourages revitalization of urban centers through a process known as ______.

a. spot zoning (aka discriminatory zoning)
b. annexation
c. infill development and redevelopment
d. downzoning

16.10 Which of the following is one purpose of the Department of Economic Opportunity (DEO)?

a. Eliminate local government authority over planning
b. Supervise funds used to attract businesses to Florida
c. Replace all municipal zoning boards
d. Administer private deed restrictions

16.11 Which element is required in a Florida comprehensive plan?

a. Securities regulation
b. Maritime insurance standards
c. Transportation and traffic circulation planning
d. Federal tax allocation formulas

16.12 The conservation element of a comprehensive plan focuses on protecting resources such as ______.

a. mutual funds and retirement accounts
b. wetlands, rivers, forests, and wildlife
c. mortgage-backed securities
d. subdivision advertising campaigns

16.13 What is the purpose of concurrency regulations in Florida?

a. To prevent new development from exceeding infrastructure capacity
b. To allow developers to ignore infrastructure limitations
c. To ensure that development occurs only in agricultural areas
d. To ensure that all projects receive automatic zoning approval

16.14 Zoning authority is delegated to counties and municipalities by the state through what process?

a. Deed restrictions
b. Enabling acts
c. Title covenants
d. Subdivision plats

16.15 Which one of the following issues do zoning ordinances typically address?

a. Stock ownership requirements
b. Mortgage interest rates
c. Building setbacks and parking requirements
d. Federal tax exemptions

16.16 A homeowner discovers his newly built house encroaches two feet into the required setback, and tearing it down would be extremely costly. To keep the structure, he would most likely seek a ______.

a. variance
b. building permit
c. rezoning
d. special exception

16.17 A small grocery store has operated at a corner for years. The area is then rezoned exclusively residential, but the store is allowed to keep operating. The store is now a ______.

a. special exception
b. nonconforming use
c. variance
d. planned unit development

16.18 A community group wants to convert an old house in a residential zone into a public library, a use not literally allowed but beneficial to the public. The zoning board would most likely grant a ______.

a. variance
b. rezoning
c. special exception
d. nonconforming use

16.19 A Florida developer's project is delayed because roads and utilities cannot yet support the new residents it would bring. This requirement reflects Florida's ______.

a. police power
b. eminent domain authority
c. deed restrictions
d. concurrency provision

16.20 A city needs private land to widen a public road and takes it, paying the owner fair market value. The city is exercising its power of ______.

a. eminent domain
b. escheat
c. zoning variance
d. police power

CHAPTER 17: ENVIRONMENTAL ISSUES AFFECTING REAL ESTATE TRANSACTIONS

Contents

- **Environmental Hazards**
- **Landmark Environmental Legislation**
- **Responsibilities, Liabilities of Transaction Parties**
- **Environmental Issues Unique to Florida**

Learning Objectives

Upon completion of this chapter, you will be able to:

1. Explain the purpose and provisions of the Comprehensive Environmental Response,
2. Compensation and Liability Act (CERCLA)
3. Explain the provisions of the Superfund Amendment and Reauthorization Act (SARA)
4. List the criteria for the innocent landowner defense
5. Describe the information contained in Environmental Assessment Phases I – III
6. Describe the disclosure requirements for radon gas
7. Identify the provisions of the Residential Lead-Based Paint Hazard Reduction Act
8. Explain the disclosure requirements for lead-based paint
9. Identify environmental issues unique to Florida

Environmental Hazards

Disclosable hazards

Health hazards occur within structures, on real estate parcels, and in the area surrounding real estate. They may occur naturally or as a result of human activity. Environmental laws regulate some, but not all, health hazards that affect real estate. Real estate agents, owners, and sellers have various responsibilities for detecting, disclosing, and remediating regulated hazards. Some important issues are reviewed below.

Lead-based paint. Lead cannot be absorbed through the skin, but it becomes dangerous when ingested or inhaled. It can be found in most homes built before 1978 and can be present in the air, drinking water, food, contaminated soil, deteriorating paint, and dust from the paint. Children are particularly susceptible because young children may be tempted to eat paint chips, allowing lead to enter their bloodstream. Homebuyers and renters must be given the EPA-HUD-US Consumer Product Safety Commission booklet, "Protect Your Family from Lead in Your Home," and informed whether lead-based paint is present in the home. Notification typically occurs through a form completed by the sellers and presented during the contract negotiation and inspection phases of homebuying. Buyers must be given at least 10 days (or as negotiated) to conduct a lead inspection or risk assessment. Sellers are not required to mitigate lead hazards prior to the sale.

Mold. This fungus grows in moist conditions and can cause an allergic reaction in some people. The presence of mold in the home must be disclosed as a latent defect. Flooding and water damage must also be disclosed, as both of those can lead to mold growth. Inspections do not always find mold because it often grows inside walls and ductwork. Most molds require professional removal.

Asbestos. While harmless in its original state, asbestos can cause lung cancer if its dust is inhaled. If it is found in a home during remodeling, it must be removed by professionals to prevent contamination. It can be found in roofing and siding, older insulation, textured paint, artificial ashes sold for gas fireplaces, some vinyl floor tiles, and coatings for older hot water and steam pipes.

Air quality. The quality of air in a home can be adversely impacted by the presence of carbon monoxide, radon, deteriorating asbestos and lead-based paint, methamphetamine production, formaldehyde, and other toxic chemicals. Homes can and should be tested for many of these contaminants prior to purchase.

Water quality. Groundwater is easily contaminated from septic tanks, agricultural runoff, highway de-icing, landfills, pesticides, animal waste, etc. Many people rely on groundwater for drinking, so they must be aware that contaminated water can cause problems from mild stomach problems to cancer and death. The Environmental Protection Agency (EPA) sets standards for protecting groundwater from contamination. It also offers advice and resources to facilitate the rehabilitation of contaminated groundwater sources. One such means of protection is to advise private well users to have the water tested at least once a year.

Carbon monoxide. This is an odorless, colorless, toxic gas that can kill a person before its presence is known. It can be caused by unvented kerosene and gas space heaters; leaking chimneys; back-drafting from furnaces, gas water heaters, wood stoves, and fireplaces; gas stoves, gasoline-powered equipment, and vehicle exhaust in garages. Carbon monoxide can be detected in a structure by a unit similar to a smoke alarm that should be included in every home, especially those with gas equipment and fireplaces or furnaces.

Faulty septic systems. Inspections of septic systems are important because these systems collect wastewater from the property, remove most contaminants, and then discharge the treated wastewater into the soil. If the system is faulty, it can release contaminated water into the soil, thereby contaminating the soil. Potential buyers and septic system users should have the county health department conduct an inspection of the system.

Illegal drug manufacturing. Manufacturing illegal drugs such as methamphetamine produces highly toxic fumes that last a long time. Continued exposure to the fumes can cause fatal burns to the lungs, can damage the liver and spleen, and can lead to learning disabilities. Any property suspected as having been a place for drug manufacturing should be investigated prior to being sold or leased, and the possible health hazards must be disclosed to the potential buyer or renter.

Radon. This is the easiest hazard to detect and mitigate. It is an odorless, colorless, and tasteless radioactive gas that is created in the ground where uranium and radium exist. Prolonged exposure to radon can cause lung cancer. It can enter the home through any cracks, gaps, or cavities, including crawl spaces and openings around pipes. It can be easily detected with a radon test, so home inspections should include it.

Urea formaldehyde. This type of hazard is found in foam thermal insulation in homes built before 1980. The formaldehyde gas emissions from the insulation decrease over time, so most homes with the insulation no longer pose a threat. The most common sources of formaldehyde in a home are pressed wood products such as particleboard, hardwood plywood paneling, and medium-density fiberboard. Plastic furniture, new carpeting, and other vinyl materials also emit formaldehyde gases during the first few months after installation. Formaldehyde can cause eye problems, nausea, breathing problems, and allergic reactions.

Leaking underground storage tanks. USTs have at least 10 percent of their volume underground and are used to store fuel oil, gasoline, and other toxic fluids. Tanks made of steel can corrode over time and leak their contents into the surrounding soil, contaminating groundwater. They also provide a potential for fire and explosion. Tank removal is expensive, so removal is not common. Therefore, potential buyers must be informed of the presence of a UST on the property and of the health and financial risks of purchasing a property that contains a UST.

Wood-destroying organisms (WDO) are such an issue in Florida that WDO inspections are often required for real estate transactions. Termites, certain beetles, and wood-decaying fungi fall under the category of wood-destroying organisms. Carpenter ants are not reportable as WDOs on the Florida report form.

Building inspections do not include WDOs. Instead, the property is inspected by a pest control company inspector who is licensed by the Florida Department of Agriculture and Consumer Services. The inspection must be completed in

Soil and water hazards. Soil, groundwater, and drinking water supplies are vulnerable to pollution from leaking landfills; improper waste disposal; agricultural runoff; industrial dumping in waterways; highway and rail spills; industrial emissions; internal combustion emissions; and underground tanks leaking fuels and chemicals, to mention a few sources. Some of the problems subject to controls are:

- dioxins, a family of compounds produced as a byproduct of manufacturing and incinerating materials that contain chlorine
- lead and mercury
- MTBE, Methyl Tertiary Butyl Ether, a gasoline additive
- PCB, Polychlorinated Biphenyl, a substance formerly widely used as an electrical insulation
- Underground Storage Tanks (USTs), regulated since 1984
- Wetlands, considered part of the natural water filtering system as well as special habitats, are subject to restrictions on development and use.

Other natural conditions. Other regulated and controlled environmental conditions include:

- Electromagnetic Fields (EMFs) created by powerlines
- noise created by airports, air, rail, and highway traffic
- earthquake and flood hazards that affect hazard insurance, lending practices, and construction requirements for buildings in designated flood and earthquake zones.

Anti-pollution Legislation

Clean Air and Clean Water Acts. The Clean Air Act of 1963, since amended several times, was designed to control air pollution at the national level. Among other things, the act authorizes the setting of standards for controlling the emission of pollutants and monitoring air quality. It identifies hazardous air pollutants such as formaldehyde and regulates their use. Importantly, the act allows private citizens to sue other citizens to enforce the law.

The Clean Water Act, officially known as the Federal Water Pollution Control Act Amendments of 1972, together with revisions contained in the Clean Water Act of 1977 and the Water Quality Act of 1987, is the primary federal law governing water pollution. It applies to all waters connected with navigable waters, but the interpretation of exactly which waters are covered remains open to dispute. The Clean Water Act does not directly deal with groundwater contamination, which is addressed in the Safe Drinking Water Act, Resource Conservation and Recovery Act, and the Superfund Act.

Safe Drinking Water Act. Congress passed the Safe Drinking Water Act (SDWA) in 1974 (amended in 1986 and 1996) to regulate and protect the public drinking water supply. The act authorizes the setting of standards, protection of water sources, training of operators, funding of improvements, and dissemination of information. Under the act, water suppliers must report health risks to the EPA within 24 hours of discovery. Hydraulic fracturing (fracking) oil and gas production poses one of the greatest current threats to groundwater.

Property sellers generally must disclose the source of the property's drinking water and the presence, type, and location of any septic system on the property. A water supply other than a municipal one and any septic system other than a standard one should be tested.

CERCLA/Superfund. Under the Comprehensive Environmental Response, Compensation, and Liability Act of 1980 (CERCLA) and the Superfund Amendments and Reauthorization Act of 1986, four main categories of potentially responsible parties (PRPs) may be held liable for hazardous waste contamination: current owners/operators, former landowners (at the time of disposal), generators of hazardous waste, and transporters who selected a specific disposal site. These parties may be held liable for environmental violations, even if "innocent" of a violation. Sellers often carry the greatest exposure, and real estate licensees may be held liable for improper disclosure. Liability can be assumed, legislation does not require proof of negligence. One or more of the noted parties may be held responsible for the entire cleanup cost. Liability is retroactive, meaning it applies even if the disposal was legal at the time.

Under CERCLA, a real property owner can be held liable for the entire cost of remediating soil, groundwater, or indoor air contamination. A tenant can be held liable for cleanup costs as an "operator" if the tenant's operations are linked to contamination.

The EPA can respond directly to releases or threatened releases, order PRPs to perform cleanup, or recover cleanup costs from PRPs.

SARA. The Superfund Amendments and Reauthorization Act of 1986 strengthened CERCLA by expanding funding for cleaning and strengthening EPA enforcement authority. SARA favors long-term, permanent solutions and requires the use of the best available technology where feasible. SARA created the Emergency Planning and Community Right-to-Know Act (EPCRA), which requires reporting of hazardous chemical storage and releases and improves emergency planning at the state and local levels. The act also gives states a larger role in cleanup decisions and expands public participation requirements.

Innocent Landowner Defense. CERCLA liability is broad, but there are limited defenses, including the innocent landowner defense. In short, this defense protects a property owner from liability if they did not know and had no reason to know about contamination at the time of purchase.

Brownfields Law. Brownfields are abandoned commercial or industrial sites that are likely to contain toxic material. The Small Business Liability Relief and Brownfields Revitalization Act (known as the Brownfields Law), passed in 2002, provides clean-up funds, liability protections, and tax incentives to reclaim contaminated properties. Under this law, owners who neither caused nor contributed to the contamination are released from liability for the cleanup.

Environmental Protection Agency. The EPA was established on December 2, 1970, to bring together federal research, monitoring, standard-setting, and enforcement activities into one agency dedicated to environmental protection. The EPA, working with state, local, and tribal governments, enforces the Clean Air and Clean Water Acts along with other environmental laws.

Landmark Environmental Legislation

National Environmental Policy Act (1969)

This act created the Environmental Protection Agency (EPA) and the Council for Environmental Quality, giving them a mandate to establish environmental standards for land use planning. The act also required environmental impact surveys on large development projects.

Clean Air Amendment (1970)

This act authorized the EPA to establish air quality standards for industrial land uses as well as for automobile and airplane emissions.

Water Quality Improvement Act (1970)

The **Water Pollution Control Act amendment** (1972) and the **Clean Water Act Amendment** (1977) addressed standards to control water pollution and industrial wastes from the standpoints of future prevention as well as remediation of existing pollution.

Resource Recovery Act (1970)

This legislation, along with the Resource Conservation and Recovery Act (1976), and the Comprehensive Environmental Response, Compensation and Liability Act (Superfund) (1980), and the Superfund Amendment and Reauthorization Act (1986 collectively addressed disposal of solid and toxic wastes and measures for managing waste. In addition, the Superfund act provided money for hazardous waste disposal and the authority to charge cleanup costs to responsible parties.

Lead-based Paint Ban (1978)

The **Lead-based Paint Ban** and the **Residential Lead-based Paint Hazard Reduction Act** (1992, 1996) banned lead in the manufacture of paint and established disclosure requirements and guidelines for testing and remediation.

As previously noted, the Lead-based Paint Act of 1992 requires a seller or seller's agent to disclose known lead problems in properties built before 1978. The licensee must give the buyer or lessee a copy of the EPA-HUD-US Consumer Product Safety Commission booklet, "Protect Your Family from Lead in Your Home."

Further, the 1996 lead-based paint regulation requires sellers or lessors of almost all residential properties built before 1978 to disclose known lead-based paint hazards and provide any relevant records available. Only a licensed lead professional is permitted to deal with testing, removal, or encapsulation. It is the real estate practitioner's responsibility to ensure compliance.

CERCLA Superfund

Under the Comprehensive Environmental Response, Compensation, and Liability Act of 1980 (CERCLA) and the Superfund Amendment of 1986, current landowners as well as previous owners of a property may be held liable for environmental violations, even if "innocent" of a violation. Sellers often carry the greatest exposure, and real estate licensees may be held liable for improper disclosure.

A real property owner can be held liable for the entire cost of remediating soil, groundwater, or indoor air contamination. A tenant can be held liable for cleanup costs as an "operator" if the tenant's operations are linked to contamination.

The National Priorities List. Under the Superfund law (CERCLA), the Environmental Protection Agency maintains the National Priorities List (NPL), a roster of the contaminated sites in the country judged to pose the greatest risk to human health and the environment. Listing a site on the NPL makes it eligible for federally funded long-term cleanup and signals to buyers, lenders, and developers that the property and its surroundings carry serious environmental liability, which is why an NPL listing is a significant red flag in due diligence.

Responsibilities, Liabilities of Transaction Parties

Disclosing hazards

Licensees are expected to be aware of environmental issues and to know where to look for professional help. They are not expected to have expert knowledge of environmental law or of the physical conditions of a property. Rather, they must treat potential environmental hazards the same way they treat other material facts about a property: by disclosing them.

The Florida disclosure duty (Johnson v. Davis). Florida's requirement that licensees disclose material facts rests on more than custom. In the landmark case Johnson v. Davis (1985), the Florida Supreme Court held that when the seller of a home knows of facts that materially affect the value of the property and that are not readily observable or known to the buyer, the seller has an affirmative duty to disclose them. The ruling set aside the old rule of caveat emptor, let the buyer beware, for known latent defects in residential sales, and Florida has since applied the same duty to real estate licensees. As a result, a licensee who knows of an environmental or other material problem, such as prior flooding, a failing septic system, or contamination, cannot stay silent; the known defect must be disclosed to the buyer even if the buyer never asks.

In sum, for their own protection, licensees should be careful to:

- be aware of potential hazards
- disclose known material facts
- distribute the HUD booklet (below)
- know where to seek professional help

Lead paint disclosure. The Lead-based Paint Act of 1992 requires a seller or seller's agent to disclose known lead problems in properties built before 1978. The licensee must give the buyer or lessee a copy of the EPA-HUD-US Consumer Product Safety Commission booklet, "Protect Your Family from Lead in Your Home," as well as a disclosure form detailing the seller's knowledge of any lead-based hazards present in homes built before 1978.

Sale of contaminated property. Selling a property with an environmental problem does not, in itself, avoid liability for the seller, although the seller and buyer may agree to share or transfer some liability. As mentioned above, sellers often carry the greatest exposure for environmental violations under CERCLA, and real estate licensees may be held liable for improper disclosure.

Phase I audits. A Phase I audit or Environmental Site Assessment (ESA) should If there is be conducted before proceeding with the transaction. A Phase I audit identifies

- prior uses
- presence of hazardous materials

The Phase I ESA reviews environmental documents; conducts a title search for environmental liens and restrictions; and includes a visual inspection of the site and surrounding properties. There is no sampling or testing. Fannie Mae, Freddie Mac, and HUD require special Phase I ESAs on certain properties.

Phase II audit. A Phase II audit (ESA) is conducted if a site is considered contaminated. This is a more detailed investigation using chemical analysis to uncover hazardous substances and/or petroleum hydrocarbons in samples of soil, groundwater or building materials.

Phase III audits. A Phase III audit (ESA) involves remediation. Intensive testing, sampling, monitoring, and modeling are applied to design plans for remediation, cleanup, and follow-up monitoring. Remediation may use a variety of techniques and technologies, such as excavation and removal, dredging, chemical treatment, pumping, and solidification. Major remediation efforts usually require extensive consultation with the surrounding community. Federal funding may be available.

Landmarks in Environmental Control Legislation

Legislation	Date	Regulated
Solid Waste Disposal Act (later part of RCRA)	1965 (1976, 1999, 2002)	landfills
Air Quality Act, Clean Air Act	1967 (1970)	air quality standards
National Environmental Policy Act (NEPA)	1969 (1970)	created EPA
Flood Control Act	amended 1969	building in flood zones; flood insurance
Resource Recovery Act	1970	solid waste disposal
Water Quality Improvement Act	1970	dumping in navigable waters; wetlands
Water Pollution Control Act amendment	1972	dumping in navigable waters; wetlands
Marine Protection Research and Sanctuaries Act	1972	offshore waste dumping
Noise control legislation	1972	airport- and transportation-related noise
Coastal Zone Management Act	1972	beaches, marine habitats
Clean Water Act	1972 (1977)	dumping in navigable waters; wetlands
Safe Drinking Water Act	1974	public water supply, lead
Resource Conservation and Recovery Act (RCRA)	1976	hazardous waste, solid waste
Toxic Substances Control Act	1976	industrial chemicals
Lead-based paint ban (US Consumer Product Safety Commission rule)	1978	lead-based paint in residences
PCB ban (EPA rule)	1979	polychlorinated biphenyls

Legislation	Date	Regulated
RCRA amendment	1984	underground storage tanks
Comprehensive Environmental Response, Compensation and Liability Act (CERCLA)	1980	hazardous waste disposal
UFFI ban	1982	formaldehyde in insulation materials
Superfund Amendment and Reauthorization Act	1986	hazardous waste cleanup costs
Asbestos ban (EPA rule)	1989	asbestos in building materials
Residential Lead-based Paint Hazard Reduction Act (EPA and HUD rule)	1992 (1996)	lead-based paint disclosure and treatment
Flood Insurance Reform Act	1994	flood insurance in flood zones
Brownfields legislation	2002	industrial site cleanup

Environmental Issues Unique to Florida

Sinkholes

Florida is one of the most sinkhole-prone states in the country because much of the state is on porous limestone. Central Florida is particularly susceptible. Over time, groundwater dissolves the limestone, which creates underground cavities that can suddenly collapse.

Sinkholes can cause foundation cracking, structural instability, road and utility damage, reduced property value, and insurance complications. Homeowners should check their homeowners policy to ensure there is adequate coverage for sinkhole-related issues.

Florida sellers must disclose any known sinkhole issues on any property they are selling.

Mold

The hot, humid climate in Florida makes mold a major real estate issue. Common causes of mold include high humidity, flooding, roof leaks, HVAC condensation, hurricane or storm damage, and poor ventilation.

While most mold is not dangerous, mold can trigger respiratory issues and allergic reactions, especially in people with pre-existing respiratory conditions.

Unlike other types of mold, the oft-mentioned "black mold" (Stachybotrys Chartarum) can produce mycotoxins that pose health risks, particularly at high concentrations. Common locations include water-damaged buildings and cellulose materials. It's important to note that mold color does not indicate mold type. In fact, most types of mold, including "black mold," are greenish-black.

Real estate professionals should avoid diagnosing mold problems. Mold identification and remediation typically requires a licensed specialist. Agents should encourage clients to request appropriate inspections and testing before purchasing a property. Sellers are required to disclose any known mold issues.

Dockage

Dockage rights in Florida are important due to the amount of waterfront property. Dockage refers to the right to construct or use docks, boat slips, mooring facilities, and marina access. Waterfront properties often command substantial premiums due to their access to navigable waters.

Dock repair, construction, or expansion may require various permits, and restrictions are in place to protect wetlands, seagrass, manatee habitats, and aquatic preserves.

Florida waterfront owners often have riparian rights, including access to navigable water, reasonable docking rights, and use of water frontage. However, these rights are regulated heavily for environmental protection.

Beach Management Fund Assistance Program

Beach erosion is a critical issue for Florida's environment and economy. Erosion directly affects property values, insurance costs, development feasibility, and coastal construction approvals.

Florida addresses these concerns through the Beach Management Funding Assistance Program administered by the Florida Department of Environmental Protection. This program provides grants (50% - 75% of the cost, depending on the project) to local governments for a number of issues:

- beach restoration
- beach nourishment
- dune restoration
- inlet management
- erosion prevention projects

FL Aquatic Weed Control Act

The Florida Aquatic Weed Control Act governs the control and management of invasive aquatic vegetation in Florida waterways. Poor aquatic vegetation management can reduce water flow, increase flooding risk, harm property values, and restrict boating access. To alleviate these issues, this law authorizes the state to control invasive aquatic weeds, protect navigation and recreation, prevent ecological damage, and protect property and water systems.

Snapshot Review for Chapter 17

The following review summarizes the key rules and concepts from Chapter 17.

ENVIRONMENTAL HAZARDS

Disclosable Hazards

- lead-based paint, mold, asbestos, radon, carbon monoxide
- contaminated water, faulty septic systems, underground storage tanks
- illegal drug manufacturing, urea formaldehyde, air-quality concerns

Florida Concerns

- WDO inspections commonly required in transactions
- wetlands, groundwater contamination, and flood hazards subject to regulation

MAJOR LEGISLATION

Environmental Protection Laws

- Clean Air Act: regulates air pollution and hazardous emissions
- Clean Water Act: regulates water pollution and wetlands protection
- Safe Drinking Water Act: protects public drinking-water supplies

Cercla (Superfund)

- imposes liability for hazardous-waste contamination
- liability may apply to current owners, former owners, generators, and transporters
- liability can be retroactive and imposed without proof of negligence
- National Priorities List (NPL): EPA's roster of the most hazardous sites eligible for Superfund cleanup

SARA

- strengthened CERCLA enforcement and cleanup authority
- expanded funding, public participation, and state involvement
- created Emergency Planning and Community Right-to-Know Act (EPCRA)

Brownfields Law

- encourages cleanup and redevelopment of contaminated sites
- provides liability protections and financial incentives

Lead-based Paint Disclosure Requirements

- applies to most residential properties built before 1978
- seller must disclose known lead hazards
- buyer or tenant must receive Protect Your Family From Lead In Your Home
- buyer given opportunity to conduct lead inspection

Exceptions

- certain housing for elderly persons
- housing for persons with disabilities
- short-term leases and specific exempt property types

LICENSEE RESPONSIBILITIES

Disclosure Duties

- disclose known environmental hazards and material facts
- recommend professional inspections when appropriate
- provide required lead-based paint disclosures and booklet
- Johnson v. Davis: Florida seller and licensee must disclose known material defects not readily observable

Environmental Site Assessments (ESA)

- Phase I: records review, site inspection, historical investigation
- Phase II: sampling and testing of soil, water, or building materials
- Phase III: remediation and cleanup planning

Innocent Landowner Defense

- owner must not know and have no reason to know of contamination
- requires appropriate environmental due diligence before purchase

Environmental Issues Unique to Florida

- sinkholes: common due to underlying limestone formations; known sinkhole conditions must be disclosed
- mold: frequent because of humidity, storms, and flooding; known mold issues require disclosure
- dockage: rights associated with docks, slips, and waterfront access; subject to environmental permitting and regulation

Environmental Programs

- Beach Management Funding Assistance Program: supports erosion-control projects
- Florida Aquatic Weed Control Act: regulates invasive aquatic vegetation

Chapter 17 Quiz: Environmental Issues Affecting Real Estate Transactions

17.1 Environmental laws generally require that known environmental hazards affecting a property be ______.

a. disclosed to buyers
b. ignored unless asked
c. repaired by the broker
d. reported to the MLS

17.2 Lead-based paint disclosure requirements apply to residential housing built ______.

a. after 2000
b. before 1978
c. after 1990
d. before 2010

17.3 Radon is best described as a ______.

a. man-made industrial solvent
b. visible black mold
c. colorless, odorless radioactive gas that seeps up from the soil
d. lead compound in old paint

17.4 Asbestos becomes a health hazard primarily when ______.

a. it is left undisturbed
b. it is painted over
c. it is buried underground
d. its fibers become airborne and are inhaled

17.5 The presence of mold in a home ______.

a. must be disclosed as a latent defect
b. never needs disclosure
c. is beneficial to air quality
d. is regulated only by the FHA

17.6 Carbon monoxide is dangerous because it is ______.

a. brightly colored and easy to detect
b. an odorless, colorless, toxic gas
c. only found outdoors
d. a radioactive solid

17.7 Leaking underground storage tanks (USTs) are a concern primarily because they can ______.

a. improve soil quality
b. increase property value
c. contaminate soil and groundwater
d. generate radon gas

17.8 The federal law that created a fund to clean up hazardous-waste sites and imposes cleanup liability is ______.

a. RESPA
b. the Fair Housing Act
c. TILA
d. CERCLA (Superfund)

17.9 Liability under CERCLA (Superfund) is generally ______.

a. strict, joint and several, and retroactive
b. limited to the current owner only
c. voluntary
d. capped at the purchase price

17.10 Brownfields are ______.

a. protected wetlands
b. abandoned commercial or industrial sites likely to contain contamination
c. federally owned parks
d. newly developed subdivisions

17.11 The innocent-landowner defense may protect a buyer who ______.

a. knowingly bought contaminated land
b. caused the contamination
c. conducted appropriate due diligence and did not know of the contamination
d. never inspected the property

17.12 A Phase I Environmental Site Assessment (ESA) is typically performed to ______.

a. set the sale price
b. obtain a mortgage
c. appraise the improvements
d. identify potential contamination before a transaction proceeds

17.13 The National Environmental Policy Act (NEPA) of 1969 is significant because it ______.

a. created the Environmental Protection Agency (EPA)
b. banned all asbestos
c. set radon limits
d. required flood insurance

17.14 Wetlands are ______.

a. exempt from all development restrictions
b. subject to restrictions on development because they filter water and provide wildlife habitat
c. always suitable for building without a permit
d. regulated only in commercial zones

17.15 A licensee who knows of an environmental hazard affecting a listed property should ______.

a. keep it confidential
b. remove it personally
c. disclose it to prospective buyers
d. cancel the listing

17.16 Which of the following is a Florida-specific environmental program?

a. CERCLA
b. NEPA
c. the Clean Air Act
d. the Aquatic Weed Control program

17.17 Environmental hazards that must be considered in a transaction may occur ______.

a. naturally or as a result of human activity
b. only from human activity
c. only in commercial buildings
d. only outdoors

17.18 Once asbestos is discovered in a home during remodeling, it ______.

a. may be removed by the homeowner without precautions
b. must be removed by trained professionals
c. must be left permanently in place
d. increases the home's value

CHAPTER 18:
PROPERTY MANAGEMENT

Contents

Learning Objectives

Upon completion of this chapter, you will be able to:

1. Explain the licensing requirements for property managers and list the exemptions from the requirements
2. Explain the definition of a community association
3. Describe the skills required of a property manager
4. Describe the steps involved in analyzing the market and the property
5. Describe the methods required by Florida Statutes, Chapter 475, to handle security deposits
6. Distinguish among the various types of leases and between a tenancy at will and a tenancy at sufferance
7. Identify the protective classes under the Federal Civil Rights Acts and the Fair Housing Act
8. Explain the Americans with Disabilities Act
9. Identify the provisions of the Florida Landlord and Tenant Act
10. Describe the types of property maintenance a manager oversees, including preventive, corrective, and routine maintenance
11. Explain the strategies a property manager uses to manage risk, including avoiding, controlling, transferring, and retaining risk
12. Describe the purpose and essential provisions of a management agreement and the agency relationship it creates
13. Distinguish between assignment and subleasing and explain the reversionary rights of an owner
14. Describe the ways a lease may be terminated and the procedures for removing unauthorized occupants

Management Functions

Property management is a specialty within the real estate profession. Many states require persons who manage real estate on behalf of other persons or entities to be licensed as real estate brokers. Other states license such persons specifically as property managers. Real estate firms that handle the sale of commercial and investment properties are in a natural position to manage those properties for their owners. Some property managers work for firms that manage multiple properties under blanket management contracts. Others are independent agents. Some are employees of the owner. They generally fall into one of the following categories:

- **individual property manager**: usually a real estate broker who manages properties for one or more owners; may belong to a small property management firm devoted to full-time property management, be self-employed, or be one of several managers in a large real estate firm.
- **individual building manager:** usually manages a single large property; may be employed by a property manager or directly by an owner; may or may not have a real estate license.
- **resident manager** (residential properties only): lives on the property and may be employed by a real estate broker, a managing agent, or an owner to manage a property on a part-time or full-time basis; may be required by state law for properties of certain types and sizes.

A manager has a fiduciary relationship with the principal and, in general, is charged with producing the greatest possible net return on the owner's investment while safeguarding the owner's investment. At the same time, the manager has some responsibilities to tenants, who want the best value and the best space for their money. Professional managers are therefore much more than rent collectors. They need technical expertise in marketing, accounting, finance, and construction.

Property managers often specialize in one type of property - apartment, office, retail, industrial, farm, single-family-and acquire specialized knowledge of that property type. Regardless of the property type or management arrangement, the manager's work involves leasing, managing, marketing, and maintaining the property. The services a manager provides thus fall into three areas: financial, physical, and administrative. Specific functions, duties, and responsibilities are determined by the management agreement, although most agreements will include at least the following functions.

Reporting

Financial reporting to the principal is a fundamental responsibility of the property manager. Reports may be required monthly, quarterly, and annually. Required reports typically include an annual operating budget (see below); monthly cash flow reports indicating income, expenses, net operating income, and net cash flow; profit and loss statements based on the cash flow reports and showing net profit; and budget comparison statements showing how actual results match the original budget.

Budgeting

An operating budget based on expected expenses and revenues is a necessity for management. The budget will determine rental rates, amounts available for capital expenditures, required reserve funds, salaries and wages of employees, amounts to be paid for property taxes and insurance premiums, and mortgage or debt service. It will indicate the expected return, based on the previous year's performance. A typical budget will include a projection, based on past performance and current market information, of income from all sources, such as rents and other services, and of expenses for all purposes, such as operating expenses, maintenance services, utilities, taxes, and capital expenditures. Operating statements itemizing income and expenses are then presented to the owner regularly so the owner can evaluate the manager's performance against the budget.

Income. The total of scheduled rents plus revenues from such sources as vending services, storage charges, late fees, utilities, and contracts is the potential gross income. Subtracting losses from uncollected rents, vacancies, and evictions yields effective gross income. Operating expenses are subtracted from this total to show net operating income. When debt service and reserves (which are not counted as operating expenses) are subtracted, the result is cash flow.

Expenses. Expenses may be fixed or variable. Fixed expenses are those that remain constant and may include operating expenses, regular maintenance costs, and administration. Variable expenses are those that may change from month to month or occur sporadically, such as specific repairs or capital expenditures.

Capital expenditures. Expected expenditures for major items such as renovation or expansion should be included as a budgeting item. Large-scale projects are typically budgeted over a period of years.

Cash reserve. A cash reserve is a fund set aside from operating revenues for variable expenses, such as supplies, redecorating, and repairs. The amount of the reserve is based on experience with variable expenses in previous years.

Renting

The property manager, whose full responsibilities include maintaining and managing the property in accordance with the owner's financial goals and seeing that the property is properly rented and tenanted. The manager may use the services of a leasing agent, whose sole concern is renting the space. In such a situation, some of the manager's tasks may be performed by the leasing agent. Renting the property includes the following tasks, regardless of who actually performs them.

Controlling vacancies. There are many possible reasons for vacancies in a building:

- rent too high or too low
- ineffective marketing
- management quality
- poor tenant-retention program
- image and appearance problems
- high market vacancy rate

Successful managers look for these factors and take steps to limit or counteract their effects.

Marketing. Finding and attracting the right kind of tenants for a property is the aim of a marketing program. A marketing plan based on the property's features and the relationship between supply and demand in the market area, and consonant with the money available, will determine the best mix of advertising and promotional activities. Marketing methods include:

- billboard advertising
- brochures and fliers
- meetings and presentations
- networking
- newspaper ads
- radio and television advertising
- signs
- tenant referrals
- websites and online services

The efficiency of marketing activities can be judged in terms of how many prospects per completed lease they generate. The lower the cost per prospect per lease, the more effective and efficient the program.

Setting rents. Rental income must be sufficient to cover fixed expenses, operating expenses, and desired return on investment. But rental rates must also be realistic, taking into account what is happening in the market. The manager must consider prevailing rents in comparable properties as well as vacancy rates in the market and in the property. The manager makes a detailed survey of competitive space and makes adjustments for differences between the subject property and competing properties before setting the rental rates for the property.

Residential apartment rates are stated in monthly amounts per unit, while commercial rates are usually stated as an annual or monthly amount per square foot. If vacancy rates in the managed property are too high, the manager may have to lower rates or identify problems in the property or its management that are contributing to the vacancy level. On the other hand, if the property's vacancy rate is significantly lower than market rates, the manager may conclude that higher rental rates are called for.

Selecting tenants. To ensure that the property produces the desired level of income from rent, it is essential to find the most suitable tenants. For commercial space, the manager must determine that:

- the space meets the tenant's needs for size, configuration, location, and quality.
- the tenant will be able to pay for the space.
- the tenant's business is compatible with that of other tenants.
- there is room for expansion if the tenant's need for space is likely to grow.

For residential space, in addition to ascertaining the tenant's creditworthiness, the manager must be careful to comply with all federal and local fair housing laws. A manager should collect the same type of information on all prospective tenants. However, even though the law prohibits discrimination on the basis of race, sex, age and other protected classes, a manager may discriminate in certain other ways. For example, a manager has the right to refuse to rent to a person who has a history paying rent late, damaging property, fighting with other tenants, or spotty employment.

Collecting rents. The lease agreement should clearly specify the terms of rental payment. The manager must establish a system of notices and records as well as a method of collecting rents on schedule. Compliance with all state laws and regulations concerning collecting and accounting for rents is a necessity to avoid unwanted legal complications. As for monies received, the manager must follow trust fund handling procedures established by law and laid out in the rental and management agreements. If authorized by the management agreement, the manager may also collect security deposits and handle them as required by law.

Maintaining tenant relations. Happy tenants remain in a rented space longer than unhappy tenants. High tenant turnover adds to increased advertising and redecorating expenses. For these reasons, it is incumbent on the manager to

- communicate regularly with tenants
- respond promptly and satisfactorily to maintenance and service requests
- enforce rules and lease terms consistently and fairly
- comply with all relevant laws, such as fair housing and ADA (Americans with Disabilities Act) regulations

Legal issues (Fair Housing, ADA, and ECOA). Fair housing laws govern landlords and tenants just as they do sellers and buyers. They ensure that persons receive fair treatment regardless of race, color, religion, national origin, sex, handicap, or familial status. Families with children must receive equal treatment with those who do not have children. Landlords cannot charge higher rents or security deposits because of the presence of children. Managers must make sure that their marketing and leasing practices are in accordance with fair housing laws.

The Americans with Disabilities Act similarly requires landlords in certain circumstances to make housing and facilities available to disabled persons without hindrance. Familiarity with this law and with the latest state, federal, and local fair housing laws is essential.

The Equal Credit Opportunity Act, which prohibits discrimination in lending, applies to how property managers evaluate potential tenants. The manager must be consistent in evaluating the creditworthiness of applicants. The same application forms and the same credit requirements should be used with all applicants.

Property maintenance

Physical maintenance of the property is one of the property manager's primary functions. The costs of services provided must always be balanced with financial objectives and the need to satisfy tenant needs. The manager will also be concerned with staffing and scheduling requirements, in accordance with maintenance objectives.

Maintenance objectives. The foremost maintenance objective is generally to preserve the value of the physical asset for the owner over the long term. Although not every property is best served by vast expenditures on top-level maintenance, it is almost always important to maintain the viability of the property as a rental. Three general types of maintenance are required to keep a property in serviceable condition: routine, preventive, and corrective.

Routine maintenance. Routine maintenance activities are those necessary for the day-to-day functioning of the property. Regular performance of these activities helps to keep tenants satisfied as well as forestall serious problems requiring repair or correction. Routine activities are such things as:

- regular inspections
- scheduled upkeep of mechanical systems-heating, air-conditioning, rest rooms, lighting, landscaping
- regular cleaning of common areas
- minor repairs
- supervision of purchasing

Preventive maintenance. Preventive maintenance goes beyond the routine in attempting to deal with situations that can become serious problems if ignored. Seasonal or scheduled replacement of appliances and equipment, regular painting of exterior and interior areas, and planned replacement of a roof are a few examples.

Corrective maintenance. When routine and preventive maintenance fail, repairs and replacements become mandatory to keep the property operational. A boiler may develop a leak, an air-conditioning unit may break down, an elevator may cease to function properly.

Maintenance contracting. Depending on building type and size, tenant needs, and budgetary constraints, a manager may decide to hire an outside firm to handle maintenance services rather than hiring on-site employees. Efficiency, competence, responsiveness, and effective cost will be major deciding factors.

Construction

Commercial and industrial property managers are regularly called upon to make alterations to existing space to accommodate a tenant's needs. They may also have to undertake or oversee construction that alters or expands common areas or the entire building itself. Again, such work may be contracted out or done by in-house employees.

Tenant improvements. Alterations made specifically for certain tenants are called build-outs or tenant improvements. The work may involve merely painting and re-carpeting a rental space, or erecting new walls and installing special electrical or other systems. In new buildings, spaces are often left incomplete so that they can be finished to an individual tenant's specifications. In such cases, it is important to clarify which improvements will be considered tenant property (trade fixtures) and which will belong to the building.

Renovations. When buildings lose functionality (become functionally obsolescent), they generally also lose tenants, drop in class, and suffer declining rental rates. Maintenance becomes more expensive because of the difficulties of servicing out-of-date building components. Renovation may solve some of these problems, but the manager will have to help the owner determine whether the costs of renovation can be recovered by increased revenues resulting from the renovation.

Environmental concerns. A variety of environmental concerns confronts a property manager, ranging from air quality to waste disposal, tenant concerns, and federal, state and local environmental regulations. The managed property may contain asbestos, radon, mold, lead, and other problematic substances. Tenants may produce hazardous waste. The manager must be aware of the issues and see that proper procedures are in place to deal with them, including providing means for proper disposal of hazardous materials, arranging for environmental audits and undertaking possible remediation. For instance, an audit may show that a building is causing tenants to become sick because of off-gassing from construction materials combined with a lack of ventilation. Remediation may consist of nothing more than replacing carpets and improving ventilation, and the manager, if empowered to do so, should take the necessary steps.

Legal concerns (ADA). The Americans with Disabilities Act requires managers to ensure that disabled employees and members of the public have the same level of access to facilities as is provided for those who are not disabled. Employers with at least fifteen employees must follow nondiscriminatory employment and hiring practices. Reasonable accommodations must be made to enable disabled employees to perform essential functions of their jobs. Modifications to the physical components of the building may be necessary to provide the required access to tenants and their customers, such as widening doorways, changing door hardware, changing how doors open, installing ramps, lowering wall-mounted telephones and keypads, supplying Braille signage, and providing auditory signals. Existing barriers must be removed when the removal is "readily achievable," that is, when cost is not prohibitive. New construction and remodeling must meet a higher standard, Managers must be aware of the laws and determine whether their buildings meet requirements. If not, the manager must determine whether restructuring or retrofitting or some other kind of accommodation is most practical.

Risk management

Many things can go wrong in a rented property, from natural disaster to personal injury to terrorism to malfeasance by employees. Huge monetary losses for the owner, in the form of civil and criminal penalties, legal costs, fines, damages, and costs of remediation can be the result. A manager must consider the possibility of such events and have a plan for dealing with them.

Risk management strategies. Depending on the nature of the risk, the size of the potential losses, the likelihood of its happening, and the costs of doing something about it, a manager and owner will generally choose one or more of the following risk management strategies:

- avoidance-removing the source of the risk, such as by closing off a dangerous area of the building

- reduction-taking action to forestall the event before it happens, such as by installing fire alarms, sprinklers, and security systems
- transference-shifting the risk to someone else by buying an insurance policy
- retention-taking the chance that the event is not likely enough to occur to justify the expense of one of the other strategies; self-insurance

Security and safety. A court may hold a manager and owner responsible for the physical safety of employees, tenants, and customers in leased premises. In addition to standard life safety and security systems such as sprinklers, fire doors, smoke alarms, fire escapes, and door locks, a manager may have to provide electronic and human monitoring systems (security cameras, security guards) and be prepared to take action against tenants who allow, conduct or contribute to dangerous criminal activities such as assault and drug use.

Insurance. Many types of insurance are available to allow for the shifting of liability away from the owner. An insurance audit by a competent insurance agent will indicate what kind of and how much coverage is advisable. Common types of insurance coverage for income and commercial properties include:

- casualty-coverage for specific risks, such as theft, vandalism, burglary, illness and accident, machinery damage
- liability-coverage for risks incurred by the owner when the public enters the building; medical expenses resulting from owner negligence or other causes
- workers' compensation-hospital and medical coverage for employees injured in the course of employment, mandated by state laws
- fire and hazard-coverage for damage to the property by fire, wind, hail, smoke, civil disturbance, and other causes
- flood-coverage for damages caused by heavy rains, snow, drainage failures, and failed public infrastructures such as dams and levies; flood insurance is not included in regular hazard policies
- contents and personal property-coverage for building contents and personal property when they are not actually on the building premises
- consequential loss, use, and occupancy-coverage for the business losses resulting from a disaster, such as loss of rent and other revenue, when the property cannot be used for business
- surety bond-coverage against losses resulting from criminal or negligent acts of an employee

The owner may opt for a multi-peril policy, which combines standard types of commercial policies and may allow special coverage for floods, earthquakes, and terrorism.

The amount of coverage provided by certain types of policies may be based on whether the property is insured at depreciated value or current replacement value. Depreciated value is its original value minus the loss in value over time. Current replacement value, which is more expensive, is the amount it would cost to rebuild or replace the property at current rates.

Commercial policies include coinsurance clauses requiring the insured to bear a portion of the loss. Fire and hazard policies usually require the coverage to be in

an amount equal to at least 80 percent of the replacement value.

Owner's policies do not cover what is owned by the tenant. Tenants should obtain their own renter's or tenant's insurance to cover personal belongings. Residential and commercial or business variants are available. The question of who owns tenant improvements is not only important when it is time for the tenant to leave the premises. It is also likely to determine whether the tenant's or the landlord's insurance company will be paying if the improvements are damaged or destroyed.

Handling of trust funds. Managers are responsible for proper handling of monies belonging to other parties that come into the manager's hands in the course of doing business. For property managers, such funds include rents collected from tenants, security deposits, and capital contributions from the property owner. State laws, usually incorporated into real estate commission rules and the state's real estate law, specify how a property manager is to manage trust funds. In general, the agent is to maintain a separate bank account for these funds, with special accounting, in a qualified depository institution. The rules for how long an agent may hold trust funds before depositing them, and how the funds are to be disbursed, are spelled out. The fundamental requirements are that the owners of all funds must be identified, and there must be no commingling or conversion of client funds and agent funds. Mishandling carries heavy penalties.

The Management Agreement

Components

The management agreement establishes an agency agreement between the manager and owner, as well as specifying such essentials as the manager's scope of authority, responsibilities, objectives, compensation, and the term of the agreement. Property managers are usually considered to be general agents empowered to perform some or all of the ongoing tasks and duties of operating the property, including the authority to enter into contracts. The agency relationship creates the fiduciary duties of obedience, care, loyalty, accounting, and disclosure. The contractual relationship ensures that the manager will strive to realize the highest return for the owner, consistent with the owner's objectives and instructions. The agreement should be in writing and include at least the basics of any real estate contract, as follows.

- **names of the parties**: owner, landlord, manager, tenant or other party to be bound by the contract
- property description: street address, unit number and location, square footage, and other information that specifies the leased premises
- **term**: time period (months, years) covered by the contract; termination conditions and provisions
- **owner's purpose:** maximize net income, maximize asset value, maximize return, minimize expenditure, maintain property quality, etc.; long-term goals for the property
- **owner's responsibilities:** management fees, plus any management expenses such as payroll, advertising and insurance that the manager will not be expected to pay
- **manager's authority:** the scope of powers being conveyed to the manager: hiring and staffing, setting rents, contracting with vendors, ordering repairs, limits on expenditures without seeking owner permission
- **manager's responsibilities**: specification of duties, such as marketing, leasing, maintenance, budgeting, reporting, collecting and handling rents; the manager should be included as an additional insured on the liability policy for the property
- **budget:** amounts or percentages of revenues allotted for operations, taxes, insurance, capital expenditures, etc.
- **allocation of costs:** who is to pay certain expenses, that is, which will be treated as expenses of the manager vs. which will be paid directly by the owner
- **reporting:** how often and what kind of reports are to be made
- **compensation:** the management fee or other means of compensation to the manager; there may be a flat fee based on square footage, a rental commission based on a percentage of annual rent, a

combination of these, or some other arrangement; in compliance with anti-trust laws, management fees are not standardized but must be negotiated by agent and principal

- **equal opportunity statement:** the HUD statement or equivalent concerning availability to all persons and classes protected by law, incorporated into the agreement in the case of a residential property

Rights, duties, liabilities

Both the manager and the landlord have rights, duties and liabilities under the terms of the management contract. How these are apportioned should be clearly stated in the agreement.

Landlord. The landlord has the right to receive rent according to the agreement, and to receive the premises in the specified condition at the end of the agreement term. The landlord and his or her agents may have the right to enter and inspect the premises, examine the books, hire and fire staff, and choose vendors. The landlord may retain or grant the power to enter into contracts, to set rents, and to select tenants. The landlord will have the right to terminate the management contract according to the terms of the contract. The landlord will have the duty to pay the agreed management fee, and to make other such payments as detailed in the agreement. State law will determine to what extent a principal is liable for the acts of the manager and the manager's employees. As owner, the landlord is liable for failures to comply with certain local, state, and federal laws, particularly the Environmental Protection Act and fair housing laws.

Manager. Depending on the degree of authority granted by the agreement, the manager may have the right to hire and fire, enter into contracts, and perform routine management tasks without interference from the owner. The manager has the duties described earlier: to maintain financial records and make reports; to budget; to find, retain, and collect from tenants; to maintain and secure the property; to meet the owner's objectives. The manager's liabilities include the consequences of mishandling trust funds, violating fiduciary responsibilities, and violating fair housing laws, credit laws, and employment laws.

Abbreviated Sample Management Agreement

Agreement made [date], between , a corporation organized under the laws of the State of

, having its principal office at [address], [city], [state], here referred to as

owner, and , a corporation organized under the laws of the State of , having its principal office at address], [city], [state], here referred to as agent.

RECITALS

1. Owner holds title to the following-described real property: [insert legal or other appropriate description], here referred to as the property.
2. Agent is experienced in the business of operating and managing real estate similar to the above-described property.
3. Owner desires to engage the services of agent to manage and operate the property, and agent desires to provide such services on the following terms and conditions.

In consideration of the mutual covenants contained herein, the parties agree:

EMPLOYMENT OF AGENT. Agent shall act as the exclusive agent of owner to manage, operate, and maintain the property.

BEST EFFORTS OF AGENT. On assuming the management and operation of the property, agent shall thoroughly inspect the property and submit a written report to owner concerning the present efficiency under which the property is being managed and operated, and recommended changes, if necessary.

LEASING OF PROPERTY. Agent shall make reasonable efforts to lease available space of the property, and shall be responsible for all negotiations with prospective tenants. Agent shall also have the right to execute and enter into, on behalf of owner, month-to-month tenancies of units of the property.

ADVERTISING AND PROMOTION. Agent shall advertise vacancies by all reasonable and proper means; provided, agent shall not incur expenses for advertising in excess of Dollars ($_____) during any calendar quarter without the prior written consent of owner.

MAINTENANCE, REPAIRS, AND OPERATIONS. Agent shall use its best efforts to insure that the property is maintained in an attractive condition and in a good state of repair. Expenditures for repairs, alterations, decorations or furnishings in excess of Dollars ($) shall not be made without prior written consent of owner.

EMPLOYEES. Agent shall employ, discharge, and supervise all on-site employees or contractors required for the efficient operation and maintenance of the property. All on-site personnel, except independent contractors and employees of independent contractors, shall be the employees of agent.

INSURANCE. Agent shall obtain the following insurance at the expense of owner, and such insurance shall be maintained in force during the full term of this agreement:

- Comprehensive public liability property insurance of______ Dollars ($) single limit for bodily injury, death, and property damage;
- Comprehensive automobile insurance of Dollars ($) single limit for bodily injury, death, and property damage;
- Fire and extended coverage hazard insurance in an amount equal to the full replacement cost of the structure and other improvements situated on the property; and
- A fidelity bond in the amount of_____________ Dollars ($) on each employee who handles cash, and workers' compensation and employer liability insurance to cover the agents and employees of both employer and agent.

COLLECTION OF INCOME. Agent shall use its best efforts to collect promptly all rents and other income issuing from the property when such amounts become due. It is understood that agent does not guarantee the collection of rents.

BANK ACCOUNTS. Agent shall deposit (either directly or in a depositary bank for transmittal) all revenues from the property into the general property management trust fund of agent, here referred to as the trust account. From the revenues deposited in the trust account, agent shall pay all items with respect to the property for which payment is provided in this agreement, including the compensation of agent and deposits to the reserve accounts as provided for. Agent shall remit any balance of monthly revenues to owner concurrently with the delivery of the monthly report.

RESERVE ACCOUNT. Agent shall establish a reserve account for the following items: taxes, assessments, debt service, insurance premiums, repairs (other than normal maintenance), replacement of personal property, and refundable deposits.

RECORDS AND REPORTS. Agent shall furnish owner, no later than the end of the next succeeding month, a detailed statement of all revenues and expenditures for each preceding month. Within days after the end of each calendar year, agent shall prepare and deliver to owner a detailed statement of revenues received and expenditures incurred and paid during the calendar year that result from operations of the property.

COMPENSATION OF AGENT. Agent shall receive a management fee equal to percent (%) of the gross receipts collected from the operation of the property. Any management fee due agent hereunder shall be paid to agent within days after the end of each month.

TERMINATION AND RENEWAL. This agreement shall be for a term commencing on [date], and ending on [date].

MODIFICATION. This agreement may not be modified unless such modification is in writing and signed by both parties to this agreement.

IN WITNESS WHEREOF, the parties have executed this agreement at [designate place of execution] the day and year first above written.

Leasing Considerations

Lease types

Recall from the chapter on leases that a leasehold estate may grant tenancy for years, from period-to-period, at will, and at sufferance.

For years. An estate for years may be for any definite period, years, months, weeks, days. When the estate expires, the lessee must return the premises to the lessor and vacate the premises. Most commercial leases grant this type of estate.

Periodic. An estate from period-to-period does not have any definite period. Such an estate begins as a lease for a definite period but continues after the expiration of the lease, as long as the lessee continues to pay rent at the regular interval, the lessor accepts it, and no one gives notice to terminate the lease. This type of leasehold is common with residential properties.

At will. A tenancy at will is similar to the periodic tenancy, except that it does not begin with a definite period. It continues, with the consent of the lessor, as long as the tenant pays rent at regular intervals. It is terminated by the death of either party. The tenancy at will is rarely, if ever, used in a written lease.

At sufferance. A tenancy or estate at sufferance comes into existence when a tenant stays beyond the expiration of another type of lease without the lessor's permission. This type of tenancy is never intentionally used in a written lease.

Leases, depending on how rent is determined, are also defined as gross, net, percentage leases, and graduated leases.

Gross. In a gross lease, the tenant pays an established, fixed rent, and the landlord pays all property operating expenses, such as taxes, insurance, utilities, and other services. This is the arrangement commonly used in residential leases.

Net. Net leases have the tenant paying rent plus some or all of the operating expenses attributable to the rented space. This arrangement is commonly used in office and industrial leases.

Percentage. A percentage lease may be gross or net, but the rent is not fixed, but depends on the income generated by the tenant in the leased property. A common arrangement is to set a fixed base rent plus a percentage of the tenant's gross income or sales at the site. The percentage calculation may take effect only when the income reaches a certain level. This arrangement is commonly used in retail leases.

Graduated. Either a gross or a net lease may also be a graduated lease, in which the rental rate increases at specified times over the lease term.

Fixed. In a fixed lease, sometimes called a flat lease, the rent stays the same throughout the entire lease term. It is the simplest arrangement and is typical of shorter residential leases. A fixed lease is the opposite of a graduated lease, in which the rent changes at set intervals.

Ground. A ground lease is a lease of land only. The tenant leases the bare site, usually for a long term such as thirty to ninety-nine years, and constructs and owns a building or other improvements on it during the lease. Because the tenant invests heavily in improvements, ground leases are long and detailed. At the end of the term, the improvements ordinarily revert to the landowner unless the lease provides otherwise.

Owned and leased inclusions

The lease should set forth items that are excluded or included in the leased property. For instance, a residential lease may include built-in appliances such as dishwashers but exclude freestanding ones, such as refrigerators. Furniture may be included or excluded. At issue for the landlord is the cost of maintenance. If a refrigerator is not included, it does not have to be maintained by the property manager.

Ownership also relates to insurance policies: one can only insure what one owns, so if a property item is destroyed by fire, the owner's policy will not provide any coverage for an item that is not included in the lease as belonging to the property. This may be of critical importance in a commercial lease where certain improvements might be owned by either the landlord or the tenant, according to the lease.

The lease should also have clear rules about making alterations. If the tenant is not satisfied with an item that is part of the property, the lease may provide for the tenant to make changes only with permission or with the obligation to return the premises to their original condition on termination, or that any alterations made to fixtures become the property of the landlord. Trade fixtures, by definition, belong to the tenant and can be removed when the tenant leaves.

Inclusions may also be of a financial nature, what is included in the rent. Principal and interest on a mortgage loan, homeowners association dues, common area maintenance charges, liability and hazard insurance, and various operating expenses are items that might be included in the lease as the owner's or the tenant's responsibilities.

Reversionary rights of owners

Like the grantor of a life estate, the grantor of a leasehold estate retains a future interest in the estate. The lease grants a number of rights to the property, including, primarily, the rights to enter, possess, and use the property for the term of the lease. The lessee does not enjoy the full bundle of rights to the property. For instance, the lessee may not encumber or sell the property. When the lease expires (a condition subsequent), all rights revert to the original owner. A common example is the leasing of an apartment for a one-year period. When the lease expires, the lessee has no further rights in the property and full ownership reverts to the lessor. Another condition subsequent that may cause reversion of rights is tenant default.

Assignment and subleasing

A tenant may wish to transfer the leased premises to another party during the lease term. There are two ways to do this, and the distinction matters.

Assignment. In an assignment, the tenant transfers the entire remaining leasehold interest to a new party, the assignee, who steps into the tenant's position and deals directly with the landlord. Unless the landlord releases the original tenant, that tenant usually remains secondarily liable if the assignee fails to pay rent or perform.

Sublease. In a sublease (or sublet), the tenant transfers only part of the interest, either a portion of the space or a portion of the remaining term, to a subtenant. The original tenant becomes a sublandlord, remains primarily liable to the landlord under the original lease, and collects rent from the subtenant.

Most leases either prohibit assignment and subleasing or require the landlord's prior written consent, often providing that consent may not be unreasonably withheld.

Statute of frauds and recording

Under the statute of frauds, a lease for a term longer than one year must be in writing and signed to be enforceable; an oral lease for a year or less is generally enforceable. In Florida, a lease for more than one year that is not in writing is unenforceable beyond the first year.

Leases are usually not recorded in the public records, because the tenant's possession itself gives notice of the tenant's rights. A long-term or commercial lease, however, may be recorded, or the parties may record a short memorandum of lease, to establish the lease's priority against later purchasers and lenders.

Landlord rights and responsibilities

State law, often incorporating or modeling the Universal Residential Landlord Tenant Act (see below) prescribes rights and responsibilities for residential landlords and tenants.

Rights. Commonly, the landlord retains the right of entry into the premises in order to perform needed repairs and maintenance on the property. The lease and/or the law may specify that a landlord may enter the tenant's property only under one or more of the following conditions:

- An emergency requires the landlord to enter.
- The tenant gives consent to enter.
- The landlord enters during normal business hours and only after giving notice to either make repairs or to show the property to prospective tenants, purchasers, or contractors.
- The tenant has abandoned or surrendered the property.
- The landlord has a court order allowing the entry.

Likewise, the landlord has the right to expect prompt payment of rent and adherence to building rules. At the end of the lease term, the landlord has the right to retake possession of the premises. In case of tenant breach or default, the landlord has the right to pursue the remedies provided by law, such as eviction, to take possession.

Responsibilities. The landlord (by way of the property manager), is expected to deliver a property that is habitable. This means that the landlord at the very least must:

- keep the heating, cooling, electrical, and plumbing systems in good working condition
- keep floors, stairways and railings safe and in good repair
- provide pest control as needed
- repair roof leaks and broken windows promptly.

Tenant rights and responsibilities

Rights. Beyond the right to quiet enjoyment (privacy) of a property received and maintained in a habitable condition, the tenant has other rights, depending on state law. For instance, a tenant may be able to take any of the following actions if a landlord fails to correct a problem that is the landlord's responsibility:

- move out without liability for back rent or the unexpired portion of the lease
- refer the problem to mediation, arbitration, or small claims court
- after giving the owner written notification of an emergency situation, call a professional repair person and deduct the cost from the next month's rent.

Responsibilities. Depending on state law, a tenant generally must:

- pay rent on time
- Follow the rules and regulations set out by the landlord
- Give a 30-day notice when terminating a month-to-month lease
- Return all door and mailbox keys when leaving the property
- Leave the unit in as clean a condition as it was at the start of the lease
- Keep the unit clean and sanitary
- Dispose of all rubbish, garbage and other waste in a sanitary manner
- Use and operate all electrical, gas and plumbing fixtures properly
- Refrain from destroying or damaging the property
- Prevent others from destroying or damaging the property
- Use the property and the rooms only for their intended purposes

Evictions

An ***actual eviction*** follows a procedure prescribed in state law and stated in the lease contract. The landlord must serve notice on the tenant a specified number of days before beginning the eviction suit. A court issues a judgment for possession, which requires the tenant to vacate. A court officer, such as a sheriff, may forcibly remove the tenant and possessions if the tenant refuses to vacate. The landlord can then enter and take possession.

In Florida, the notice and court steps of a residential eviction are specific. When the tenant fails to pay rent, the landlord must first serve a *three-day notice* giving the tenant three days, not counting weekends and legal holidays, to pay the rent due or surrender possession. For other lease violations, a different notice, commonly seven days, applies. If the tenant neither cures nor leaves, the landlord files an eviction action. When the landlord prevails, the court enters a judgment for possession and issues a *writ of possession*, which is delivered to the sheriff. After the writ has been posted for the period set by statute (24 hours in Florida), the sheriff may remove the tenant, and the landlord may retake possession. A landlord may not use self-help, such as changing the locks or shutting off the utilities, to force a tenant out.

A ***constructive eviction*** occurs when a tenant vacates the leased premises and declares the lease void, claiming that the landlord's actions have made the premises unfit for the purpose described in the lease. The tenant must prove that it was the landlord's actions that were responsible and may be able to recover damages.

Removal of unauthorized occupants

Florida law distinguishes between a tenant, who has or had a rental agreement and must be removed through the formal eviction process, and an unauthorized occupant, sometimes called a squatter, who never had permission to occupy the property. Under Section 82.036, Florida Statutes (created by House Bill 621, effective July 1, 2024), a residential property owner, or the owner's authorized agent, may ask the county sheriff to immediately remove an unauthorized occupant by filing a verified complaint, without going through a full eviction lawsuit, when the statutory conditions are met. Those conditions include that the person entered without authorization, there is no current or former tenancy dispute, and no related lawsuit is pending. The law also created new criminal penalties, for example making it a felony to present a false lease or other document to obtain or stay on a property, to cause significant damage as an unauthorized occupant, or to list or advertise a property for sale or rent without authority. In 2025 the Legislature extended comparable expedited-removal protections to commercial property and to transient occupancy such as hotels.

This remedy does not replace the eviction process for true tenants, and it does not eliminate the doctrine of adverse possession, but it makes it far harder for a squatter to occupy a property and resist removal. A property manager should be able to tell the difference between a tenancy dispute, which requires eviction, and an unauthorized occupant, who may be removed through the sheriff under Section 82.036.

Tenant improvements

As discussed earlier, leased spaces are often modified to a tenant's specifications. Such alterations may be made by the landlord on the tenant's behalf or by the tenant. Buildings usually have "standard" improvements that any tenant improvements must equal or improve on. Many leases have a clause that requires the tenant to return the premises to the condition in which they were received at the end of the lease term. Who pays for improvements and who owns them are major matters for negotiation.

Termination of a lease

Like contracts in general, leases may terminate in a number of ways. Principal among these are the following. See the chapters on leases and contract law for more information.

Expiration. A lease with a term (estate for years) automatically expires at the end of the term.

Performance. Any contract terminates when all parties have performed their obligations.

Agreement. The parties may agree to terminate the lease before the end of the term.

Abandonment. The landlord may retake possession and pursue the tenant for default if the tenant abandons the premises and fails to fulfill lease obligations. The tenant's obligation to pay rent continues.

Default or Breach. A default occurs when either the tenant or landlord violates any of the terms or covenants of the lease. The damaged party may sue for damages, specific performance (of the breached obligation), or cancellation of the lease. When the default arises from the tenant's failure to pay rent or maintain the premises, the landlord may sue for possession and for eviction. Before filing suit, the landlord must give proper notice and allow the tenant to remedy the breach. The most common form of landlord default is failure to maintain the property and provide services. The tenant may vacate the premises and declare the lease canceled if the landlord's default has made the premises unoccupiable. This action is called constructive eviction.

Notice. A periodic leasehold or tenancy at will may be terminated by proper notice given by either party.

Destruction. Property destruction is grounds for termination of the lease. Condemnation. Eminent domain proceedings terminate leases.

Foreclosure. Foreclosure actions terminate lease obligations.

Death. A tenancy at will terminates on the death of either party. The landlord's death terminates any lease if the landlord held the leased property under a life estate, since the landlord cannot convey an interest that extends beyond the landlord's life.

Security deposit procedures

As previously mentioned in the context of handling trust funds, state laws, real estate commission rules, and the state's real estate laws usually specify how a property manager is to manage security deposits. Such funds are normally held in a special trust account and may not be used for any purpose other than the intended one. Whether the deposit can earn interest, and to whom that interest belongs, are likewise prescribed by law. The law also prescribes when the deposit must be returned to the tenant, and under what circumstances any of it may be withheld. The contract language should clearly state, among other things, the rules governing what happens to the deposit when the lease terminates.

Uniform Residential Landlord-Tenant Act (URLTA)

The Uniform Residential Landlord and Tenant Act (URLTA) is a model law enacted as a blueprint for state laws to regulate leasing and management practices of landlords with residential properties. Numerous states have enacted tenant-landlord regulations in response to the law.

The act aims to:

- equalize and standardize landlord and tenant rights
- protect tenants from unethical practices
- prevent unfair, complex leases and their enforceability

One important effect of URLTA is that it prompted legislation at the state level that empowered the courts to nullify residential leases that violated URLTA guidelines, particularly where a lease gave unfair advantage to the landlord.

URLTA Areas of regulation

URLTA legislation primarily addresses the lease contract, deposits and advances, obligations of landlord and tenant, the landlord's rights of access, and standards for eviction.

Lease agreements. URLTA sets standards for improving oral, vague, or unbalanced lease agreements. The law's positions on these issues are:

- unclear lease term: becomes a periodic tenancy
- rent amount: fair market value or the court's opinion
- waiving of rights: certain rights cannot be waived

The law aims to prevent irregularities and vagueness in lease terms and rent obligations, as these can lead to excessive claims by landlords for rent due from a defaulting tenant. A vague lease term can also lead to a dispute about the duration of a tenant's possession rights. A landlord, for example, could claim that a lease has expired in order to acquire a higher-paying tenant. URLTA also discourages the landlord practice of persuading tenants to waive rights they do not understand or are unaware of.

Deposit and advance. URLTA requires leases to be clear about:

- maximum deposit amount
- the tenant's right to earn interest on the deposit
- commingling deposit or advance with other monies
- deadline for returning deposits
- procedures and criteria for return of the deposit to the tenant

Although URLTA applies to how landlords can handle deposits and advances, state laws also strictly regulate how brokers and agents may handle tenant monies.

Landlord's obligations. Under URLTA, a landlord must:

- bargain in good faith with the tenant
- provide required maintenance
- make repairs
- comply with local building codes
- provide access and safety services: elevator; fire escapes, etc.
- provide a procedure for delivery of official notices

Tenant's obligations. A tenant must:

- bargain in good faith
- maintain the condition of the leased premises
- abide by (legitimate) rules and regulations of the building
- refrain from abusing or causing destruction to the property
- limit uses to those approved
- avoid unduly disturbing other tenants

Access. URLTA attempts to balance the landlord's right to access the premises with the tenant's right of quiet enjoyment. The landlord has the right to enter the premises at any time when acting to prevent damage or destruction; to make repairs or show the property, on giving proper notice; if the purpose is not arbitrary and the time is reasonable The tenant may not refuse the landlord entry for acceptable reasons such as emergencies, repairs, inspections, and showings.

Default and eviction. URLTA attempts to establish equitable procedures for handling lease defaults. Upon landlord default, a tenant may sue for damages, terminate the agreement, or negotiate a rent abatement. Tenants generally are not released from liability for rent during a dispute. Rents, however, may be paid to a court impound pending judgment. Upon tenant default, the landlord may terminate and evict, but must comply with eviction regulations.

Exemptions. State laws based on URLTA generally do not apply to transient occupancies, such as hotel and motel rentals, proprietary leases in cooperatives, or to occupancy in a residence that is under a contract for deed.

Florida Landlord and Tenant Act

Florida's own statute, Chapter 83, Florida Statutes, governs landlord-tenant relationships in the state and is divided into two parts.

Residential tenancies (Part II). The Florida Residential Landlord and Tenant Act applies to the rental of dwelling units. It requires the landlord to comply with applicable building, housing, and health codes and to keep the structure, plumbing, heating, and common areas in working order. The tenant, in turn, must keep the unit clean and sanitary, dispose of garbage, and not destroy or deface the premises. The Act regulates security deposits in detail: a landlord who intends to keep any part of a deposit must notify the tenant in writing within a set period after the tenant moves out, and must return the balance within a set period after that. It also fixes the notice periods for terminating tenancies and for eviction, including the three-day notice for nonpayment of rent.

Nonresidential tenancies (Part I). The Florida Nonresidential, or commercial, Landlord and Tenant Act governs the lease of commercial and other non-dwelling property. Commercial tenancies rely far more on the negotiated terms of the lease and carry fewer statutory tenant protections than residential ones. The Act gives a commercial landlord a statutory lien on the tenant's property located on the premises for unpaid rent, and it provides the procedures, including notice and a writ of possession, for recovering possession when a commercial tenant defaults.

The Management Business

Sources of business

Property management is increasingly a specialization within real estate. There is a growing need for skilled managers because of the increasing number and complexity of properties.

Specialist opportunities. Property managers with specialized training are in demand in a wide variety of property types, including shopping centers, commercial buildings, residential properties, and industrial parks. Within these property specialties are opportunities to specialize even further in such areas as:

- **leasing:** a leasing specialist focuses on residential or commercial properties, with duties such as marketing vacancies, showing properties, screening tenants, and negotiating and preparing leases
- **asset management**: asset managers oversee real estate investments to maximize profitability and long-term value; duties include monitoring financial performance, budgeting and forecasting, evaluating market conditions, improving occupancy rates, and developing investment strategies
- **corporate property management:** corporate property managers oversee real estate owned or leased by corporations; property types include retail chains, banks, healthcare companies, and restaurant groups; duties may include site selection, lease administration, maintenance oversight, vendor management, and facility operations
- **resort management:** resort managers supervise hotels and resort properties, vacation ownership communities, guest services, rental programs, food and entertainment operations, and property maintenance; resort managers must understand hospitality operations, seasonal tourism trends, revenue management, and customer service
- **association management:** association managers work with condominium, homeowners, and cooperative associations; duties include enforcing governing documents, managing budgets and reserves, coordinating maintenance, supervising vendors, organizing board meetings, and handling owner communications

- **housing program management** : housing program managers administer public or affordable housing programs; these programs involve rental assistance, community development, workforce housing, senior housing, and federal housing grants
- **mobile home park management**: managers oversee tenant relations, lot rentals, community maintenance, utility systems, rule enforcement, and regulatory compliance; this specialty area requires understanding Florida mobile home laws, long-term resident relations, age-restricted housing issues, and community amenities management
- **office building management:** office building managers supervise commercial office properties; duties include tenant retention, building maintenance, security coordination, lease compliance, budget management, vendor supervision, and common area operations

Owners and investors in these various property types are among the consumers of management services who represent potential clients for a professional property manager. Such owners and investors may be individuals, corporations, developers, landlords, banks, trusts, homeowners' associations, condominium associations, or investment syndicates.

Securing business

Reputation, demonstrated competence, professional training, and smart advertising are keys to finding management business. Before entering into a management agreement, the manager should ensure that the owner's management objectives are clear and realistic.

Management plan. Developing a management plan is a necessary step in launching a management project, and it may also be required to obtain a management contract. The manager must consider the owner's objectives, including financial goals; the competitive market for the property, both local and regional, depending on the property type; and the features of the particular property. The plan will take into account market indicators such as vacancy rates, occupancy rates, absorption rates, and new supply coming onto the market. It will also include a budgetary component that considers sources of revenue and anticipated expenses. Finally, the plan will indicate what the manager intends to do with the property, given these considerations, to manage it in a way that meets the owner's objectives.

Professional development

A number of organizations provide valuable information and training on property management topics. The certifications and designations provided by these organizations are often viewed as valuable signs of competence and can be a significant factor in getting hired as a manager. Important associations include:

- IREM-The Institute of Real Estate Management, offering the CPM (Certified Property Manager) designation
- BOMA and BOMI-The Building Owners and Managers Association International and the affiliated Building Managers and Owners Institute International, offering the RPA (Real Property Administrator), SMA (Systems Maintenance Administrator), and FMA (Facilities Management Administrator) designations
- NAA-The National Apartment Association, offering designations in apartment building management, maintenance, leasing, portfolio supervision and other related areas
- NARPM-The National Association of Residential Property Managers, offering the RPM (Residential Property Manager), MPM (Master Property Manager) and other related designations

- ICSC-The International Council of Shopping Centers, offering designations in retail property leadership, management, marketing, leasing, and development
- NACM-The National Association of Condominium Managers, offering the RCM (Registered Condominium Manager) designation

Other Property Management Issues

Americans with Disabilities Act of 1990

Purpose. The Americans with Disabilities Act (ADA), which became law in 1990, is a civil rights law that prohibits discrimination against individuals with disabilities in all areas of public life, including employment, education, transportation, and facilities that are open to the general public. The purpose of the law is to make sure that people with disabilities have the same rights and opportunities as everyone else.

The Americans with Disabilities Act Amendments Act (ADAAA) became effective on January 1, 2009. Among other things, the ADAAA clarified that a disability is "a physical or mental impairment that substantially limits one or more major life activities." This definition applies to all titles of the ADA and covers private employers with 15 or more employees, state and local governments, employment agencies, labor unions, agents of the employer, joint management labor committees, and private entities considered places of public accommodation. Examples of the latter include hotels, restaurants, retail stores, doctors' offices, golf courses, private schools, day care centers, health clubs, sports stadiums, and movie theaters.

Components. The law consists of five parts.

- Title I (Employment) concerns equal employment opportunity. It is enforced by the U.S. Equal Employment Opportunity Commission.
- Title II (State and Local government) concerns nondiscrimination in state and local government services. It is enforced by the U.S. Department of Justice.
- Title III (Public Accommodations) concerns nondiscrimination in public accommodations and commercial facilities. It is enforced by the U.S. Department of Justice.
- Title IV (Telecommunications) concerns accommodations in telecommunications and public service messaging. It is enforced by the Federal Communications Commission.
- Title V (Miscellaneous) concerns a variety of general situations, including how the ADA affects other laws, insurance providers, and lawyers.

Real estate practitioners are most likely to encounter Titles I and III and should acquire familiarity with these. In advising clients, licensees are well-advised to seek qualified legal counsel.

Requirements. The act requires landlords in certain circumstances to modify housing and facilities so that disabled persons can access them without hindrance.

The ADA also requires that disabled employees and members of the public be provided access that is equivalent to that provided to those who are not disabled.

- Employers with at least fifteen employees must follow nondiscriminatory employment and hiring practices.
- Reasonable accommodations must be made to enable disabled employees to perform essential functions of their jobs.

- Modifications to the physical components of a building may be necessary to provide the required access to tenants and their customers, such as widening doorways, changing door hardware, changing how doors open, installing ramps, lowering wall-mounted telephones and keypads, supplying Braille signage, and providing auditory signals.
- Existing barriers must be removed when the removal is "readily achievable," that is, when cost is not prohibitive. New construction and remodeling must meet a higher standard.
- If a building or facility does not meet requirements, the landlord must determine whether restructuring or retrofitting or some other kind of accommodation is most practical.

Penalties. Violations of ADA requirements can result in citations, business license restrictions, fines, and injunctions requiring remediation of the offending conditions. Business owners may also be held liable for personal injury damages to an injured plaintiff.

Licensing requirements

In Florida, property management activities involving rentals and leasing for others are general considered real estate services under state law. Many property managers must hold a Florida real estate license (sales associate or broker) because Florida does not have a single general “property manager” license.

A license is required when a manager performs any of the following tasks:

- lease or rent property for others
- collect rent for others
- negotiate leases
- advertise rental property
- manage property for compensation

A real estate license is likely not required when managing personally owned property, managing property for a single employer under a salaried agreement, or when duties are strictly clerical or maintenance-related.

Association governance and reserves. Property managers who work with community associations should also be aware of the post-Surfside condominium safety requirements (milestone inspections and structural integrity reserve studies) and the 2024 Homeowners' Association Act reforms, both summarized in Chapter 11. These reforms affect reserve funding, special assessments, recordkeeping, member access to records, and director and manager education, all of which bear directly on day-to-day association management.

Snapshot Review for Chapter 18

The following review summarizes the key rules and concepts from Chapter 18.

MANAGEMENT FUNCTIONS

Property Manager Role

- fiduciary relationship with owner; goal is to maximize return while protecting the asset
- financial, physical, and administrative responsibilities
- skills in marketing, accounting, finance, construction, and tenant relations

Financial Management

- reporting includes budgets, cash-flow reports, and profit-and-loss statements
- potential gross income → effective gross income → net operating income → cash flow
- expenses classified as fixed, variable, capital expenditures, and reserves

Renting and Tenant Relations

- controlling vacancies through marketing, rent setting, and tenant retention
- selecting qualified tenants and collecting rents
- compliance with Fair Housing, ADA, and ECOA requirements

Property Operations

- maintenance categories: routine, preventive, and corrective
- construction may include tenant improvements, renovations, and remediation
- risk management through avoidance, reduction, transfer, or retention

Management Agreement

- key components: parties, property description, term, owner objectives; manager authority, responsibilities, reporting requirements; budget, compensation, allocation of costs, Equal Opportunity statement

Rights and Responsibilities

- landlord: receive rent, inspect property, enforce lease terms, comply with laws
- manager: maintain records, collect rents, manage operations, handle trust funds, meet owner objectives

Leasing Considerations Lease Types

- for years: fixed term
- periodic: renews automatically until terminated
- at will: continues with consent of both parties
- at sufferance: tenant remains after lease expiration
- gross, net, percentage, and graduated leases based on rent structure
- fixed (flat) lease: rent stays level for the entire term
- ground lease: long-term lease of land only; tenant builds and owns the improvements
- reversionary right: the lessor retains a future interest that returns full ownership when the lease ends

Lease Transfers and Form

- assignment: tenant transfers the entire remaining lease; usually stays secondarily liable

- sublease: tenant transfers part of the space or term; remains primarily liable to the landlord
- statute of frauds: a lease over one year must be in writing; leases may be recorded for priority

Landlord and Tenant Responsibilities

- landlord provides habitable premises and required maintenance
- tenant pays rent, follows rules, maintains premises, and avoids property damage

Lease Termination

- expiration, performance, mutual agreement, abandonment
- breach or default, notice, destruction, condemnation, foreclosure, death

Security Deposits

- handling governed by Florida law, FREC rules, and lease terms
- trust-fund requirements strictly enforced

Florida Landlord-tenant Law

URLTA

- model law regulating residential leasing practices
- protects tenants and standardizes landlord-tenant rights
- establishes rules for leases, deposits, access, defaults, and evictions

Florida Landlord and Tenant Act

- Chapter 83, F.S.: Part II governs residential tenancies; Part I governs nonresidential (commercial)
- residential: code-compliance duties, detailed security-deposit rules, and statutory notices
- commercial: governed mainly by the lease; landlord has a statutory lien for unpaid rent

Evictions

- actual eviction follows statutory notice and court procedures
- Florida: three-day notice for unpaid rent; sheriff serves the writ of possession
- constructive eviction results from landlord failure to maintain habitable conditions
- unauthorized occupants (squatters): expedited sheriff removal under s. 82.036, separate from formal eviction

Management Business

- sources of business: residential, commercial, office, retail, resort, and association management; clients include owners, investors, corporations, developers, associations, and trusts
- community association managers must apply post-Surfside condo safety (milestone/SIRS) and 2024 HOA reforms (see Chapter 11)
- professional development: reputation, competence, training, and effective marketing; professional designations offered through industry organizations

Americans with Disabilities Act

- prohibits discrimination based on disability
- requires reasonable accommodations and accessible facilities
- applies to employment and public accommodations

Florida Licensing Requirements

- license required to lease, rent, advertise, negotiate, collect rent, or manage property for others

- exemptions include personally owned property, salaried employees of a single owner, and purely clerical or maintenance duties

Chapter 18 Quiz: Property Management

18.1 The document that creates an agency relationship between an owner and a property manager is the ______.

a. management agreement
b. lease
c. listing agreement
d. deed

18.2 A property manager authorized to handle the ongoing operations of an owner's property typically acts as a ______.

a. special agent
b. general agent
c. subagent
d. transaction broker

18.3 Maintenance intended to prevent problems before they become serious, such as seasonal servicing of systems, is ______.

a. corrective maintenance
b. deferred maintenance
c. preventive maintenance
d. cosmetic maintenance

18.4 Day-to-day upkeep necessary for a property's normal functioning is ______.

a. preventive maintenance
b. construction maintenance
c. corrective maintenance
d. routine maintenance

18.5 The four general strategies for managing risk are to avoid, control, transfer, and ______.

a. retain the risk
b. ignore the risk
c. insure everything
d. sell the property

18.6 The lessor's future interest that returns full ownership when a lease ends is the ______.

a. leasehold estate
b. reversionary right
c. remainder to the tenant
d. security deposit

18.7 When a tenant transfers the entire remaining leasehold interest to a new party, this is a(n) ______.

a. sublease
b. novation
c. assignment
d. reversion

18.8 When a tenant transfers only part of the space or part of the remaining term to another, this is a ______.

a. assignment
b. reversion
c. novation
d. sublease

18.9 Under the statute of frauds, a lease for a term longer than one year must be ______.

a. in writing and signed to be enforceable
b. recorded within 10 days
c. approved by FREC
d. notarized

18.10 An estate for years is a leasehold that ______.

a. automatically renews forever
b. has a definite beginning and ending date
c. has no fixed term
d. cannot be created in writing

18.11 A periodic tenancy (estate from period-to-period) ______.

a. has a fixed expiration with no renewal
b. lasts exactly one year
c. continues from period to period until proper notice is given
d. requires court approval to end

18.12 In Florida, when a residential tenant fails to pay rent, the landlord must first serve a ______.

a. 30-day notice
b. 10-day notice
c. 24-hour notice
d. three-day notice

18.13 An actual eviction ______.

a. follows a legal procedure with proper notice to remove a tenant
b. lets the landlord change the locks immediately
c. requires no notice
d. is illegal in Florida

18.14 A constructive eviction occurs when ______.

a. the tenant pays rent late
b. the landlord's failure to maintain the premises makes them unfit and the tenant vacates
c. the landlord sells the property
d. the lease expires normally

18.15 A landlord who wants to remove a tenant generally may NOT ______.

a. serve a proper legal notice
b. file an eviction action in court
c. use self-help such as shutting off utilities to force the tenant out
d. follow the lease terms

18.16 The Uniform Residential Landlord-Tenant Act (URLTA) primarily governs ______.

a. commercial leases
b. property taxes
c. zoning
d. residential landlord-tenant relationships

18.17 Under a typical residential lease, the landlord is generally obligated to ______.

a. maintain the premises in a habitable condition
b. pay the tenant's utilities
c. furnish the unit
d. waive all rent

18.18 A tenant's typical obligations include ______.

a. making structural repairs
b. paying rent on time and not damaging the premises
c. paying the landlord's mortgage
d. managing other tenants

18.19 A foreclosure on a rental property generally ______.

a. has no effect on existing leases
b. increases the rent automatically
c. can terminate the existing lease obligations
d. transfers the security deposit to the tenant

18.20 Which federal law requires that places of public accommodation be accessible to persons with disabilities?

a. RESPA
b. URLTA
c. the Fair Housing Act only
d. the Americans with Disabilities Act (ADA)

18.21 A gross lease is one in which the ______.

a. landlord pays most or all of the property's operating expenses
b. tenant pays all operating expenses
c. rent is based on sales
d. tenant owns the building

18.22 Managing a client's rental property for a fee in Florida generally requires the manager to ______.

a. be a licensed attorney
b. hold an active real estate license
c. own the property
d. be a certified appraiser

18.23 Security-deposit funds a property manager collects on the owner's behalf must be ______.

a. mixed with the manager's personal funds
b. spent on repairs immediately
c. handled and accounted for according to Florida law
d. returned to the owner at once

18.24 Risk that a property manager shifts to an insurance company is being ______.

a. avoided
b. retained
c. ignored
d. transferred

18.25 A percentage lease is most commonly used for ______.

a. retail tenants, who pay base rent plus a percentage of sales
b. single-family homes
c. government offices
d. vacant land

18.26 Preventive maintenance differs from corrective maintenance in that preventive maintenance ______.

a. is performed only after a breakdown
b. is scheduled to avoid problems before they occur
c. is never planned
d. applies only to landscaping

18.27 A property management firm's primary fiduciary duty is owed to ______.

a. the tenants
b. the government
c. the property owner (client)
d. the general public

18.28 When a lease term expires and the tenant must return possession to the landlord, this reflects the landlord's ______.

a. security interest
b. lien rights
c. leasehold estate
d. reversionary interest

Florida Broker Practice Exam

1. The primary purpose of the Americans with Disabilities Act is to ______.
   a. regulate brokerage commissions
   b. prohibit discrimination against individuals with disabilities
   c. control zoning decisions to ensure that every individual with disabilities has adequate parking
   d. establish fair housing financing rules

2. The Fair Housing Act prohibits discrimination based on ______.
   a. income level only
   b. political affiliation
   c. protected classes such as race and religion
   d. occupation

3. Florida law prohibits advertising that _____.
   a. is overly detailed
   b. is informative
   c. has any exaggerations
   d. is false, deceptive, or misleading

4. The primary purpose of an escrow (trust) account is to ______.
   a. hold brokerage operating funds
   b. hold funds belonging to others until properly disbursed
   c. hold brokerage commission income
   d. pay office and other operating expenses

5. Which institution may serve as a qualified escrow depository in Florida?
   a. Any private business that's been licensed and bonded
   b. A licensed brokerage only
   c. A bank, credit union, or savings and loan association
   d. A title company only

6. A sales associate who receives an earnest money deposit must deliver it to the employing broker ______.
   a. immediately
   b. by the end of the next business day
   c. within three business days
   d. within one week

7. Brokers are generally required to deposit escrow funds ______.
   a. by the end of the third business day after receipt
   b. within ten calendar days
   c. on the closing date
   d. within thirty days

8. Which Florida real estate license category allows a person to perform real estate services independently for compensation?
   a. Sales associate
   b. Broker associate
   c. Broker
   d. Property manager

9. A broker associate is best described as a person who ____.
   a. holds a sales associate license only
   b. holds a broker license but works under a broker
   c. owns a brokerage company
   d. works only for developers

10. Which of the following is a general qualification for Florida real estate licensure?
   a. Florida residency
   b. U.S. citizenship
   c. High school diploma or equivalent
   d. College degree

11. An applicant for licensure must disclose _____.
   a. only felony convictions
   b. only real estate-related offenses
   c. only offenses occurring within the last five years
   d. any prior disciplinary action involving a license

12. Which agency reviews applicants whose background checks reveal criminal history?
   a. HUD
   b. FREC
   c. IRS
   d. FHA

13. A sales associate applicant must complete ____.
   a. a FREC-approved pre-license course
   b. a broker pre-license course
   c. a post-license course before examination
   d. continuing education before licensure

14. A sole proprietorship brokerage is owned by ______.
   a. two or more partners
   b. one individual
   c. a corporation
   d. a trust

15. In a general partnership brokerage, at least one partner must be ______.
   a. An attorney
   b. A CPA
   c. A licensed broker
   d. A developer

16. A limited partnership includes ______.
    a. at least one general partner and one limited partner
    b. only general partners
    c. only limited partners
    d. corporate shareholders

17. Which business structure generally protects partners from liability for another partner's actions?
    a. Sole proprietorship
    b. General partnership
    c. Joint venture
    d. Limited liability partnership

18. A brokerage corporation must have at least one _____.
    a. licensed sales associate officer
    b. active broker serving as an officer or director
    c. CPA on its board
    d. property manager

19. Team advertising must _____.
    a. omit the brokerage name and use the team name instead
    b. use "Realty" in every team name
    c. be supervised by the broker and identify the brokerage
    d. be approved by FREC before publication

20. Real estate advertisements should clearly indicate _____.
    a. the advertiser is a real estate licensee
    b. the broker's commission rate
    c. the seller's motivation
    d. the property tax history

21. The Florida Americans with Disabilities Accessibility Implementation Act _____.
    a. replaces the national Americans with Disabilities Act
    b. incorporates ADA accessibility requirements into Florida law
    c. applies only to residential property
    d. eliminates accessibility standards

22. Multiple licenses are required for ______.
    a. sales associates only
    b. broker associates only
    c. those licensees who have their broker's written permission
    d. brokers who serve multiple entities

23. Fair housing laws are intended to _____.
    a. limit where people may live
    b. ensure equal housing opportunity without discrimination
    c. preempt local zoning laws and building codes to favor people with disabilities
    d. regulate brokerage structures

24. When may licensees use the name or insignia of a real estate association?
   a. Only when it appears on social media
   b. Only when they receive authorization to do so
   c. Only when it is part of a team name
   d. Only when they see others using it

25. A DBPR office inspection may be _____.
   a. conducted only after a complaint
   b. conducted only with advance notice
   c. announced or unannounced
   d. conducted only by FREC members

26. A complaint against a licensee must generally be _____.
   a. oral and confidential.
   b. written, signed, and legally sufficient.
   c. filed only by a consumer.
   d. approved by FREC first.

27. What is the primary purpose of the Probable Cause Panel?
   a. To determine guilt or innocence
   b. To determine appropriate fines
   c. To determine whether a license should be renewed
   d. To determine whether probable cause exists

28. A summary suspension may be issued when _____.
   a. a license expires
   b. the public is in immediate danger
   c. a broker changes offices
   d. a complaint is withdrawn

29. An informal hearing is appropriate when _____.
   a. facts are disputed
   b. criminal charges are pending
   c. facts are not disputed
   d. the complaint is anonymous

30. Real estate consists of _____.
   a. land only
   b. improvements only
   c. Improvements and personal property
   d. land plus permanently attached improvements

31. Which of the following is considered a physical characteristic of land?
   a. Scarcity
   b. Utility
   c. Heterogeneity
   d. Demand

32. What does the physical characteristic of immobility mean?

a. Land cannot be insured.
b. Land cannot be moved from one location to another.
c. Land cannot appreciate.
d. Land cannot be improved.

33. The physical characteristic of indestructibility helps explain why _____.

a. land is viewed as a long-term investment
b. land depreciates
c. land is considered temporary
d. land can be relocated

34. Heterogeneity means _____.

a. all land is identical
b. land supply changes rapidly
c. land is immobile
d. no two parcels of land are exactly alike

35. An appraisal is primarily conducted to _____.

a. determine property taxes
b. establish an estimate of value
c. create legal ownership
d. transfer title

36. Which factor commonly requires an adjustment in the sales comparison approach?

a. Owner's income tax bracket
b. Property insurance premium
c. Location
d. Owner's credit score

37. When the costs of repairing an item are less than or equal to the resulting increase in the property's value, this is known as ______.

a. functional obsolescence
b. economic obsolescence
c. incurable deterioration
d. curable deterioration

38. The cost approach is most applicable to _____.

a. vacant land only
b. recently constructed properties
c. short sale properties only
d. residential homes

39. Reproduction cost refers to _____.

a. building a precise duplicate
b. building a functional equivalent
c. buying an existing structure
d. renovating an older structure

40. Which type of depreciation results from wear and tear?

a. Functional obsolescence
b. Economic obsolescence
c. Physical deterioration
d. External depreciation

41. Economic obsolescence is generally caused by _____.

a. poor floor plans
b. deferred maintenance
c. interior remodeling
d. external influences outside the property

42. A CMA is primarily used to _____.

a. determine property taxes
b. help sellers determine a listing price
c. issue title insurance
d. produce a formal appraised value

43. Which of the following does market value assume?

a. a forced sale
b. related parties
c. a willing buyer and willing seller
d. seller financing only

44. Market price differs from market value because market price ______.

a. is always higher
b. is the actual price at which the property sells
c. requires an appraisal
d. excludes financing terms

45. A broker's opinion of value differs from an appraisal because a broker's opinion of value ______.

a. may not be used for federally related transactions
b. must follow USPAP standards
c. must always be performed by a certified appraiser
d. is used for loan origination purposes

46. Which source is commonly used to obtain CMA data?

a. MLS records
b. Census reports only
c. Building permits
d. Mortgage applications

47. Expired listings can indicate ______.

a. increasing market demand
b. properties were likely overpriced
c. properties sold too quickly
d. a shortage of inventory

48. To qualify as a comparable in a CMA, the property should generally ______.

a. be in another market area
b. be larger than the subject
c. have sold recently
d. be currently listed

49. If a comparable is inferior to the subject, the appraiser ______.

a. deducts value from the comparable
b. adds value to the comparable
c. adjusts the subject downward
d. makes no adjustment

50. In a stock sale, the buyer generally acquires ______.

a. inventory only
b. real estate only
c. equipment only
d. complete ownership of the business entity

51. Which of the following is an intangible asset?

a. Accounts receivable
b. Inventory
c. Patent
d. Equipment

52. Which financial statement reports revenues and expenses over a period of time?

a. Balance sheet
b. Income statement
c. Cash flow statement
d. Statement of equity only

53. A balance sheet provides ______.

a. a snapshot of financial condition
b. future projections
c. tax calculations
d. marketing information

54. One common purpose of a business appraisal is to ______.

a. determine zoning compliance
b. obtain title insurance
c. calculate property taxes
d. establish a fair market value for sale

55. The last step in the business appraisal process is ______.

a. data collection
b. financial analysis
c. finalization of the appraisal report
d. establishing the appraisal date

56. How long after a licensee pleads guilty or nolo contendere to a crime must he or she generally report it to the DBPR?

a. Within 20 days
b. Within 30 days
c. Within 45 days
d. Within 60 days

57. An interest-bearing escrow account may be used only when ______.

a. the broker approves it
b. the buyer requests it
c. all transaction parties agree in writing
d. all involved licensees agree in writing

58. When conflicting demands are made for escrow funds, what should the broker do?

a. The broker must notify FREC within 5 business days only.
b. The broker must notify FREC within 10 business days.
c. The broker must notify FREC within 15 business days.
d. The broker must notify FREC within 30 business days.

59. Mediation is best described as ______.

a. An informal trial held outside of a courtroom
b. an informal dispute-resolution process using a neutral third party
c. a criminal proceeding
d. a FREC disciplinary hearing conducted by an administrative law judge

60. Commingling occurs when ______.

a. escrow funds earn interest without the parties' written authority
b. escrow funds are transferred at closing
c. opposing clients have the same agent
d. personal or business funds are mixed with escrow funds

61. Which of the following describes conversion?

a. It's the final step in reviewing an escrow account or conducting an escrow account audit.
b. Trust funds are used for personal purposes.
c. Trust funds are deposited late, incurring a penalty.
d. It's the process that occurs in a 1031 exchange.

62. Sara is a broker in Tampa. How long is she required to retain escrow records?

a. 2 years
b. 3 years
c. 5 years
d. 10 years

63. Which of the following duties does Tallahassee broker Jake, who's acting as the buyer's agent, owe to a property owner?

a. Loyalty
b. Obedience
c. Confidentiality
d. Dealing honestly and fairly

64. In which of the following situations can a licensee practice real estate without an active license?

a. Only with the licensee's broker's verbal permission
b. Only with the licensee's broker's written permission
c. Only with a written exemption from FREC
d. This is never allowed.

65. Most real estate brokerage relationships are ______.

a. special agency relationships
b. universal agency relationships
c. general agency relationships
d. dual agency relationships

66. Which fiduciary duty survives termination of the agency relationship?

a. Compensation
b. Loyalty
c. Confidentiality
d. Obedience

67. An agent's duty of obedience requires ______.

a. following all client instructions, legal or illegal
b. following lawful instructions from the client
c. negotiating without client involvement
d. guaranteeing results

68. Florida law prohibits ____.

a. dual agency
b. transaction brokerage
c. buyer representation
d. seller representation

69. Under Florida law, the presumed brokerage relationship is ______.

a. single agency
b. no brokerage relationship
c. universal agency
d. transaction brokerage

70. In a transaction broker relationship, the broker owes ______.

a. limited representation to both parties
b. undivided loyalty to both parties
c. full fiduciary representation
d. representation to the seller only

71. A contract entered into under fraud or duress is generally ______.

a. void
b. voidable
c. executed
d. unenforceable only

72. Which is NOT a requirement for contract validity?

a. Valuable consideration
b. Mutual consent
c. Legal purpose
d. Recording

73. In Florida, a minor's contract is generally ______.

a. void
b. illegal
c. voidable
d. executed

74. Mutual consent is also known as ______.

a. assignment
b. good faith
c. novation
d. meeting of the minds

75. Which of the following is generally required of a contract that conveys an interest in real estate?

a. It may be oral if all parties agree.
b. It must be recorded.
c. It must be in writing.
d. It must be witnessed by at least one licensed broker.

76. The Statute of Frauds primarily concerns contract ______.

a. validity
b. enforceability
c. fairness
d. time frames

77. A lease for one year or less may generally be ______.

a. oral
b. void
c. illegal
d. recorded

78. A counteroffer ______.

a. accepts all terms
b. creates a binding contract immediately
c. extends the original offer
d. terminates the original offer

79. Hypothecation refers to ______.

a. conveying title to the lender
b. foreclosing a mortgage
c. recording a lien on a property
d. pledging property as security while retaining ownership

80. Florida is considered a _____.

a. title theory state
b. trust theory state
c. lien theory state
d. mortgage theory state

81. The promissory note serves as evidence of _____.

a. the debt
b. ownership
c. market value
d. title insurance

82. The borrower under a mortgage is known as the ____.

a. mortgagee
b. beneficiary
c. mortgagor
d. trustee

83. Under a mortgage, the lender is called the _____.

a. mortgagee
b. mortgagor
c. trustor
d. grantor

84. A vacation home is generally considered a residence when personal use exceeds ______.

a. 7 days or 5% of rental days, whichever is greater
b. 14 days or 10% of rental days, whichever is greater
c. 30 days per year
d. 45 days per year

85. The simplified home office deduction allows ______.

a. $2 per square foot
b. $3 per square foot
c. $5 per square foot
d. $10 per square foot

86. To qualify for the principal residence gain exclusion, the property generally must have been used as a primary residence for at least ______.

a. 1 of the last 5 years
b. 2 of the last 5 years
c. 3 of the last 5 years
d. 5 years

87. A purchase contract becomes enforceable when it is ______.

a. delivered
b. notarized
c. fully executed
d. recorded

88. Earnest money received by a sales associate must be delivered to the broker by ______.

a. the end of the next business day
b. midnight on the third business day
c. the end of the fifth banking day
d. the day before closing

89. A title search is conducted primarily to ______.

a. determine value
b. verify ownership and uncover title defects
c. estimate taxes
d. calculate commissions

90. The general relationship between risk and return is ______.

a. lower risk usually produces higher returns
b. risk and return are unrelated
c. higher risk guarantees higher returns
d. higher potential return generally requires greater risk

91. An investment that can be converted to cash quickly with minimal loss is ______.

a. liquid
b. leveraged
c. appreciating
d. amortized

92. A primary goal of land use control is ______.

a. preserving property values
b. eliminating private property ownership
c. increasing tax rates
d. restricting all development

93. Florida's Community Planning Act encourages _____.

a. unregulated development
b. infill development and redevelopment
c. elimination of zoning
d. state ownership of land

94. The legal authority for zoning is derived from ______.

a. eminent domain
b. escheat
c. taxation
d. police power

95. Carbon monoxide is particularly dangerous because it is:

a. visible, but odorless
b. radioactive
c. found only outdoors
d. colorless and odorless

96. CERCLA liability is notable because it ______.

a. can be retroactive
b. requires proof of negligence
c. applies only to future contamination
d. applies only to industrial properties

97. Lead-based paint is most likely to appear in properties built before ______.

a. 1978
b. 1988
c. 1996
d. 2001

98. A latent defect is ______.

a. obvious
b. not visible
c. readily observable
d. found on a survey

99. Preventive maintenance is intended to _____.

a. eliminate routine maintenance
b. reduce rent levels
c. replace insurance coverage
d. address problems before major repairs become necessary

100. A management agreement typically establishes ______.

a. the key elements of the Florida Residential Landlord and Tenant Act
b. the lessor-lessee relationship between a property owner and a tenant
c. an agency relationship between owner and manager
d. a dual agency relationship between the property manager and the tenant

End-of-Chapter Questions — Answer Key

Chapter 1: Becoming a Licensed Real Estate Broker

1.1 (b) Broker, sales associate, and broker associate
1.2 (c) Broker
1.3 (b) has obtained a broker's license
1.4 (b) Advertising real property for another for compensation
1.5 (c) Broker appraisals do not substitute for licensed appraisal services.
1.6 (b) A general partner of a brokerage partnership
1.7 (b) Be a Florida resident
1.8 (c) To ensure compliance with child or spousal support
1.9 (b) Prior aliases or "also-known-as" names
1.10 (b) falsely acted as a licensee within one year prior to applying
1.11 (c) 90 days
1.12 (c) Two years
1.13 (c) 63 hours
1.14 (d) Inactive
1.15 (b) Associate with a broker and activate the license
1.16 (b) held an active sales associate license for 2 years within the past 5 years
1.17 (d) Time working under an owner/developer
1.18 (b) 14 hours
1.19 (c) Active
1.20 (c) Brokers must renew each multiple license separately.
1.21 (a) obtain a Florida license without completing Florida's pre-license education requirement
1.22 (c) It is an agreement allowing licensees of one state to obtain a license in another state without completing the full licensing process.
1.23 (b) A group license
1.24 (d) complete a 45-hour post-license course
1.25 (a) March 31 or September 30
1.26 (c) a licensee on involuntary inactive status fails to renew within two years
1.27 (b) 10 days
1.28 (d) An owner who sells his or her own real property
1.29 (a) involuntarily inactive
1.30 (c) a FREC-prescribed 28-hour education course and pass the end-of-course exam

Chapter 2: Opening a Real Estate Office

2.1 (c) Sole proprietorship
2.2 (b) At least one partner must be a licensed broker
2.3 (d) The partnership registration is canceled.
2.4 (c) They are liable only if they manage the business or are named.
2.5 (b) All partners may participate in management
2.6 (d) Their own acts and their employees' acts
2.7 (b) Sales associates and broker associates
2.8 (c) 60 days
2.9 (b) At least one officer or director must be an active broker.

2.10 (c) They must file annual reports
2.11 (b) Corporation sole
2.12 (c) The brokers are already licensed.
2.13 (d) They mislead the public.
2.14 (b) Obtain a new license
2.15 (c) Using the associate's real name only
2.16 (c) Office must be in stationary construction.
2.17 (c) When closings are conducted there
2.18 (c) New brokerage business may not be performed
2.19 (b) One
2.20 (c) an active licensed broker
2.21 (d) FDACS and the Attorney General
2.22 (b) At least one enclosed room
2.23 (c) Work under one employing broker
2.24 (b) the brokerage name is omitted
2.25 (b) opt-out options

Chapter 3: Owning, Managing, and Supervising a Real Estate Office

3.1 (d) No specific minimum capital requirement
3.2 (b) Financial responsibility and stability
3.3 (c) 6 months of expenses
3.4 (b) Licensing and registration
3.5 (b) A security deposit and first month's rent
3.6 (a) Errors and omissions
3.7 (c) Critical start-up cost consideration
3.8 (b) Provide a roadmap for operations and financial success
3.9 (b) Mission statement and key objectives
3.10 (c) The firm's purpose and goals
3.11 (b) Average sales price and days on market
3.12 (b) cash flow
3.13 (c) Overestimate expenses and undervalue income
3.14 (a) Property management fees
3.15 (b) They remain relatively constant regardless of activity.
3.16 (c) Variable expenses
3.17 (c) Brand recognition and standardized systems
3.18 (b) Royalty and franchise fees
3.19 (c) 5 years
3.20 (b) 2 years
3.21 (c) They are not considered income unless they include commission funds.
3.22 (c) When it is received
3.23 (b) Adequate supervision of affiliated licensees
3.24 (c) Respect for rules and procedures
3.25 (a) Licensee
3.26 (a) ensure the associates are properly trained and supervised
3.27 (d) keeps 100% of subsequent commissions

3.28 (b) vicarious liability

Chapter 4: Escrow Management

4.1 (b) An account held by a third party to hold funds belonging to others
4.2 (c) is not required to open a trust account
4.3 (c) $1,000
4.4 (a) end of day Monday
4.5 (b) By the end of the third business day following receipt
4.6 (c) When the sales associate receives the funds
4.7 (c) The third party's name, address, and phone number
4.8 (d) 10 business days
4.9 (c) the funds are held by a title company or attorney
4.10 (b) 15 business days of the last demand
4.11 (c) 30 business days
4.12 (c) The parties reach a written agreement signed by both.
4.13 (a) They are binding if agreed to in writing.
4.14 (d) It requires the broker to deposit funds with the court, removing the broker from the dispute.
4.15 (b) The broker claims part of the escrow funds
4.16 (c) A condominium buyer timely cancels under Florida Condominium law
4.17 (a) A broker mixes personal or business funds with trust funds beyond permitted limits.
4.18 (b) Using another party's escrow funds for personal purposes
4.19 (c) Only the bank statement balance
4.20 (b) the bank statement balance
4.21 (b) notify FREC and follow one of the settlement procedures
4.22 (d) all parties consent in writing and agree on who receives the interest
4.23 (c) up to $5,000

Chapter 5: Office Inspections, Disciplinary Process, and the Real Estate Recovery Fund

5.1 (c) An initial written summary of alleged license law violation
5.2 (b) Depositing excess personal or business funds in an escrow account
5.3 (d) A licensee's personal use of a client's escrow funds
5.4 (c) may affect a party's decision to enter a transaction
5.5 (c) The defendant accepts a conviction without admitting guilt.
5.6 (b) An emergency suspension to prevent public danger
5.7 (c) In writing, signed, and legally sufficient
5.8 (d) 20 days
5.9 (a) Decide whether probable cause exists
5.10 (b) Dismissal of the case
5.11 (b) An Election of Rights form
5.12 (c) Formal hearing
5.13 (b) FREC approves it
5.14 (b) Permanent license revocation
5.15 (d) When the case is heard before FREC, and material facts are not disputed
5.16 (b) A recommended order
5.17 (b) 30 days

5.18 (c) Revocation of license
5.19 (a) Notice of noncompliance with 14 days to correct
5.20 (c) Up to $5,000 fine and/or 5 years in prison
5.21 (b) The claimant obtained a final civil judgment and met statutory requirements.
5.22 (d) $50,000 total per transaction
5.23 (a) The license is suspended until repayment with interest
5.24 (b) The claimant is the spouse of the offending licensee
5.25 (c) A guilty plea, nolo contendre plea, or conviction in any jurisdiction
5.26 (a) They may be either announced or unannounced.
5.27 (c) $150,000
5.28 (a) fees charged to licensees
5.29 (b) the District Court of Appeal
5.30 (d) held a current, valid, active real estate license when the act was committed
5.31 (b) two members
5.32 (c) a reasonable basis or concrete evidence that a violation may have been committed
5.33 (a) culpable negligence
5.34 (d) breach of trust
5.35 (c) fraud

Chapter 6: Overview of Real Estate Valuation

6.1 (b) The surface of the earth, everything beneath it to the center, natural attachments, and the air above extending outward
6.2 (a) A fixture that is permanently attached to the land
6.3 (c) Heterogeneity
6.4 (c) Prices decrease as the market becomes saturated
6.5 (d) Dwelling units
6.6 (c) Substitution
6.7 (b) A state-certified appraiser
6.8 (d) The Appraisal Foundation
6.9 (c) Contains only the results and is intended solely for the client
6.10 (b) The price agreed upon under normal conditions in an arm's length transaction
6.11 (a) immobility
6.12 (d) purchasing power
6.13 (c) yields the greatest value for the site
6.14 (d) conformity
6.15 (a) anticipation
6.16 (b) contribution
6.17 (c) progression
6.18 (d) plottage value
6.19 (b) cost
6.20 (c) reproduction value
6.21 (d) investment value
6.22 (b) assessed value
6.23 (a) value in use
6.24 (b) identify the problem to be solved
6.25 (c) client

Chapter 7: Sales Comparison, Cost-Depreciation, and Income Approaches

7.1 (c) The market data approach
7.2 (d) Substitution
7.3 (b) Identifying comparable sales
7.4 (c) Within six months
7.5 (a) A seller lists a home on the open market and sells it to an unrelated buyer.
7.6 (b) Total net value of all adjustments
7.7 (b) Recently constructed properties
7.8 (d) The improvements
7.9 (c) Depreciation occurs at a constant rate over the economic life.
7.10 (d) Total operating expenses
7.11 (a) adds an amount to the comparable's price
7.12 (c) subtracts from the comparable's price
7.13 (d) the sale prices of the comparables are known while the subject's value is not
7.14 (a) paired-sales analysis
7.15 (d) financing terms
7.16 (b) an exact duplicate of the improvements
7.17 (c) older structures with outmoded features
7.18 (d) the quantity survey method
7.19 (a) economic obsolescence
7.20 (b) functional obsolescence
7.21 (c) economic (external) obsolescence
7.22 (b) the depreciated cost of the improvements
7.23 (b) net operating income divided by the cap rate
7.24 (c) $750,000
7.25 (b) vacancy and collection losses
7.26 (d) debt service (mortgage payments)
7.27 (a) monthly rent
7.28 (c) annual gross income
7.29 (d) weighs the indications according to their reliability
7.30 (a) the sales comparison approach

Chapter 8: Comparative Market Analysis

8.1 (b) The highest price a buyer would pay and the lowest price a seller would accept under normal conditions
8.2 (c) The property is exposed on the open market for a reasonable time.
8.3 (c) Market price is the sales price, while market value is an estimate of probable value.
8.4 (b) Recently sold properties
8.5 (d) They may indicate that properties were overpriced for the market.
8.6 (b) Substitution
8.7 (a) A recently sold property with similar size, design, and location
8.8 (d) Deduct value from the comparable's sale price
8.9 (c) Physical characteristics
8.10 (d) An AVM uses mathematical modeling and property databases to estimate value.
8.11 (a) an estimate of value that is not a formal appraisal

8.12 (c) is not an appraisal and may be prepared by a real estate licensee
8.13 (d) help decide on short sales or foreclosures
8.14 (b) expired
8.15 (c) the competition the subject will face
8.16 (d) recently sold and pending properties
8.17 (b) the comparable properties
8.18 (a) help a seller establish a realistic listing price
8.19 (c) weighs the values based on how comparable each property is
8.20 (d) cannot physically inspect the property's condition

Chapter 9: Business Valuation

9.1 (b) Effecting the sale or exchange of an existing business
9.2 (c) The sale of a small business that usually involves assets and lease assignment
9.3 (c) Business brokerage involves transferring goodwill and income.
9.4 (d) Goodwill
9.5 (b) The value expected from ongoing operations and profits
9.6 (c) Existing liabilities
9.7 (b) The business entity plus liabilities
9.8 (d) Non-compete agreement
9.9 (c) Balance sheet
9.10 (d) Inventory
9.11 (b) Prices paid for similar businesses
9.12 (a) Business transactions may involve the sale of securities such as stocks
9.13 (c) To protect creditors when a business sells its inventory
9.14 (b) Analysis of the collected data
9.15 (d) Horizontal analysis
9.16 (c) asset approach
9.17 (b) the income statement
9.18 (c) adjust for unusual, non-recurring, or discretionary expenses
9.19 (a) goodwill
9.20 (d) routine daily bookkeeping

Chapter 10: Brokerage Relationships and Disclosure Requirements

10.1 (a) principal
10.2 (d) customer
10.3 (b) special (limited) agency
10.4 (b) dual agency, which Florida prohibits
10.5 (c) residential sale transactions
10.6 (d) transaction broker
10.7 (a) loyalty
10.8 (d) limited confidentiality
10.9 (c) that the seller will accept less than the asking price
10.10 (b) disclose all known facts materially affecting value that are not readily observable
10.11 (b) disclosing known material facts not readily observable
10.12 (c) non-residential transactions where the buyer and seller each have assets of $1 million or more

10.13 (d) sign a statement that their assets meet the $1 million requirement
10.14 (a) obtain the customer's consent (Consent to Transition to Transaction Broker)
10.15 (c) honesty, fairness, and disclosure of known material facts
10.16 (b) the case of Johnson v. Davis
10.17 (d) advise the seller and recommend that the buyer investigate further
10.18 (a) even when there is no brokerage relationship with the customer
10.19 (c) universal agency
10.20 (d) client (principal)
10.21 (b) deal honestly and fairly and use skill, care, and diligence
10.22 (a) completion (performance) of the agency's purpose

Chapter 11: Real Estate Contracts

11.1 (a) an agreement between parties that is enforceable by law
11.2 (b) valuable consideration
11.3 (c) of legal age and sound mind
11.4 (d) good consideration that does not satisfy a valid contract
11.5 (a) void
11.6 (b) in writing to be enforceable
11.7 (c) express contract
11.8 (d) implied contract
11.9 (a) bilateral
11.10 (b) unilateral
11.11 (c) executed
11.12 (d) executory
11.13 (a) void
11.14 (b) voidable
11.15 (c) mutual consent (a meeting of the minds)
11.16 (d) a counteroffer that voids the original offer
11.17 (a) at any time before the offeree communicates acceptance
11.18 (b) enforceable
11.19 (c) unless the agreement specifically prohibits assignment
11.20 (d) novation
11.21 (a) cancels the contract and returns the parties to their pre-contract position
11.22 (b) compel the defaulting party to comply with the contract's terms
11.23 (c) forfeiture of the buyer's earnest money deposit as liquidated damages
11.24 (d) specific performance, damages, or cancellation
11.25 (a) regardless of who procures the buyer during the listing period
11.26 (b) only to the broker who procures the buyer
11.27 (c) any amount received above the seller's stated net price
11.28 (d) include a definite expiration date
11.29 (a) vendee; vendor
11.30 (b) cancel the contract and recover the deposit if the specified loan is not obtained
11.31 (c) has the right, but not the obligation, to purchase the property
11.32 (d) the seller retains legal title while the buyer holds equitable title

Chapter 12: Financing Real Estate

12.1 (a) the borrower's written promise to repay the loan
12.2 (b) pledge the property as security for the loan
12.3 (c) hypothecation
12.4 (d) mortgagor
12.5 (a) lien-theory state
12.6 (b) satisfaction of mortgage
12.7 (c) the date each was recorded
12.8 (d) acceleration clause
12.9 (a) demand full repayment if the borrower transfers the property without approval
12.10 (b) without a prepayment penalty
12.11 (c) defeasance (release) clause
12.12 (d) subordination clause
12.13 (a) the loan amount and the property's value
12.14 (b) the property's value minus the debt owed against it
12.15 (c) 1 percent
12.16 (d) cover the cost of processing the loan
12.17 (a) protects the lender against loss when the down payment is small
12.18 (b) escrow (impound) account
12.19 (c) primary mortgage market
12.20 (d) secondary mortgage market
12.21 (a) Ginnie Mae (GNMA)
12.22 (b) government-sponsored enterprise in the secondary market
12.23 (c) judicial foreclosure
12.24 (d) deed in lieu of foreclosure
12.25 (a) the lender agrees to accept less than the balance owed on the loan
12.26 (b) gross income
12.27 (c) other recurring debt payments
12.28 (d) not insured or guaranteed by a government agency
12.29 (a) conforming loan
12.30 (b) insured by the Federal Housing Administration
12.31 (c) eligible veterans and service members
12.32 (d) seller financing
12.33 (a) the seller remains personally liable on the original loan
12.34 (b) discrimination against credit applicants based on protected characteristics
12.35 (c) the annual percentage rate (APR) and finance charges

Chapter 13: Closing Real Estate Transactions

13.1 (a) transfer title to the buyer and disburse funds to the seller
13.2 (b) confirm the seller can convey marketable title
13.3 (c) closing (settlement) agent
13.4 (d) verify the property's condition before title transfers
13.5 (a) clarify settlement costs and eliminate kickbacks
13.6 (b) referral fees and kickbacks among settlement service providers
13.7 (c) within three business days of the loan application

13.8 (d) itemizes the final loan terms and closing costs for the borrower
13.9 (a) the Truth-in-Lending Act
13.10 (b) an amount a party owes or must pay at closing
13.11 (c) debit to the buyer and a credit to the seller
13.12 (d) credit to the buyer
13.13 (a) debit to the seller
13.14 (b) debit to the seller
13.15 (c) is charged entirely to one party
13.16 (d) dividing continuing expenses between buyer and seller as of the closing date
13.17 (a) in arrears
13.18 (b) credit to the buyer and a debit to the seller
13.19 (c) 360-day (30-day-month) method
13.20 (d) $1,800
13.21 (a) $300
13.22 (b) $0.70 per $100 of the sale price
13.23 (c) $2,100
13.24 (d) $0.35 per $100 of the loan amount
13.25 (a) $500
13.26 (b) protects the buyer against defects in the title
13.27 (c) uncover unrecorded code-enforcement and utility liens
13.28 (d) $129,900

Chapter 14: Federal Income Tax Laws

14.1 (c) It encourages investment activity through faster deductions and lower taxable income.
14.2 (d) Bonus depreciation was reinstated and made permanent at 100%.
14.3 (c) The near doubling of the standard deduction
14.4 (d) $10,000
14.5 (c) $750,000
14.6 (c) The rental income is not taxable.
14.7 (a) A self-employed individual with a regularly used exclusive business area
14.8 (b) 14 days or 10% of rental days, whichever is greater
14.9 (b) 27.5
14.10 (a) Replacement property must be identified within 45 days after closing on the relinquished property
14.11 (a) two of the last five years
14.12 (b) 39 years
14.13 (c) the land
14.14 (d) defer capital-gains tax on the exchanged property
14.15 (a) only when the property is sold

Chapter 15: Investment Real Estate

15.1 (a) the income or profit the investor receives
15.2 (b) leverage
15.3 (c) relatively illiquid
15.4 (d) active, hands-on management
15.5 (a) hedge against inflation

15.6 (b) allowable expenses, deductions, and exclusions
15.7 (c) deduct a portion of the property's value each year
15.8 (d) only for income-producing property
15.9 (a) the improvements (building), not the land
15.10 (b) $10,000
15.11 (c) $250,000 for a single filer and $500,000 for married filing jointly
15.12 (d) operating expenses
15.13 (a) $60,000
15.14 (b) annual debt service
15.15 (c) $15,000
15.16 (d) the investor's tax liability
15.17 (a) subtracted from potential rental income
15.18 (b) property management and maintenance costs
15.19 (c) debt service (mortgage payments)
15.20 (d) a user property
15.21 (a) duration (time-horizon) matching
15.22 (b) financial qualifications and investment objectives
15.23 (c) the landlord
15.24 (d) some or all of the property's operating expenses
15.25 (a) taxes, insurance, and maintenance
15.26 (b) base rent plus a percentage of business revenue
15.27 (c) the actual space the tenant occupies and uses
15.28 (d) a proportionate share of the common areas
15.29 (a) the percentage added to usable space to arrive at rentable space
15.30 (b) 1,150

Chapter 16: Zoning, Planning, and Environmental Controls

16.1 (c) It helps protect property values, public welfare, and environmental quality.
16.2 (b) Balance individual property rights with the public good.
16.3 (c) Administration by a planning commission
16.4 (b) Provide guidelines for long-term growth and land use.
16.5 (d) Availability of sanitation facilities and utilities
16.6 (b) Traffic patterns and environmental impacts
16.7 (c) Plan development
16.8 (a) Approving site plans and ruling on zoning issues
16.9 (c) infill development and redevelopment
16.10 (b) Supervise funds used to attract businesses to Florida
16.11 (c) Transportation and traffic circulation planning
16.12 (b) wetlands, rivers, forests, and wildlife
16.13 (a) To prevent new development from exceeding infrastructure capacity
16.14 (b) Enabling acts
16.15 (c) Building setbacks and parking requirements
16.16 (a) variance
16.17 (b) nonconforming use
16.18 (c) special exception

16.19 (d) concurrency provision
16.20 (a) eminent domain

Chapter 17: Environmental Issues Affecting Real Estate Transactions

17.1 (a) disclosed to buyers
17.2 (b) before 1978
17.3 (c) colorless, odorless radioactive gas that seeps up from the soil
17.4 (d) its fibers become airborne and are inhaled
17.5 (a) must be disclosed as a latent defect
17.6 (b) an odorless, colorless, toxic gas
17.7 (c) contaminate soil and groundwater
17.8 (d) CERCLA (Superfund)
17.9 (a) strict, joint and several, and retroactive
17.10 (b) abandoned commercial or industrial sites likely to contain contamination
17.11 (c) conducted appropriate due diligence and did not know of the contamination
17.12 (d) identify potential contamination before a transaction proceeds
17.13 (a) created the Environmental Protection Agency (EPA)
17.14 (b) subject to restrictions on development because they filter water and provide wildlife habitat
17.15 (c) disclose it to prospective buyers
17.16 (d) the Aquatic Weed Control program
17.17 (a) naturally or as a result of human activity
17.18 (b) must be removed by trained professionals

Chapter 18: Property Management

18.1 (a) management agreement
18.2 (b) general agent
18.3 (c) preventive maintenance
18.4 (d) routine maintenance
18.5 (a) retain the risk
18.6 (b) reversionary right
18.7 (c) assignment
18.8 (d) sublease
18.9 (a) in writing and signed to be enforceable
18.10 (b) has a definite beginning and ending date
18.11 (c) continues from period to period until proper notice is given
18.12 (d) three-day notice
18.13 (a) follows a legal procedure with proper notice to remove a tenant
18.14 (b) the landlord's failure to maintain the premises makes them unfit and the tenant vacates
18.15 (c) use self-help such as shutting off utilities to force the tenant out
18.16 (d) residential landlord-tenant relationships
18.17 (a) maintain the premises in a habitable condition
18.18 (b) paying rent on time and not damaging the premises
18.19 (c) can terminate the existing lease obligations
18.20 (d) the Americans with Disabilities Act (ADA)
18.21 (a) landlord pays most or all of the property's operating expenses

18.22 (b) hold an active real estate license
18.23 (c) handled and accounted for according to Florida law
18.24 (d) transferred
18.25 (a) retail tenants, who pay base rent plus a percentage of sales
18.26 (b) is scheduled to avoid problems before they occur
18.27 (c) the property owner (client)
18.28 (d) reversionary interest

Florida Broker Practice Exam — Answer Key

1. **(b)** prohibit discrimination against individuals with disabilities
2. **(c)** protected classes such as race and religion
3. **(d)** is false, deceptive, or misleading
4. **(b)** hold funds belonging to others until properly disbursed
5. **(c)** A bank, credit union, or savings and loan association
6. **(b)** by the end of the next business day
7. **(a)** by the end of the third business day after receipt
8. **(c)** Broker
9. **(b)** holds a broker license but works under a broker
10. **(c)** High school diploma or equivalent
11. **(d)** any prior disciplinary action involving a license
12. **(b)** FREC
13. **(a)** a FREC-approved pre-license course
14. **(b)** one individual
15. **(c)** A licensed broker
16. **(a)** at least one general partner and one limited partner
17. **(d)** Limited liability partnership
18. **(b)** active broker serving as an officer or director
19. **(c)** be supervised by the broker and identify the brokerage
20. **(a)** the advertiser is a real estate licensee
21. **(b)** incorporates ADA accessibility requirements into Florida law
22. **(d)** brokers who serve multiple entities
23. **(b)** ensure equal housing opportunity without discrimination
24. **(b)** Only when they receive authorization to do so
25. **(c)** announced or unannounced
26. **(b)** written, signed, and legally sufficient.
27. **(d)** To determine whether probable cause exists
28. **(b)** the public is in immediate danger
29. **(c)** facts are not disputed
30. **(d)** land plus permanently attached improvements
31. **(c)** Heterogeneity
32. **(b)** Land cannot be moved from one location to another.
33. **(a)** land is viewed as a long-term investment
34. **(d)** no two parcels of land are exactly alike
35. **(b)** establish an estimate of value
36. **(c)** Location
37. **(d)** curable deterioration
38. **(b)** recently constructed properties
39. **(a)** building a precise duplicate
40. **(c)** Physical deterioration
41. **(d)** external influences outside the property
42. **(b)** help sellers determine a listing price
43. **(c)** a willing buyer and willing seller

44. (b) is the actual price at which the property sells
45. (a) may not be used for federally related transactions
46. (a) MLS records
47. (b) properties were likely overpriced
48. (c) have sold recently
49. (b) adds value to the comparable
50. (d) complete ownership of the business entity
51. (c) Patent
52. (b) Income statement
53. (a) a snapshot of financial condition
54. (d) establish a fair market value for sale
55. (c) finalization of the appraisal report
56. (b) Within 30 days
57. (c) all transaction parties agree in writing
58. (c) The broker must notify FREC within 15 business days.
59. (b) an informal dispute-resolution process using a neutral third party
60. (d) personal or business funds are mixed with escrow funds
61. (b) Trust funds are used for personal purposes.
62. (c) 5 years
63. (d) Dealing honestly and fairly
64. (d) This is never allowed.
65. (a) special agency relationships
66. (c) Confidentiality
67. (b) following lawful instructions from the client
68. (a) dual agency
69. (d) transaction brokerage
70. (a) limited representation to both parties
71. (b) voidable
72. (d) Recording
73. (c) voidable
74. (d) meeting of the minds
75. (c) It must be in writing.
76. (b) enforceability
77. (a) oral
78. (d) terminates the original offer
79. (d) pledging property as security while retaining ownership
80. (c) lien theory state
81. (a) the debt
82. (c) mortgagor
83. (a) mortgagee
84. (b) 14 days or 10% of rental days, whichever is greater
85. (c) $5 per square foot
86. (b) 2 of the last 5 years
87. (c) fully executed
88. (a) the end of the next business day

89. **(b)** verify ownership and uncover title defects
90. **(d)** higher potential return generally requires greater risk
91. **(a)** liquid
92. **(a)** preserving property values
93. **(b)** infill development and redevelopment
94. **(d)** police power
95. **(d)** colorless and odorless
96. **(a)** can be retroactive
97. **(a)** 1978
98. **(b)** not visible
99. **(d)** address problems before major repairs become necessary
100. **(c)** an agency relationship between owner and manager

Index

If you liked Florida Broker Postlicensing, check out the other titles of Performance Programs Company!

Looking to complete your Florida 60-hour broker postlicensing requirement? Go with Performance Programs Company's Florida Broker Postlicensing!

Florida Broker Postlicensing is a 60-hour review and applied principles course for newly-licensed brokers beginning their real estate careers in Florida. Successful completion of this course will satisfy your one-time postlicense requirement as a broker actively practicing real estate in Florida.

Where can you buy Florida Broker Postlicensing?
Florida Broker Postlicensing is available as a printed book or e-book through nearly all online retailers.

Needing to complete your 14 hours of CE? Performance Programs Company has you covered!

Where can you buy Performance Programs Company's 14-Hour Florida Real Estate Continuing Education (FLA.CE) program?
Our FLA.CE Program is available through licensed real estate schools

Looking for a Florida-specific real estate principles textbook? Get what all the students love -- Principles of Real Estate Practice in Florida!

Principles of Real Estate Practice in Florida is invaluable reference material for real estate professionals. Its 540-pages contain the essentials of real estate law, principles, and practices taught in real estate schools and colleges across Florida.

Where can you buy Principles of Real Estate Practice in Florida?
Principles Real Estate Practice in Florida is available as a printed book or e-book through nearly all online retailers.

Cramming for the Florida real estate sales associate exam? You need Florida Real Estate License Exam Prep!

Where can you buy Florida Real Estate License Exam Prep?
Florida Real Estate License Exam Prep is available as a printed book or e-book through nearly all online retailers.

Publisher Contact
Ryan Mettling
Performance Programs Company
6810 190th Street East, Bradenton, FL 34211
941-677-6043
ryan@performanceprogramscompany.com
www.performanceprogramscompany.com

www.ingramcontent.com/pod-product-compliance
Lightning Source LLC
Chambersburg PA
CBHW061154240926
51846CB00006B/1008
9781965482667